Giving Predestination a Decent Burial

NEW AND COMPELLING REASONS TO PUT THE GHOST OF JOHN CALVIN TO REST FOREVER

BILL MAULDIN

ATRADUMS
RIGA, LATVIA
2020

Published in Latvia by Atradums
www.atradums.lv
Printed in Latvia by Latgales druka
www.druka.lv
Graphic design by Aigars Truhins
Cover photos used by permission of DreamsTime.com and Can Stock Photo

ISBN: 978-9934-8826-4-7

Acknowledgements

It would be impossible to mention everyone who has been a part of the preparation of this book, but I would be remiss not to mention four who have been particularly pivotal. The first was my New Testament professor, Dr. Jim Christie, who viewed my early observations on Ephesians 1, and recognized in them a line of reasoning that had never before been explored. Years later, a conversation with a friend in Latvia, Igors Rautmanis, pushed me to make this an immediate priority, after he started observing ideas of predestination creeping into the Latvian church for the first time ever, and causing division. Then, when I actually took time to do the deeper research at Fuller Theological Seminary, Dr. Dan Shaw also recognized the importance of what I was discovering, and acted as an informal advisor as I studied. Finally, my wife, Donna, has been an indispensable part of the entire journey, enduring my tendency to work too much, and providing invaluable help along the way, with every part of the journey. May God reward them, and all the others who helped, in ways that only he can do.

Table of Contents

Introduction
Connecting the Dots: A Brief Summary of the Book

Is this book for you?

Is it readable?

Does it say anything new?

If so, what?

This book is about connecting the dots, the way we did as kids to make a clear picture appear from what beforehand appeared to just be a bunch of random points. Like the picture that appears from the dots, the purpose of the book is to bring clarity from confusion.

It appears to me that most Christians accept the teachings of their particular church without ever really examining them. That includes most Calvinists, and most of those opposed to Calvinism. At least partially, this is because much of the material written about theological issues is written for other theologians, so it is hard for the ordinary Christian to understand.

But it doesn't have to be that way.

In this book, I describe my journey away from Calvinism, attempting to show the thinking process that fueled that journey, and I try to do it in a way that any person of basic intelligence can understand. I tend to dislike big words myself, so if I have to use one that has a specific "theological" meaning or that I think some people won't understand, I immediately explain it. Beyond that, I try to build my case step by step, with no assumption that the reader already has any specific "Bible" or "theological" education.

To provide a historical foundation, the first chapter gives a brief introduction to John Calvin himself and the times in which he lived. In the next chapter, I go in a completely different direction, reflecting on how culture shapes our worldviews, how we know what we know, and how we determine what is truth and what is not. This is important because the culture and worldview of the writers of the New Testament were so different from those of Calvin's era, and from ours today, that misunderstandings are hard to avoid. For me, it was learning to understand my own thinking better, and learning to compare it to the thinking of other cultures, that started my reexamination of what I believed about Calvinism. Learning to put my beliefs through the tests for truth was a necessary part of my journey, because Calvinism, like all other religious teaching, claims to be true.

The third chapter shows why the foundation laid in the first two chapters is necessary. It reflects on the difference between truth and theology, with theology simply being any organized human system for understanding the truth about God. Calvinism then, like all other theologies, is shown to be one human way among many of understanding Scripture, and like all other theologies, it is shown to be the logical result of the time and place from which it arose – its "context." Chapter 4 traces the history of the Church's thinking about predestination that led up to the time and place – the context – from which John Calvin and his beliefs arose, then Chapter 5 traces the legacy of that context and its effect on our own, through the impact it had on the Bibles we use today.

A primary point of Chapter 5 is that what we see in our Bibles today about the "chosen" and the "elect" are inadequate translations of the concepts that were contained in the original words from which those words are translated. Translation experts much brighter than me recognize that "Bible translation is an ideological act" so that the words we see in our Bibles today are more a reflection of the time and place when the Bible was first being translated into the local European languages, than they are of the meaning the original writers were trying to communicate. When the broader meanings of the original words are understood, what we see in our Bibles changes dramatically.

As the dots start to come together, I examine the two places in the New Testament that are normally used to support "predestination of salvation for individuals," putting those two passages within the larger argument being made by the writer of those two books. When the overall argument is considered, it becomes clear that John Calvin never really understood what the original author was saying. But it goes beyond that.

In the next chapter, the longest by far in the book, I consider various concepts that together form the basic biblical worldview – everything from the purpose of creation, to the sovereignty of God, to circumcision, the spiritual battle, prayer, redemption, the problem of evil, and many others. The purpose of this mini-theology course is to show both the interrelatedness of the concepts – the amazing consistency of what the Bible teaches – and how incompatible they are with what John Calvin believed and taught. For example, if God in his sovereignty "renders all things certain" as Calvin taught, then the spiritual battle, prayer, and personal development are all complete nonsense. We appear to have free will, but actually don't. We appear to make decisions and take actions that affect the future, but we actually don't. Why pray for God's will to be done on earth as it is in heaven, when it already is? Why practice birth control, when what eventually happens has already been determined before the foundation of the earth? Why evangelize when those individuals who will be saved were already determined in eternity past? Why teach a kid not to run out in the street?

These inconsistencies are examined in more depth in Chapter 8, primarily by asking questions that Calvinism cannot answer logically. Then I show the conclusions I have come to, based on almost 20 years of studying this subject and working with cross cultural translation. Briefly, I reflect on how each part of the argument I have made, applies to Calvinism. Overall, for me, the evidence has become completely overwhelming. Calvinism presents such an inadequate view of God and his plan for the ages, that rather than disclose truth, it obscures it. When the dots are connected, the picture becomes too clear to ignore.

Chapter 1
Who is John Calvin, and Why Does it Matter?

If anything matters, everything matters.
– Wm. Paul Young[1]

The noise of the carnage in the ship's engine room was muffled in the crew cabins, not likely to awaken anyone that far away. Yet the father was instantly awake. Was it the sudden stillness that woke him, or the loudspeaker on deck spouting commands? Or both? The constant vibration was missing, replaced with distant shouts of scrambling crew. The father groped for a light switch, but it didn't respond. The emergency lighting illuminated the door, but not much more. As his eyes adjusted, he could see a little light seeping through the porthole, so it must be morning, but barely so. Had they docked? Not likely – they were supposed to be two weeks away from anywhere. And the engines never shut off, even in port. Something didn't fit.

He sat on the side of his bunk for a moment, listening for sounds from the two adjacent cabins. Nothing. That was good. All four kids must *still be asleep. He was relieved that they were already starting to adjust. His mind slid back over the events that had him sitting in the dark on a container ship, somewhere in the Pacific.*

In February, when he and his wife had celebrated their fifteenth wedding anniversary, she was not as energetic as usual. He had planned a weekend of hiking, returning to their hotel each evening to clean up and enjoy time alone. She hadn't complained, but the schedule seemed to exhaust her – she joked about being out of shape. Over the next several weeks, the tiredness got worse, but things were busy so she tried to ignore it. Then one day she had been really sick, with aches and pains all over her body and nausea when she tried to walk. Probably the flu, but he took her to see the doctor anyway. It was not flu – it was advanced bone cancer. Less than two months later, she was gone, leaving the entire family numb with shock.

They had managed to get through the last few weeks of school, aware that summer would bring a whole new set of problems. Without the mother, the fabric of the family was unravelling. Finally, somebody suggested getting away for the summer, to regroup and heal. A cruise, maybe? The father checked into cruises, but the more he checked, the more they realized that most cruises were too expensive, too public, and too short for healing. Then an ad offered a different type of cruise – around the world on a freightliner. Older ships had been reconditioned to carry containerized freight, and fewer crew members meant empty crew cabins. One company was experimenting with converting the extra cabins into comfortable quarters for travelers who wanted a long, glitz-free cruise – maybe writers or artists. It sounded perfect for the grieving family, so the father made arrangements for a leave of absence, and they packed their bags with a variety of clothes, anticipating a range of weather conditions over the next several weeks. They had embarked two weeks ago. They were the only ones on the ship other than the crew.

Now what?

The passageway was as dimly lit as the room. He weaved his way to the bridge, where he found the captain and several crew. In the background, now, he could hear a diesel engine – a standby generator no doubt, for just such occasions.

When he opened the door, the conversation stopped, and everybody looked at him. To the crew, the captain said, "You know what to do. Do it." To the father, he said, "You're wondering what happened?"

"I noticed the engines quit," the father said.

"They didn't just quit. We can't get in there to see, but we think a bearing to the prop failed, so the main shaft broke loose and threw metal through several bulkheads. The two crew got out and locked the engine room down, but it's already full of water, and now it's coming into the main hold. The damage is under three layers of containers, and even if we could get to it, we couldn't fix it underwater. We think we have about two hours before that hold is full, but when it is, the ship will be unstable. The nearest help is about four hours away, so it looks like we're gonna be in lifeboats for awhile. You need to get your kids to the foredeck. The crew already have the lifeboats ready to launch."

It took the father less than ten minutes to be back to the foredeck with two of his kids. Crew members helped them put on lifejackets, and were about to help them into one of the bright orange, fully enclosed lifeboats, when the captain appeared. He visibly counted the crew, and to the one in charge, he said, "Crew is all accounted for. As soon as you get everybody loaded, launch the lifeboats. You and I will go in the last one." To the father, he said, "Are all your kids ready to go?"

"I brought the ones who're going," the father replied.

"The ones who're going? What does that mean?"

"Two are still sleeping. I brought the two who are going."

The captain looked at the father as if he had heard something wrong. "Two of them are still sleeping? Go wake them up. We're ready to launch, but there's plenty of time. We'll wait."

In a quiet but firm voice, the father replied, "No, I've already brought the two I've chosen. The other two stay."

Jehan Cauvin was born 10 July, 1509, in the town of Noyon in the Picardy region of France. His father prospered working for the church court so it was natural for him to want his sons to be priests. Jehan was exceptionally bright, and even as a child, devoutly religious. By age 12, he was working as a clerk for the bishop, and had shaved his head according to the tradition of the priests, a symbol of dedication known as tonsure.[2]

At age 14 Jehan went to Paris to study in preparation for university. While in Paris he changed his name to its Latin form, Ioannis Calvinus, which in French became Jean Calvin. English history knows him as John Calvin.

When Calvin finished the preparatory courses at Collège de la Marche, he transferred to the Collège de Montaigu as a philosophy student. The Collège de Montaigu had come under the influence of the humanist Jan Standonck in the 15th century, so by the time Calvin started his studies there, it was attracting reformers from within the Roman Catholic Church. The influence of Calvin's contacts there prepared him for his later participation in the Protestant Reformation.

Before Calvin finished at the Collège de Montaigu, his father advised him to study law rather than theology, so around 1528 he moved to Orleans to study civil law, a humanist education which involved studying in various places and under various scholars.[3] By 1532 Calvin finished his law studies and published his first work, which was a commentary of Seneca the Younger's De Clementia. Published at his own expense, it showed that he was a humanist in the tradition of Erasmus with a thorough understanding of classical scholarship.[4] We will see more of Erasmus later.

The following year Calvin was forced to flee Paris because of his opposition to the Roman Catholic Church. He spent the next three years in hiding in various places outside of France. By 1536 he had completely broken with the Roman Catholic Church, begun work on the first edition of his famed *Institutes*, and left France permanently. He initially landed in Geneva, where he pastored for the first time, even though he had not been officially consecrated.[5] Within two years, he was asked to leave because of theological conflicts.[6] He settled in Strasbourg for three years, during which time he married a widow with two children from her first marriage. By 1541, changes in Geneva had altered the political climate, so the Council of Geneva requested that he return, which he did.[7] Soon after their arrival in Geneva, his wife gave birth prematurely to their only child together, who did not survive. Calvin's wife died in 1549, and Calvin never remarried. He remained in Geneva until his death on 27 May, 1564. Those 23 years were filled with deep controversy, opposition, and political wrangling, as well as a heavy workload – lecturing, preaching, and writing.

In his early years, Calvin deeply respected Martin Luther, including writing his own catechism based largely on Luther's Large Catechism.[8] In later years, however, Calvin was aligned with Ulrich (or Huldrych) Zwingli from Zurich in a doctrinal dispute with Luther, and Calvin actively participated in the polemics that were exchanged between the Lutheran and the Reformed branches of the Reformation movement.[9] Polemics, in case the term is unfamiliar, is a form of theological argument similar to apologetics, except in polemics, the purpose of the argument is to conclusively prove the opponent wrong.

The unusual and lasting influence of John Calvin can be traced to at least eight factors, which strengthened his local influence, and extended it beyond his local area and beyond his lifetime:

1. his exceptional intelligence;[10]
2. his sermons, which were popular and numerous – he preached over 2000 during his time in Geneva;[11]
3. his copious writings, which rival what can be done in the same time with computers today;[12]

4. his recognition of the importance of music and his use of it to teach and support Scripture;[13]

5. the school and academy which he started in Geneva in 1559, which later became Collège Calvin and eventually the University of Geneva;[14]

6. the fact that he gave shelter in Geneva to exiles from Scotland and England during the Catholic reign of Mary I in England and Ireland (later known as "Bloody Mary"), including John Knox and William Whittingham and others, who later returned to their homelands and became influential proponents of Calvin's doctrine;[15]

7. the fact that he deliberately exported his views, sending over 100 ministers as missionaries into France between 1555 and 1562 to promote his reforms, funded by the church in Geneva;[16] and,

8. the fact that he "identified his own view with the cause of God," which was consistent with his oligarchic view of leadership, that only an elite group of the upper class are given the divine right to make radical changes in the social order – a view that either stemmed from an innate confidence, or gave him an innate confidence, that enabled him to lead even to the point of having his opponents executed.[17]

Several incidents reveal the culture of Geneva in Calvin's day, and his participation in it.

On 27 June 1547, a letter threatening the church leaders was found at the pulpit of St. Pierre Cathedral where Calvin preached. Under torture, a suspect confessed, was condemned to death by the civil court, and beheaded. John Calvin supported the decision.[18]

In 1551, a Geneva physician named Jérôme-Hermès Bolsec accused Calvin of making God the author of sin with his doctrine of predestination. As a result, Bolsec was banished from the city. After

Calvin's death, Bolsec wrote a biography severely castigating Calvin's character.[19]

Around 1546, Calvin started corresponding with Michael Servetus, a Spanish physician and Protestant theologian who had openly criticized the doctrine of the trinity and infant baptism[20] and as a result, was tried in absentia by Catholic church authorities. To avoid his sentence of "death by slow burning," Servetus went into hiding.[21] Over a period of time, he and Calvin exchanged some 30 letters debating doctrine,[22] with each concealing his true identity for fear of future recriminations, but both, apparently, fully aware of whom they were debating. Eventually Calvin became outraged at Servetus and stopped responding. When Servetus mentioned coming to Geneva, Calvin wrote to William Farel, the man who had originally convinced him to stay in Geneva, that if Servetus came, "as far as my authority goes, I would not let him leave alive."[23] Servetus did come to Geneva on 13 August, 1553, and was arrested and sentenced to death by the Protestant controlled civil authorities, at Calvin's urging.[24] On 27 October, Servetus was burned alive at the Plateau of Champel outside Geneva.[25]

During February, 1555, elections in Geneva strongly favored Calvin and his supporters. In May, their opponents staged a drunken protest that included attempting to burn down a house full of Calvin's supporters. As the insurrection was suppressed, the leaders fled the city, and four others involved were identified and executed, with Calvin's approval. This effectively ended opposition to Calvin's leadership, so his authority was practically uncontested during his final decade.[26] Under his authority, every luxury in goods and clothing was forbidden and public theaters were closed.[27]

John Calvin's contributions to the Protestant Reformation are second only to those of Martin Luther, so his influence can hardly be overstated. It is the skeleton of his doctrine, however, for which he is famous, and which has kept him at the center of controversy for almost 500 years. He maintained that the following teachings are contained within the Bible, and form the basis for understanding all of Scripture: 1) That humans are totally depraved – heart, emotions, will, mind, and body, are all affected by sin; 2) that God, by his sovereign grace, predestines certain people to salvation; 3) that Jesus died only for the predestined; 4) that God works within predestined individuals so they are able to and want to respond to the gospel; and 5) that it is impossible for those who are redeemed to lose their salvation.[28] In English, the word TULIP forms a five-letter acronym to make the five points of Calvinism memorable:

Total Depravity – that every part of every human is depraved, affected by sin

Unconditional Election – that God sovereignly elects some for salvation and not others

Limited Atonement – that Jesus died only for the elect

Irresistible Grace – that those predestined cannot fail to respond to the call of God

Perseverance of the Saints – that once the chosen are saved, they cannot lose their salvation

---

When I was 45 years old, and my wife Donna was 41, we made the decision as a family to leave our businesses and home, and commit the next several years of our lives to Christian mission work. It was not made lightly. We both had experienced a clear sense of calling that made the upheaval of the family justified in our minds. Almost immediately, we started the process of divesting ourselves of our businesses and helping employees find new sources of income, which proved to take almost two full years. Donna returned to college to finish her degree, which she had postponed to devote herself to family and business responsibilities. At the time, our two daughters were 13 and 10.

When we were free of business obligations, I entered seminary in Canada, following a series of events that we interpreted as the clear leading of the Lord for us to do so. It proved to be a crucial step in the journey to my current understanding of Scripture.

The seminary was small, but a couple of things made it unique, and appropriate for where we were on our journey of faith. For one, it had been founded by a man of great faith and great spiritual wisdom, and his legacy lived on. For another, the seminary was very cross cultural. I personally had professors from China, Brazil, Sweden, the United States, and Canada, and there were others from other countries. The students came from all of those same countries, and more – Jamaica, the Netherlands, India, Korea ....

Because the students represented a wide variety of ethnic and denominational backgrounds, the seminary was known for trying to teach "how to think" rather than "what to think." In other words, they were trying to press us to develop our own walk with God, and our own understanding of Scripture, so we could formulate our own theology and know why we believed it. Often a professor would present different denominational perspectives, and force us to deal with them ourselves, rather than telling us which one was "right." We had discussions, sometimes heated, about "mythology in Genesis" and whether "the Fall" in the Garden of Eden could be symbolic without the rest of the gospel message falling apart. One thing was consistent about my professors, though. All who allowed their own doctrinal leanings to be known, were Calvinistic. I entered the seminary from a distinctly Calvinistic church; I thought I understood the reasoning on which Calvinism rests, and I believed it.

So I entered seminary believing Calvinism, spent two and a half years studying under professors who believed Calvinism, and by the time I graduated and left seminary behind, I had also left Calvinism behind. I think I am now as far away from Calvinism as it is possible to get. More importantly, I know why. This book will relate what led me to change my mind, and where my thinking has gone since those earlier days.

As a basic premise of any worldview, it matters whether we believe in God, or not. It affects what we do.

As I have come to realize, it also matters what we believe about God. It affects what we do. John Calvin believed very differently from the Catholics of his background, very differently from many other Protestants of his day, very differently from Michael Servetus and others of his opponents, whose deaths he contributed to, whose deaths were simply for believing differently. John Calvin was a product of the culture of his day, but his legacy is part of the culture of our day. It's time to examine that legacy from a new perspective.

Endnotes

[1] Wm. Paul Young, *The Shack* (Los Angeles, CA: Windblown Media, 2007), 235, 248.

[2] Thomas Henry Louis Parker, *John Calvin: A Biography* (Oxford: Lion Hudson PLC, 2006), 3.

[3] Karin Maag, https://calvin.edu/about/history/john-calvin.html?dotcmsredir=1, accessed 19 June 2016.

[4] Wulfert De Greef, *The Writings of John Calvin: An Introductory Guide* (Louisville, KY: Westminster John Knox Press, 2008), 41; Bernard Cottret, *Calvin: A Biography*, transl. from French [*Calvin: Biographie, 1995*] by M. Wallace McDonald (Grand Rapids, MI: Wm. B. Eerdmans, 2000), 63-65; Alister E. McGrath, *A Life of John Calvin* (Oxford: Basil Blackwell, 1990), 60-62; David C. Steinmetz, "Calvin as Biblical Interpreter Among the Ancient Philosophers", *Interpretation* 63 (2) 2009: 142–153.

[5] Cottret, *Calvin*, 170-171.

[6] Cottret, *Calvin*, 129-131; McGrath, 98-100; Parker, *Calvin*, 2006, 85-90.

[7] Parker, *Calvin*, 2006, 103-107.

[8] Cottret, *Calvin*, 120.

[9] T. H. L. Parker, *John Calvin* (Tring, Hertfordshire, England: Lion Publishing Plc, 1975), 162-163.

[10] His sermons lasted more than an hour, and he preached without using notes. Dawn DeVries, "Calvin's Preaching," in *The Cambridge Companion to John Calvin*, ed. Donald K. McKim (Cambridge: Cambridge University Press, 2004), 106-124.

[11] DeVries, "Calvin's Preaching," 106-124; Parker, *Calvin*, 2006, 116-123.

[12] Parker, *Calvin*, 2006, 161-164.

[13] Cottret, *Calvin*, 172-174; Parker, *Calvin*, 2006, 92-93, 112-115.

[14] Cottret, *Calvin*, 256-259; Alexandre Ganoczy, "Calvin's Life," trans. David L. Foxgrover, in *The Cambridge Companion to John Calvin*, ed. Donald K. McKim (Cambridge: Cambridge University Press, 2004), 19-20; Jeannine Olson, "Calvin and social-ethical issues," in *The Cambridge Companion to John Calvin*, ed. Donald K. McKim (Cambridge: Cambridge University Press, 2004), 158-159; Parker, *Calvin*, 2006, 157-160.

[15] Parker, *Calvin*, 2006, 170-172.

[16] McGrath, *Life of Calvin*, 1990, 182-184; Parker, *Calvin*, 2006, 178-180.

[17] Ganoczy, "Calvin's Life," 10-12, 20.

[18] Cottret, *Calvin*, 190-191; De Greef, *Writings*, 30-31; John Thomas McNeil, *The History and Character of Calvinism* (Oxford: Oxford University Press, 1954), 170-171; Parker 2006, 136-138.

[19] Cottret, *Calvin*, 208-211; Richard C. Gamble, "Calvin's Controversies," in *The Cambridge Companion to John Calvin*, ed. Donald K. McKim (Cambridge: Cambridge University Press, 2004), 198-9; McGrath, 16-17.

[20] Roland H. Bainton, *Hunted Heretic: The Life and Death of Michael Servetus, 1511-1553* (Revised edition edited by Peter Hughes and jointly published in Providence, RI by Blackstone Editions and the Unitarian Universalist Historical Society, 2005), 141. (Original publication Boston, MA: The Beacon Press, 1953).

[21] Parker, *Calvin*, 2006, 140-150.

[22] Michael Servetus, "Thirty letters to Calvin," *Christianismi Restitutio*, Part 4.

[23] Cottret, *Calvin*, 216-217; Leonard W. Levy, *Blasphemy: Verbal Offense Against the Sacred from Moses to Salman Rushdie*, (Chapel Hill, NC: Univ. of North Carolina Press, 1995), 65; Parker 2006, 147-148.

[24] Ganoczy, "Calvin's Life," 18.

[25] Cottret, *Calvin*, 222-225; McGrath, *Life of Calvin*, 1990, 118-120; Parker, *Calvin*, 2006, 150-152.

[26] Cottret, *Calvin*, 195-200; Scott M. Manetsch, *Calvin's Company of Pastors: Pastoral Care and the Emerging Reformed Church, 1536–1609, Oxford Studies in Historical Theology*, (New York: Oxford University Press, 2013), 187; Parker 2006, 154-157.

[27] Ganoczy, "Calvin's Life," 19.

[28] John Calvin, *Institutes of the Christian Religion* [Originally published in Latin in 1564 as *Institutio Christianae religionis*], translated by Henry Beveridge (Grand Rapids, MI: Wm. B. Eerdmans Publishing Company, 1989). Calvin's *Institutes* can be found online at this link: http://www.ntslibrary.com/PDF%20Books/Calvin%20Institutes%20of%20Christian%20Religion.pdf

Chapter 2
How We Know What We Know

A person wearing tinted glasses can avoid the conclusion that the entire world is tinted only by being conscious of the glasses themselves.
– Justo L. Gonzalez[1]

Paul Harvey was famous for interjecting interesting stories and his own opinions into his "News and Commentary" broadcasts.[2] When a madman shot people at random on a university campus, Paul Harvey would comment, "If you could understand people who do such things, we'd have to worry about you, too." After telling a story from another part of the world that he knew would seem particularly bizarre to his audience, he would often say, "It's not one world, you know." That comment leads us to this question:

What makes it "not one world"?

Cultures and Worldviews

The answer lies in the concept of *worldviews*. Simply stated, our worldview is the way we see and interpret the world. It includes all of our assumptions, conscious and unconscious, about the way the world works – past, present, and future. One way of thinking about worldviews is to imagine them as lenses through which we see the world, or mental glasses. Worldviews are made up of many different assumptions, which individually are often called *paradigms*. Both of these ideas are important, worth spending some time on.

Even if we have never heard the words *worldview* or *paradigm* before, we intuitively understand the ideas if we've ever encountered people from other cultures. It's obvious to us that tribal people without cars or clocks, see the world very differently from, say, people in Switzerland or Germany, where high speed trains are punctual to the millisecond. Let's look at some examples to show what worldviews are, and how they affect things.

One writer tells about a western Peace Corps nurse teaching microbiology to nursing students in a developing country. The students listened respectfully, took notes, and passed all the tests, but when the final exam was over, one girl raised her hand and said, "Miss, I know you taught us about polio, but would you like to know how people *really* get it?" Then she proceeded to describe the role of the spirit world in causing disease and death. The teacher later commented that she was saddened by their lack of understanding. The *writer*, in relating the story, commented that the teacher's perspective was as limited as that of her students, because she was as blind to the personal nature of evil and the impact of the demonic world on health, as she assumed her students were to the realities of microbiology.[3]

In this story, we see three different worldviews:
- The animistic worldview of the nursing students, in which the

spirit world animates and controls the physical world, including causing disease and death, or healing;

- The secular worldview of the teacher, which sees the physical world as all there is, so any belief in a spirit world is ridiculed and all solutions to problems are achievable only through scientific understanding and human effort;

- The biblical worldview of the writer relating the story, which sees both the physical and spiritual worlds as reality, and sees a connection between the two worlds, including interaction and interdependence between them, so disease and death operate in the physical world in which microbes live, but can be influenced by spirit beings in a world cannot be detected through current scientific means.

Let's briefly consider how these worldviews will affect the behavior of those who hold them. The nursing students, with an animistic background, will be tempted to do something to appease the spirits if someone in their family gets ill. The secular teacher will seek medical treatment, and the writer evaluating the other two, will be tempted to pray about the illness, but will also probably seek medical help. Each is experiencing the same situation, but different worldviews will lead to different actions in response to it.

It matters what we believe. It affects what we do.

Another example, briefly, from the same writer. He relates a personal experience:

When I first came to Food for the Hungry, I visited some friends who were working in a beautiful, almost alpine valley called Costanza in the Dominican Republic. It has many farms and a temperate climate year-round. As we drove, I remarked, "This almost looks like paradise." The people we were working among were some of the poorest in the country, yet I saw some beautiful villas on a hill with a majestic view of the countryside. "Who owns these houses?" I asked. My companions replied, "There are some Japanese families here." It turned out that these Japanese had come to the Dominican Republic right after the war, with *nothing*. Like the locals, they labored as poor farmers. Yet after just a few decades they were prosperous, while the Dominicans still struggled to eke out a living in the midst of a breathtaking setting. The difference was not physical; it was worldview. The Japanese settlers have a social value called *gambere*, which roughly translates, "Try harder, don't give up, never give up." .... The local farmers were fatalistic, believing, "whatever will be, will be."[4]

Here we see two more conflicting worldviews, made more obvious by the fact that they were present at the same time and place:

- The worldview held by the Japanese, that humans can control nature;
- The worldview held by the Dominican farmers, that nature controls humans.

The belief concerning humans and our relationship with nature is a part of every worldview, whether we realize it or not. Since these two views are polar opposites of each other, they can be shown on a continuum, something like this:

Nature controls humans	*Humans affect nature*	*Humans* control nature
⟵	*Nature affects humans*	⟶

Since everybody has this belief as part of their worldview, everybody falls on that line somewhere. People with completely fatalistic worldviews will be on the extreme left, and optimists with a western secular worldview will be somewhere near the far right. Most of us raised in western nations are more balanced, so we say that humans can overcome certain aspects of nature, but some we cannot. For example, we recognize that irrigation can make a desert into an agricultural haven, and irresponsible urbanization can pollute the air, causing forests nearby to die. We recognize that we do have an effect on our physical world, but we do not have total control. We can clean up the air from the city and replant and cultivate the forest, but we can't prevent the hurricane or tornado that comes through and levels both the city and the forest.

Both of these two illustrations come from a person who has spent his life working with poor people in various parts of the world, trying to help them overcome the forces that keep them poor. It's obvious to a person in that line of work that different worldviews create different expectations about how things work, so they determine how efforts are directed, so they produce different outcomes.

This can be illustrated in a very simple way:

Beliefs or ideas $\longrightarrow$ behavior or actions $\longrightarrow$ results or outcomes

We said that we quickly observe differences in worldviews whenever we see people of different cultures. So what is culture? To combine a couple of definitions, culture is the *integrated system* of "language, habits, ideas, beliefs, customs, social organization, inherited artifacts, technical processes, and values,"[5] "which binds a society together and gives it a sense of identity, dignity, security, and continuity."[6] Culture is the composite of those things that make a group of people think of themselves as separate from other people groups, and which enable them to automatically understand one another. The "language, habits, ideas, beliefs," etc. are all patterns which have been assigned a common meaning, locally.[7] Culture and worldview are deeply interrelated – in essence, culture is the environment which shapes the thinking process of the individuals within it, so they share the same way of thinking about the world. The culture produces the worldview, and the worldview produces the culture.

One of the ways we can think of our worldviews is as maps in our minds.[8] For example, let's imagine that I'm going on a business trip to Budapest, Hungary, and I've recently watched a Dracula movie that mentions Hungary, so while I'm there, I want to see everything I can about this infamous person. As I do some research in anticipation of my trip, I find that the historical person the movies show as "Dracula" spent time in prison in Visegrád Hungary, so I plan to visit Visegrád and see the castle where he was imprisoned. I'm excited at the prospect!

In actual fact, Visegrád is a small castle town about 45 km north of Budapest on the right bank of the Danube River, and was home to the Royal Palace of the King of Hungary during Hungary's glory days (1308-1490), but I don't know that, so I order a map of Hungary, and when it arrives, I search for Visegrád, and I find the name marking a city about 120 km *southwest* of Budapest, about 15 km north of a large lake named Balaton. Now I'm more than excited – I'm elated! I make my travel plans, to include renting a car and scheduling an entire day to drive down to the Lake Balaton area and visit the castle at Visegrád.

ONE OF THE WAYS WE CAN THINK OF OUR WORLDVIEWS IS AS MAPS IN OUR MINDS

The time comes, I take my trip, do the business I came for, and the day arrives for my Dracula tour. Finally! The weather is nice, it's going to be a great day! I get the rental car, and with my trusted map in hand, I drive to the place the map shows as Visegrád, and I look for the famous castle. I see a lot of beautiful things, but I don't find the castle, and people keep telling me I'm in the wrong city. When I show them my map, they shake their heads and point to a place north of Budapest which the map says is Veszprém. I never find what I'm looking for, so I go home deeply disappointed, and my one free day is gone, so I never get to see what I wanted to see. It's only later that I realize that my map, 99.9% accurate, had just two tiny errors. Somehow the names of two cities had been switched – Visegrád and Veszprém.

To understand what just happened, we have to consider the concept of *reality*. My imaginary trip to Hungary was deeply disappointing because what my map showed did not accurately reflect the *reality* that was on the ground. Made personal, I have to admit that since I trusted the map, *my understanding* did not match the reality that was on the ground. The *map in my mind* did not match the reality that was on the ground.

Let's look at another illustration that is commonly used to make this point.

This time, we're invisible observers on the bridge of a military ship, on a mission, travelling at night. The officer on duty sees a flashing light ahead, just coming over the horizon. As he watches it, he sees it coming directly toward them, so he notifies his captain and asks for instructions.

Wanting to avoid a collision, the captain gives his duty officer instructions to send a message to the other ship, "Change course 20 degrees starboard" (to the right). The reply came back, "Unable to comply. For your safety, suggest you change course 20 degrees starboard." Time is passing, and the light is getting closer, so the captain gives the instruction to send the message again, "Change course 20 degrees starboard." Again the reply came back, "Unable to comply. For your safety, you should change course 20 degrees starboard." Angry now, the captain sends the message, "I am a military destroyer. I insist that you change your course 20 degrees starboard." The reply came back, "Unable to comply. For your safety, you should change course 20 degrees starboard. I am a lighthouse."

What the captain was visualizing in his mind, did not match the reality that was "out there."

Both of these illustrations make the point that our understanding can be different from what is actual reality. For simplicity, we can use the letter "r" to stand for "reality," so the reality that is "out there" we can call "Big R" and the reality that is in our minds, "in here," is "little r." When "little r" does not match "Big R" then we have the potential to fail, as I did on my imaginary search for Dracula, or we can even place ourselves in the path of danger, as our ship's captain was doing. This concept is well understood in all the social sciences today, but it was not always so. It is obvious that many people never really consider that what they "know" may be a very poor or even completely false reflection of the reality "out there."

I remember the first time I was ever confronted with this concept. I was barely 18 years old, and had just entered college. Sitting in a Sociology class just days into that first semester, we were presented with the idea that "We don't respond to situations as the situations are, but as we perceive them to be." Think about how much useless information we are presented with in four years of college, and how much we forget, and you get a sense of the impression that statement made on me. Decades later, I still have a visual image of that class, instructor up front, other students all around me, as I realized for the first time that the world might actually be different from the way I saw it. (I had a lot of German influence in my background.)

What happened that day was the start of a process for me, of seeing the world differently. It was the start of a paradigm change. Thomas Kuhn was the one who really introduced this idea of paradigm change to the world in 1962 in a book called *The Structure of Scientific Revolutions*.[9] We tend to think of progress as being made through a process of accumulating facts. But, Kuhn said, it's not so simple. It is not the new facts that enable progress, it's that those new facts enable us to visualize new options. It's the new way of looking at things, the paradigm change that the new facts produce, that enables progress.

At any particular time and place, the circumstances that exist – the knowledge that is available, and the way the world is viewed – produce both the possibilities that can be explored, and their limits. This explains the extreme differences in the fortunes of the Japanese farmers and the Dominican farmers that we considered earlier. Kuhn observed that it's not that other options are considered and discarded, it's that other options are never even considered, because they cannot even be conceptualized. That's why Food for the Hungry was working in the Dominican Republic in the first place – to give the local people new options that they had never even visualized before. Kuhn makes the point that as new information is gathered and assimilated, it produces a new, changed perspective, a new paradigm, a new way of seeing the world from which new options can be envisioned, which can then be explored. With that exploration, the learning we acquire from it enables us to envision even newer possibilities, so we explore them, and on and on it goes. But within the changing perspective that new information provides, Kuhn observed, *the vast majority of all intellectual effort is spent defending what is already believed, rather than in exploring new possibilities.* In 1633, Galileo experienced that backlash, and spent the last nine years of his life under house arrest. He was fortunate that he was not killed. For most people, most of the time, it feels safer to protect the maps in our minds, than to amend them to better fit the information that is accumulating.

THE VAST MAJORITY OF ALL INTELLECTUAL EFFORT IS SPENT DEFENDING WHAT IS ALREADY BELIEVED, RATHER THAN IN EXPLORING NEW POSSIBILITIES

As the story of the Japanese and Dominican farmers illustrates, the maps in our minds determine our success in life. If our "little r" is very close to "Big R," then we see the world generally the way it is, so as long as we do what we know to do, we tend to be successful. However, the further away from "Big R" our "little r" gets, the more we are actually trying to interact with a world that is not the way we think it is, so the more we are prone to failure.

- Accidents result: "I thought I had the right of way."
- "I thought the limb was strong enough to hold my weight."

- Disappointment occurs: "I thought the assignment was due on Monday."
- "I thought he actually loved me."
- Failure occurs: "He thought he was sober enough to drive."
- "When she started smoking, nobody knew that cigarettes cause cancer."

When our "little r" is very different from "Big R," we are interacting with an imaginary world. The world, as we see it, does not exist in reality; it exists only in our minds. Since this is true, it makes sense to try to get our "little r," the maps in our minds, as close as possible to "Big R," the reality that is "out there," on the ground.

This idea will not go away. It applies to all of us, in all areas of this life and beyond, and it will be important as we examine the claims of Calvinism.

Knowing

Having established that our understanding can be different from reality, let's think about the whole idea of knowing. The purpose of this section is not to plumb the depths of epistemology – the theory of knowledge – its purpose it to introduce an element of humility into our thinking. Let's say that in one area of life, our "little r" perfectly matches "Big R." In that case, we can say that we *know* this particular thing, because our belief exactly matches reality. But if we're both humble and realistic, we have to admit that life is rarely that certain. We use the word "know" with casual confidence, usually without giving it any real thought, when in actual fact, we are often dealing more with *degrees of certainty* than with really *knowing*.

When we think about it, we realize that what we know, or consider ourselves to know, comes from three possible sources: the testimony of others, our own experiences, and the reasoning processes in our own minds.[10] If we're honest, we will admit that all of these sources are fallible. We have all been lied to by others, or given false information in good faith, so we're aware that the testimony of others is not always reliable. We've also had occasions when we experienced something, but later realized that something went wrong in the recording process, so that the way we remembered it does not match other sources, maybe even a photographic record. So at least occasionally, our own memories, our own experiences, are not reliable. And of course, we've all experienced occasions when we've used our own reasoning, only to find out that we've come up with the wrong answer. This is common in math classes, more so for some than others. So, even our own reasoning process is subject to failure. When we consider these things in a practical sense, it shows how potentially uncertain our knowledge actually is. Malcolm Muggeridge summed this up precisely when he said, "We know that we can't know."[11]

To illustrate this, ask yourself if you really know who your own biological mother is. Everything you assume that you know about your ancestors is hearsay, that is, it's based on the testimony of others. You assume you lived through your own birth, but have no memories of it, so you can't rely on your own experience there. Your logic might indicate that the people who raised you were in fact your parents, but there are cases of infants being swapped in hospitals,[12] and we've also known of cases where adopted children never knew they were adopted until later in life. You might take the position that you could use DNA testing to prove kinship, but even that is open to question, in that you would then be relying on (1) the validity of the test itself, which is based on the testimony of others, and (2) the reading of the test, which is based on the testimony of the technician, who might have been drunk or tired at the time the test results were read, or maybe just inept or poorly trained.

When we actually consider these issues, we realize that virtually all that we consider ourselves to know we're actually accepting as true based on the testimony of others. This includes our schooling, the news we hear, our understanding of the way the universe is built, and the way the world works. It creates a dilemma when we think about it, because we come to realize that ultimately, what we believe is all suspect to some degree. In a sense, then, we as individuals ultimately become the final judges of what we accept as true, and what we don't.

We will get to know more about William James later, but for now, it might be helpful to include an observation he made. In regard to knowing, he pointed out that the field can be divided into two teams: those who believe that we can not only know, but we can know that we know, and those who believe that we can know, but not know for certain that we know. Then James points out that all of us, by what he calls instinct, act like those who are completely certain that they know ("dogmatize like infallible popes").[13] In other words, in the practical, day to day way we function, we automatically assume that we know, and that we know that we know. We can accept at the theoretical level that our knowing may be suspect, even impossible to prove beyond doubt, but for practical purposes, it works well to accept that we know, and to act accordingly.

For ordinary, daily life, this works well. But if something is critically important, it may not be good enough. This brings us back to the dilemma that everything we believe is suspect to some degree, so we as individuals ultimately become the final judges of what we believe – what we accept as true, and what we don't.

Since we are faced with that dilemma, it makes sense to understand the issue of truth, so we can decide how to manage the part we play in this process of determining what we believe.

Truth

We've looked at culture and worldviews, and tried to show how their connection with the reality that is "out there" affects our success. Now let's look at how this is related to *truth*.

Ravi Zacharias says that there are three basic tests for truth: *logical consistency, empirical adequacy,* and *experiential relevance*.[14] We're going to look at each of these in more detail, but first, let's get the last two into simpler terms. By *empirical adequacy*, he means that a "truth claim" – whatever is stated as truth – can be verified by observation or experience rather than just in theory or by pure logic. By *experiential relevance*, he means that if we try to use this truth in a practical way, it will work. We can experience how this idea connects to the real world.

As we look at the idea of truth, and how we test for it, I will break some of Zacharias's three broad categories down into more specific tests, and bring in ideas from other sources.

Going back to my imaginary trip to Hungary, let's think of what might have happened after I got the map, but before I actually took the trip. I was excited, so I would talk about my upcoming trip with anybody who would listen. I would pull out my map and show them what I planned to do – rent a car, drive southwest of Budapest for a couple of hours to the Lake Balaton area and visit the castle at Visegrád where the

TRUTH IS SIMPLY AN ACCURATE EXPRESSION OF THE WAY THINGS REALLY ARE

formidable Dracula spent years languishing in squalor in the dungeon of a medieval castle. "Think about it! Isn't this going to be exciting?"

So I would enthuse about my plans, but was I telling the truth?

The answer is no, because (to be profound), truth must be true to be truth. The most basic definition of truth is that it is an understanding or statement that accurately describes reality. Truth is not reality itself, it is a *description* of reality. We can say, then, that *truth is simply an accurate expression of the way things really are.* As I bore my friends with the details of my upcoming trip, I am not telling them the truth, because I don't have it myself. I think I do, but time is going to prove me wrong. Regardless of how confident I am of my information, if it does not accurately reflect the reality that is out there, it is not truth. Being certain is not the same thing as having the truth. Certainty is contained within "little r," truth is an accurate reflection of "Big R."

A critical point here is that our *belief* about reality has no bearing on the actual reality that is out there. William James realized this as well: "Throughout the breadth of physical nature," he said, "facts are what they are quite independently of us."[15] What we *believe* about a thing does not change that *thing*. What we believe may change the way we interact with it, but it doesn't change the reality itself. Consider the statements we made earlier:

> "I thought the limb was strong enough to hold my weight."
>
> "I thought the assignment was due on Monday."
>
> "When she started smoking, nobody knew that cigarettes cause cancer."

The strength of the limb, the due date for the assignment, and the poisons in cigarettes are not affected by what we think about them. Imagine a man brought to a hospital, unconscious. When he awakens later, it's dark. Groggy, and with his head aching, he stumbles to the window and looks out into the darkness. He can see reflections off water about three floors below, so he concludes that the building is on the edge of a river. In his disoriented state, he reasons that he can jump out of the window into the river, swim to safety, and get on with life. So he takes the leap. The next time he wakes up, he's back in the hospital, but now his legs are in casts. In dim light, a street that is wet from a recent rain may look like a river, but it isn't. And concrete is still hard, regardless of what we call it, or what we believe about it. Our beliefs affect how we interact with reality, but don't affect the reality itself.

So from this starting point, we can make this argument:

Reality is reality:
– Whether we understand it or not
– Whether we agree with it or not
– Whether we like it or not

Consider a young lady who had an assignment due on Friday (reality, "Big R"), but thought it was due the following Monday (her belief, "little r"). Maybe she had a conversation with a classmate on Thursday, and they discuss when the assignment is due. She says she's glad it's due on Monday, so she can work on it over the weekend. At this point, the assignment is actually due on Friday, but she doesn't *understand* that. Her friend say it's due on Friday, but she's confident that she's right, so she insists, "No, it's due on Monday." In reality, it's still due on Friday, but she doesn't *agree* with it. Her friend pulls out the class calendar and shows her that the assignment is due on Friday, seriously raising her stress level, because she needs the weekend to get it done. It's too much to do in one day. The assignment is still due on Friday, even though she doesn't *like* it.

We have a hard time escaping from the reality of reality, regardless of what we believe about it, or how we respond to it. The problem extends to truth. Any time we are confronted with an accurate description of reality – whether we understand it or not, whether we agree with it or not, or whether we like it or not – it is still true.

As we attempt to understand the way life works, these ideas become more and more important. Living based on wrong understanding, is a form of bondage. We are held captive by beliefs that do not accurately explain the way things are. Success is impossible in that prison. We need to escape.

Let's say that when the two classmates discuss the due date of the assignment, they disagree. The fact that they disagree does not affect reality, so the problem is in the understanding of reality, that is, in their different perspectives that they both regard as the truth. So now we are presented with a deeper question – how do we *confirm* truth? In this case, the classmate pulls out the class calendar, appealing to an outside source that they both respect, and that settles the question. But it's not always so easy. Fortunately, we're not the first people to think about such things, so there are some logical ideas that can be applied. We can call them tests for truth. There are several, and they overlap to a degree. Let's look at them and see if they're helpful.

One test for truth is that it is *consistent with observable reality*, or as Ravi Zacharias put it, it has empirical adequacy. If this sounds obvious, that's because it is. When Mark Twain was reported to have died in London in 1897, he responded with, "the report of my death was an exaggeration."[16] Sometimes deciding what is true is as simple as pointing to something and saying, "How do you explain this?" At other times, reality is not easily observable, so we have to go deeper. Think, for example, about trusting a statement a person makes, when we have no way to check it out. What we may be able to do is to check to see if other statements the person has made have proven to be true. If so, it increases the chances that this statement is true as well, and so this test is not a guarantee, but it has some merit. What we're being told is consistent with observable reality, that is, that this person's word is reliable. It doesn't give us final proof, but it's still helpful. In court trials, the credibility of the witness is important. In the religions arena, this test is used to scrutinize the literature upon which a religion is based. If we are being asked to wager our eternal destiny on a belief system, we want to check out the reliability of the source. Is it consistent with observable reality?

Another test for truth is that it is *consistent with other truth*. This is very similar to the first test. Let's say, for example, that a friend tells us that he spent last night on the moon. In the past, his statements have been reliable, so he has, to some degree at least, passed the first test. We didn't spend the night watching him, so we don't really know where he spent the night. We do know that other people have spent time on the moon, so his contention is not beyond the realm of possibility. However, we do have some idea of the cost and complexity of getting to the moon and back, and as far as we know, our friend does not have either that amount of money or that capability, and as far as we know, he also doesn't have the contacts who could provide those things for him. Realistically, we're probably not going to believe him. His story seems to be inconsistent with other truths that we know.

A third test for truth is *internal coherence*. This, combined with the previous one, is Zacharias's logical consistency. Let's say that in the process of hearing our friend talk about his night out, we ask him some questions. He tells us that he left for the moon about midnight, and got back about 6 in the morning. We ask him how fast he was travelling, and he gives us a speed. We ask him if he knows how far it is to the moon, and he gives us an answer that agrees with what we remember from high school science. We do some quick mental calculations, and we realize that his speed doesn't work. If he had travelled at that speed, it would have taken him about two days each way, so he could not have left at midnight, travelled at the speed he says, and returned by early morning. At this point, his story is both inconsistent with other truth and lacks internal coherence. It fails the test for truth in two ways.

A fourth test is whether the truth claim is *complete* or not. Sometimes we may have only part of the picture. Maybe what we have is accurate, but if we had the whole picture, it would show something very different. A husband might tell his wife that he will be home late because he has to work late to get ready for a special event the next day, which is the truth. He knows he will have to work an extra hour or so. But he's actually going to get home four or five hours late, because he has also made arrangements to meet an old high school friend at a bar after work, and he doesn't think his wife would approve. Especially since the old friend is a female.

A lot of advertising uses this technique. We're told the benefits of the product, but not the true costs, or the side effects. This is also common in religions, including the way Christians use Scripture. People have used 1 Corinthians 7:29 (which says in part, "From now on, those who have wives should live as if they had none") to justify divorce or being so busy that family life is ignored. However, when we look at all that Scripture has to say about marriage relationships and family life, we can see that their understanding is reached by having only a small part of the entire picture. This principle is going to be important in our look at Calvinism.

Another test for truth is that it is *eventually provable*. This is Zacharias's experiential relevance. Some things can be verified quickly: "This pill will make your headache go away." Others take more time: "The rhythm method works for birth control. Trust me." "You can recover the Sahara desert by planting trees around the outside, then gradually working your way in." "Sperm cryogenically preserved in liquid nitrogen tanks can survive for thousands of years."

Truth is eventually provable. Murder cases are being solved today that could not be solved when they were committed 30 or 40 years ago. Witnesses come forward who were afraid to testify; new forensic methods are developed. Just because we cannot prove something today, does not mean it is not true, or that it can never be proven. A person who murdered somebody is still the murderer (truth), even if it cannot be proven today. The opposite is also happening. People who were convicted of crimes years ago sometimes have their sentences reversed. They were innocent all along (truth), but could not prove it. New evidence describes reality differently, so the courts decide their story really is true, after all. They get to go home.

Since there is such a direct relationship between truth and the reality that is out there, eventually it becomes obvious whether something is true or not. Anyone willing to wait thousands of years to see how well the sperm survives, can prove or disprove the claim. Simply put, truth works; falsehood doesn't. Over the years, I have observed three major areas of life that have the most success using falsehood – religion, politics, and education. In each field, statements can be made that will take years to prove. By the time the inaccuracy is obvious, the one who promoted it is gone, or the one who learned it is gone, so there is no accountability. And it may be too late to correct the mistake. This is especially true of religion, which can only be ultimately proven at death. But be assured, it will be proven at death. We will discuss later how to improve our chances of confirming our beliefs before that event occurs.

While we're on this subject of testing truth, though, let's make the case that it's always easier to prove a positive statement than a negative one. To prove a positive statement, all we have to do is produce one conclusive piece of evidence. To prove a negative statement, we have to eliminate all possible positive evidence, and that is often impractical or impossible. Let's look at an example.

Suppose I go to Canada to visit my daughter and her family in Edmonton. After I've been there a few days, I realize that I have not seen a single black cat since I arrived. All other colors, but never solid black. I mention it, and my daughter assures me that there are black cats around, I just haven't seen any. Unconvinced, I continue to watch, and the more I watch, the more certain I become that Edmonton is unusual, in that it has all other colored cats, but no solid black ones. So I bring the subject up again, and again I am assured that there are black cats in Edmonton. This time I stand my ground. I'm certain there are no black cats in Edmonton. My daughter is equally certain there are. My daughter could prove her point simply by showing me exactly one black cat in Edmonton. Or, she could even present convincing evidence to support her position by producing a photo of someone holding a black cat in front of a clearly recognizable Edmonton landmark. I, on the other hand, have a formidable challenge to prove my point. I not only have to examine every cat in Edmonton to prove that none of them is black, but I have to examine every place that a cat could hide in Edmonton to make sure that every cat has been eliminated, and I even have to secure every place that I have already checked to make sure a cat couldn't circle around behind my back and change hiding places from one I haven't checked to one that I have.

The point of this book is not to challenge atheism, but if it were, this argument would the one to use. The person who seriously takes the position that "there is no God" is equating himself with God, in that he is essentially saying that he has omniscience (all knowledge) and omnipresence (the ability to be everywhere at once). To take the position that there is no God, one would have had to have lived for eternity and been everywhere in the universe at the same time. Otherwise, God might be hiding just beyond the edge of the atheist's limits of comprehension. Or, when the atheist searches one place, maybe God sneaks around behind his back and hides where he has already looked. The atheist also has to know everything, because he must recognize God when he sees him – or her. Maybe God masquerades as the irritating woman next door. So the atheist must not only be everywhere at once, but he must know for certain what God would look like if he existed, and be able to demonstrate that nothing in the universe could be God in disguise.

Even if we doubt the existence of God, the atheist's position is difficult to defend. A more realistic choice is to take the agnostic position – those who say the existence of God is questionable because they don't see enough convincing evidence to cause them to believe. To be an atheist takes more faith than it does to believe that there is a God, because the atheist is trusting in a negative conviction that is impossible to prove, while people who believe in God can point to large bodies of evidence to support their positive conviction.

From a practical perspective, then, it becomes obvious that proving a positive proposition can often be done easily, while proving a negative one is much more difficult.

This principle, as well as the other tests for truth, will become important as we start to examine what Calvinism teaches. Consider how this principle can help us in our theological thinking. As I write this, I have just seen a news article in which a well known Christian leader made the statement that a certain politician is a Christian because the Christian leader knows the politician has made a profession of faith. Immediately, an acquaintance of ours posted on social media, "Making a profession of faith does not make a person a Christian. To be saved, a person must . . ." and he outlined his denomination's stance of what constitutes salvation, which includes water baptism. If baptism is *necessary* for salvation, as he contends, then we can reword his statement into a negative form, so that it says, "No person is saved if he/she has not been baptized." Now all we have to do is find one black cat, one statement in the Bible that says a person is saved without baptism, and the negative statement is disproven. Is there such a statement? Certainly, if being in paradise equals salvation. In Luke 23:43, after one of the thieves crucified with Jesus expressed faith in him, Jesus answered him, "I tell you the truth, today you will be with me in paradise." One black cat. Our acquaintance's theological statement, that baptism is necessary for salvation, does not withstand the test for truth. It needs to be re-thought at the personal level even if the denomination is not willing to do that.

Let's go back to our example of the two classmates disagreeing over the due date of the assignment. We said that maybe one classmate pulls out the class calendar, appealing to an outside source that they both respect, and that settles the question. But what if they did not both respect the outside source? Maybe our young lady pulls out her own copy of the class calendar, and it supports her contention that the assignment is due on Monday. Now we are no longer dealing with one proposition that we want to test for truthfulness – now we actually have to decide between two contradictory claims of truth. It's a problem we face every day, now.

We are in the information age. There is a glut of information available today, and all of it is contradicted by someone. If we are not aware of some tests for truth, and how to use them, we will find the diversity of ideas overwhelming. In sorting out contradictory claims, I have found three ideas helpful.

First, we need to ask ourselves which way the bulk of the evidence points. Another writer supports the tests for truth by describing three general characteristics of evidence: *quality, logical consistency*, and *quantity*.[17]

Quality has to do with our first and second tests for truth – whether the evidence is consistent with observable reality and with other truth, that is, is it publicly verifiable. Zacharias called this empirical adequacy. Mark Twain was personally visible when he was protesting the premature report of his death. His "aliveness" was objectively, publicly verifiable.

Logical consistency matches Zacharias's. It is the characteristic of evidence that, in our tests for truth earlier, we called internal coherence. The best evidence has no logical contradictions.

The final general characteristic of evidence is the *quantity*. If one opinion explains more of the available data, or if it is supported by more evidence, then it is likely a better opinion. Most changes in understanding start as a minority opinion, and gather support over time. Galileo, again, is the classic example, with his unpopular conviction that the sun, not the earth, was the center of the solar system. The reason minority opinions gather support is because they explain more of the available data than the previous understanding. As the evidence accumulates, more of it points in one direction than in any other. This is the basis on which juries find defendants guilty or innocent – the jury is instructed to render a decision when they are convinced "beyond all reasonable doubt." The preponderance of the evidence points in one direction. It is also the process by which science changes over time, as it has in relation to Galileo's beliefs. It is why I abandoned Calvinism.

A second idea I have found helpful is to understand the difference between proof and evidence. My Criminology degree proves useful here.

We tend to think that we know things that have been proven to us. That's why we do experiments in science class. We are taught a concept in the classroom (testimony of others), then in the lab class, we "prove" it (see it for ourselves, personal experience), and we conclude that the concept is true (the logic within our own minds). Now we "know" it. That process happens thousands of times over a lifetime, as we build our knowledge and reshape our belief systems, amending the maps in our minds, trying to make sense of the world. When we interact with that world, we want it to work. When a particular belief produces consistent results, we conclude that it is true and that we "know" it. The ultimate test of truth is consistent results. Remembering that truth is simply an accurate description of reality, then the ultimate test for truth is: does it work? Does it have experiential relevance? When the man jumped out of the hospital window into the street, it didn't work. A wet street may look like a river to a foggy mind, but it isn't. Nowhere is this concept more important than in religion, which purports to answer questions of eternal importance. Jesus understood this: "You will know the truth, and the truth will set you free" (John 8:32).

Like "knowing" though, proof is elusive, because both of them imply that they are conclusive. In actual fact, we seldom have proof. We use the word "prove" as a matter of practical convenience, as I have been doing, even though we recognize that what we have proven may not be fully conclusive. What we really have is *evidence* that points us toward a conclusion. When the evidence for a particular belief is consistent, then we consider it to be conclusive. Again, we believe it, and consider ourselves to know it. In simple, everyday situations, that works well enough, but the larger the concept, the less likely it is that all the evidence will point in the same direction, so we have to evaluate the evidence to see which is more compelling. This is the situation we are in with all the "existential" issues of life – questions like, how did things originate, why are we here, what happens after death, and so on.

Before we go to the next helpful idea, let's make sure our definitions are clear. *Proof is conclusive.* There is no doubt, no more room for argument. Evidence is not conclusive. *Evidence simply points toward a conclusion.* There may be contrary evidence. There is still room for doubt or further argument.

This leads us to the final idea that I have found helpful. It's the *importance* of what we are wanting to prove.

It's odd which things stick in our memories, and which don't. Another of those very few things I remember from college is the way our minds process contradictory information. It's called "cognitive dissonance." In everyday language, it means "contradictory information." Strangely enough, the mind in the western world learns early that the "Law of Non-Contradiction" is true, even if we've never heard of it. That law, officially taught in the logic classes that most people hate and avoid, says that two statements that contradict each other cannot both be true at the same time. As an aside, eastern cultures don't hold to this same belief to the same degree. They can tolerate more ambivalence in their thinking, which explains why the sciences developed in the west and not in the east. In the west, historically, when things were seen to disagree, effort was made to find out why. In the east, it was simply accepted without further exploration.[18]

The difference in cognitive dissonance and generic contradictory information, is that with cognitive dissonance, the new information contradicts something we already *believe*. That's what makes it cognitive (the thinking part of our brain) dissonance (out of harmony).

Earlier we looked at the statement, "When she started smoking, nobody knew that cigarettes cause cancer," as an illustration of how our understanding ("little r") can be different from reality ("Big R"). But the dangers of cigarette smoking is now common knowledge. That means for every person about whom that statement was true – that they did not know of the danger – at some point, they became aware of the new information. At that moment, cognitive dissonance occurred: "I've always thought cigarettes were harmless. Now you're telling me I'm killing myself by smoking."

At this point, the mind of the smoker has three basic options: 1) it can accept the new information; 2) it can reject the new information; or 3) it can decide that the matter is not important, so it can allow the dissonance, the ambiguity, the contradiction, to exist without attempting to resolve it.

When we encounter cognitive dissonance, the maps in our minds are being challenged. That is what happened on my imaginary trip to Hungary. The local people in Veszprém kept telling me I was in the wrong city, but my map said I was in Visegrád, and I had already invested a lot in what the map told me, so I was hard to convince. If I had accepted their contradictory information early in the day, I would have had time to recover, to retrace my path and see the real Visegrád. By rejecting the new information, I wasted the day, and failed to satisfy my morbid fascination with Dracula.

WHEN WE ENCOUNTER COGNITIVE DISSONANCE, THE MAPS IN OUR MINDS ARE BEING CHALLENGED

How about the due date on the assignment? Let's say that another classmate is a witness to the disagreement, but she has already turned in her assignment. She thought it was due on Friday, but since she has already submitted hers, she leaves before they pull out the class calendars and try to clear it up. It's simply not important enough for her to worry about.

What about the smoker? If she decides the new information is true, she has to make the effort to quit smoking, or suffer the consequences of her lack of discipline. If she decides the new information is false, she will continue to enjoy smoking, until the day the bill comes due. Or she may decide the issue is not important enough to worry about – after all, when you're young, sixty is a long way off.

This issue of cognitive dissonance, and how we resolve it, is deeply tied to the third idea I have found helpful in deciding whether or not to believe something – *how important is it?* We can safely be wrong about insignificant things, or simply blow them off. In the overall scheme of things, my trip to see the Dracula dungeon is not critical. I'm disappointed, and I've wasted some time and money, but nothing more. In the case of smoking, evidence shows that for each cigarette our lady smokes, she takes about that same amount of time off her life. Each cigarette reduces her life expectancy by about 11 minutes.[19] In this case, the issue is a matter of life and death, much more important than the due date on an assignment, or a day trip in Hungary.

Again, we are not the first people to consider these things.

Pascal's Wager

One of the most well known is Blaise Pascal (1623-1662). No physics or math student ever graduates without being introduced to Blaise Pascal. His history is well known. His father was a French tax collector. At the age of 12, Pascal started writing about geometry without ever having a class on it. At age 16, he published a work on new geometric theorems; at age 17 he published a work on sections of cones; at age 19 he built the world's second ever mechanical calculator (unaware of the existence of the first one). He was the first to prove the existence of the vacuum. He studied atmospheric pressure and pressure in liquids, leading to the principles of hydraulics known today. He laid the foundation to the theory of probability. He solved many other mathematical problems that are beyond the grasp of most of us. After an accident in 1654 (age 31) in which his horses bolted and left his carriage hanging over the edge of a bridge, followed soon after by a profound religious experience, Pascal pledged his life to Christianity, and started devoting his brilliant mind to religious topics. His most famous writing is *Pensees* (Thoughts), a book on the philosophy of religion. In it, he addressed this issue of *importance* in deciding what to believe. His argument has become known as Pascal's Wager, and is one of the most famous arguments in the philosophy of religion.[20]

Pascal reasoned that there are only two possibilities regarding the existence of God – either there is a God, or there is not. We do well to remember that he lived in France in the 17th century, where the Catholic version of Christianity dominated. The reality that existed in his mind was based on the culture from which it had arisen, so the God he envisioned was the God of Christianity. As a biblical extension of the existence of God, he believed in the possibility of heaven and hell. He envisioned three possibilities of what might happen to a person after death – heaven, hell, or non-existence. If God exists, then there is the possibility of spending eternity in either heaven or hell, but if God does not exist, those possibilities also logically don't exist, in which case the person dies and ceases to exist.

From Pascal's perspective, the advantage of eternity in heaven, compared to either of the other alternatives, was obvious. He concluded, much as we discussed earlier, that "knowing" if God exists is not possible with the rational mind alone, so the choices are similar to gambling. He essentially suggested betting for the existence of God rather than against that possibility. If we bet *for* the existence of God, he reasoned, and there is no God, we lose nothing, because there is nothing to lose. But if we bet *against* God, and lose, we lose everything. His worldview, based on his background, led him to assume that God sends unbelievers to hell for eternity – the ultimate loss. Conversely, he reasoned, if we bet *against* the existence of God and win, we gain nothing, because there is nothing to gain. But if we bet *for* the existence of God and win, we gain everything – everything that eternal life and heaven have to offer.

Pascal's Wager, in summary, looks like this:

	God exists	God does not exist
Wager for God	Gain everything	Lose nothing
Wager against God	Lose everything	Gain nothing

There have been many objections to Pascal's wager over the centuries, especially the past few decades, mostly because it is based on a biblical worldview. It fails to take into consideration the possibility of many gods, or reincarnation rather than heaven or hell, and so on. Our purpose is not to argue for or against the complete validity of Pascal's Wager (although the objections usually have equally plausible responses), but simply to show that thinking people realize that the more important the consequences of a decision, the more important it is that the decision be made well, and to make good decisions, we need to base our choices on truth. Our decisions need to be aligned with reality.

Proof vs. Evidence

Another thinker who recognized this was William James, whom we have already heard from a couple of times. Like Pascal, to describe William James as brilliant is an understatement. He was born in the United States in 1842 to wealthy parents, so in his youth James travelled extensively, becoming fluent in five languages by the time he was 19. At 27, he graduated from Harvard as a medical doctor. Later in life, he earned two more doctor's degrees. He taught anatomy, physiology, psychology, and philosophy at Harvard for 35 years. With no formal education in psychology, he became the first professor of psychology in America. He said, "The first lecture in psychology that I ever heard was the first I ever gave (1875)."[21] He authored multiple books on

As you consider this book, whether to simply discard it, or scan its contents, or actually read it and consider the evidence, all I can hope for is that you are like the Bereans, willing to examine the Scriptures to see if the evidence presented is true. If you find the case I make compelling enough to recommend the book to others, it is available in both print and Kindle form on Amazon. It is reasonably priced because money is not the issue, the message is.

May God guide your consideration of the evidence offered in this book, and ultimately, may the Holy Spirit guide you to all truth.

Sincerely,

Bill Mauldin

Bill Mauldin
mauldin.book@gmail.com

20 Sep 2021

Dr. David Turner
Grand Rapids Theological Seminary
1001 E. Beltline Ave NE
Grand Rapids, MI 49525

Dear Dr. Turner,

You did not request a copy of this book, but I am sending it because I think you might be interested in the topic. The book is the story of my journey from being a Calvinist to one who now believes that "predestination of individuals for salvation" was never taught in Scripture, as the Bible was originally written. The book documents the process and the research that has led me to that conclusion.

As you would expect, my journey started out with "cognitive dissonance," which happens any time we are presented with new information that appears to contradict what we already believe. But my experience was not new. Luke recorded two very different responses to it in the book of Acts. Rather than examine the evidence, the Thessalonians attempted to destroy the one challenging their existing beliefs. The Bereans, in stark contrast, "were of more noble character than the Thessalonians, for they received the message with great eagerness and examined the

Psychology and Philosophy, and how those fields relate to the religious nature of humans. He was a strong believer in the validity of religious experiences.

In his essay, "The Will to Believe," which "has been argued to be not only the most influential individual article in the philosophy of religion ever published but also the most widely read essay ever written by an American philosopher,"[22] William James originated the idea of *precursive faith*.[23] The word "precursive" simply means "to come before." The idea is that in certain circumstances, the wisest thing we can do is to believe, *before* we have the evidence necessary to justify that belief.

To allow our belief to run ahead of the evidence, James suggested, requires that three conditions be met. He set up his argument like this. First, he pointed out, to believe implies a choice, and a choice implies options. The three conditions, then, are options. Summarized, his argument says:

It is rational to believe beyond the available evidence, if and only if:

– It is a *live* option: It is within the bounds of believability

– It is *forced* option: To not choose has the same consequences as a negative choice

– It is a *momentous* option: Something of great importance is at stake

Said in a different way, if something is genuinely believable, and very, very important, and if not choosing will have the same results as choosing against the possibility, then it is rational (logical and wise) to choose to believe before we have evidence to justify that belief.

Tom Morris, the popular Professor of Philosophy at the University of Notre Dame for many years, gave an example to illustrate the three conditions included in William James's precursive faith.

Imagine that you can't swim well and are on a boat dock completely alone when you see a sole swimmer out in the water get into trouble and begin to go under. The swimmer is too far out for you to make it there unassisted. And there is no one else around at all. The swimmer calls for help. You notice that an old, rickety rowboat is pulled up onto the shore right beside you. The evidence is not clear as to whether it will make it all the way out there to the drowning swimmer or not. But there are no evident holes. It just looks real bad.[24]

– Using the boat to try to save the swimmer is a live option. It is within the bounds of believability that the boat can be used safely.

– It is also a *forced* option. To *not decide* if the boat is safe will have the same results as deciding it is not safe.

– It is also a *momentous* option – a life is at stake. If you don't trust in the reliability of the boat before you have evidence to believe, the swimmer will drown.

In these circumstances, according to James, the wisest thing is not to demand evidence of the boat's seaworthiness, but rather to push it into the water in an effort to save the swimmer. This is precursive faith. It is belief that runs ahead of the evidence. It is justified because of the *importance* of what we are being asked to believe.

William James' ideas about precursive faith have taken about as much criticism over the years as Pascal's Wager has, but both of them still make the point that when something is really, really important, it matters how we think about it. One point of James's precursive faith is that some matters in life are too important to ignore – failing to make up our minds has the same effect as if we had made up our mind against the idea.

In some important matters, we don't serve ourselves well by ignoring them, by failing to give them the consideration they deserve. Having the truth about important matters, is, well, important.

Life is easier when we are only aware of one option. That's rarely the case nowadays. Globalization has removed the scales from our eyes, as it were. In today's information age, there is not only a glut of information, but everything is contested. This is precisely why words like pluralism and relativism have crept into our language and consciousness. Without some way to guide our thinking, we become disoriented, because each perspective seems to have equal value.

To sort through these contradictory claims, I have attempted to demonstrate that we need to be capable of testing information for truthfulness. To begin with, it helps to recognize that we're looking for evidence, not proof. We ask ourselves which way the bulk of the evidence points. To find some stability, we learn to question the long term dependability of the sources, then follow sources with a good track record. We're left with one final question: how much evidence is enough?

The answer is: enough to justify a commitment.

Throughout the 1980s, Lee Iacocca was the head of Chrysler Corporation. He had been hired at a time when Chrysler was losing millions of dollars a year, and appeared to be on the verge of complete corporate death. His leadership literally turned the company around. Chrysler not only avoided bankruptcy, but became one of the world's leading car companies. One of Iacocca's strategies relates to what we are discussing. Among other things, he attributed his success to making right decisions. He once confronted a corporate executive for hesitating to make a decision when he had 95% of the information he needed. Iacocca told him it would take another six months to get the remaining 5%, to be absolutely certain he was making the right decision. By then, likely, the opportunity would be lost. [25] It's true for all of us. Sometimes we cannot get 100% of the information needed to make a right decision, or, if we do, as Iacocca pointed out, it will take an inordinate amount of time. Iacocca's success over the years demonstrated the wisdom of his logic. He was not looking for proof, he was looking for *enough evidence to justify a commitment.*

It's the way life works. Proof is elusive. We are not looking for proof. We are looking for *enough evidence to justify a commitment.*

The commitment, however, needs to be made with integrity. The human mind is masterful at believing what it wants to believe. The whole concept of *confirmation bias* is based on that tendency. We tend to believe information that confirms what we already believe, or what we want to believe, and discard what is contradictory. It is a tendency we have to fight against, because our ultimate goal is to achieve good results, over the long term, from the commitments we make.

> WE ARE NOT LOOKING FOR PROOF. WE ARE LOOKING FOR *ENOUGH EVIDENCE TO JUSTIFY A COMMITMENT*

Our tendency toward confirmation bias gets worse when we have an agenda. With an agenda, our commitment is not to truth, but to what we already believe, or to what we want to accomplish. When we already have a commitment, our objectivity is diminished, so we are more likely to reject contradictory information. Every committed Calvinist who reads this book will face this temptation, as I did in seminary.

Interpretive Frameworks and Anchor Premises

One of the unavoidable results of growing up is that we develop biases, commitments, agendas, before we even know what they are. Think about how our understanding grows.

The basic idea of the human mind as a "blank slate" can be traced back as far as Aristotle.[26] It was brought into Christian thinking in the 13th century by Thomas Aquinas, then into Enlightenment thinking in the 18th century by John Locke.[27] Even though no reputable psychologist today argues for the "blank slate" theory, we all know that babies are born without the level of mental ability that they will have later in life. Mental ability is developed over time, as the brain matures, and as the child encounters new information. The brain seems to be organically configured primarily for detecting patterns, and figuring out what those patterns mean. Physical coordination is a series of patterns. Speech is a series of patterns. Acceptable use of emotions is a series of patterns. The brain starts by detecting a pattern, building a framework of understanding based on that observation, then over time, filling in the complex connections within that framework.

Here is the critical point. The framework is necessary before other understanding can be added. I call it our "interpretive framework," or our "framework of assumptions." Meaning can only be assigned in relation to what is already known, or assumed to be true. We use what we already believe, to interpret new, incoming information. Others call these frameworks "plausibility structures."[28]

Let's examine this idea a little. The brain is the part of the body in which our consciousness resides. But the brain has access to the outside world only through the senses. Sensory data comes into the brain through our sight, hearing, smell, etc. The brain takes that sensory data and makes sense of it. In the reality of our minds ("little r"), there is only sensory data, and the interpretation of that data. At this point, it's the interpretive process that we're interested in.

We can say that our interpretive frameworks have two sources: one is the environment in which we develop them, and the other is our own unique way of interacting with the incoming data. The evidence is strong that newborns are innately different in many ways. There are at least nine different congenital temperaments that are present at birth, and that affect the way we interact with our environment.[29] For example, some babies have a general tendency to welcome new stimuli into their world, whereas others tend to withdraw from new things. These tendencies connect with an idea called an "anchor premise" that affects those things that come after it. If a baby comes into the world with a welcoming approach to life, the anchor premise is that the world is generally a friendly place. To the baby who tends to withdraw, the anchor premise is the opposite – that the world is generally unfriendly. From that initial starting point, patterns are assigned meaning, or interpreted. This process continues throughout life. The interpretive frameworks develop in complexity, and hopefully, in internal coherence. As cognitive dissonance occurs, the interpretive frameworks are modified. Or not.

Culture plays a major role in the development of our interpretive frameworks, of our plausibility structures. We can say that all belief is socially conditioned, and that social conditioning is itself based on presuppositions within the culture. The growing child learns to use its powers of reasoning only by interacting with other people, so the development of both beliefs and reason (how to interpret incoming information) is conditioned to a large degree by the experiences, discoveries, debates, etc. of those who have gone before us, who surround us as we develop.[30] This impact of culture on how we reason, explains why Geert Hofstede found more tolerance of rational ambiguity in the east than in the west.

Consider the difference in an American and a Russian at the height of the Cold War. Both considered the other dangerous, not to be trusted. In America, higher education was not free, but it was freely available to anyone, and any person could work in any job in which he or she could get hired. In Russia, higher education was free, but not freely available. Access was controlled by the state. Christians who were devout in beliefs outside the state-sanctioned Orthodoxy, for example, were prevented from studying in certain areas, and prohibited from holding certain jobs. This policy was both based on certain plausibility structures (that certain Christians were dangerous, subversive elements in society), and created certain plausibility structures ("If I convert to Christianity, it will limit my education and career opportunities").

Our interpretive frameworks, our plausibility structures, tell us at a fundamental level what is possible and what is not. They are what William James called a "live option." Some ideas we never consider, because they are outside the limits of what we believe is actually possible, or at least, what is realistic. Anytime we believe one thing to be true or untrue, that plausibility structure affects future beliefs.

A simple way of describing this process is to say that our assumptions determine our conclusions. This explains why different people, viewing the same evidence, come to different conclusions. The difference is not in the evidence – the data – it is in the assumptions, the interpretive framework, the plausibility structures, that are used to evaluate the data. It can be illustrated like this:

Assumption A ⟹ Data ⟹ Interpretation A ⟹ Conclusion A

Assumption B ⟹ Data ⟹ Interpretation B ⟹ Conclusion B

This point is clearly recognized by people who work cross culturally. Eugene Nida, who is famous for his work in translation theory, understood it. Charles Kraft summarizes it precisely in his seminal book, *Christianity in Culture*, starting with a quote from Nida: "'The fundamental processes of reasoning of all people are essentially the same, but the premises on which such reasoning rests and the basic categories that influence judgment of different people are somewhat different. . . . [People] differ . . . not so much in their reasoning as in their starting points.' That is, the members of different cultures arrive at different conclusions concerning reality because they started from different assumptions."[31] It is true for people from different cultures; it is equally true for people from different religions, from different theological persuasions, from different perspectives concerning the existence of anything beyond the visible, material world.

The critical point is that the interpretive framework always precedes the evaluation of the data. If you follow the interpretive framework back far enough, you will always find an anchor premise – some basic position that the individual is not willing or not able to give up, that will always influence the way they view the world. It can be that the world is basically an unfriendly place, or it can be that there is no God, or it can be that God has written the entire human script from before the foundation of the earth. Whatever it is, and each person has hundreds, if not thousands of them, our most basic assumptions, our anchor premises, determine our interpretations of the events and ideas we encounter.

Consider a statement I read recently. It was made by two writers who are Calvinists, stating their view on their theological opponents' defense of free will:

> The Arminian insistence upon the inviolability of the human free will and their willingness to define God's ability to redeem human beings such that it cannot violate free will creates an anthropological idol and demeans the power and rights of God.[32]

These authors are making the point that Arminians (typically thought of as the theological opposites of Calvinists) hold "human free will" as an anchor premise – it is "inviolable." The Arminians, the authors are saying, are not willing to release that point. But the authors' view is affected by an assumption of their own – that of equating their own thinking with objective reality.

Notice two things about their statement: 1) the high tone of the language, including big words that make the statement hard to understand by one who is not highly educated – "inviolability" and "an anthropological idol" and "demeans"; and 2) how this statement is presented as a fact. "Their insistence creates an idol and demeans God's power and rights." But, realistically, *does* it? Or is it somebody's *opinion* that it does? They are addressing a much debated question that is not likely to be resolved this side of heaven, so their perspective on the question is simply an *opinion,* one of a number of possible opinions. It's not even the majority opinion.

This debate is why I'm writing this book – to give people more tools they can use to help think these things through. If those authors had wanted to be more accurate and honest (and humble), they would have said, "The Arminian insistence upon . . . human free will . . . , *in the minds of Calvinists*, creates a human idol and takes away the power and rights of God." The fact that it creates a human idol and takes away from God *in the minds of Calvinists* (their "little r"), does not mean that it does so in reality ("Big R"). This attitude is the actual problem in this debate, and it was even more a problem in Calvin's day. It is the danger of equating our beliefs with objective reality (my "little r" = "Big R"). Those who are strong advocates of their position hold their position, not because they are right, but because they see the world so clearly through the lenses of their own worldview, that they lack the ability to imagine it otherwise. They *know* they are right, not because there are not other perfectly logical explanations, but because they either lack the ability to imagine those other explanations, or because they simply refuse to consider them.

TO A LARGE DEGREE, OUR ANCHOR PREMISES, AND FROM THEM OUR ENTIRE INTERPRETIVE FRAMEWORK – OUR WORLDVIEWS – ARE ASSIGNED BY THE CULTURE IN WHICH WE GROW UP

The maps in our minds provide us with a sense of security. They tell us what the world is like. It can be scary to think they may be wrong. The closer cognitive dissonance gets to the deepest of our beliefs, to the very anchor premises on which everything else depends, the more threatening it becomes. Historically, and even to many today, it is often easier and safer to destroy those who disagree with us, than to go through the process of re-examining our own mental maps.

To a large degree, our anchor premises, and from them our entire interpretive framework – our worldviews – are assigned by the culture in which we grow up. Most people simply accept them as true, and never examine them for validity by comparing them to alternative perspectives. That is the nature of worldviews. To break out of the prison of our worldview, we have to look out from between the bars and witness scenes that make us realize there is more to the world than what we have experienced. The person who checks, will find the prison door unlocked. Freedom is possible. Our fellow prisoners will attempt to discourage us from opening the door. They will argue with us, shame us, and in times past, they would kill us, as Calvin and his contemporaries did their opponents. That is human nature. Still, there is a world out there, bigger than the cultural prison in which we were born. We may find that world to be a mirage, or dangerous, or filled with falsehood, so we may eventually return to our cell, but the initial exploration is worth the risk. What we may do is actually experience freedom out there, so we may return to our cell only to try to help others escape as we have. To make that offer is the nature of love, but we can only offer what we have ourselves.

"You will know the truth, and the truth will set you free."
– Jesus of Nazareth.[33]
"The function of freedom is to free someone else."
– Toni Morrison[34]

Endnotes

[1] Justo L. Gonzalez, *The Story of Christianity* (Peabody, MS: Prince Press, 1999), xvii.

[2] Paul Harvey Aurandt, known publicly as just Paul Harvey (Sep 4, 1918 - Feb 28, 2009).

[3] Darrow L. Miller with Stan Guthrie, *Discipling Nations: The Power of Truth to Transform Cultures* (Seattle, WA: YWAM Publishing, 2001), 31-32.

[4] Miller, *Discipling Nations*, 65.

[5] H. Richard Niebur, *Christ and Culture* (New York: Harper and Row, 1951) section 1.3.2.

[6] "Lausanne Occasional Paper No. 2," *The Willowbank Report – Gospel and Culture*, (Wheaton, IL: LCWE, 1978), 7.

[7] Early recognition of this was by Ruth Benedict, *Patterns of Culture* (Abingdon-on-Thames, UK: Routledge and Kegan Paul, 1934).

[8] I an indebted for the "map" analogy to M. Scott Peck, *The Road Less Traveled: A New Psychology of Love, Traditional Values and Spiritual Growth* (New York: Simon & Schuster, 1978), 26. "Our view of reality is like a map with which we negotiate the terrain of life."

[9] Thomas Kuhn, *The Structure of Scientific Revolutions* (Chicago, IL: University of Chicago Press, 1962).

[10] For much of the logic here, I am indebted to Tom Morris, *Philosophy for Dummies* (Hoboken, NJ: Wiley Publishing, 1999), 57-61.

[11] Malcolm Muggeridge, *The End of Christendom* (Grand Rapids, MI: Wm. B. Eerdmans, 1980), 28.

[12] In 1975, two times, infants were switched at birth in the same hospital, and it was not discovered for 41 years. http://www.foxnews.com/world/2016/08/28/two-friends-from-remote-canada-discover-were-switched-at-birth-41-years-ago.html.

[13] William James, "The Will to Believe," in William James, *The Will to Believe: And Other Essays in Popular Philosophy and Human Immortality* (Cambridge MA: Harvard University Press, 1979), 21. Originally presented as an address to a combined meeting of the Philosophy Clubs of Yale and Brown Universities, then published in the *New World*, June, 1896.

[14] From the Question and Answer session following Zacharias's lecture on "What does it mean to be human?" October 15, 2015, Soldiers & Sailors Memorial Hall, Pittsburgh, PA.

[15] James, "The Will to Believe," 26.

[16] From a note Twain wrote in London on May 31, 1897, to reporter Frank Marshall White, quoted in Shelley Fisher Fishkin, *Lighting Out For the Territory: Reflections on Mark Twain and American Culture* (Oxford University Press, 1996), 134.

[17] Robert J. Spitzer, *Ten Universal Principles: A Brief Philosophy of the Life Issues* (San Francisco, CA: Ignatius Press, 2011), 8.

[18] Geert Hofstede has done remarkable work in this area of uncertainty avoidance and tolerance or intolerance of ambiguity, among other important differences in cultures. See *Cultures and Organizations: Software of the Mind* (London: McGraw-Hill, 1991), or the updated edition with Gert Jan Hofstede, 2005.

[19] British Medical Journal, 2000 Jan 1; 320 (7226): 53. Report on a study conducted by Mary Shaw, Richard Mitchell, and Danny Dorling at the University of Bristol, UK, in which life expectancy was compared between smokers and non-smokers in England and Wales. The study examined mortality ratios of 34,000 doctors over 40 years, and the difference was a shorter life expectancy of 6.5 years for smokers.

[20] There is a wealth of information on the Internet about Pascal, including translations of his writings, and objections to and defenses of his ideas. One good source is Stanford University's Encyclopedia of Philosophy.

[21] Ralph Barton Perry, *The Thought and Character of William James*, vol. 1, (1935), (Nashville, TN: Vanderbilt Univ. Press, 1996 edition), 228.

[22] Rydenfelt, Henrik, and Sami Pihlström, eds., *William James on Religion* (Basingstoke, Hampshire, England; New York: Pelgrave Macmillan, 2013), 7.

[23] James, *The Will to Believe*, 14.

[24] Morris, *Philosophy*, 79.

[25] Lee Iacocca with William Novak, *Iacocca: An Autobiography* (New York: Bantam Books, 1984), 50.

[26] Aristotle, *De Anima* ("On the Soul", translated by J.A. Smith), 429b30-430a2, in Jonathan Barnes, ed., *Complete Works of Aristotle, Volume 1: The Revised Oxford Translation* (Princeton, NJ: Princeton University Press, 1984), 683.

[27] Forrest E. Baird and Walter Kaufmann, *From Plato to Derrida* (Upper Saddle River, NJ: Pearson Prentice Hall, 2008), 527–529.

[28] Cf. Lesslie Newbigin, *The Gospel in a Pluralist Society* (Grand Rapids: Eerdmans, 1989), 8, and throughout.

[29] Ross Campbell, *How to Really Love Your Child* (Colorado Springs: Chariot Victor Publishing, a division of Cook Communication, 1977), 17-18, from Stella Chess and Alexander Thomas, *Temperament and Behavior Disorder in Children* (New York: University Press, 1968).

[30] Newbigin, *Gospel*, 54.

[31] Charles Kraft, *Christianity in Culture: A Study in Dynamic Biblical Theologizing in Cross-Cultural Perspective* (Maryknoll, NY: Orbis Books, 1979), 57, quoting Eugene A. Nida, *Message and Mission* (New York: Harper & Row, 1960 and reprinted by William Carey Library in South Pasadena, CA in 1972), 90-91.

[32] Robert A. Peterson and Michael D. Williams, *Why I Am Not an Arminian* (Downers Grove, IL: InterVarsity Press, 2004), 143-135.

[33] John 6:32.

[34] Quoted in Lamott, *Bird by Bird*, 193.

Chapter 3
Calvinism as a Contextual Theology

He who knows but one culture, knows none.
– John Gration[1]

In the book of Acts, Luke shows that persecution of the followers of Jesus started immediately after Stephen was killed at the hand of an angry mob (Acts 8:1). This explains why many believers moved out of Jerusalem. Philip went to Samaria, and Peter and John joined him there. Then Peter went to Lydda and from there to Joppa. While in Joppa, Peter had the vision that led him to visit Cornelius, who was the first clearly Gentile convert (the Samaritans who were converted earlier were half-Jews). Note that the story of Peter and Cornelius gets told *three times* in the book of Acts (in detail twice in chapters 10 and 11, then retold in shorter form again in chapter 15).

This suggests that Luke thought it was *really* important. It was – and is. This story explains why the church became totally inclusive of Gentiles, which involved "reinterpreting" itself and establishing its own identity, separate from Judaism.[2]

This process of reinterpreting itself and establishing a new identity, has been the story of the church throughout history. Let's look at a few examples.

Soon after the Cornelius incident in Acts, Luke takes us to Antioch (Acts 11:19), where four significant things happened:

(1) the good news was clearly presented to Gentiles, rather than primarily to the Jews;

(2) the message was changed slightly to fit the new cultural context (The good news was no longer about "Jesus, the Messiah," but about "the Lord Jesus." "Lord" was the way the pagans referred to their cult divinities, so the message was "contextualized" for this new audience.);

(3) at Antioch, followers of Jesus were called "Christians" for the first time, confirming their new identity as the "church" rather than just a part of the local synagogue, and also establishing their exemption from the Jewish law and the temple rituals at Jerusalem;[3] and

(4) Paul and Barnabas were sent out on their first missionary journey, with the deliberate intention to target Gentiles with the good news.

This is the second time the church reinterprets itself – the first was to freely *include* Gentiles into what had been a purely Jewish movement. Now, the movement becomes "the church" made up of "Christians" in which Jews and Gentiles have equal status and there is no obligation to keep the Jewish law.

With this second reinterpretation, the church becomes completely separate from Judaism. Paul explains that process theologically in the book of Ephesians, and shows the practical implications it has. We will spend more time on Ephesians later, because it is not only critical to Calvinism, but to understanding why John Calvin was wrong.

As a side note, it should be pointed out that from this start in the book of Acts, the church would expand in ways that are not well documented in history. For example, Christian communities have existed in southern India for much longer than written history can explain. The Christians there actually attribute their origins to the work of the apostle Thomas, as does the Christian church in Pakistan. For our purposes, though, it will be sufficient to look briefly at the development of the church as history has recorded it.

The church's third major reinterpretation of itself occurred when Constantine ended the persecution of the church that had lasted much of the previous three centuries. A case can even be made that the church in its new privileged position used pagan models as the basis for developing its new identity. [4] It built buildings, formed choirs, and established a clear hierarchy that separated the clergy from the ordinary person, just like the local pagan religions. It adopted formal dress for the clergy, and introduced a lot of pomp and ceremony. Leadership resulted in prestige, rather than persecution and possible martyrdom. As the power of the hierarchy was consolidated, it started settling disputes by councils, rather than by apostolic authority.

One of the earliest major disputes was settled at the Council of Ephesus (431 C.E.), when the doctrinal teachings of Nestorius, the Patriarch of Constantinople, were in question. Nestorius was condemned as a heretic. Rather than changing his views, his followers separated from the larger church, becoming known as the Assyrian Church of the East, which still exists today. Twenty years later, another similar split occurred, again with the splintered group still in existence today. The point is that both of the splinter groups reinterpreted themselves as separate from the larger church. Within the larger church, as it became more affluent, some saw the increasing pomp, privilege, and affluence as being contrary to the model of Jesus, so they reacted to it by developing monasteries where those who wanted to dedicate themselves solely to God could do so within a community of like-minded believers. In this case, we see the reinterpreting, or redefining of what the church looks like, being done within the church, by segments of the greater church. That process would continue, but so would the breaking apart of the church into separate "churches" with their own identities.

The biggest division occurred in 1054 in what is known as the Great Schism, effectively creating what has become known as the Orthodox Church in the East and the Roman Catholic church in the West. This split resulted from differences in several areas (theological, linguistic, political, and geographical) that had been escalating for centuries. With the split, each side of the schism reinterpreted itself within its new context, including choosing names that implied *they* were the only true church. The process would repeat itself a few centuries later in the West with the Protestant Reformation. In this latter case, initially, the differences were not political or geographical, but primarily theological. When the division was complete, the Catholic Church had to reinterpret itself again, and the Protestants had to start from the beginning to define who they were. That process would take decades, and would result in the Protestants dividing into several branches themselves. Those divisions, their causes, and their continuing effect, is the reason this book was written.

The big point from this short history lesson is that *social change and the rebirth of the church* are ultimately connected.[5] As societies change, the thinking of the people within the societies change. It is an interrelated cycle. With new understanding, society changes. As society changes, thinking changes. As thinking changes, social behavior changes. It is inevitable that those changes will be reflected in areas like religious thought and practice. We might like to think that with the Holy Spirit present and at work, Christianity would be immune to these cultural changes, but history argues against that. Theology develops from within a cultural worldview. It does not stand above it. We can say that truth is "supracultural" or beyond culture, but not theology. Theology is a human attempt to understand truth, but it is always human, and since humans are taught to think by their culture, theology will always reflect the thinking of the culture from which it originated.

Evolving Theology

Let's look, briefly, at a couple of the major theological shifts that have occurred over time within Christianity.

The early understanding of the work of Jesus described redemption in terms of a battle. By his death and resurrection, Jesus conquered Satan, thereby freeing humanity from slavery to Satan as they became believers. The early church father, Irenaeus (who died in 202 C.E.), reflected this view in his writings.[6] This view made perfect sense during the time it developed, which was when the church was still undergoing persecution, so evidence of the spiritual battle was constant.

Irenaeus' view prevailed until the Middle Ages, when Anselm of Canterbury proposed the Satisfaction theory, which was related to the honor of God, and was more fitted to feudalism and the cultural conditioning of the Germanic legal systems.[7] Physical evidence of that feudal system is still very visible in many parts of Europe today. We have lived in Latvia for years, where castles, palaces, and manors in various states of splendor or decay can be seen throughout the country. Each one represents an "overlord" who was responsible for his region, and everybody within that region was under the authority of that overlord.

Anselm thought of God as the overlord of the world. As such, the world owed him a debt of honor. Failure to pay the debt was sin, but humans were incapable of paying such a high debt, so God had to make the payment himself. Anselm simply proposed a "better" understanding of the work of Jesus, because it made more sense to him based on the cultural conditions that had shaped his worldview. And since it also made sense to his audience, it became the general understanding until it was itself replaced or modified by other, later understandings.

The Reformers came along with the Penal Substitution theory, which was related to justice rather than the honor of God, because within their context, that made more sense to them. In the earlier Satisfaction theory, the debt owed to God was one of honor. In the Penal Substitution theory, sin was related to the holiness, not the honor of God, so it deserved appropriate punishment. Since the holiness of God was so great, the only appropriate payment was the life of the sinner. Christ paid that debt, and the payment was substituted for the debt of the sinner when he accepted it by believing.

Constants and Contexts

Stephen B. Bevans and Roger Schroeder, in *Constants in Context*, trace the development of Christian theology through the centuries, and how that development has impacted mission efforts. They show that Christian theology always addresses six basic questions. These are the constants – they are the questions that are always present:

1. What does the Bible say about *Christ*? (Christology)

2. What does the Bible say about *humanity*? (Anthropology)

3. What does the Bible say about *culture*? (Culture)

4. What does the Bible say about *salvation*? (Soteriology)

5. What does the Bible say about *the church*? (Ecclesiology)

6. What does the Bible say about *end times*? (Eschatology)

Bevans and Schroeder then trace the way these constants have been understood in various times and places throughout the history of Christianity. These are the contexts. Their study shows three different veins through which theology has generally flowed through the centuries.[8] One vein can be traced back to the North African city of Carthage and the early Christian apologist, Tertullian (c. 155 - c. 240 C.E.). It reflects Roman cultural thinking, and has a general focus on law. The second vein goes back to the Egyptian city of

Alexandria and the early theologian, Origen (184/185 - 253/254 C.E.). It reflects Greek cultural thinking, and has a general focus on truth. The third vein can be traced to the city of Antioch, from which Paul embarked on his missionary journeys, but its early proponent was Irenaeus (c. 125 - 202 C.E.), who grew up in the Smyrna mentioned in Revelation 2:8 and who later was the bishop in the area that is now Lyon, France. This perspective reflects Near Eastern cultural thinking and has a general focus on history as the way God reveals himself.

These three veins of theology can be traced through various theologians, through the centuries, and are still visible today. Calvinists, along with other orthodox Protestants and Christian fundamentalists, tend to be in the vein that comes from Carthage, and focuses on the law. Liberal Protestants tend to follow Origen from Alexandria, and the third vein can be traced through Martin Luther and John Wesley to their followers.[9] In a very general sense, these three dominant veins, and their fractured derivatives, are the explanation for the variety of denominations present today. People group themselves with others who see things the same way they do, so they can worship together without dissent and conflict.

> CHRISTIAN THEOLOGY HAS NEVER BEEN STATIC. IT HAS ALWAYS CHANGED AS CULTURAL THINKING HAS CHANGED, AND CONTINUES TO DO SO

It should be noted that while these three veins have been visible through the centuries, and still are today, their boundaries are often fuzzy and sometimes overlap, and within denominations, elements of all three may be visible. The fact that they are often seen together, however, does not mean they are compatible. They are, in actuality, the basis for much of the division that has characterized Christianity through the ages.

My purpose, here, is not to argue for or against any one of these veins of theology. It is simply to demonstrate that Christian theology has never been static. It has always changed as cultural thinking has changed, and continues to do so. It brings us to one of the critical questions I am attempting to deal with. At what point does a Christian belief system cease to point people to the true and living God, and instead, pushes them away?

As we think about that question, this might be a good time to ask: What is theology, anyway? Does a Christian have to subscribe to some particular "theology"? The truth is, most Christians don't give their theology much thought. They leave that to the theologians and church leaders, and they simply accept what they are taught. That's not to say that they would not kill over their beliefs. But it's still not *their* theology as a result of having examined the issues, thought them through, and arrived at where they are – it's *their* theology because it's what they were raised with, and the thought of revising the maps in their minds is more intimidating to them than killing the one who is threatening those maps.

Essence and Form

It helps to realize that all theologies are of human origin – theologies are simply human attempts to organize the truths of Scripture in a way that is logical, coherent, memorable, and teachable. But here's the rub – different cultures approach the Scriptures from different viewpoints, so what is seen as logical and coherent in one culture is not in another.

I have seen this problem illustrated as two circles, one inside the other, so the figure looks like a donut. The inner circle represents the truth of Scripture, and the outer circle represents the way in which that truth is understood and expressed. Sometimes the circles are called the "essence" and the "form." The essence, the inner circle, is the truth that does not change; the form is the way it is understood and communicated, and it does change. The form is what is visible.

It changes based on the "context." This concept is very similar to the "form" that expresses the deeper "meaning" in languages that Eugene A. Nida described in multiple books on translation.[10] The *form* is the way *meaning* is expressed in languages; it is the way *truth* is expressed in theology.

Think about how changes to that visual illustration can be used to represent reality. In some churches, the inner circle would be very small, and the outer circle large – they have a well organized religious system (form), but there is very little truth contained within it. Or maybe in the minds of some people, the two circles are the same – they equate their whole religious system with the truth, not recognizing the potential for different perspectives to produce legitimate but different ways of expressing the same truth. They don't understand how culture and context affect thinking, and they don't understand the difference in essence and form. This is true of almost anybody to whom the term "fundamentalist" applies. There is nothing wrong with holding firmly to the fundamentals; there is something wrong with equating them with the form in which they are expressed. This is the basic problem with radical Islam, but it has been equally true within Christianity over the centuries. It fails to recognize that all forms of expression, including religious ones, are derived from the context within which they arose.

So what is context? As a simple noun, it is a close synonym of the word "situation" except it is a much broader word. We might say of a family in financial trouble, that they are "in a bad situation." But to understand all that is involved, we need to know the context. What brought them to this position, and what all will it affect? Context brings into the picture the whole overall scenario, including time, place, circumstances, etc. Generally, when we are talking about context, we are talking about all of them: time, place, culture, and the immediate situation.

Earlier, we considered the idea that social changes bring about changes in thinking, and therefore changes in behavior. Now, we can say that *culture conditions our thinking, so thinking is always derived from the context in which it develops.* This explains why the church has had a variety of theological veins over the centuries, why the divisions and schisms have occurred, and why the church has had to "reinterpret" itself in different times and places. It's all related to context.

Through the ages, the church has not just reinterpreted itself in terms of its identity and theology, but in its understanding of its purpose, and how to accomplish that purpose.

The book of Acts shows the early disciples basically gathered in Jerusalem following Jesus' ascension, continuing to worship together and impact their immediate neighbors, until the stoning of Stephen started a wave of persecution that compelled many to leave Jerusalem. During that time in Jerusalem, the argument can be made that mission efforts primarily focused on disciple-making and helping the poor among the local Jews.[11] After persecution dispersed the church from Jerusalem, their efforts looked more like Paul's – missionary efforts to carry a message of "apocalyptic eschatology" to all people. For those of us who are not theologians, that means Paul was convinced that the return of Jesus was imminent and was going to be an earth-shattering event, and he was offering the opportunity for others to share in all that it promised.[12]

Paul's view dominated the mission efforts of the early church. For at least two centuries, "healer-missionaries, miracle workers, and itinerant preachers" emulated Paul. That's the way mission work was done.[13] That early style has been replaced by at least five other periods in which the purpose of the church was generally viewed through different lenses, and therefore mission was done differently.[14] Particularly visible changes can be seen with the monasteries being the main form of mission work for centuries, followed by colonialism, then mission in the wake of the Enlightenment, with its sense of optimism, its reliance on reason and human strategy, and its focus on the Great Commission.[15] Once again, the idea is that the way Christianity sees itself has been consistently connected with the context, and has been dynamic, not static.

This is directly related to our examination of Calvinism.

As kids, all of us have gone through the exercises of connecting the dots, to make a picture that was not fully visible at first. So now, we can connect some dots, to expand the major point that was made earlier: that *social change and the identity of the church* are ultimately connected. We can now say that *theological understanding and cultural conditioning* are also ultimately connected, and that *both theology and culture reflect themselves in the way the church expresses itself, in missions.*

My personal journey beyond Calvinism started while I was in seminary, as two realizations converged: 1) that John Calvin and his successors viewed the world very differently from Paul and his contemporaries, and as a result, 2) that the concept of "chosen" in the first chapter of Ephesians would not have been understood by Paul's initial readers as it was understood by John Calvin and his successors. The first realization also impacts the understanding of "chosen" in Romans. Combined, those two realizations gave me a new paradigm through which I now read Scripture, and I find that the new paradigm fits the evidence in Scripture, and the tests for truth, much better than Calvinism ever did. I will deal with "chosen" in Ephesians and Romans later, but for now, I want to revisit the issue of worldviews, and how different Paul's and Calvin's were.

Collectivism vs. Individualism

There would be many differences between Paul's and Calvin's worldviews, but two in particular are critical to our discussion – and, I will argue, to understanding Paul's writings. The first is the tendency of societies to view the world either in communal or individual terms. Until just recently, this difference was not understood at all. Now, among sociologists and anthropologists, it is well understood. Geert Hofstede calls it "a fundamental issue in human societies: the role of the individual versus the role of the group."[16] He points out, "The vast majority of the people in our world live in societies in which the interest of the group prevails over the interest of the individual."[17] Hofstede calls these societies *collectivist*, and he defines the two dimensions in this way:

> Individualism pertains to societies in which the ties between individuals are loose: everyone is expected to look after himself or herself and his or her immediate family. Collectivism as its opposite pertains to societies in which people from birth onward are integrated into strong, cohesive in-groups, which throughout people's lifetimes continue to protect them in exchange for unquestioning loyalty.[18]

There is clear consensus among historians and anthropologists, that first century societies in Palestine were communal/collectivist in nature. It was true of both first century Rome and first century Israel. Historic evidence shows that communal thinking was gradually replaced in Western Europe by individualistic thinking, starting generally around the end of the first millennium. There was a gradual progression away from the ancient worldview, collectivist in nature, through a worldview generally based on Greek philosophical thought, to one which was logical and empirical, known as positivism. "Positivism is an attempt to acquire certain, objective knowledge about the material world."[19] As certainty and objectivity became the new standard for credibility, positivism separated the natural from the supernatural in order to study the natural. Over time, since the supernatural could not be studied with certainty and objectivity, it was dispensed with – that which could not be objectively known was labeled as superstition. One of the effects was that *tradition*, the ancient repository of knowledge and wisdom, lost its credibility. Since tradition resides in the corporate knowledge and wisdom of the group, with time, authority was transferred from the group to the individual. [20] Individualism, as Calvin experienced it, and as we experience it in the western world today, was non-existent in Paul's world. As Geert Hofstede has already stated, it is still non-existent in most of the world today.

The reason it is important to understand communal thinking is that Paul wrote from that perspective. In his day, and in his thinking, people got their identity from the group to which they belonged. More than any other reason, this explains the persecution Christians experienced for the first three centuries. For individuals to change groups was a threat to the entire society. Societies existed and survived because members were loyal to the group. In return, the society gave the individual a sense of belonging and a sense of security – if one individual was threatened, the whole group came to the rescue. This explains a lot of behavior in the world today that seems inexplicable to many of us. As I write this, a current news story tells of a mother in Pakistan burning her daughter alive for marrying outside the boundaries approved by the family.[21] When individualistic thinking and communal thinking come into contact, there tends to be a lot of misunderstanding and confusion. The daughter, in the news story, was acting individually. Her mother was interpreting her actions communally, and acting communally. From her communal worldview, the daughter's actions brought dishonor to the family, so killing her was justified. The girl's brother helped his mother carry out the death sentence.

While I was in seminary in Canada, I shared responsibilities with another seminary student as the youth pastor for a Korean church. Every other week I spoke in their English service and taught the "high-school, college, and career" Sunday School class. After the young, second generation Korean Canadians came to trust me, they shared with me their complaints against their parents and the older people in the church. To a large degree, the complaints centered around the fact that the older generation Koreans gossiped constantly, and minded everybody else's business. The younger generation found that to be a severe invasion of their privacy. One of the reasons the older generation wanted someone like me in their youth ministry, was because they felt they were losing their kids to the world, and they did not know how to combat it. What I realized was that the problem was a conflict of cultures. The older Koreans were communal in their thinking. They weren't gossiping and minding other people's business, they were living life together, sharing everything of common interest, and getting their identity from being part of the group. The younger generation had been influenced enough by their contact with the media and the Canadian culture through their public school experience, that they were much more individualistic. They wanted to make their own career and relationship choices, and they wanted to be able to visit friends and go places on Saturday night without having to explain it both in advance and afterward to their parents. The parents wanted them all to share their lives with each other, as past generations had always done. The result was that both generations had a sense of being misunderstood and not being loved or trusted.

It was the Renaissance that changed Europe from communal/collectivist thinking, to individualistic. The Renaissance began in Italy around 1300 and lasted about three hundred years. Essentially, it was the rediscovery of classical Greek philosophy, such as that of the agnostic Protagoras (c. 490 – c. 420 B.C.E), who is credited with being the originator of the philosophy of relativism. Since he believed that humans cannot verify the existence of "the gods," he concluded that "Man is the measure of all things: of the things that are, that they are, of the things that are not, that they are not."[22] He laid the foundation of the idea that each individual is the measure of how things are perceived by that individual. Essentially, he said that the individual's "little r" is the final judge. Bevans and Schroeder show how this Renaissance thinking impacted the worldview of an entire continent: "Interest in the study of human nature itself would develop into an understanding of a person more as an individual than as a member of a group."[23] By the time John Calvin attended Collège de Montaigu, individualism was a part of the European culture.

Both of the illustrations given above – the Pakistani mother burning her daughter, and my experience with the two generations of Korean Canadians – reflect the differences between Paul's thinking and the thinking of John Calvin. Paul was not an individualistic thinker, so he never envisioned predestination of individuals for salvation, nor did he write from that perspective. John Calvin *was* an individualistic thinker, so he never envisioned anything *but* predestination of individuals for salvation, and that is the perspective from which he both read and wrote. As Paul wrote, he had groups in mind; as Calvin read, he had individuals in mind. The result is a complete misunderstanding of certain texts in Scripture, then the creation of an entire theological system that attempts to reconcile all of Scripture to that erroneous understanding. As we shall see, that reconciliation cannot be done. It results in multiple cases of internal inconsistency, and the weight of the evidence does not support it. As this book progresses, I will attempt to show that, in detail.

The second important difference between Paul's and Calvin's worldviews relates to how they interpreted the world in terms of determinism, or fatalism. I'm convinced that Paul attempts to make it clear that he believes people have free will, and that their choices change history and eternity. I could use any of his letters to support this, but Romans works, since it comes first in the New Testament. In Romans, we find: The gospel is the power of God for the salvation of *everyone who believes* (Rom 1:16); God's wrath is being revealed against those who *suppress* the truth (Rom 1:19); the *thoughts* of people who don't have the law accuse or defend them (Rom 2:15); the righteousness of God comes from *faith* in Jesus Christ to *all who believe* (Rom 3:22); God will credit righteousness to us who *believe* (Rom 4:24). And on and on. Since we have been justified by *faith*, we have peace with God, and we have gained access to our Lord Jesus Christ by *faith* (Rom 5:1-2); *everyone* who calls on the name of the Lord will be saved, but how can they call on one they have not *believed* in, and how can they *believe* if they have not heard, and how will they hear if no one tells them (Rom 10:13-14)?

I will make the argument that this viewpoint is consistent throughout Paul's writings. At the same time, I am also aware that however we see Paul – as a staunch defender of free will, or as one who believes in predestination of individuals for salvation – our view is complicated by the fact that all of us who read him, are doing so through lenses of our own.

As I have already stated, for many years I was one of those who saw predestination in Paul's worldview. But I also saw the emphasis on believing. I was taught to rationalize the inconsistencies between free will and predestination – to rationalize the lack of internal coherence. "Free will and being chosen are two sides of the same coin. We just can't see both sides at the same time." Or, "We approach the door of salvation and see a sign over the door that says SALVATION TO EVERYONE WHO BELIEVES. Once we enter, we look back and see a sign that says CHOSEN BEFORE THE FOUNDATION OF THE EARTH." And of course, the ultimate fallback verse when questions are asked about the apparent contradictions, "As the heavens are higher than the earth, so are my ways higher than your ways and my thoughts than your thoughts, declares the Lord" (Isa 55:9). My theology professor in seminary told us on one occasion that appealing to that verse is often simply a cover up for sloppy thinking. The more I understand, the more I agree with him.

What I now realize is, that when we read Paul's writing through the lenses of *his* culture, there are no inconsistencies. There are not two sides of the same coin, there are not different signs over the same door. Paul was a brilliant scholar who was deeply in tune with the Holy Spirit. Both of those characteristics favor coherence. If we see inconsistencies in Paul's writings, it is either because Paul was a sloppy thinker, or because we are. I don't believe Paul was, and I believe I can show that we don't have to be. We can learn to read Paul through his own lenses, and when we do, we will not only find coherence in his writings, we will find coherence between his writings and the rest of Scripture. Why could Calvin not see the same things?

John Calvin was a product of his time, as we all are. His thinking was shaped by the culture and the education system in which he grew up.

Aristotle, Humanism, and Fatalism

Wendy Helleman reflects on the connection between Greek classical culture and the education of Calvin's day:

> ... the literary education typical of Renaissance humanism, with its focus on the classical texts, influenced Calvin in his approach to Scriptures . . . Most Calvinist theologians thus were ready to make judicious use of the pagan authors, especially Aristotle, be it in purified form, justifying this use by indicating that all truth has its source in God or that the pagans had received their wisdom from Moses by way of the Egyptians.[24]

In case someone does not understand the term, "humanism" was the intellectual and cultural movement associated with the Renaissance in Europe, already discussed above (14th - 17th centuries), that turned away from medieval scholasticism due to the rediscovery of classical Greek philosophy. The Renaissance not only moved Europe toward individualism, but it moved scholars to value human reasoning above spiritual discernment. Even among religious scholars, humanism had two important elements: 1) devotion to a body of accepted authors, and 2) a recognized methodology for conducting study and debate.[25] It was "a humanist tradition of scholarship that searched for truth using non-theological sources and methods."[26]

One of the accepted perspectives of Calvin's time was that fatalism was logically true. The argument for fatalism can be traced back to Aristotle,[27] whose teachings, as Helleman points out, were basic to education in Calvin's day. Essentially, fatalism says that if something can truly be known in advance, then when the time arrives for that event to happen or that decision to be made, it cannot occur other than the way it was known to be ahead of time. The argument is logical, and was accepted as true by both John Calvin and Martin Luther, as well as Huldrych Zwingli.[28] Applied to salvation, it follows that if God knows the decision we are going to make ahead of time, then when we are faced with the decision, we can only make it the way God knows ahead of time that we will.

I want to deal with this on two levels: first, with simple solutions to the logical dilemma that such a fatalistic view presents, then at a deeper level in Chapter 7 by looking at current views on the foreknowledge of God.

C.S. Lewis is one of many thinkers who challenges fatalism by attacking the idea of God knowing *ahead of time*. He says:

> If God foresaw our acts, it would be very hard to understand how we could be free not to do them. But suppose God is outside and above the Time-line. In that case, what we call "tomorrow" is visible to Him in just the same way as what we call "today." All the days are "Now" for Him. He does not remember you doing things yesterday; He simply sees you doing them, because, though you have lost yesterday, He has not. He does not "foresee" you doing things tomorrow; He simple sees you doing them: because, though tomorrow is not yet here for you, it is for Him. You never supposed that your actions at this moment were any less free because God knows what you are doing. Well, He knows your tomorrow's actions in just the same way – because he is already in tomorrow and can simply watch you. In a sense, He does not know your action till you have done it: but then the moment at which you have done it is already "Now" for Him. [29]

Lewis suggests that God is outside of time, so even though he knows our decisions before we make them in our time, it is not *ahead of time* for him. In his existence, all things are present time. His "foreknowledge" is simply because he can watch us making that decision in real time for us, an eternity before we exist, because all time is real time for him. That's one possible explanation that breaks the binding effect of the logic of fatalism. It is also consistent with Einstein's theory of relativity and recent scientific conclusions, that time is related to gravity and is not the constant we thought it was just decades ago. In the absence of gravity, apparently, time passes very differently than it does in the presence of gravity, with the strength of the gravity affecting the speed at which time passes.[30] This is the premise on which the *Planet of the Apes* movies were based. Space travelers gone from earth for only a few years, as time was passing for them, return to find that time on earth has advanced by several hundred years, so apes have evolved beyond humans and are ruling the earth.

From our human perspective, we lack the ability to state definitively how this applies to God, but it is entirely logical to suggest that he who created both time and gravity, is beyond them both. There are other ways of resolving this fatalistic logic as well, which will be discussed in Chapter 7, but the point is this: deterministic thinking is not a logical necessity.

A second simple solution to fatalism is the observation that even if God knows our decisions ahead of time, that does not mean he determines our decisions. Foreknowledge and predestination are not the same thing.[31] This is consistent with Lewis's observation that God is outside of time. God can know ahead of time what we will do, not because he predetermines it, but because that is what we choose to do, and he simply observes it. It is also consistent with the theology of the vast majority of Christians.

In the same way that Charles Darwin proposed the theory of evolution before things like the complexity of the living cell were understood, and before anyone had attempted to calculate the amount of time it would take for random chance to produce the complexity of the world we live in, John Calvin lived in a world where alternatives to Aristotle's logic of fatalism were not available.

From Calvin's worldview, conditioned as it was by the culture in which he lived, both individualistic thinking was normal and unchallenged, and fatalism was logical and largely unchallenged. When you take those two perspectives and impose them on Paul's writings, the natural outcome is

LIKE ALL OF US, JOHN CALVIN WAS A PRODUCT OF HIS CULTURE

Calvinism. It was logical to Calvin because he had been educated to view the world through Aristotle's lenses, although it was not necessary. Others, notably the entire Catholic Church, the entire Orthodox Church, and other Christian leaders like Jacob Arminius, avoided interpreting Paul's writings that way, and avoided imposing that perspective on the whole of Scripture. In John Calvin's context, his perspective made sense, but the logic was determined by the context.

Consider Eddie Gibbs's observation:

> Due to the fact that culture's presence is so pervasive and that we are all shaped by the culture in which we are nurtured, we are often unaware of the extent to which our culture influences our thinking, attitudes and actions. No theological tradition is immune from the influence of culture. Every person, to a greater or lesser extent, is shaped by his or her own context. The evangelical movement has been as much influenced by culture as has the liberal tradition within Christianity. For the most part we remain unaware of our cultural biases until someone from another culture is sufficiently frank or angry to confront us with the issues that we have either chosen to ignore or have been unable to see.[32]

Like all of us, John Calvin was a product of his culture. The characteristics of his thinking that are visible today, are only visible because we do not see the world through the lenses his culture taught him to use. Remember, culture not only teaches us *what* to think, but also *how* to think. As Gibbs points out, we can never completely separate ourselves from our culture, because it shapes our thinking so profoundly.

Theology and Context

One of the most difficult challenges for the Christian of any era is to allow the Bible to be the judge of what our culture teaches, rather than the other way around. The process is complicated because we approach the Bible through cultural lenses in the first place. That problem will never be completely solved, but if it is ever solved even to a degree, it will be because we use clear scriptural teaching to help us understand less clear passages, rather than simply reading Scripture through our cultural lenses and interpreting it in a superficial way. Ideally, we will identify the deeper truths of Scripture (the essence), use them to clarify unclear portions of Scripture, and process those truths through the grid of our cultural thinking (unavoidable), and come out with a way to express those truths (form) in a way that is both understandable within our culture, and consistent with the original truth. That is contextualization. It is the way *all* contextual theologies are developed. In fact, as Gibbs says, it is the way *all theology* is developed. Once we understand the degree to which our culture shapes our thinking and provides the lenses through which we view reality, we realize that *all theologies are contextual theologies.* That means Calvinism is a contextual theology. It has never been anything other than that. It was logical in its day, but now, with a more coherent understanding, it can be relegated to the grave.

When I was a child, I heard a country preacher teaching from Luke 9:62, where Jesus says, "No one who puts his hand to the plow and looks back is fit for service in the kingdom of God." The preacher used the passage to challenge us to keep our eyes ahead, fixed on the goal, because, he said, if you're plowing behind a mule, and you look back, you end up with a crooked furrow rather than a straight one.

The preacher was using his personal experience as a Texas farm boy to interpret Scripture, even though his experience was nothing like the world in which words were originally spoken. There is a sense in which that is all we can do, but there is also the potential to put more prayerful thought into the process so that we come up with a better understanding. I was about 10 at the time, and I knew very little about first century Jewish farming practices, but from the parable of the sower, I reasoned that they probably broad sowed their seed rather than planting them in rows. I wondered at the time if Jesus cared enough about straight rows to address it in the Bible.

Years later, attempting to understand that passage, I asked two questions, which I think the preacher could also have done: 1) what larger subject was Jesus talking about when he used that illustration? And 2) what common knowledge would he and his audience have shared that would enable them to understand his illustration without further explanation? The answer to question 1 is supplied by the prior text. Luke is relating Jesus' response to three potential disciples. Jesus had detected reservations in all of them about making a total commitment. For each excuse, Jesus had a further comment, and his statement about the plow was in response to the one who wanted to go back and say good-bye to his family. That's question 1 answered – the context.

Question 2 is, what common knowledge would Jesus and that Jewish man have shared about plows and looking back? The likely answer is the story of Elisha in 1 Kings 19. Elisha was a commercial farmer, plowing with twelve yoke of oxen, the twelfth pair of which he was driving himself. Whether Elisha was the owner of all the oxen, or just the ones he was plowing with, is not clear. What is clear is that when Elijah called Elisha, Elisha put his hand to the plow, literally, but not to plow straight furrows. He slaughtered his oxen, cooked them on the wood from the plows, distributed the meat to neighbors so it would not go to waste, then he went and followed Elijah. He put his hand to the plow and then did not look back.

Why include that story in the Old Testament in the first place? Because it shows total commitment to the call. It was an ancient parallel of the story of Hernán Cortés in his quest to conquer Mexico in 1519. Whether the story is true or not, he is reputed to have burned the ships on which he and his men arrived in Mexico.[33] He removed their opportunity to go back. His commitment was total, just as Elisha's was. And, in contrast to the preacher's challenge to plow a straight furrow and keep our eyes on the goal ahead, the Elisha illustration fits perfectly with the situation Luke was describing. Jesus was making the same point in Luke 9 that he makes in more detail in Luke 14, that true discipleship requires a total commitment. The one who wants to hedge his bet, to have one foot in discipleship and one foot in other enterprises, to keep open some avenue of escape if things don't work out as hoped, is not a true disciple. Note that such an understanding is consistent with the rest of Scripture, providing clarity by allowing Scripture to interpret the unclear portion, rather than allowing a foreign cultural understanding to do it.

On a matter of much less importance, the country preacher was guilty of the same thing Calvin was.

Rene Padilla addresses the trap they fell into. "If in the process of interpretation, any of the values or premises of the culture that are incongruent with the Gospel are included in that interpretation in such a way as to affect its content, the result is syncretism. In every syncretism, there is the accommodation of the Gospel to some value prevalent in the culture. . . ."[34] I am convinced that Calvin imposed both fatalism and individualism on his interpretation of Scripture, accommodating Scripture to the values "prevalent in the culture" of his day. The result was an aberrant understanding of Scripture that would be completely foreign to the ones who wrote it.

Calvinism and the Worldwide Church

The proponents of Calvinism often teach it as if it's the final and complete truth from God. In reality, it appeals only to people who have a certain worldview, the one that arose in western Europe as a result of the Renaissance. It appeals to people who have a low tolerance for ambiguity or uncertainty, who tend to be black and white (dichotomistic) thinkers.[35] Calvinism made perfect sense to a small minority of Christians when it was developed, and it still does today. However, the critical point is "small minority." Calvinism still reflects the views of only a small minority of the worldwide Christian church, and that minority is shrinking every day. If we attempt to visually portray the development of Calvinism and its position today, in relation to the history of the worldwide church, it looks like this:

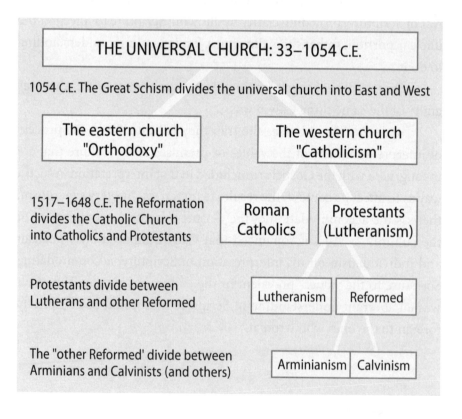

As the divisions occurred, we see the church first separating between the East and the West, over what we now understand to be primarily cultural issues. Some five hundred years later, the Western Church divided again, this time over primarily theological issues. Within the next few decades, the Protestants divided into two groups – those who followed Martin Luther, and those who did not. Those reformers who did not join Luther's group divided again, this time as followers of Jacob Arminius and John Calvin and others, such as the Anabaptists. In light of all the people and issues involved in these divisions, and the time involved in the various processes, my diagram is very simplistic. It is offered, however, to demonstrate that the followers of Calvin were, originally, and continue to be, a very small minority in comparison to all the rest of Christianity. Often, however, they maintain a strict loyalty to their group, and a strict conviction that they are right and everybody else is wrong. When you are "the chosen," it makes sense to avoid contamination by the unchosen, in the same way the Jews were doing in Jesus' day. But avoiding contact with others is not unique to Calvinists.

One of my observations is that *most* Christians in the western world stay pretty much within the church circles in which they were raised, or which they first entered as a new believer. There is little or no consideration of other ways of seeing things.

Recently, I read an online article written by a theologian. I found myself interested in who had written the article, so I checked out his credentials. The writer was proud of the fact that he was raised in a religious home loyal to one of the smaller and more exclusive Protestant denominations in the United States. He was educated in a private school affiliated with the denomination, attended a private college run by the denomination, then a seminary that prepared leaders for the denomination. Now, with his Ph.D. and access to the Internet, he is doing his best to convince the world that his denomination's perspective on reality is the right one.

When I was in college, my parents moved to a new location and rented a house owned by an older couple. The husband – the landlord – was proud of the fact that he had never, in his entire 70 years, been out of the rural Texas county in which he had been born.

The uneducated landlord and the theologian with his Ph.D. have one thing in common – their ignorance. They are not well informed about the world that is out there, and their worldviews reflect their lack of understanding. The landlord was probably harmless. The theologian is not.

"IF I STAY IN MY LOCAL AREA AND LIMIT MY INPUT TO SOURCES THAT SUPPORT WHAT I ALREADY BELIEVE, I CAN DEFEND BELIEFS THAT DO NOT ACCURATELY REFLECT ALL THAT IS OUT THERE IN THE WORLD."

I was raised in rural churches with a "fundamental" stance. By the time I finished college, I could see that their views were too narrow, and their boundaries too rigid, to explain all there is in the world. I could no longer be a part of it. Many years later, I attended a large non-denominational church that attracted affluent, professional people. It was Calvinistic in its theology. After awhile, I realized that they limited their input and their pastors to two specific non-denominational institutions – a certain Bible institute, and a certain seminary. After finding myself in trouble with the church leadership for asking a question that challenged what the church believed, I realized that not everybody is questioning what they have always been taught. Even affluent, well educated people.

Now we live in a world that faces a constant threat from various terrorists – who never question what they have always been taught.

As I was reflecting on the similarities between these two positions, the Calvinists and the terrorists, I wrote a statement in my journal that explains all four of the examples I just used – the landlord, the theologian, the Calvinists, and the terrorists: *"If I stay in my local area and limit my input to sources that support what I already believe,*

I can defend beliefs that do not accurately reflect all that is out there in the world." It's easier to defend the maps in our minds than to revise them, but it is not always the right thing to do. It's easier to defend those maps if we never encounter the information that confronts the flaws in the maps. Those of us who travel a lot, and who read widely, find it increasingly difficult to defend beliefs that simply do not address huge swaths of the information that is out there. If our commitment is ultimately to truth, new information should not threaten us.

Andrew Walls, British Christian theologian and missiologist, professor of History of Mission, and long time missionary to Africa, reflects on the reality of Christianity in culture. He points out, as we have already discussed, that all theology is both *occasional* and *local* in character,[36] or, to use the terms I have used, it is always contextual, a product of a *time* and *place*. He also points out that there are two principles at work between Christianity and culture. One he calls the *indigenizing* principle, that God accepts us as we are, which includes our culture, and the other is the *pilgrim* principle – the fact that certain universal truths always apply, so God not only accepts us as we are, but he does so in order to transform us, including our culture.[37] Walls's point is that Christianity is always understood through the lenses of the local culture (the indigenizing effect), and yet Christianity always stands in opposition to the local culture (the pilgrim effect), at least in opposition to certain aspects of the culture. Christianity is always both *at home* in every culture, and *an outcast* in every culture. The truths never change, but they are understood very differently in different cultures.[38]

In applying these ideas to current reality, Walls observes that over the past half century, the center of the Christian world has shifted globally from the northern hemisphere to the southern, so over time, theological understanding will also originate from there and will be based on cultural conditions there.[39] This has already started, with Liberation Theology already a potent actor on the stage of the global south,[40] and other contextual theologies emerging around the world –

black theology, Hispanic theology, feminist theology, Asian theology, various African theologies, etc.[41]

Notable with this shift to the global south is also the fact that Pentecostalism is the dominant way Christianity is being expressed among the majority of Christians today, pushing Calvinism even further into an outdated, minority status.

That which made sense in 16th century western Europe, does not resonate with the vast majority of Christians today. As we continue to examine the issues, it will become more and more apparent why.

Endnotes

[1] From a lecture by Dr. John Gration, Christianity and Culture course, Prairie Graduate School., June, 2001.

[2] Stephen B. Bevans and Roger Schroeder, *Constants in Context: A Theology of Mission for Today* (Maryknoll, NY: Orbis Books, 2004), 23-25.

[3] Bevans and Schroeder, 27.

[4] Frank Viola and George Barna, *Pagan Christianity?: Exploring the Roots of Our Church Practices* (Carol Stream, IL: BarnaBooks, 2008).

[5] Frei Betto, "Gustavo Gutiérrez – A Friendly Profile," in Marc H. Ellis and Otto Maduro, eds., *The Future of Liberation Theology: Essays in Honor of Gustavo Guitiérrez* (Maryknoll, N.Y.: Orbis Books, 1989), 33.

[6] Bevans and Schroeder, 64, citing Irenaeus, *Against Heresies*, 3.18.6. Original source can be found at Irenaeus, *Against Heresies*, Book 3, Ch. 18, para. 6. https://carm.org/irenaeus-heresies3-15-25. Accessed 14 Nov 2016.

[7] Bevans and Schroeder, 64, citing Anselm of Canterbury (1033-1109) in his book, *Cur Deus Homo* (lit. "Why the God Man?"); Original source can be found at Anselm, *Cur Deus Homo*, Ch. 19-20, in *Saint Anselm: Basic Writings*, translated by S. N. Deane (La Salle, IL: Open Court Publishing, 1962), 222-228.

[8] For a more thorough treatment of these three veins of theology, see Justo González, *Christian Thought Revisited: Three Types of Theology* (London: SCM Press; Philadelphia, PA: Trinity Press Int'l, 1990).

[9] Bevans and Schroeder have a chart on p. 37 that summarizes the six constants and the three types of theology that the rest of the book deals with in detail.

[10] Although Nida's work has been expanded upon and even heavily critiqued in the past several decades, he is still recognized as having jump-started the massive advances that have been made in translation theory in recent times.

[11] See David Bosch, *Transforming Mission: Paradigm Shifts in Theology of Mission* (Maryknoll, NY: Orbis Books, 1991), 56-122.

[12] Bosch, 170-8.

[13] Bosch, 191.

[14] Bosch uses the six paradigms suggested by Hans Küng to show how theological changes throughout history have reflected themselves in different ways of doing mission. These paradigms are reflected in Küng's writings: Hans Küng and David Tracy, *Theologie – wohin? Auf dem Weg zu einem neuen Paradigma* (Zürich-Cologne: Benziger Verlag, 1984), 25; Hans Küng, *Theologie im Aufbruch: Eine* ökumenische *Grundlegung* (Munich: Piper Verlag, 1987), 157.

[15] Bosch traces these movements in detail in chapters 5-11 of his monumental work.

[16] Geert Hofstede and Gert Jan Hofstede, *Cultures and Organizations: Software of the Mind* (London: McGraw-Hill, 2005), 75.

[17] Hofstede, 75.

[18] Hofstede, 76, italics are in the original.

[19] Paul G. Hiebert, *Missiological Implications of Epistological Shifts: Affirming Truth in a Modern/ Postmodern World* (Harrisburg, PA: Trinity Press Int'l, 1999), 7.

[20] Hiebert traces this progression succinctly, 1-8; see also Bevans and Schroeder, 230, on how the "breakdown" in communal thinking has affected Christian missions efforts.

[21] http://www.cnn.com/2016/06/08/middleeast/mother-sets-pakistani-woman-on-fire-police-say/

[22] Carol Poster, "Protagoras," *Internet Encyclopedia of Philosophy*, http://www.iep.utm.edu/protagor/, accessed 16 July 2016.

[23] Bevans and Schroeder, 139.

[24] Wendy E. Helleman, ed., "Introduction," *Christianity and the Classics: The Acceptance of a Heritage* (Lanham, MD: University Press of America, 1990), 22-23. Charles Kraft treats that position as assumed: "Since European culture has been greatly influenced by Greek-type thinking, we Euro-Americans are naturally attracted to those portions of the Scriptures that are directed to Greek-speaking peoples." Charles Kraft, *Christianity in Culture* (Maryknoll, NY: Orbis Books, 1979), 9.

[25] Nicholas Mann, *The Origins of Humanism* (Cambridge University Press, 1996), 1-2; Jacques Barzun, *From Dawn to Decadence :500 years of Western Cultural Life* (New York: HarperCollins, 2000), 45.

[26] Stanley H. Skreslet, *Comprehending Mission: The Questions, Methods, Themes, Problems, and Prospects of Missiology* (Maryknoll, N.Y.: Orbis Books, 2012), 52.

[27] http://plato.stanford.edu/entries/fatalism/#5.

[28] Frank A. James III, *Peter Martyr Vermigli and Predestination: The Augustinian Inheritance of an Italian Reformer* (Oxford: Clarendon, 1998), 30; Ewald M. Plass, *What Luther Says*, Selection 1353 (Saint Louis, MO: Concordia Pub. House, 1959), 458; *Carl R. Trueman, Luther's Legacy: Salvation and English Reformers, 1525-1556 (Oxford: Clarendon, 1994), 69.*

[29] C.S. Lewis, *Mere Christianity* (New York: The MacMillan Co., 1953), 133.

[30] Cf. http://physicsworld.com/cws/article/news/2010/feb/17/gravitys-effect-on-time-confirmed, accessed 3 Nov 2016.

[31] Tom Morris, p. 134.

[32] Eddie Gibbs, *ChurchNext: Quantum Changes in How We Do Ministry* (Downers Grove, IL: InterVarsity Press, 2000), 27-28.

[33] Ross Hassig, *Mexico and the Spanish Conquest* (London: Longman Group UK Limited, 1994), 53–54.

[34] C. Rene Padilla, "The Contextualization of the Gospel," *Journal of Theology for Southern Africa* No. 24 (September, 1978): 12-30. Quote p. 16.

[35] As Hofstede describes, 163-205, and as addressed in Sherwood G. Lingenfelter and Marvin K. Mayers, *Ministering Cross-Culturally: An Incarnational Model for Personal Relationships* (Grand Rapids: Baker Book House, 1986), 53-68.

[36] Andrew F. Walls, *The Missionary Movement in Christian History: Studies in the Transmission of Faith* (Maryknoll, NY: Orbis Books, 1996).

[37] Walls, 7-9.

[38] Hiebert makes these points equally clearly, 111.

[39] Walls, 10.

[40] Cf. Gustavo Gutiérrez, *A Theology of Liberation: History, Politics, and Salvation* (Maryknoll, N.Y.: Orbis Books, 1973).

[41] For summaries, see Daniel G. Groody, *Globalization, Spirituality, and Justice* (Maryknoll, NY: Orbis Books. 2007), 202-207. For more, see Virginia Fabella and R.S. Sugirtharajah, eds., *Dictionary of Third World Theologies* (Maryknoll, NY: Orbis, 2000).

Chapter 4
Predestination Through the Centuries

**The glory of human nature lies in our seeming
capacity to exercise conscious control
over our own destiny.**
– Winston Churchill[1]

Predestination did not originate with John Calvin, although he systematized the theology that bears his name. Predestination is a form of religious determinism that has had parallels in the thinking of certain cultures at least since the days of Aristotle. In Chapter 1, we saw how the fatalistic thinking of the local farmers in the Dominican Republic kept them in poverty. But fatalistic thinking has shown up even among modern academics. As Charles Kraft points out, "The positions of White and Skinner within the behavioral sciences [that humans are not autonomous but are controlled totally by environmental influences] are not dissimilar from the theological determinism advanced by those who hold to extreme views of predestination."[2] The essence of the religious doctrine is that all events have been willed by God, usually with reference to the eventual fate of the individual soul. The "anchor premise" on which the doctrine rests, is that God is sovereign in all affairs both in heaven and earth. In Chapter 7, we will consider the Plan of God, including how his sovereignty is involved in that plan, but in this chapter, we will briefly trace the history of predestination within Christianity.

To begin with, it should be noted that in Romans 8:28-30, the Apostle Paul writes,

> And we know that in all things God works for the good of those who love him, who have been called according to his purpose. For those God foreknew he also predestined to be conformed to the likeness of his Son, that he might be the firstborn among many brothers. And those he predestined, he also called; those he called, he also justified; those he justified, he also glorified.

In Chapter 6, we will look at the letter to the Romans in some detail to try to determine what Paul actually meant by these verses, within the larger setting of the book. For now, however, the point is to establish that the original concept of predestination within Christianity originated in the New Testament itself, in the writings of Paul. If we believe that the entire Bible is inspired of God, then we have to conclude that this statement is as well, and is therefore both true and worthy of our understanding.

The problem is, of course, that Paul's teaching has been understood differently at different times in different cultures. And those varying interpretations tend to run along denominational lines. We will look at that briefly, below. For now, however, let's look at the history of the thinking.

The earliest attempt to describe what Paul meant by predestination shows up in the writings of Origen (c. 184 - c. 253 C.E.). Origen lived a life of rigid frugality so he could study and teach without distraction. Eusebius, writing less than a hundred years later, reported that Origen literally castrated himself to avoid being tempted sexually.[3] He was a prolific writer who had several ideas that led to his teachings being denounced as heretical at the Second Council of Constantinople in 553, including his belief in the pre-existence of souls and in a final form of universalism, in which all creatures, including Satan himself, would be reconciled to God.[4] In the first half of the third century, he wrote that God's providence extends to every individual and that God's predestination was based on God's foreknowledge.[5]

Augustine of Hippo (354 - 430) was born almost exactly a hundred years after Origen died. Augustine is considered to be the father of predestination as Calvin taught it, and as we have it today. In his earlier years, he believed that predestination was based on God's foreknowledge of whether or not individuals would believe.[6] Later though, in his response to Pelagius, Augustine argued that God's choice has nothing to do with the individual, but is based on God's will alone.[7] Pelagius (c. 360 - c. 418) was a monk and theologian of British or Irish origin who spent most of his life in Rome and northern Africa. He was convinced of human free will to the extent that "nature retains the ability to conquer sin and to gain eternal life even without the aid of grace."[8] His views were condemned as heresy at the Council of Ephesus in 431, but Augustine's rebuttal lived on.

Whether Augustine's teaching implies double predestination or not, is a matter of continuing debate, with some Protestant and secular scholars arguing that it does, and Catholics tending to deny it.[9] In case someone is not clear on what is meant by "double predestination," it is the belief that God not only deliberately predetermines who will be saved, but also who will not. In other words, it eliminates the possibility that people remain unsaved by God's passive will, clearly making their damnation God's active determination.

One statement of Augustine's that seems to reflect the view of double predestination, is in Book XXII of his *City of God*: "What will God give to those whom he has predestined to life, if he has given all these [blessings of nature] to those predestined to death?"[10] Voices were raised in opposition, including those of Julian (c. 386 - c. 455), bishop of Eclanum, near what is now Benevento, Italy, and Vincent of Lérins, (the group of four Mediterranean Islands off the French Riviera coast, near Cannes).[11] The institutional Church never interpreted Augustine's position to include predestination of the condemned, although individual priests and theologians certainly did. Around 475 to 480 (the historical record is not clear on the date), a Council held in Arles, in what today is southern France, condemned the teachings of the priest Lucidus "that some have been condemned to death, others have been predested to life."[12] In 529, the Second Council of Orange also condemned the position "that any are foreordained to evil by the power of God."[13]

Some two hundred years later, John of Damascus, best known for his defense of religious icons,[14] taught a doctrine of predestination that emphasized the freedom of the human will, arguing that people's actions are not caused by God, but may work in cooperation with him.[15]

In the ninth-century, Gottschalk, a Saxon monk from Mainz, Germany, was sent to the Orbais Abbey in what is now northeastern France. He became known as Gottschalk of Orbais. As he studied the writings of Augustine, he became a committed believer in double predestination. He interpreted Augustine's remarks in *City of God*, mentioned above, to mean that God predestines some people to hell as well as some to heaven. Despite being condemned by several synods, he never recanted his view, and as a result, he spent the rest of his life imprisoned in the monastery of Hautvillers. His views were tenacious, however, so the archbishop of Reims asked Irish theologian John Scottus Eriugena to write a rebuttal of Gottschalk. Eriugena attempted to reconcile Augustine's earlier and later teachings on predestination by explaining that God predestines people based on his foreknowledge of their choices and excusing Augustine's statement of "predestined to death" as simply meaning "not predestined to eternal life."[16]

Three hundred years later, in the twelfth century, Thomas Aquinas wrote prolifically, including his *Summa theologiae*, in which he taught that God "governs all the acts and movements that are to be found in each single creature"[17] which includes predestining certain people to what the Catholics and certain other denominations call the "beatific vision" – the final state in which individuals personally see God and can communicate with him directly. Aquinas taught that predestination is based solely on God's own goodness rather than that of created beings, so "why He chooses some for glory, and reprobates others, has no reason, except the divine will".[18] Aquinas also believed people are free in their choices, fully cause their own sin, and are solely responsible for it.[19] Aquinas makes a distinction between God's direct will (which produces good), his indirect will (which results in evil consequences for human choices), and what he permits (evil itself). Following Augustine, Aquinas believed that God "neither wills evil to be done, nor wills it not to be done, but wills to permit evil to be done".[20]

As Aquinas interprets 1 Timothy 2:4 (which teaches that God "wants all men to be saved"), he draws from John of Damascus's teaching, that God's will regarding rational creatures can be divided into 'antecedent' and 'consequent'. *Antecedent* simply means to precede in time or sequence. "God's antecedent will, according to which he wills the salvation of all, is his will as the giver of being and salvation. God's consequent will has to do with rational creatures 'as they exist in themselves', and in this regard God justly wills the everlasting punishment of those who freely and permanently reject his saving work."[21] Humans contribute nothing to God's plan, since "whatsoever is in man disposing him towards salvation, is all included under the effect of predestination; even the preparation for grace."[22] In Aquinas's reckoning, God's 'antecedent' will shows that God is the cause of predestination, and his 'consequent' will shows that he is not the cause of reprobation. The rational creature's sin is the cause of reprobation.[23]

A reprobate is one who is degenerate, without a moral compass, and without hope of recovery. Reprobation is the process that leads to that state. The question is whether God is responsible for a person being in that state. Aquinas thought not. We will return to the possibility of God having more than one "will" in Chapter 7 as we consider the overall Plan of God.

In the fourteenth century, William of Ockham, an English Franciscan friar, through a complex series of logical arguments, arrived at the conclusion that God's will does not cause human choices, so predestination must stem from divine foreknowledge. Ockham went further than believing that predestination was based on God foreseeing one's belief, to foreseeing their works, or "merit." He argued that God is not compelled to do this, however, so the result is still a free gift. If God left some out of his predestination, without considering their sinful choices, he would be punishing them before they even exist, let alone commit sin.[24] According to James Halverson, rather than Ockham's argument supporting predestination based on foreseen merit, it supports the premise that "God offers grace to all and a person's predestination depends on the response to grace."[25]

Roughly two centuries after Ockham, Martin Luther and John Calvin entered the picture. Luther was deeply influenced by the Catholic monastic Augustinian Order, in which he was a monk.[26] When the Order was founded in 1244, it had nothing to do with predestination, but later it did. Initially, the Order simply set out to follow Augustine's ideas on how monastic life should be lived. He had left written instructions on everything from charity to care of the sick, poverty, fasting and abstinence, detachment from the world, monastic division of labor, obedience, fraternal charity, common prayer, and much more.[27] Since the Augustinians studied Augustine's writings, they became familiar with his views on predestination, so by the time Martin Luther was being mentored by Johann von Staupitz, who was the leader of the Augustinian Order in Germany at the time,[28] Staupitz had already written what Michael Horton calls "a marvelous tract" defending Augustine's position on predestination.[29]

John Calvin picked up the strain that Augustine had started, and with the timing of the Reformation and the printing press, propelled the teaching from being consistently condemned by church councils, to being the dominant belief among certain Protestants. As I have already attempted to establish, that acceptance was dependent on two major factors: 1) a foundational belief in fatalism, courtesy of Aristotle, and 2) an individualistic worldview. These two preconditions melded with the resentment of the abuses of the institutional Church and the availability of mass printing to make conditions ripe for Calvin to broadly disseminate, and certain people to accept, a theology that interpreted Scripture contrary to fifteen centuries of church doctrine.

Calvin rejected Aquinas's idea that God permits rather than actively decrees evil, including the damnation of sinners, calling it an "evasion that this is done only by the permission, and not also by the will of God."[30] When Calvin encountered contradictions between his beliefs, rather than revisiting his understanding of Scripture as I will be suggesting, he attributed his inability to comprehend to "the feebleness of our intellect." For example, he considered it an unfathomable mystery that God seems to simultaneously will sin and to also not will sin.[31] Though he insisted that God's predestination applies to damnation as well as salvation,[32] Calvin affirmed that for the damned, "though their perdition depends on the predestination of God, the cause and matter of it is in themselves."[33] By contrast, he said, the salvation of the saved is caused solely by God.[34]

Aristotle Rises Again

There is a common thread among all the major proponents of divine determinism throughout church history – a deep familiarity with Aristotle's writings. Augustine was heavily influenced by the

Greek philosophical tradition, so there is a consistent similarity between his thinking and that of Aristotle.[35] Thomas Aquinas was a staunch defender of Greek philosophy, and his copious commentaries on the works of Aristotle reveal the degree to which he was steeped in Aristotle's teachings.[36] The connection is equally clear of William of Ockham, even though Ockham's conclusion is less deterministic than that of Augustine and Aquinas.[37] Luther actually taught Aristotle's *Nichomachean Ethics* at Wittenberg,[38] and we have already established the connection between Calvin and Aristotle. Without detracting any from Aristotle's brilliance, it appears clear that, as the father of fatalism, his paradigm on this matter was passed along with his other philosophy.

On a global scale today, Calvinism is being overshadowed with a growing Pentecostal presence. However, Calvinism has experienced a resurgence in the USA in the early 21st century, according to *Time Magazine* religious writer David Van Biema. He connects the renewed interest in Calvinism's "austerely demanding God" to several passionate and widely broadcast spokespersons who offer a God "unaffected by human action or decision" as an alternative to the "doctrinal drift" of many churches. A certain number of young people who grew up "in a culture of brokenness, divorce, drugs or sexual temptation," apparently find security there.[39] Still, the vast majority of people worldwide who call themselves Christians, do not adhere to the convictions of John Calvin, as we established in Chapter 3.

For those interested in a deeper look at the differences between major Christian denominations on the issue of predestination, Appendix D provides a brief summary of those basic beliefs.

At this point, however, it is sufficient to note that almost all of the major Churches have some form of a "doctrine of election." The staunch Calvinists are on one extreme; the Charismatics are on the other. Most Churches are in between, either with the idea of *prevenient grace*, or with what is called *compatibilism*, the view that human free will is somehow compatible with divine determinism.

For anyone not familiar with the term *prevenient grace*, it simply means divine grace that precedes human decision. Like the word *antecedent* we encountered earlier, *prevenient* simply means to come before something in time or sequence. The concept will be dealt with in detail in Chapter 7, but for now, it is sufficient to say that, theologically, the reality and necessity of prevenient grace is accepted by most denominations. Compatibilism, on the other hand, is not.

Regarding this, Peter Thuesen quotes Allen Guelzo, that compatibilism "always has an air of unreality to it, of talk that somehow masks the obvious."[40] As I have studied this issue, I have come to realize that the air of unreality is justified. In the next two chapters, I will attempt to show why that unreality is there and why it masks the obvious. With the mask removed, the obvious becomes clear, and all of the efforts that have been made over the centuries to reconcile irreconcilable views of God, suddenly become unnecessary.

Endnotes

[1] Quoted in Morris, *Philosophy*, 134.

[2] Charles Kraft, *Christianity in Culture* (Maryknoll, NY: Orbis Books, 1979), 61.

[3] Eusebius, *The Church History,* Book 6, para. 8, in Paul L. Maier, transl., *Eusebius – The Church History: A New Translation with Commentary* (Grand Rapids, MI: Kregel Publications, 1999), 212-213.

[4] Matthew Levering, *Predestination: Biblical and Theological Paths* (Oxford: Oxford University Press, 2011), 41, citing Origen, *On First Principles*, trans. G. W. Butterworth, orig. pub. 1936 (Notre Dame, IN: Ave Maria Press, 2013), Book III, Ch. VI, p. 321ff, "The Consummation of the World".

[5] Levering, *Predestination,* 38-40.

[6] Levering, *Predestination,* 48, citing Augustine, *On the Predestination of the Saints,* in Augustine, *Anti-Pelagian Writings*, trans. Peter Holmes and Robert Ernest Wallis (1887), translation revised by Benjamin B. Warfield (Peabody, MA: Hendrickson, 1995), 500.

[7] Levering, *Predestination,* 44-48, citing Augustine, *On the Predestination of the Saints,* 499-517.

[8] Catholic Encyclopedia: Pelagius and Pelagianism. http://www.newadvent.org/cathen/11604a.htm, accessed 25 Aug 2016.

[9] James, *Peter Martyr Vermigli,* 102.

[10] Levering, *Predestination*, 72, citing Augustine, *City of God*, trans. Henry Bettenson (New York: Penguin, 1984,) Book XXII, Ch. 24, p. 1075.

[11] Henry Chadwick, *The Early Church*, rev. ed. (London: Penguin Books, 1993), 232-233.

[12] Levering, *Predestination*, 37, citing Henry Denzinger, *The Sources of Catholic Dogma*, trans. Roy J. Deferrari from the Thirtieth Edition (1957) of *Enchiridion Symbolorum* (Fitzwilliam, NH: Loreto Publications, 2002), 65, Council of Arles, Letter of submission of Lucidus, the priest.

[13] Levering, *Predestination*, 37, citing Denzinger, 81, Second Council of Orange, canon 25.

[14] Mike Aquilina, *The Fathers of the Church: An Introduction to the First Christian Teachers*, illus. ed. (Huntington, IN: Our Sunday Visitor Publishing, 1999), 222.

[15] Levering, *Predestination*, 60.

[16] Johannes Scotus Eriugena, *Treatise on Divine Predestination*, trans. Mary Brennan (Notre Dame, IN: University of Notre Dame Press, 1998), 76; Levering, *Predestination*, 69-74.

[17] Levering, *Predestination*, 78, citing Thomas Aquinas, *Summa theologiae*, trans. Fathers of the English Dominican Province (Notre Dame: Christian Classics, 1981), Part I, question 22, answer 3, *sed contra*.

[18] Levering, *Predestination*, 80, citing Aquinas, Part I, ques. 23, ans. 5, ad 3, then quoting Part I–II, ques. 93, ans. 4, ad 1.

[19] Levering, *Predestination*, 78, citing Aquinas, Part I, ques. 22, ans. 4; Part I, ques. 105, answers 4-5.

[20] Levering, *Predestination*, 78-79, citing Aquinas, Part I, ques. 19, ans. 9, then quoting Aquinas Part I, ques. 19, ans. 9, ad 3.

[21] Levering, *Predestination*, 81, citing Aquinas, Part I, ques. 19, ans. 6, ad 1.

[22] Levering, *Predestination*, 81, citing Aquinas, Part I, ques. 23, ans. 5.

[23] Levering, *Predestination*, 81, citing Aquinas, Part I, ques. 23, ans. 3, ad. 1-3.

[24] Levering, *Predestination*, 84-89, citing William of Ockham, *Philosophical Writings*, ed. and trans. Philotheus Boehner, OFM, rev. Stephen F. Brown (Indianapolis, IN: Hackett, 1989), 125-135, and William of Ockham, *Predestination, God's Foreknowledge, and Future Contingents*, trans. Marilyn McCord Adams and Norman Kretzmann (Indianapolis, IN: Hackett, 1983), 48-77.

[25] James Halverson, "Franciscan Theology and Predestinarian Pluralism in Late-Medieval Thought," *Speculum* 70 (1995): 1–26. Quote p. 17.

[26] Albrecht Beutel, "Luther's Life," *The Cambridge Companion to Martin Luther*, ed. Donald K. McKim (Cambridge, UK: Cambridge University Press, 2003), 4.

[27] Jean Besse, "Rule of Saint Augustine," *The Catholic Encyclopedia*, Vol. 2 (New York: Robert Appleton Company, 1907). Online at http://www.newadvent.org/cathen/02079b.htm, accessed 31 Aug 2016.

[28] Beutel, "Luther's Life," 6.

[29] Michael Horton, *For Calvinism* (Grand Rapids, MI: Zondervan, 2011), 19.

[30] Levering, *Predestination*, 102, citing John Calvin, *Institutes of the Christian Religion*, trans. Henry Beveridge (reprint, Grand Rapids, MI: Eerdmans, 1989), Book I, Ch. xviii, p. 199.

[31] Levering, *Predestination*, 103-104, citing Calvin, *Institutes*, Book I, Ch. xviii, p. 199.

[32] Levering, *Predestination*, 105, citing Calvin, *Institutes*, Book III, Ch. xxi, p. 202.

[33] Levering, *Predestination*, 105-106, citing Calvin, *Institutes*, Book III, Ch. xxiii, p. 232.

[34] Levering, *Predestination*, 107, citing Calvin, *Institutes*, Book III, Ch. xxii, p. 214.

[35] Cf. Stanford Encyclopedia of Philosophy, http://plato.stanford.edu/entries/augustine/, accessed 26 Aug 2016.

36 Cf. Stanford Encyclopedia of Philosophy, http://plato.stanford.edu/entries/aquinas/, accessed 26 Aug 2016.

37 Cf. Stanford Encyclopedia of Philosophy, http://plato.stanford.edu/entries/ockham/, accessed 26 Aug 2016; Levering, Chapter 3, The Medieval Period: Seeking a Balance, endnote 88.

38 Beutel, "Luther's Life," 6.

39 David Van Biema, "The New Calvinism," *Time Magazine*, 12 Mar 2009. http://content.time.com/time/specials/packages/article/0,28804,1884779_1884782_1884760,00.html, accessed 31 Aug 2106.

40 Thuesen, *Predestination,* 5, quoting Allen C. Guelzo, *Edwards on the Will: A Century of American Theological Debate* (Middleton, CN: Wesleyan University Press, 1989), 10.

Chapter 5

History and Translation of our Bibles

If we are to break free from the undue weight of tradition, we must begin by understanding what that tradition is, how we came to be where we are, and how particular elements in our past color our view of the present.

– Justo L. Gonzalez[1]

The pastor raised both hands in an upward motion, arms outstretched, palms up, fingers carefully together. The entire congregation rose to their feet. Just in case someone failed to understand the motion, the pastor intoned, "Let us all rise for the reading of God's Word."

In both Judaism and Christianity, the Bible is considered to be the Word of God. There is some disagreement, however, as to what that Word of God includes.

All major religions, including Judaism and Christianity, have their own canons. The word "canon" comes from a Greek word for a measuring instrument, so it is used to describe a collection or list of accepted sacred books – they have been "measured" and determined to be genuine. "The Bible is not a single book, written in one language, during a short period of time in history. The Bible is an entire library, written during a period of many centuries . . . ."[2] For mainstream Judaism, the official Hebrew Bible today consists of the twenty-four books of the Masoretic Text,[3] which gained dominance because of the reputation of the scribes and scholars who preserved it. The Masoretes, working between the 7th and 11th centuries C.E., developed a system and reputation for accuracy in their copying that gave their texts an authority above all others. "The prestige of the Masorah material cut across all Jewish groups . . . and was adopted even in those transmission circles which held on to a Bible text that differed from the Masoretic Text."[4] The dates by which the Hebrew canon was fixed is debated, with some scholars arguing for as early as 140-40 B.C.E.[5] and others for as late as the second century C.E. or even later.[6]

Among Christians, the canons differ among the Orthodox, Catholics, Church of England, and Protestants. All Christians accept the Hebrew Bible, calling it the Old Testament, and adding another section to it called the New Testament, which was written since the time of Christ. The word "testament" is simply a synonym of the word "promise" or "covenant", so in a broad sense, these two major sections of the Christian Bibles are considered to represent binding covenants God has made with his people.

Protestants limit their Old Testament to exactly those books that are in the Hebrew Bible, but the Orthodox, Church of England, and Catholics include several more books that Protestants refer to as the

Deuterocanonical Books or the Apocrypha (the word "apocrypha" means obscure or hidden). The Protestant Old Testament is made up of 39 books that contain the same material that is in the 24 books of the Hebrew Bible. The difference in number is because the Hebrew Bible has combinations of several books that are separated in the Christian Old Testament.

Among the churches that include the Deuterocanonical Books, or Apocrypha, there is variation as to which books they include, and the degree of authority they give them. Some give them the full authority of Scripture, while others include them for reading and edification, but do not use them in the formulation of church doctrine. The reason certain churches include these books is because they were included in the Septuagint, the first Greek translation of the Hebrew Bible. It was well respected in Jesus' day. Most of the Old Testament quotes found in the New Testament are from the Septuagint (over 80%)[7], so, the argument goes, if Jesus and the writers of the New Testament considered the Septuagint as inspired Scripture, including the Apocrypha, we should, too.

The development of the Christian canons was a gradual process that can be traced through the writings of early church leaders. The Old Testament consistently coincided with the Hebrew Bible, with differences limited to whether the churches used the Septuagint as their base, or the Hebrew texts. The acceptance of New Testament writings as Scripture was initially determined by local congregations, based on whether or not they experienced the voice of God through the writings. It was a highly subjective process that included a certain amount of debate, but was defended as being led by the Holy Spirit. A few books were accepted by some churches but questioned by others, but by the middle of the third century the consensus was fairly solid.[8] Centuries later, what had already happened informally was codified by official church councils.

Although the Septuagint was the first complete translation of the Bible, translation itself is no doubt as old as civilization itself. Bilingual word lists have been discovered for working between the Sumerian and Akkadian languages "from the earliest times of writing"[9] and the Rosetta Stone of the second century B.C.E. is evidence of translation in ancient Egypt.[10] In the Bible itself, Joseph is shown talking with his brothers through interpreters when they first came to Egypt to buy grain (Gen 42:23), and in the book of Esther, King Ahasuerus (Xerxes) "sent dispatches to all parts of the kingdom, to each province in its own script and to each people in its own language" (Est 1:22 NIV). It is very likely that as Ezra read from the "Book of the Law of God" and several Levites "instructed the people . . . so that the people could understand what was being read" (Neh 8:8 NIV), the Levites were actually translating into Aramaic what Ezra was reading in Hebrew. During the 70 years in exile, many of the younger Jews would have lost their familiarity with the Hebrew to some extent, if not entirely.

This trend continued, so that by the third century B.C.E., many Jews in places like northern Africa spoke no Hebrew at all, so they had no access to their own Scriptures. To correct that, the decision was made to translate them into Greek. The story of the translation of the Septuagint is told in the *Letter of Aristeas*, a document whose author is unknown, but which has been dated from about the second half of the second century B.C.E.[11] to 125 B.C.E.[12]

As Aristeas tells the story, Demetrius was the librarian of Alexandria, Egypt, at the time. He brought to the attention of the king, Ptolemy II Philadelphus (285-247 B.C.E.), that the library had no copy of the Hebrew Scriptures. Out of concern for the considerable number of Jews living in Egypt, the king commissioned a translation of the Jewish Torah (the first five books of the Bible) from Hebrew into Greek. Agents were sent to Eleazar, the high priest in Jerusalem, requesting six scholars from each of the twelve tribes of Israel to do the work. Equal representation was requested from all the tribes to assure that the translation would be accepted by all Jews as having equal authority to the Hebrew original. When the scholars arrived in Alexandria, they were isolated on the island of Pharos in order to work without interruption. In exactly 72 days the 72 translators finished and presented the translation to Ptolemy.[13] Aristeas does not make the claim that the Greek translation was as divinely inspired as the Hebrew original, but later writers do. A hundred or so years later, for example, Philo described the translators in *de vita Mosis* 2.37 (140): "They seemed to be in ecstasy, and all rendered the same text, word-for-word, as though they were listening to an unseen prompter."[14]

The time and date of the translation of the first five books of the Septuagint that Aristeas reports seems likely, placing it in the early third century B.C.E.[15] The rest of the story is not so likely, not least of which is the ability to come up with six bilingual scholars from each of the twelve tribes of Israel, considering the northern ten tribes had been completely dispersed centuries earlier. The translation of the remaining 19 books of the Septuagint occurred over a period of about two hundred years,[16] and shows evidence of a variety of translators, based on the "very different types and styles."[17]

The word "Septuagint" means seventy and the title is often abbreviated by the Roman numerals LXX. The explanation for that title, considering the original numbers were given as 72, has never been resolved.[18]

Even though translation of Scripture started with the Septuagint, it obviously did not stop there. The need for the Scriptures in Aramaic had already been established in the time of Nehemiah (c. 532 B.C.E.), mentioned earlier. Aramaic was the common language of the Babylonian empire, so after 70 years of exile, the younger Jews, as third generation immigrants, would have spoken Aramaic as their first language, possibly their only language. As time passed, more Jews completely lost their Hebrew. As a result, Scripture reading in the synagogues would be in Hebrew, followed by oral translation into Aramaic. Eventually, starting in about the second century B.C.E.,[19] a written translation of the Hebrew Scriptures was made into Aramaic. It is referred to as the *Targum* (or more properly, the *Targumim*, plural).

The translation of the Septuagint and then the *Targum* established a principle that was carried forward from Judaism into Christianity, and explains to a large degree Christianity's exponential growth from its obscure beginnings to being the largest body of faith believers in the world today – that the translation of the holy word into the common language of the people is not only possible, but is the best way to enable them to understand the biblical texts.[20] As this principle of the translatability of Scripture moved into Christianity, it had two important consequences: first, it helped disconnect the new movement from its Jewish roots at the same time that significant aspects of those roots were being promoted, and second, it destigmatized the Gentile culture, giving value to non-Jewish culture as a repository worthy of the very word of God.[21]

Many theologians and writers today attribute the Pentecost event recorded in Acts 2, with impressing this principle on the church at its origin. As the Holy Spirit fell on the assembled believers, they "began to speak in other tongues as the Spirit enabled them." The "God-fearing Jews from every nation under heaven . . . each one heard them speaking in his own language" (Acts 2:4-6). Peter stood up and addressed the crowd that had gathered (Acts 2:14), and when he finished, "Those who accepted his message were baptized, and about three thousand were added to their number that day" (Acts 2:41 NIV). It was an impressive beginning, and it crossed linguistic and cultural barriers.[22] The translatability of Scripture as a cornerstone of Christianity had been laid.

Since then, the history of Bible translation can be divided into four periods:[23]

I.   The late 6th century B.C.E. to the 8th century C.E. (from 532 B.C.E. until 700 C.E).;

II. The period of the Arab Islamic empire from 700 to 1500 C.E.;

III. The Renaissance and Reformation period covering the 16th, 17th, and 18th centuries;

IV. The modern era covering the nineteenth century up to the present.

The first period started with the *Targumim* as oral translations in public Jewish worship. The Septuagint was the first written translation, followed by the written *Targumim*, then translations into Syriac, a regional dialect of Aramaic. About mid-way through this period, the Jews rejected and eventually condemned the Septuagint, replacing it with the *Aelia Capitolina* (c. 112 C.E.). The Septuagint had become too Christian.[24]

Apparently the Parthians who were present on the day of Pentecost in Acts 2 took the gospel back to the area of modern day Iran, and created a church there. By 225 C.E., there were more than 20 regional bishops.[25] Evidence of translation into the Persian language can be found as early as 340 C.E. but the church did not flourish because it was mainly composed of ethnic non-Persians.[26]

In 436 C.E., the Armenian Bible was published, which first required inventing an alphabet. It was motivated by official persecution of Christians, which involved closing schools, outlawing all Greek learning, and burning all Greek books, especially the Scriptures.[27] Within the next few decades, the Gospels were apparently translated into Georgian, with the translation most likely being done from the Armenian.[28]

It was during this period that Jerome translated the Bible into Latin. He entered the picture at a pivotal time, as Christianity was consolidating itself as an institutional religion following the end of centuries of persecution. He was born around 347 and educated in Rome in rhetoric, theology, Greek, and Latin grammar and literature. Then he moved to Antioch and studied Hebrew. At the time, there were many Latin translations of the Bible, but they were often of questionable quality. The institutional church needed one which would standardize the text and become the basis for doctrine. In 382, Jerome was apparently asked by the bishop of Rome to provide that text, one which would accurately reflect the Greek of the Septuagint in the Old Testament.

Long before Jerome could finish, the bishop for whom he was working died, and the new bishop and Jerome did not get along, so Jerome moved to Bethlehem in 385. He had started working from the Septuagint, as requested, but from his position in the Holy Land, he decided it would be better to work from the original Hebrew. From that point, it is clear that his translation was his own work, not one officially commissioned by the church. He found a protégé, Rufinus the Syrian, and together they completed what later became known as the Latin Vulgate (meaning the 'vulgar' or most common text). In his day, and for centuries afterward, Jerome was highly controversial. He exhibited an "extremely nasty temper,"[29] was ambitious and given to deceptive self-promotion,[30] was seen as a "spiritual seducer of aristocratic women"[31] for financial reasons, and his "character and doctrine remain disputed"[32] to this day, as do his linguistic capabilities.[33] As a result, it took centuries for Jerome's translation to replace the Old Latin translations, but by the ninth century, it had become dominant. It was officially declared the authoritative Bible of the Roman Catholic Church at the Council of Trent in 1546, as defense against the Protestant vernacular translations that were challenging it.[34]

The second period of translation (700 to 1500 C.E.) includes translation efforts that are not commonly recognized. For example, in the late 800s, the Hebrew Bible was translated into Arabic. Around the same time, translation was started into Slavonic (around 863), but history is vague until the complete Bible was officially published six hundred years later (the earliest surviving text of the whole Bible is from 1499).[35] Slavonic continues to be used by the Russian Orthodox Church today.

The third period of Bible translation is the one of primary interest to an evaluation of Calvinism. Two events in the 1450s played a crucial role in preparing the world for this period. The first was the development of the printing press in Mainz, Germany, by Johannes Gutenberg.[36] The second was the relentless advance of the Islamic Turks on the outposts of Christendom, with Constantinople falling in 1453 following a long siege.[37] Constantinople, known today as Istanbul, Turkey, had been made the capital of the Roman empire in 330 by the same Constantine who became a Christian and ended the persecution against Christianity. For centuries, it was the largest city in Europe, important as a cultural and religious center and as a natural bridge between Asia and Europe and between Africa and Europe. It was the center of Greek culture at the time. The fall of Constantinople in 1453 resulted in an exodus of hundreds of Greek scholars who fled to the West, taking with them their treasury of Greek manuscripts. The reintroduction of these Greek classics into western Europe triggered the Renaissance and from it, the Protestant Reformation.[38] The importance of this chain of events cannot be overstated, so its impact will addressed in more detail later.

This period ended the general prohibition against Bible translation. Just prior to the Reformation, Erasmus produced a new Greek Bible alongside a new Latin translation. As part of the Reformation and the resulting Catholic "Counter-Reformation," the Bible was translated into many vernacular languages, especially in Europe. Among them were Luther's German Bible, Calvin's French Geneva Bible, and the King James Version of the Bible in English, all of which are worthy of more attention, later.

The fourth period of translation would be considered the modern era. Although it is not as important for our study as the previous period, it is still worthy of a quick review. What happened in this fourth period is to a large degree the result of what happened in the previous one.

In Chapter 3, I made the point that the church has reinterpreted itself over the centuries, including how it saw its purpose, and how it carried out that purpose. In this final period of Bible translation, it would not be an overstatement to say that Bible translation became one of the highest priorities in mission efforts, and one with the most far-reaching effects. This was the period that saw the establishment of the British and Foreign Bible Society (1804) and the American Bible Society (1816), and the growth of the Protestant missionary movement, which had been slow getting started after the Reformation. The Catholics participated very little in this wave of new Bible translations, for two reasons: 1) the modern missionary movement was primarily a Protestant enterprise; and 2) the Catholics were more interested in producing liturgical and catechetical materials than in Bible translation.[39]

Between 1800 and 1885, complete Bible translations were published for the first time in at least 60 languages: 12 in Europe, 31 in Asia and the Pacific, 11 in Africa and Madagascar, 3 in the Americas, and 3 in interregional languages.[40] Since 1885, the complete Bible has been translated into over 460 additional languages, so that now, of over 7000 known languages, over 550 have complete Bibles, over 1300 have complete New Testaments, and over 2900 have at least some of the Christian Scriptures.[41] This fourth period of Bible translation has been truly remarkable, not only in the number of translations, but in their apparent affect on world affairs. "The Bible in the people's tongue was a religious act that produced irrepressible social and cultural consequences."[42] It altered the political power structure.

Without doubt, one of the ugliest of human traits is the tendency of powerful people to dominate and exploit others. Within recent centuries, this expressed itself in the colonizing efforts of various European nations. The end of that era, however, can be traced directly to missionaries' efforts to translate the Christian Bible into local languages. Most of the receptor languages were not even written, so translation had to be preceded by literacy work – establishing an alphabet and creating a written language, then teaching people how to read it. This literacy and translation work empowered the local people in a new and unique way. It gave speakers of local languages a new sense of ethnic identity that developed into a new sense of nationalism. People educated in mission schools emerged as the leaders in national causes, eventually ending the colonial rule.[43] At one time, secular sociologists sought other explanations for these events, but rarely today.

In a widely lauded article of statistical research about democracy, Robert Woodberry has documented a connection between Protestant missions and democracy that is consistent in different continents and subsamples, and the correlation is supported through more than 50 controls and instrumental variable analyses. Woodberry says that "conversionary Protestants heavily influenced the rise and spread of stable democracy around the world" through their "unique role in spreading mass education, printing, civil society, and other factors that scholars argue fostered democracy." Woodberry shows that while both Muslims and Catholics were conversionary, their influence did not promote democracy because they attempted to control public discourse and religion. The conversionary Protestants were interested in giving indigenous people spiritual freedom, but in the process, they also gave them the tools to achieve freedom from colonial domination and establish stable democracies.[44] This is an important point to which we will return.

Bible translation had a remarkable impact on the world, but it was not, and even today is not, without its difficulties. Communication across languages is never precise, so the success of translations has varied. William Carey is heralded as one of the most successful and influential missionary translators ever, yet even he experienced the frustrations of translation. With no formal preparation, he sailed from Britain to northeastern India in 1793. While supporting himself by working in an indigo factory, he began learning and translating local languages. After he was joined by other missionaries, they set up a printing press in Serampore and made Bible translation and printing their primary focus. He is credited with translating the Bible into Bengali, Oriya, Marathi, Hindi, Assamese, and Sanskrit, and with the help of other translators, into many more languages, including Chinese. By the time he died, they had printed new Bible translations in 34 languages, and printed several supporting grammars and dictionaries. His translation into Marathi was less than a resounding success, however. Apparently the translator he hired to help had such a localized dialect, that when the translation was finished, no one could read it beyond the local district the translator was from.[45]

Translation is a complex undertaking, but two aspects of the complexity are of concern in evaluating Calvinism. The first is the differences in languages themselves. It was Eugene Nida, remember, who laid the substantial foundation upon which all translation theory has been built over the past several decades. He recognized that since "no two languages are identical, either in the meanings given to corresponding symbols or in the ways in which symbols are arranged in phrases and sentences, it stands to reason that there can be no absolute correspondence between languages. Hence, there can be no fully exact translations."[46] This is worthy of more attention.

The second important complexity of translation, is related to worldview. Philip Noss, editor of the extensive *A History of Bible Translation*, points out that "Bible translation is an ideological act," that "translators are engaged in a cultural act, and this is manifestly evident in Bible translation today."[47] To the common person, it is not manifestly evident. At the time of the Protestant Reformation, both sides of the divide recognized how much potential there is for printed material to change the religious and political worlds, when it is gotten into the hands of the common person. Both sides attempted to control that potential. The differences in religious and political perspectives can be summarized in one word – ideology. When ideology changes, the intellectual world changes in all its dimensions – socially, politically, and religiously. That which shapes ideology, shapes the society's worldview, shapes the future. This is also worthy of more attention.

Translation and accuracy

I have spent almost 20 years involved with translating and publishing Christian books and teaching materials into the Latvian and Russian languages. With almost every translation project, some questions arise. Often they are directly related to the differences with which languages deal with the same concepts. For example, consider the decisions that have to be made to translate just one verse of Scripture, 2 Peter 1:3, from English into Latvian. In English, it says, "His divine power has given us everything we need for life and godliness through our knowledge of him who called us by his own glory and goodness." In both English and Greek (the language the verse was originally written in) each of the words *life* and *knowledge* appear as one word, and the verse makes perfect sense to the English or Greek reader. In English, both of the words, *life* and *knowledge*, are broader words than they are in Latvian. In Latvian, the "range of meaning" contained in those English words has been broken down into more specific concepts. In Latvian, there are two ways to say "life": *dzīvība* and *dzīve*. *Dzīvība* means the life that is in us, and *dzīve* means the life we are living. If we said in English, "We watched the life fade from his body," that would be *dzīvība*. If we said, "With their wealth, they must have an easy life," that would be *dzīve*.

THIS INABILITY TO ENCAPSULATE IN THE RECEPTOR LANGUAGE THE MEANING OF WHAT IS A BROAD WORD IN THE SOURCE LANGUAGE, IS ONE OF THE MOST PROBLEMATIC ISSUES WITH TRANSLATION

When the Latvian translator reads, "His divine power has given us everything we need for life and godliness" she has to decide which of the two Latvian words to use for *life*. And if the original meaning intended by the author included both of the Latvian concepts, then the meaning in Latvian has just been distorted, narrowed in a way that does not really do justice to the original meaning. This inability to encapsulate in the receptor language the meaning of what is a broad word in the source language, is one of the most problematic issues with translation, and we will return to it later.

Then the Latvian translator gets to the word "knowledge" and has the same dilemma. In Latvian, there are three words that are contained within the range of meaning of the one English word – *pazīt, saprast,* and *zināt.* So if we ask the question in English, "Do you know French?" the translator has to decide which of three ways to translate the sentence into Latvian: "Are you acquainted with French?" "Do you understand French?" or, "Do you have a knowledge of French?" Obviously, we can break the meaning down into specific ideas in English as well, but the word *know* is a broader word that contains all of the more specific meanings. Latvians don't have that broad word. Generally, they associate *acquaintance* with people, so if we say, "Yes, I know John" that would be *pazīt* – I am acquainted with John. If we say, "We know what you mean" we're saying that we *understand,* so that would be *saprast.* If we say, "I know how tall that building is" that would be *zināt,* the *knowledge of a fact.*

So which one of the narrower Latvian words fits best in 2 Peter 1:3? Is our "knowledge of him who called us by his own glory and goodness" something factual, or more like understanding, or personal acquaintance with "him who has called us"? In English, we might argue about this point, and even divide up into denominations over the theological implications of it, but for the Latvian, the decision is made when the translation is done. When the Latvian reads it, there are not three possibilities, there is only one, so the meaning of the verse is established in that culture. This is why Philip Noss says that "Bible translation is an ideological act." If the translator has an ideological or theological position that can be reflected in the choice of words used in the translation, that position *will* be reflected – it cannot be otherwise. It is why Bible translations in major languages are done by large committees today, but in most Bible translations throughout history, that was not the case. It was not the case when Jerome translated the Vulgate, and it was not the case in the days of the Protestant Reformation, and that fact is important even to this day. We will look at its implications more closely.

Let's consider some of the words that have created confusion or controversy over the years because of the way they have been translated. In many cases, the confusion or controversy has been caused by the narrowing of a broader word. Many words, particularly nouns, have what translators call "semantic components". Often those semantic components are actually inseparable in the original language: for example, bachelor = man + unmarried; widow = woman + dead husband; wife = woman + married. If the receptor language does not have a word for bachelor or widow or wife, then the translator is tasked with deciding what to do – to use the closest word, or use a phrase to communicate the entire concept.

One of the most familiar examples in Bible translation history is the word in Isaiah 7:14 that has been translated either as *virgin* or as *young woman*. In the NIV, the verse reads, "Therefore the Lord himself will give you a sign: The virgin will be with child and will give birth to a son, and will call him Immanuel." In the original Hebrew, the word was *'almâh*, which means *young woman*. In the Septuagint, when the Hebrew was translated into Greek, the word used was *parthenos*, which means *virgin*. When the Jews rejected the Septuagint and replaced it after the Christians started using it to support their beliefs, the Jews made sure the word for virgin was eliminated in their replacement translation – they used the word *neanis* which means *young woman* in Greek, and is a more precise translation of the original Hebrew word.[48] In recent times, whenever a translation into English follows the Jews' lead in this, a firestorm of protest erupts. The accusation is made that the translation is "liberal" and even heretical. Let's digress for more clarification, and then return to this.

Every translator has to decide how literal the translation should be. Considerations include how important specific words might be, compared to the broader concepts they represent. This difference in translation styles has been recognized for centuries. Marcus Tullius Cicero (106-43 B.C.E.) understood this well before the time of Christ. He was a Roman philosopher, politician, lawyer, orator, political theorist, consul, and constitutionalist.[49] A master of both Greek and Latin, his influence on the history of European literature and ideas is said to have been greater than any other prose writer has ever had in any one language.[50] He is regarded as being the founder of Western translation theory, since he is the first writer to ever record this principle. In reflecting on how he translated literary works from Greek into Latin, Cicero observed that he did not translate the words as if counting out coins, but as if paying according to value.[51]

In general, if a translation is very literal, word for word – counting coins – it is called "formal correspondence." If it is much freer, paying according to value, it is usually called "dynamic-equivalent" or "functional equivalent." Dynamic or functional equivalent Bible translations are often called "paraphrases." The more different the receptor culture is from the source culture, the more important it is to use functional equivalents. For example, to contrast the wisdom of building on rock or sand (Matt 7:24-27) in a culture that lives in swamps and builds on stilts, doesn't compute. To use a snake as a contrast to a fish as a good gift (Matt 7:9-11) in a culture where a fish is a dietary staple and a snake is a delicacy, doesn't communicate the lesson embedded in the original message. Bible translation is like walking a tightrope, a balancing act with the danger of falling off both sides. The goal is to be as faithful to the original as possible – but sometimes being faithful to the *words*, is not being faithful to the *message* those words communicated to the original audience. This tension has been recognized as far back as the recording of the Talmud. *Talmud* is Hebrew for "instruction." The Talmud is a massive collection of ancient Jewish writings regarding ethics, philosophy, customs, history, etc. recorded from oral tradition following the destruction of the temple in 70 C.E. The Talmud

> CICERO OBSERVED THAT HE DID NOT TRANSLATE THE WORDS AS IF COUNTING OUT COINS, BUT AS IF PAYING ACCORDING TO VALUE

contains this statement: "He who translates a verse literally is a liar; but he who adds to it is a blasphemer."[52]

An amusing example of counting coins can be found in the original English KJV. In Isaiah 37:36, the angel of the Lord put to death 185,000 Assyrian soldiers in the night. The original KJV translated the verse word for word from the Hebrew, so the second half of the verse said "when they arose early in the morning, behold, they were all dead corpses." As Gordon Campbell observes in his work commissioned for the 400th anniversary of the KJV, "The notion that the Assyrians got up in the morning before noticing that they were dead is exceedingly unhelpful. . . . The meaning could be captured by translating the second phrase as 'at dawn it became clear that they were all dead', but the KJV translators preferred literal fidelity to interpretative translating."[53]

So decisions regarding how to translate words is a constant part of the translation process. Sometimes it requires breaking the words or concepts down into their semantic components in order to get the original message across.

This is the situation in the "virgin" verse in Isaiah: "The virgin will be with child and will give birth to a son." For the literalist, the word needs to be *young woman*, because that is the most literal translation. But does it do justice to what the original audience would have understood? Consider that in the Law of Moses, a sexually active unmarried woman was worthy of the death penalty. So any young unmarried woman was presumed to also be a virgin. Only women get pregnant, and all babies are born to women, so nothing is gained in the prophecy by stating who gets pregnant and gives birth, unless it is significant. It is not unusual if a woman gets pregnant and has a baby, but it is unusual if a virgin does. If the original writer had not intended to imply a virgin, he could have simply said that a *woman* would be with child and would give birth to a son, or more likely, he would have simply said that a child would be born. Again, the fact that the prophecy includes both pregnancy and birth is important only if there is something unusual about them. The *young woman* is what makes it unusual – the understanding includes virginity. One of the synonyms for *young woman* in English is *maiden*. They are not perfect synonyms, but very close, so if the translator had translated the original word as *maiden*, rather than either *virgin* or *young woman*, the implication of virginity would have been retained but not spoken, much closer to the original. The literalist, counting coins, wants to see *young woman*. The functional equivalent, paying according to value, recognizes that the original audience would have understood the young woman to be a virgin. To translate it as *virgin*, then, communicates the original message better than the more literal word, especially considering translators now have later events to consider in making their word selection.

This situation is repeated a number of times in our Bibles. Two of the most common words that have deeply impacted later understanding, are the words *Christ* and *baptism*. The word *christos* meant *anointed one* in Greek, equivalent to *messiah* in Hebrew, and it was the way the Septuagint translated the concept.[54] But later vernacular translations did not translate the word at all. They simply transliterated the Greek word, so almost all translations now use some version of *Christ*. The result has been a significant loss of meaning in some passages. This is an important point that will be dealt with in more detail when we look at John Calvin's understanding of Ephesians 1, in Chapter 6. It is the same with the word *baptism*.

The word *bapto* in Greek, from which *baptizō* (to baptize) and *baptisma* (baptism) come, simply means to fully cover with a fluid – to dip, immerse, or submerge. Ships sank, people drowned, and Naaman dipped himself seven times in the Jordan River (2 Kings 5:14) using these words.[55] But by the time vernacular translations started in Europe in the fifteenth and sixteenth centuries, the church had been baptizing by "sprinkling" for centuries. To suddenly translate the Greek word literally into the local languages would have raised uncomfortable questions, so the word was not translated at all. It was transliterated, so the receptor languages got a new word with only one association – the church's established practice of water baptism. The new word had the definition the church gave it. This is why translation experts say that "Bible translation is an ideological act." If water baptism were the only thing affected by this transliteration, it might not be critical, but the practice obscures understanding when the Greek word was used to mean *immerse* without any water being involved.

Consider the difference in these two translations of the Great Commission, Matt 28:19-20:

(1) "Therefore go and make disciples of all nations, *baptizing* them in the name of the Father and of the Son and of the Holy Spirit, and teaching them to obey everything I have commanded you. And surely I am with you always, to the very end of the age."

BIBLE TRANSLATION IS AN IDEOLOGICAL ACT

(2) "Therefore go and make disciples of all nations, *immersing* them in the name of the Father and of the Son and of the Holy Spirit, and teaching them to obey everything I have commanded you. And surely I am with you always, to the very end of the age."

In the first translation, water seems to be the obvious mental picture, especially since many of us have heard "I baptize you in the name of the Father and of the Son and of the Holy Spirit" dozens of times in association with water baptism. But what if the word actually meant to *immerse* here, with no water involved? We know people can *immerse* themselves in their work or study. Maybe we can *immerse* ourselves in God. When the word *name* is also considered for a more functional equivalent translation, then the likelihood of water gets even more remote. We understand that a name in Hebrew culture was more than a way of addressing a person, it was connected with their identity, with all that they were. The Hebrews called on "the name of the Lord." God sometimes told people to give their children specific names that had special meaning (like Ishmael and Isaac and the children of Hosea). He sometimes changed people's names (like Abram and Sarai and Jacob), and often people's names indicated their character or their calling (like Jesus himself). If that very Jewish understanding was in Jesus' mind and in the minds of his disciples when he gave them this commandment, then they would have heard something more like this:

> "Therefore go and make disciples of all nations, *immersing* them in *everything about* the Father and the Son and the Holy Spirit, and teaching them to obey everything I have commanded you. And surely I am with you always, to the very end of the age."

Suddenly, the verse has a very different meaning, but one much more consistent with the word *disciples* just before *immerse*, much more consistent with "teaching them to obey *everything* I have commanded you," and much more consistent with what discipleship means, as reflected in Luke 14. A simple translation decision can make a massive difference in what later generations hear.

I think this same issue may also be true of Romans 6. Paul frequently uses word plays, where he deliberately uses the same word in close proximity to mean different things, playing on that relationship between the various uses of the word. In Romans 6, it appears to me that Paul uses the word *baptized* two times related to our identification with Christ in a spiritual sense, of fully participating, being *immersed* in his being and in his death spiritually. Then he uses the word *baptism*, playing on the previous understanding, showing how we go through the physical act of water baptism as a demonstration of our death to our old life and the beginning of our new life, in the same way that Jesus now has a new and different kind of life since his resurrection. He builds his argument with the idea of being *immersed* into, or placed under, or completely identified with Christ or his death or burial. The transliteration of the Greek word obscures the way those verses tie in with the rest of the chapter.

Evidence of the word being used to mean *immersed into*, or *completely identified with*, with no water involved, is strengthened by 1 Corinthians 10:2, where Paul says the Israelites leaving Egypt were "baptized into Moses in the cloud and in the sea." They had to make a total commitment to go with Moses, or die at the hands of the advancing Egyptian army. No water, but complete immersion into a new destiny, and evidence that the original word was used consistently with its original meaning rather than the meaning assigned to it by the translators.

I have encountered two other words where the prevailing translations don't seem to work well. In Philippians, Paul uses the generic Greek word for *safety* three times: 1:19, 1:28, and 2:12. Those three verses are translated this way in the King James Version:

> Phil 1:19 For I know that this shall turn to my *salvation* through your prayer, and the supply of the Spirit of Jesus Christ,

> Phil 1:28 And in nothing terrified by your adversaries: which is to them an evident token of perdition, but to you of *salvation*, and that of God.

> Phil 2:12 Wherefore, my beloved, as ye have always obeyed, not as in my presence only, but now much more in my absence, work out your own *salvation* with fear and trembling.

At the time the New Testament was being written, there was no exact Greek word for *salvation*, so as the Christians would talk about life after death, they would just use the word *safety*, which was a broad word that easily extended to include spiritual safety.[56] That means every time translators encounter that word, they have to decide whether the writer meant something like physical safety, or spiritual salvation, or some other related concept included in the word, like protection, or mercy, or health, or inner well-being that even included personal self-esteem.

In the NIV, the first time the word *safety* is used in Philippians, it is translated as *deliverance*. Paul was talking about getting out of prison, so the translation should be closer to physical *safety* than spiritual *salvation*, so the NIV seems more accurate than the KJV. The second time Paul uses the word, he is talking about his readers being persecuted, so again, the better word is probably *safety*, although this one could go either way. The NIV uses the word *saved*, which can apply either to their physical safety or their spiritual destiny. The third time Paul uses the word, the subject is still persecution, and he makes the famous statement that is inconsistent with all evangelical understanding about salvation. He says (KJV), "work out your own *salvation* with fear and trembling" and (NIV) "continue to work out your *salvation* with fear and trembling." If the word is translated as *salvation*, then confusion arises. But if it is translated as *safety*, the word the original readers would have heard, then it makes perfect sense in light of what Paul is advising them. "You're being persecuted," he says, "so don't do anything stupid. Work out your *safety* with fear and trembling, without complaining or arguing (with those persecuting you), without fault in a wicked and depraved generation, in which you shine like stars in the universe."

The problem with the prevailing translation is that it removes from Scripture some very good advice that could be important to people facing persecution. How many people have been martyred over the centuries because they were brash and confrontational rather than "working out their safety with fear and trembling" and living through the persecution to serve God another day? There may come a time when a crucial stand has to be taken, and one must be willing to die for what one believes, but there are also times when the confrontation can be avoided. Jesus did this several times, and Paul did, including leaving Damascus over the city wall in a basket at night. As Paul writes this statement to the Philippians, he has already told them to use Jesus as an example, and he is going to tell them later in the letter to follow his own example. He has already told them in the first chapter of Philippians how *he's* handling persecution. Yet generation after generation, pastors read a translation of questionable accuracy and join the circus, jumping through intellectual and exegetical hoops trying to justify from other Scripture how we "work out our salvation," when the rest of Scripture says our salvation is not related to what we do. Salvation is not something we work out. Safety is.

The translation of this word is problematic in at least one other location. Below, we will look more closely at how the translator's understanding affects translation, but we can see it now, as well, in connection with this word *safety*. 1 Timothy 2:15, in the NIV, reads: "But women will be saved through childbearing – if they continue in faith, love and holiness with propriety." The subject that Paul is dealing with is how things should function in the church. He makes it clear that he is giving Timothy instruction as a young pastor (1 Tim 1:3-7) so that he may "fight the good fight" (1 Tim 1:18), which we can probably interpret as "to persevere with integrity" or "to be diligent and faithful even under opposition." Then in chapter 2, he starts with some principles of how things should function in the church. "First," he says, "pray for everyone." He finishes with this principle by giving it a masculine twist, saying, "I want men everywhere to lift up holy hands in prayer, without anger or disputing" (2:8). Then he immediately transfers his attention to women, giving instruction on adorning themselves with "good deeds" rather than being flashy in their jewelry, hairstyles, or dress (2:9-10). He follows this up with instructions for women to "learn in quietness and full submission," then he points out that he does not allow women to teach men or exercise authority over them (2:11-12). He says this pattern of female submission can be traced all the way back to creation (2:13-14), then he tacks on this problematic verse: "But women will be saved through childbearing – if they continue in faith, love and holiness with propriety" (NIV).

This translation has the same problem that "working out our salvation" does. It seems to connect salvation with something additional, which appears to contradict all the rest of Scripture. Anytime we encounter such an apparent contradiction, we should look for another explanation. I am convinced that this verse, understood as Paul's original audience would have heard it, makes perfect sense. It is used to support Paul's larger argument, which is how things should function in the church. He has just said, "Women are not to have leadership positions in the church, over men." Now, he is giving women an alternative means of finding fulfillment that is consistent with the roles established at creation. In the NIV, three translation problems obscure his message of hope for women.

First, the word *women* is not there in the original. The NIV translators have substituted the word *women* (a third person *plural noun*) for the word *she* (a third person *singular pronoun*) that Paul used. The change makes the word *women* consistent with the later use of the pronoun *they* (third person plural) in the same verse, but by doing so, the attempt to clear up the meaning actually obscures the one that fits Paul's argument better. Keeping in mind that pronouns are normally used *after* the noun that they substitute for, it is logical that the pronoun *she* refers back to the third person *singular* noun used in the previous verse ("the *woman* who was deceived"), and the pronoun *they* refers back to the children borne by the woman.

The second translating problem here is with the word under consideration, which in Greek was *safety*, the broad word introduced above that applied to a wide variety of circumstances. As well as physical safety and spiritual salvation, the word also included such meanings as to *find protection,* to *do well* (prosper), and to *be made healthy or whole,* which included *inner well-being,* or *a sense of personal self-esteem.*[57] If this last meaning of the word is used instead of *salvation,* then Paul is saying that the woman, *she,* singular, will *be made whole,* or *be completed,* or *be fulfilled* – will *have a sense of personal value or self-*

esteem – if *they, her children,* plural, continue in faith and holiness, not if *she* does. It is logical that *fulfillment* has ongoing conditions that must be met, but *salvation* does not.

The third complication in the verse is the word translated as *childbearing.* The Greek word from which that word is translated was also a much broader word, which included *all that is related to childbearing and child raising.* The semantic components = giving birth + maternal responsibilities of raising children to adulthood. [58] We can not get that word into English without using several. It's like starting with the word *widow* (= woman + dead husband), and translating it into a language without such a word. We either settle for the word *woman* or we have to include an explanation. In this verse, the translators settled for a single word that captures only a part of the original meaning – they exchanged a coin for a coin, rather than paying according to value.

When all three of these translation problems are addressed, the verse makes perfect sense in terms of Paul's bigger argument, which is how things should function in the church. He says that men were created for leadership, and women were created for all that is related to childbearing and child rearing, and the two separate roles are not to be confused in the church. I am convinced that 1 Tim 2:15, accurately translated, paying according to value, would read: "But she will be fulfilled through all that is related to bearing and raising children, if they continue in faith, love, and holiness with propriety."

One other such word has come to my attention, and this is another one that directly bears on the examination of Calvinism. It is the use of the word *spirit*, especially in Paul's writings. One of the most basic problems of any translation is that if the translators don't understand what the original message means, they certainly can't translate it accurately. Idioms are among the biggest problems – expressions like "twisting your arm" or "pulling your leg" or "tongue in cheek." Several years ago, we were looking through the Latvian translation of a book originally written in English. The author said "Love is not a four letter word," probably a rebuttal of the song written by Bob Dylan and made popular by Joan Baez. Both the song and the author were making a word-play on the fact that profanity in English is often called "four letter words" since most curse words have exactly four letters, and the fact that one such "four letter word" is used to signify the act of "making love," of having sex. In Latvian, the word for *love* is *mīlestība*, so the statement was translated literally, as "Mīlestība is not a nine letter word." The translator counted coins, when she should have paid according to value, but since she did not understand the English idiom, she could not translate it correctly.

I'm actually convinced that, like Cicero, the Apostle Paul understood this concept, and gave advice on how to use it. Paul wrote two letters to Timothy, giving him pointers on how to carry out his responsibilities as a young pastor. Starting in the middle of 2 Timothy 2:14 and continuing through 2:15, Paul says: "Warn them before God against quarreling about words; it is of no value, and only ruins those who listen. Do your best to present yourself to God as one approved, a workman who does not need to be ashamed and who correctly handles the word of truth." First he tells Timothy to warn people about arguing over words, that is, don't count coins. "It is of no value, and only ruins those who listen."

Secondly, Paul apparently pulled a term out of his tent making vocabulary to explain how to actually do it. Like making tents from skins, Paul said, you have to "cut it straight" – you have to cut each piece correctly so that it fits together with all the others to make a whole – *correctly handling* the word of truth. One skin is not the issue – the tent is the goal. Don't obsess over one skin. Make a tent. That's paying according to value. It is what makes Christianity so effective. The concepts that are resident in the character of God, and that were perfectly reflected in the life of Jesus, are the solutions to all problems in all cultures. But they have to be integrated into the culture in a way that makes sense in that culture, properly fitted together to make a unified whole. Translators are charged with providing the tools to do that. Those tools are not contained in words, but in concepts. As Grant Osborne points out, "No two languages express themselves or use words the same way."[59] "Meaning," he emphasizes, "is not an inherent property of words ... in reality, words are arbitrary symbols that have meaning only in a context."[60] The words are negotiable, the concepts they symbolize are not.

Another way translators can fail to provide the proper tools is when meaning is distorted because the translator applies an understanding that did not exist at the time the original work was written. A well known example is the word *martyr*, which originally meant *witness*, but since so many witnesses were executed for their testimony, it came to have its current meaning – one who dies for a cause.[61] This is called a *semantic anachronism*: semantic = meaning of a word; ana = after + chrono = time. "The meaning originated after the time." Before looking at Paul's use of the word *spirit*, let's consider John's use of the word in the first chapter of Revelation, since it appears in tandem with one such semantic anachronism.

> WORDS ARE ARBITRARY SYMBOLS THAT HAVE MEANING ONLY IN A CONTEXT. THE WORDS ARE NEGOTIABLE, THE CONCEPTS THEY SYMBOLIZE ARE NOT

The Apostle John is starting to record an experience so bizarre that he needs to first explain to the reader who he is, how he came to have this information, and what it means. In Revelation 1:9-10, he does exactly that. He says, "I, John, your brother and companion in the suffering and kingdom and patient endurance that are ours in Jesus, was on the island of Patmos because of the word of God and the testimony of Jesus. On the Lord's Day I was in the Spirit, and I heard behind me a loud voice like a trumpet. . ." To the original readers, that was all they needed to know to understand the rest of the book, but to the modern reader, the introduction is obscured by three things:

1) a lack of familiarity with the Old Testament idiom, "the day of the Lord," 2) the fact that the idiom is translated as "the Lord's Day," with *Day* capitalized, and 3) the fact that the word *Spirit* is capitalized. The muddled translation of the introduction may account for why the book is so often poorly understood today.

The "day of the Lord" was well known to the Jews from the prophets of old – it meant the day of judgment, the day when the wrath of God would descend on the world, and the wicked would get their due. It is a familiar theme in many of the Old Testament prophets (e.g. Isa 2:11, 7:18, 24:21; Joel 1:15, 2:1, 2:31; Amos 5:18,20), and it was even brought into the New Testament (2 Thes 2:2; 2 Pet 3:10). Grammatically, "the Lord's Day" and "the day of the Lord" are essentially identical, but when both of those phrases are idioms in different cultures, the word order makes a difference. And the capital letters make a difference – on both the words *Day* and *Spirit*.

> In the notes of my study Bible, to be helpful, this is what it says:
>
> **1:10** *the Lord's Day.* A technical term for the first day of the week – so named because Jesus rose from the dead on that day. It was also the day on which the Christians met (see Ac 20:7) and took up collections (see 1 Cor 16:2). *in the Spirit.* In a state of spiritual exaltation – not a dream, but a vision like Peter's in Ac 10:10.[62]

I think everything about that "helpful" explanation is wrong, but the translation lends itself to such misunderstanding. I don't know when Sunday became known as "the Lord's Day," but I suspect it would have been much later than when John was writing this. And why would it be significant what day of the week John experiences this? History tells us that John was exiled to the island of Patmos as part of ongoing persecution, so the first verse (v. 9) is clear enough, but the meaning of the second one (v. 10) is obscured by the translation, and made worse by the added explanation in the Study Bible notes. If I could paraphrase John's introduction, to make sure the meaning is clear, it would say: "I,

John, your brother and companion in the suffering and kingdom and patient endurance that are ours in Jesus, was exiled on the island of Patmos because of my witness to the word of God and the testimony of Jesus. I was transported into the future in a disembodied state and witnessed the day of the Lord, that great and terrible day of judgment. The experience started when I heard a loud voice like a trumpet behind me. . ." That seems to much more accurately fit with the rest of the book and the rest of the Bible, than what the capitalized words and the study notes reflect. The day of judgment is significant, the day of the week is not. Good translation is only possible with good understanding.

The issue of understanding is tied to the so-called science of hermeneutics. (The word "hermeneutics" simply means "interpretation.") One of the most basic fallacies of Bible hermeneutics is that a word has one basic meaning,[63] so a word used by the same author in the same book is assumed to have the same meaning each time. This idea seems to have prevailed in the KJV, which explains why the word *safety* was consistently translated as *salvation* in Philippians, as I explained above. But the error seems to continue to plague Bible translators.

GOOD TRANSLATION IS ONLY POSSIBLE WITH GOOD UNDERSTANDING

For example, in both Romans 8 and 2 Corinthians 3, Paul uses the word *spirit* in a variety of ways, which English translators seem to consistently miss. Paul appears to deliberately play on the different uses of the word. He uses the word in at least four different ways, to mean: 1) our spirit (that is, our new regenerated nature), 2) the Holy Spirit (the Spirit of God), 3) the principle behind written laws (the essence or spirit of the law), and 4) an attitude or approach to life (as in, she has a kind and gentle spirit). The translators demonstrate that they don't understand the argument Paul is making, because they use the word *Spirit* in most places, capitalized to reflect divinity, implying that it refers to the Holy Spirit. Even in places where Paul's argument is clearly a contrast between the spirit of the law and the letter of the law, such as Romans 2:29 and 7:6, and 2 Corinthians 3:6, the word is translated as *Spirit*, with a capital letter. Even when Paul is clearly contrasting our sinful nature (flesh) and our new nature (spirit) the word *Spirit* is capitalized (Rom 8:4-9, 12-13). The message is obscured or even altered by the way the translator's understanding, or lack of it, is imposed on the work.

Translation and ideology

The examples above do not imply evil intent on the part of the translators. It is inevitable that the understanding of the translator is reflected in the translation. Sometimes it is the best a translator can do, but sometimes it is a deliberate choice, such as the transliteration of *baptizō*.

As we think about this, it should be kept in mind that the original manuscripts are not available for us to refer to. Everything we have available is from multilingual copies of copies, "some of them quite fragmentary, many of them contradictory, and most requiring interpretation in terms of non-sacred texts from the same periods."[64] Often, when someone encounters that fact for the first time, they ask, "Then how do we know that what we have is accurate?" The answer is provided by a common illustration: If a teacher dictated a story to a class of 40 students, and they all wrote it down, the finished transcripts would have some differences. There would be some mistakes made in the transcribing process. But when the 40 different transcripts are compared, the differences will be visible, and the errors will be detectable, but the consistent similarities will be sufficient to reconstruct the original. That is the way the accuracy of the biblical text is confirmed. There are enough copies of copies that to a large degree, the original can be figured out. There are some questions that cannot be solved, but none of such importance that the basic message is corrupted or even questionable. However, within the solidity of the basic text, understanding can be different, and translation can affect the way the understanding is taken into other languages.

A couple of things have complicated arriving at the solidity of the basic text which we now have. One is that the ancient Hebrew texts were written entirely in consonants, to conserve space. The reader had to supply the vowels, which was done by familiarity with the oral tradition, and by the context. An example is the consonants MLK, which could have vowels supplied to be MeLeK to mean king, or MoLeK, which was the wicked god of the Ammonites. It was the Masoretes, mentioned earlier in connection with the development of the Hebrew canon, who supplied the vowels and additional markings between the sixth and tenth centuries C.E. that converted the ancient manuscripts into actual written Hebrew. The result of their efforts is what is known as the Masoretic text.[65] Even with their careful work, the meaning of some words remains unclear, but those unresolved questions do not affect the basic message.

The second thing that has complicated working with the copies of early biblical manuscripts, is that most of the available copies from the early Christian period until about the tenth century, were written in *uncial* script. It was a rather untidy script consisting entirely of capital letters with no punctuation or even spaces between words.[66] In uncial script,

ASENTENCEWOULDLOOKSOMETHINGLIKETHIS
EXCEPTTHELETTERSWEREHANDWRITTENSOTHEY
WERENOTUNIFORMTHENEXTSENTENCEWOULD
STARTWITHOUTABREAKANDSOONANDSOON

If you tried to decipher the two sentences above illustrating uncial script,[67] you notice that, among other challenges, at the end you are presented with the choice of reading "and soon and soon" or "and so on and so on." That is exactly what the scholars have been dealing with over the centuries. Sometimes, the meaning is determined simply by where the Bible scholar inserts the punctuation. Let's consider an example that will be important to our understanding later.

In the NIV, Romans 8:17 reads like this: "Now if we are children, then we are heirs – heirs of God and co-heirs with Christ, if indeed we share in his sufferings in order that we may also share in his glory."

Consider what changing just one comma does to the meaning.

The verse is written with the comma after the word "Christ," so it says that if we are children, then we are heirs of God and co-heirs of Christ, on the condition that we share in his suffering, etc. In this construction, being an heir of God and co-heir with Christ is the same thing, based on a common conditional statement – if we share in his suffering, etc.

But change the comma to be after the word "God," and it reads: "Now if we are children, then we are heirs – heirs of God, and co-heirs with Christ if indeed we share in his sufferings . . . ." It changes the meaning so that being children makes us heirs of God, with no condition attached, but to become a co-heir with Christ, there is the condition that we share in his suffering, etc.

"Now if we are children, then we are heirs of God, and we may also become co-heirs with Christ if we share in his sufferings in order that we may also share in his glory." That's enough difference to affect doctrinal statements of denominations. From just one comma.

In a humorous book written to show how important punctuation is, Lynne Truss says, "Punctuation is a courtesy designed to help readers to understand a story without stumbling."[68] For centuries, Bible copyists did not extend that courtesy to their readers. Like the example from Scripture above, Truss shows what a difference a simple punctuation change can make to the meaning of a sentence. Even the title of her book makes the point. *Eats, Shoots and Leaves.* Is it about panda bears, or gunrunners? Consider another comparison she makes:

"A woman, without her man, is nothing. A woman: without her, man is nothing."[69]

If this sentence were drawn from an uncial manuscript, historically, the first option would have been automatic. Now, however, the choice of how to translate it would fall directly on the sides of a line separating feminists from supporters of traditional gender roles. The battle lines would be drawn. Bible translation is an ideological act. If those words appeared in the Bible, whichever way they were translated today, there would be an outcry.

As we consider this later in evaluating Calvinism, one point to keep in mind is that the source language, for the New Testament at least, was Greek. Unlike English,[70] Greek has a grammatical system that uses *cases*, so word endings change based on how the word is being used in the sentence. That pattern only shows up in English in personal pronouns and in possessives – the difference in a *car*, as a noun, and a *car's* door, when the car is in a possessive position (known as the *genitive* case, from *genesis*, or source). When languages use cases, the ending of a noun as the subject of a sentence (the *nominative* case, or the *name* of the item) usually has a basic ending which changes when the same noun is used in other ways in the sentence, for example, as the object of the sentence (the *accusative* case, from the one *accused* or acted upon). So the spelling of both *car* and *John* would be different in these two statements: "The car hit John" and "John hit the car." As the words change position in the sentence (change cases), the ending of the words change, so a reader is given a hint of how the words should be interpreted. We personally know of languages that have as many as 14 cases, so there are 28 different endings for every noun – fourteen when the word is singular, and fourteen more when it is plural.

Since Latvian uses cases, prepositions are rarely needed. A preposition is a word that "pre-positions" the word that comes after it. Prepositions are words like *in*, *on*, *under*, *before*, etc. Latvians can say that this package is *in* the post office (*locative* case, giving the location), simply by changing the last letter of the word *post office*. Or they can say that this package is *for* John (*dative* case, from a Latin origin relating to giving) simply by changing the ending of John's name. When we were studying Latvian, we had a teacher whose strength was in her Latvian, not her English. She repeatedly told us, "In Latvian, word order is not so principle." That's because they use cases. Like Latvian, Greek uses cases. Since it does, that eases the burden on translation somewhat, but not entirely. Translation decisions still have to be made where there are two or more perfectly legitimate options, and the ideological leanings of the translator will sway the decision.

Because translation is such a critical issue in understanding why Calvinism exists, let's pursue this just a little more.

It is often the relationship between adjoining phrases and clauses that is not clear. Punctuation is one tool used to show these relationships, so when it is missing, there is potential for confusion, as Lynne Truss's examples show, and as the verse we considered in Romans shows. Another tool that languages use to deal with this problem is connecting words, like *and*, *but*, *if*, or *therefore*, *similarly*, *now*, etc. These conjunctions, or conjunctive adverbs, show the relationship between what they connect. When such words are missing, decisions have to be made regarding coordination or subordination – are these clauses or phrases equal, so they should stand alone, or is one of them subordinate to the other one (based on, conditional to, etc.). If one is subordinate, which one is it? How should this be shown in the receptor language? Since there are no conjunctive words in Romans 8:17, the comma that we moved determines what the conditional clause is subordinate to. When these conjunctive words are missing, it is called *parataxis*. When they are present, so subordination is clear, it is *hypotaxis*. A hypotactic sentence without punctuation may still be clear, but a paratactic one without punctuation presents a real problem, unless other indicators, like the changing cases of words, give some clarification. This brings us back to an earlier conclusion.

Reality: translation, Bible or otherwise, is not black and white. Because that is true, *Bible translation is an ideological act*. Paul

Hiebert talks about "Western cultural biases . . . and how these have shaped the way we understood Scripture, theology,"[71] etc. At the risk of being tedious, I have laid this groundwork because it is important in understanding the worldview behind Calvinism and how it has impacted the Bibles the world uses today. With this foundation, let's return to the history of our Bibles.

Erasmus

No history of the Bible or of Bible translation, would be complete without Erasmus. He was a pivotal figure. Born Desiderius Erasmus in Rotterdam probably in 1466, he was the illegitimate child of a Catholic priest and a woman who was likely the priest's housekeeper. At age 25, poverty forced Erasmus into the priesthood, which he apparently had no interest in, but it proved fortuitous, because after three years, he was given a stipend and sent to study at the same school in Paris that John Calvin would attend some 30 years later. The Collège de Montaigu was already moving toward humanism, based on the rich heritage of Greek logic and reason, in contrast to the more mystical medieval scholasticism. The effect of the school on Erasmus was much the same as it would be on Calvin. He came under the effect of influential humanists, and it changed his worldview, his future, and the future of the world.[72]

In 1499, Erasmus got the opportunity to visit England where he was welcomed by, and impressed by, the English humanists.[73] While there, he "conceived the plan . . . of turning humanistic learning to the service of religion by purifying theology and practical piety of false teaching, obscurity and superstition" through the "scientific study of sacred literature."[74] He went back to France in 1500, studied Greek, then returned to England in 1505, where "he was welcomed in all learned circles as a gifted humanist."[75] He went to Italy in 1506 and stayed until 1509, when he learned that Henry VII had died, and his personal friend

Prince Henry had become Henry VIII, King of England. He returned to England at once, hopeful of reward for "scholarly labours under the Prince who had grown up among the brightest of English humanism."[76]

During this time in England, soon after the start of Henry VIII's reign, Erasmus wrote *Encomium Moriae* (*In Praise of Folly*), "an original and biting satire on the stupidity and self-contradiction of human nature" that "contained serious and damaging criticism of the Church," including "Scholasticism, Bishops and mendicant friars . . . even the Curia itself . . . . Apart from the identification of the Papacy with Antichrist, much of the scorn which Luther was to pour out on the reigning abuses can be found in this early work of Erasmus."[77] Although Erasmus never left the Catholic Church and never personally participated in the Protestant Reformation, he furnished the material that Luther used to ignite the fire, and that all the Reformers used to keep it burning.

This satirical criticism of the Church was the first of two crucial contributions Erasmus made to the Reformation. The second was his parallel Greek and Latin New Testament, published in 1516. Erasmus's original plan had been to re-work Jerome's Vulgate, which he was convinced had become deeply corrupted over time. In one letter, in which he attacked both Jerome and those who copied his work, he said, "But one thing the facts cry out, and it can be clear, as they say, even to a blind man, that often through the translator's clumsiness or inattention the Greek has been wrongly rendered; often the true and genuine reading has been corrupted by ignorant scribes, which we see happen every day, or altered by scribes who are half-taught and half-asleep."[78]

In another letter, Erasmus gave an update on his progress: "My mind is so excited at the thought of emending Jerome's text, with notes, that I seem to myself inspired by some god. I have already almost finished emending him by collating a large number of ancient manuscripts, and this I am doing at enormous personal expense."[79] As he stated, to amend Jerome's work, Erasmus first had to work on the Greek on which it was based. He did not have access to a complete, single manuscript, so from the various Greek manuscripts he had available,[80] he created one. It became the first complete Greek New Testament ever published,[81] printed in parallel with his updated Latin translation. It was republished in 1519 with some corrections, then republished in 1522 with more corrections. Martin Luther used the second edition in his German translation of the New Testament, and William Tyndale used the third edition in his English translation.[82] Erasmus's parallel Greek and Latin New Testament provided a critical foundation upon which the Reformers built, in more ways than one.

As Erasmus created his parallel Latin and Greek New Testaments, he introduced new words for the traditional Latin in several places. For example, in the gospels, Gabriel greeted Mary, not with *Ave gratia plena* ("Hail, full of grace"), but with *Ave gratiosa* ("Hail, graceful one"). The difference implies that the grace was already there, rather than that she had been filled with grace. The implication was shocking. He also translated the Greek word for repentance in Matthew 3:2 as *risipicite,* to "be penitent," in place of the traditional *penitetiam agite,* to "do penance." One implies a changed attitude, the other is something you do. As Christopher de Hamel points out, "There is an enormous difference between those two meanings. Erasmus was not one of the Protestant Reformers, and he always remained Catholic. However, his *Novum Instrumentum* in 1516 laid out a technique for interpreting the Greek which the Lutheran reformers would find very valuable."[83]

Martin Luther

Although eighteen editions of German Bibles had been published before Martin Luther got involved,[84] his was the first to be based on the original texts[85] and his was written in a much more contemporary style.[86] It's "fluent literary style" included "select vocabulary which was as neutral and mainstream as possible" and "had an enormous influence in promoting the Reformation in Germany."[87] Luther's New Testament was translated while he was in protective custody at Wartburg castle in 1522 and published in September of that same year. With the help of Philipp Melanchthon, the Old Testament joined it in 1534 to make a complete Bible.[88] By the time Luther's Bible was published, other countries had already embraced the Lutheran Reformation, so the influence of Luther's Bible rapidly extended into those countries. The Danish Bible, completed in 1550 in Copenhagen, was heavily influenced by Luther's. Since the Danish and Norwegian languages were even closer to each other than they are today, it has been described as "the main translation event for Denmark and Norway prior to the Enlightenment."[89] The first complete Swedish Bible, published in Uppsala in 1541, followed Luther's closely, and remained the standard church Bible in Sweden for over 350 years.[90] The Icelandic New Testament published in 1540 was based largely on Luther's Bible, and that New Testament was later included in a complete Bible in 1584, which was again based largely on Luther's.

The first Latvian Bible was translated in 1685 by Johann Ernst Glück in Alūksne, relying heavily on Luther's German Bible. Glück was born in Germany and studied theology at Wittenberg University,[91] where Luther had taught for many years, and which is now named in his honor. The Glück translation was the only Bible available in Latvian until 1965, when the United Bible Societies in London updated it.[92] In addition to the Bible, Glück also translated the Lutheran Book of Worship, the Small Catechism, and the Book of Prayer into Latvian. Glück was apparently a remarkable linguist – he was fluent in at least German, Latin, Latvian, and Russian, and had a working knowledge of Hebrew, Greek, and Estonian.[93]

To diverge for a moment, it may well be said that Johann Ernst Glück's influence on Russia, albeit indirectly, was greater than his influence on Latvia. Glück married the daughter of a Baltic-German army officer who was serving in Latvia, had several children of his own, and took in a peasant girl named Marta Skovronska, whose Polish parents had apparently died of plague when Marta was three. Marta's aunt moved to Alūksne, the small town in northeastern Latvia where the Glück family lived, taking Marta with her. Marta was later taken in by Glück to help his wife with their children. In 1702, the Swedish army was pushed out of Alūksne, and the occupying Russian army took the Glück family to Moscow as prisoners. Because of their class and Glück's education, they were treated well, and Glück was given an influential teaching position. His step-daughter, Marta, apparently due to her exceptional beauty and wit, came to the attention of the tsar, Peter I, who made her his mistress and later married her. Based on numerous surviving letters, the two had a strong, loving relationship. She was crowned as Catherine I, the Empress of Russia, and when Peter died, she ruled for two years until her own untimely death at 43 from an abscessed lung. She was the first woman to rule Imperial Russia.[94] By taking Marta in, and by taking her to Russia as part of his family, Glück was the conduit through which she eventually ascended to being empress. Her legacy lived beyond her through her daughter Elizabeth and her granddaughter-in-law, Catherine the Great. Glück never made it back to Latvia. He died only three years after his deportation to Russia, but his legacy, and that of Martin Luther, remains in Latvia to this day.

Luther's influence also extended to the Finnish Bible. It was published in 1642 based on translation work done in the mid-1550s by a Lutheran reformer and friend of Luther.[95] Since Finland was part of Sweden at the time, Luther's influence had arrived with the publication of the Swedish Bible a hundred years earlier. To this day, Finland has two official languages, Swedish and Finnish, and over 96% of Finns who are affiliated with any church, are Lutherans.[96] The first Polish New Testament appeared in 1553, done by a friend of Luther.[97] The first complete Slovenian Bible was translated by a Lutheran pastor, and published in Wittenberg in 1584, where Luther had pastored and taught for years.[98]

In 1556, Dutch Calvinists produced a Bible based on the Zürich Bible, which was itself based on Luther's translation, to the extent it had been completed at the time. It became the Bible of the Dutch Mennonites and Lutherans.[99]

Luther's influence also extended to the English Bible, from the very first one, to those of today. That trail of influence, and its importance, will be traced in more detail.

> **LUTHER UNDERSTOOD THAT *BIBLE TRANSLATION IS AN IDEOLOGICAL ACT*, AND DID NOT SHRINK FROM USING IT TO FURTHER HIS INFLUENCE**

Biographies and other works on Martin Luther point out why all this influence is important – there were other German Bibles, but Martin Luther clearly tailored his translation to his own doctrine. "Where the Greek text seemed to allow it, Luther gladly chose words consistent with a Protestant interpretation ..."[100] Luther was aware of what he was doing, and when criticized for it, defended his actions as justified.[101] In his mind, no doubt, they honestly were justified – it was even the moral thing to do. His reasoning was similar to that demonstrated above regarding the use of the word *virgin* in Isaiah 7:14. I hasten to add, at this point, that this is not an attempt to criticize Luther. I have the utmost respect for him. Still, the point is that Luther understood that *Bible translation is an ideological act*, and did not shrink from using it to further his influence.

John Calvin

The story is similar with John Calvin.

The first French Protestant Bible was prepared by Pierre Robert Olivétan, a cousin and friend of Calvin. Its New Testament was based on the 1523 French translation of Jacques Lefèvre d'Étaples, who, like Erasmus, was a slightly earlier reformer who never actually separated from the Catholic Church. Olivétan's Bible was first published in 1535 with two forewords in it by Calvin that contained explicit anti-Roman Catholic comments.[102] Between the publication of Lefèvre's Bible and Olivétan's, several reformers were burned at the stake in France for their leanings toward Lutheranism.[103] As a result, many reformers, at one time or another, were in hiding.

Like Calvin, both Lefèvre and Olivétan were French refugees to Strasbourg at different times. A brief look at Strasbourg helps show the political situation of the time. Today, Strasbourg is in the extreme eastern edge of France, separated from Germany only by the Rhine River. Over the centuries, though, the city has been under the rule of a variety of governments, most recently, Germany and France. At the time of the Protestant Reformation, it was part of the Holy Roman Empire, a complex confederation of hundreds of cities, feudal territories, and kingdoms in central and western Europe.[104] The Holy Roman Empire existed continuously for over 800 years, until it was abolished in 1806 by Napoleon's rise to power. It was what is commonly referred to as Christendom, since until the Protestant Reformation it had a single religion, Roman Catholicism, and the religious and political powers were deeply intertwined. In theory, the Empire was governed by an Emperor, but power struggles between the civil government and the pope were frequent.[105] From 1262, Strasbourg was a Free Imperial City, so it had a seat at the Imperial Diet, the assembly of territorial leaders from throughout the Empire that originated to advise the Emperor, but which over time gained power so that it replaced the Emperor as the final civil authority. As a Free Imperial City, Strasbourg had self-rule, and answered only to the Imperial Diet, rather than to a king or some overlord, which could have been either a territorial ruler or a church appointed bishop. Strasbourg converted early to Lutheranism, in the 1520s, so it became a refuge for Protestants persecuted by church and civil authorities in other parts of the Empire.

A few years after Olivétan died in 1538 (age 32), his French Bible was revised by Calvin himself. Sources disagree on the date the revision was initially published, but there is agreement that it was republished in 1553 by the printer Robert Estienne of Geneva using his system of dividing the text into numbered verses. This was the first time Estienne's system was ever used throughout an entire Bible.[106] After Calvin died in 1564, his French Geneva Bible went through several more revisions before being standardized in 1588 by a committee of Geneva pastors led by Théodore de Bèze and Corneille Bertram. Bèze was the one selected by Calvin to head up the schools Calvin started in Geneva, and who subsequently became the leader of the Calvinist movement after Calvin died.

Although Calvin's influence on the Bible was not as extensive as Luther's, it was not limited to the French translation. As mentioned earlier, he welcomed refugees from England and Scotland to Geneva during the repressive reign of Bloody Mary. His influence on them resulted in their taking his brand of Reformed Theology back with them when they returned home, and it showed up in the subsequent English Bibles.

John Wycliffe

The first English translation of the Bible was through the efforts of John Wycliffe (c. 1324 - 1384) around 1382. Wycliffe was a forerunner to the Protestant Reformers. He was an English priest, theologian, and seminary professor at Oxford. He was also an outspoken opponent of many church practices of his day, and a close follower of Augustine, so his doctrine was strongly predestinarian. He was called "John of Augustine" by his pupils.[107] His English Bible was among the earliest Bible translations in Europe after Jerome's Vulgate a thousand years earlier.[108] His influence on later events cannot be overstated. Some thirty years after his death, the 1415 Council of Constance, in the southwest corner of Germany, dealt with two major issues: first, the Western Schism (which was related to three simultaneous, rival popes), and second, reforms aimed at limiting the teachings of John Wycliffe. Wycliffe was declared a heretic, and the order was issued for his remains to be removed from consecrated ground and his writings to be burned. This same Council also condemned Jan Hus, the Czech priest and professor who was a follower of John Wycliffe's teachings, to be burned at the stake. Hus's sentence was carried out immediately, and the order regarding Wycliffe was carried out in 1428, when his corpse was exhumed, burned, and the ashes thrown into the river. Wycliffe's influence can be traced to Jan Hus, and Hus in turn had a dramatic impact on Martin Luther.[109] Hus's followers, known as the Moravians, were dispersed by Catholic armies attempting to annihilate them, so they had a significant impact in many other parts of Europe, including Latvia, and including England and North America through the legacy of John Wesley and the Methodists. Wycliffe had a tremendous impact on the later Reformers, and through them, on the Bible itself. Although his Bible was the first in English, it was not, however, the most influential. That credit goes to William Tyndale.

William Tyndale

Tyndale was born around 1494 near Gloucestershire, England, 106 years after Wycliffe died. He was educated at Oxford and Cambridge and worked as a chaplain and private tutor. He was a gifted linguist who, in addition to his native English, became fluent over the years in French, German, Italian, and Spanish, as well as Latin, Hebrew and Greek.[110] Tyndale's views proved to be controversial, resulting in some harsh confrontations. In the most famous of them, a "learned man" is reported to have said to Tyndale, "We had better be without God's laws than the Pope's." Tyndale responded: "I defy the Pope, and all his laws, and if God spare my life, ere many years, I will cause the boy that driveth the

plough, shall know more of the Scriptures than thou dost!"[111] Tyndale
went to London in 1523 hoping to get official permission to translate
the Bible into English. When he was unsuccessful, he went to Germany.
Despite disagreement among writers concerning the evidence, it is
reasonably certain that Tyndale was at Wittenberg during part of 1524
and 1525.[112] According to Henry Hoare, "The unanimous evidence of
his contemporaries supports the view that he was at Wittenberg with
Luther, and that he worked there on his translation."[113] Hoare says,
"Speaking generally it may be said that up to the year 1523 Tyndale
remained more or less the disciple of his earliest instructors, John Colet
and Erasmus. Thenceforward he felt very strongly the influence of
Luther."[114]

Tyndale is frequently credited with translating his New Testament
directly from Erasmus's Greek rendering, but the textual evidence
suggests that he translated directly from Luther's New Testament, using
Erasmus only as a supporting aid. After comparing Tyndale's work with
Luther's, Franklin Gruber says, "That Tyndale bodily incorporated,
by merely translating them from the German, whole pages of Luther's
writings . . . is an open secret, as we could easily show. And what appears
later from our comparisons between the New Testaments of Luther and
Tyndale, should be evidence enough, that Tyndale did abundantly rely
upon, and freely use, Luther's New Testament."[115] David Daniell agrees,
but challenges which source was primary: "He follows Luther, but only
when he chooses to do so. His primary source is the Greek."[116] Regardless
of which source was primary, it is clear that Luther's influence entered
the English Bible somewhere around 1526 in Tyndale's first printing.

As soon as Tyndale's New Testament was published, he turned
his attention to the Old Testament, with the help of an assistant, Miles
Cloverdale. Together, they worked on the Pentateuch, but Tyndale's New
Testament made him a wanted man, so he and Cloverdale separated
and Tyndale went into hiding and continued to work on other Old
Testament books. Cloverdale was not able to translate from Hebrew

and Greek, but with the several translations he had available, which included Luther's German Bible, Zwingli's Zürich Bible, and three Latin versions, he was able to publish the first complete English Bible in 1535, while Tyndale was still in hiding. Cloverdale was actually supported financially ("patronized") during this time by Anne Boleyn, the second of Henry VIII's six successive wives, who was openly sympathetic to Protestantism. About the same time Cloverdale's Bible was being published in England with the King's favor, Tyndale was betrayed in Antwerp and imprisoned near Brussels until August, 1536, when he was convicted of heresy and condemned to death. Mercifully, his executioner strangled him with the chain being used to tie him to the stake, then his body was burned. He had no way of knowing what was already happening in England with Cloverdale and the royal family. His last words were, "Lord, open the King of England's eyes."[117]

Tyndale's life on earth ended at the stake in 1536, but his influence did not. Soon after Cloverdale's first Bible was published, another was published by John Rogers in 1537, known as the Thomas Matthew Bible, an anglicized version of the name of a French Calvinist whose "militantly Protestant attack on the mass, religious images, free will, the priesthood, confession, holy days, purgatory, and every other doctrine that separated the widening gulf between Catholics and Protestants" had been included along with Calvin's two prefaces in Olivétan's French Bible that had been published two years earlier.[118] The Matthew Bible was based directly on Tyndale's work.[119]

Almost immediately, Miles Cloverdale started work on the Great Bible, the first authorized version issued by the Church of England after it separated from the Catholic Church over Henry VIII's divorce issues. Rather than revising his own earlier Bible, Cloverdale revised the Matthew Bible, so the Great Bible of 1538 was based on Tyndale's New Testament and his incomplete work on the Old Testament.[120] When Bloody Mary took the throne in 1553 and returned England to the Roman Catholic faith, many reformers (including William

Whittingham and John Knox) fled the country,[121] settling in Geneva, as we have already seen. From there, they used the Great Bible and Tyndale's to come up with a revision they compared to the original languages,[122] and produced the Geneva Bible in 1560,[123] not to be confused with the French Geneva Bible. William Whittingham was in charge of the project, but Miles Cloverdale was also involved, as was John Knox, the Scottish reformer.[124] When Mary's reign ended after only five years, Elizabeth I reinstated the Church of England and recognized the need for a new Bible that was a little more "episcopal" than the Geneva Bible,[125] so she authorized the Bishop's Bible, a revision of the Great Bible from thirty years earlier. The Bishop's Bible, published in 1568, never replaced the enormously popular Geneva Bible among ordinary people. Because the Geneva Bible was small and inexpensive, it was published in more than seventy editions between 1560 and 1640.[126]

In response to the popularity of the Geneva Bible, the Catholics produced the Douay-Rheims version, even though they did not yet acknowledge the right of the laity to read the Bible in their own language.[127] The New Testament was published in 1582 and the Old Testament was finished in 1610.[128] Even though it claimed to be based on the Vulgate, comparisons show about 80% of the Douay-Rheims text to be directly from Tyndale's.[129]

As already mentioned, Elizabeth I reinstated the Church of England when she took over from her half-sister, Bloody Mary, in 1558. The Protestants who had fled the country returned, but after their experience in Europe with a "purer" form of Protestantism, they were no longer comfortable with the formalism of the Church of England. They became known as "puritans." Elizabeth's government was firm in limiting their influence, but when she died in 1603 and King James of Scotland ascended to the English throne, the puritans presented their case to him. In response, he authorized a new translation of the Bible which was officially published in 1611, and which became known as the King James Version (KJV).

The King James Version and Beyond

The KJV, on its title page, claimed to be "Newly translated out of the Originall Tongues"[130] but in the preface, it said the purpose of the translators "was not to make a new translation . . . but to make a good one better."[131] In fact, the very first of the fifteen rules by which the translation was to proceed, was that the Bishop's Bible was to be followed, and "as little altered as the truth of the original permit."[132] And that is precisely what the evidence shows.

Remember the sequence: Tyndale translated directly from Luther, the Matthew Bible used Tyndale as its base, Cloverdale created the Great Bible using the Matthew Bible as its base, the Bishop's Bible was a revision of the Great Bible, and the KJV was a revision of the Bishop's Bible.

According to Brian Moynahan, "A complete analysis of the Authorised Version, known down through the generations as 'the AV' or 'the King James' was made in 1998. It shows that Tyndale's words account for 84% of the New Testament and for 75.8% of the Old Testament books that he translated" before his execution.[133] Joan Bridges says, "He [Tyndale] is the mainly unrecognised translator of the most influential book in the world. Although the Authorised King James Version is ostensibly the production of a learned committee of churchmen, it is mostly cribbed from Tyndale with some reworking of his translation."[134]

Earlier, we looked at the comparison Franklin Gruber made between Luther's German New Testament, and Tyndale's. In concluding his comparison, Gruber says, "... both in form and substance, Tyndale generally very closely, and in places minutely, follow's Luther's New Testament.... It is also seen that justly to value or to magnify the importance of Tyndale's translation by pointing to the fact that it survives to so large an extent in King James's Version, as well as in the Revised Version, is therefore inadvertently also to emphasize an inherent dependence of those English versions upon Luther's great original Protestant Version. And, moreover, to emphasize the extent to which that translation lies at the basis of the English language even of our day, is in a sense to emphasize the extent to which the features of a parent are reproduced in the child."[135]

The reason the trail of influence has been traced in such detail, is this: Martin Luther, as well as Huldrych Zwingli, held the same double predestinarian views that have made John Calvin so controversial for the past 500 years.[136] The difference is that Calvin made that point the "anchor premise" on which all the rest of his theology rested. Luther believed the same way, but refused to make it central to his teachings. He said, "A dispute about predestination should be avoided entirely ... I forget everything about Christ and God when I come upon these thoughts and actually get to the point to imagining that God is a rogue. We must stay in the word, in which God is revealed to us and salvation is offered, if we believe him. But in thinking about predestination, we forget God ... However, in Christ are hid all the treasures (Col 2:3); outside him all are locked up. Therefore, we should simply refuse to argue about election."[137]

> MARTIN LUTHER, AS WELL AS HULDRYCH ZWINGLI, HELD THE SAME DOUBLE PREDESTINARIAN VIEWS THAT HAVE MADE JOHN CALVIN SO CONTROVERSIAL FOR THE PAST 500 YEARS

To make sure we are clear on what double predestination means, let's look at Calvin's position. He said, "By predestination we mean the eternal decree of God, by which he determined with himself whatever he wished to happen with regard to every man. All are not created on equal terms, but some are preordained to eternal life, others to eternal damnation; and, accordingly, as each has been created for one or other of these ends, we say that he has been predestinated to life or to death."[138]

Because the double predestinarian view is so divisive, Calvinists have never been able to avoid disputing about it, in contrast to Luther. Even so, since "Bible translation is an ideological act," Luther's leanings toward double predestination logically showed up in his translation. We said earlier that if the translator has a theological position that can be reflected in the choice of words used in the translation, that theological position *will* be reflected – it cannot be otherwise. Where there are two or more perfectly legitimate translation options, a translation decision has to be made and the ideological leanings of the translator will sway the decision. By his own admission, Luther understood that and even consciously allowed his theological understanding to influence his translation. If the translator is a person of integrity, it is even the moral thing to do, as I have already observed. The pattern was carried down even in the preparation of the KJV. There were both Calvinists and those opposed to predestination on the committee who prepared the KJV, but most of them were Calvinists, so their view tended to prevail. In at least one case, they used an etymological analysis by Theodore Beza (Théodore de Bèze), Calvin's direct successor, to settle a dispute over the choice of *foreknown* or *foreordained*. The word was entered as *foreordained* but has been changed in several more recent translations.[139]

> THERE WERE BOTH CALVINISTS AND THOSE OPPOSED TO PREDESTINATION ON THE COMMITTEE WHO PREPARED THE KJV, BUT MOST OF THEM WERE CALVINISTS, SO THEIR VIEW TENDED TO PREVAIL

Proposing Changes

Any time a change is made in a new translation, there is always an outcry. The familiar translations are part of the maps in our minds. We memorize Scripture, and embrace it as "authoritative in all matters of faith and practice." Changes require that we re-think what we believe. It is easier to reject the change than to revise the maps in our minds. And, sometimes there is good reason for the outcry. For example, if the use of the word *virgin* is eliminated from Isaiah 7:14, there is concern that over time, the virgin birth will be eliminated, and if that happens, then Jesus was not divine, and if he was not divine, then he cannot save. Each new translation seems to favor one perspective while eroding concepts that support a conflicting one. It takes a certain amount of courage to propose such a change. Anthony Pym explains why.

The Bible is a sacred book, Pym says, not from anything about its linguistic characteristics, but because of how it has been received throughout the ages. "Over the centuries, the Bible has thus been the site of so much human effort, both for and against particular readings, that its status is necessarily special. It has gained a cultural weight, heavy with scholarship, revelation, mystery, elegance, cleverness, cunning, bigotry, blindness, and persecution. And that accumulated weight, if nothing else, affects the way any translator approaches the text."[140]

I attempted to give a very abbreviated history of the Bible above. If I had put in more of the details that are available, it would be obvious that no translator ever approached Bible translation with only one source to work from, unless there was only the one available. Bible translators always compare the main source from which they are working, with what others before them have done. It is still true today. Even if a particular translation is questionable, if it has been consistently translated a certain way over the centuries, it will almost certainly continue to be translated that way. The accumulated weight Pym refers to, affects the way translators approach the text.

Occasionally, though, an alternative translation is suggested, as with the word *foreknown*, above. Changes always tend to favor one theological position over another one, as we established above, so certain Bible translations are used by certain denominations, and others by others. Any creative change proposed is subjected to scholarly scrutiny, and even the scrutiny will tend to follow theological or ideological lines that support certain positions. Consider an example.

In recent years, Bible translations supporting gender equality have become more common. If the equality is in terms of value and importance to the plan of God, there will be little argument, because those principles are supported by careful exegesis of the text (*exegesis* means to get the meaning out of the text, *eisegesis* means to introduce meaning into the text). But if gender equality implies equality in roles, then it pits one ideological perspective against another – egalitarianism against complementarianism, feminism against traditional gender roles. (Egalitarianism supports gender equality in everything, complementarianism supports gender equality in value and importance, but differences in roles – roles are seen as complementary). When a change is proposed, evidence will be presented for each viewpoint, and the tests for truth that we discussed in Chapter 2 will have to be applied. Is it consistent with other truth? Is the proposed change more consistent with other Scripture, or less? Where does the bulk of the evidence point? If the change is accepted, what change in practice will necessarily follow? If we implement this new practice, what will the long term result be? In other words, ultimately, will it work?

Here is a summary of the problem with proposed changes: they always challenge the previous translation, and with the change, they challenge the maps in our minds and the way those maps affect what we do. This book opens with the epigraph that "if anything matters, everything matters." The maps in our minds form a logical network of ideas (even, at the biological level, a neurological network) which are interrelated and interdependent. Change the location of one city, and it affects other things. The maps in our minds are sometimes illustrated by a spider web. It is a flexible whole, such that if one strand is snipped, all the rest of the web will sag. The one strand does not ruin all the rest of the web, but it *affects* all of it. So we tend to protect even the details of the maps in our minds.

The principle extends to theology. For every theological perspective, over time, the system is constructed in such a way that it is coherent – if you change one detail, it requires rethinking the way that change affects all the rest of the theological construct. If the Garden of Eden is mythological, then the whole argument falls apart about Adam transmitting sin to all subsequent people, so the need for redemption by the second Adam, Jesus, is unnecessary, so the whole Christian argument about being reconciled to God has to be rethought. Proposed change has to be approached very carefully, and both theologians and translators are aware of that.

Because change can be so dangerous, the justification for that change has to be credible, so the proposed change must be scrutinized. Galileo proposed change, that the earth might revolve around the sun, rather than the other way around, but what he proposed was seen as theologically subversive, so it was rejected until the evidence became so overwhelming that it was accepted, and the previous understanding was determined to not be critical to the rest of the theological construct. Such scrutiny of any proposed change is justified.

Consider the case we mentioned above, regarding gender roles. In the 1980s, there was a considerable debate over that issue, based to a large degree on an article[141] that challenged the meaning of just one word in the New Testament, in just one passage – the Greek word which means *head* (κεφαλή, *kephalē*), in 1 Corinthians 11. In the past, the word has consistently been understood to mean *authority*. The authors of the article suggested the use of *head* as in *the head of a river*, so that the word implies *source*, not authority. Such a change would completely alter the understanding of 1 Corinthians 11:3: "Now I want you to realize that the head of every man is Christ, and the head of the woman is man, and the head of Christ is God."

Using the proposed change, the verse could now be rendered as, "Now I want you to realize that the source of every man is Christ, and the source of the woman is man, and the source of Christ is God." However attractive such an idea may be ideologically, it has to withstand the normal, intense scrutiny to be accepted. In this case, it does not. Scholars point out that the idea is based on only one example of the suggested usage, found in a lexicon that is for classical Greek rather than for New Testament studies, and even that one example is textually uncertain and could be translated in other ways.[142] According to Wayne Grudem, this means there is a complete absence of any clear usage in any ancient Greek literature to support the idea of head as 'source without authority', compared to over 50 to support 'person in authority over'.[143] Then when the suggested rendering is set into the biblical text in which it is found (1 Cor 11:3-16), it proves to be inconsistent with the overall argument of the passage, which is clearly related to authority, not source. To paraphrase Daniel's statement to Belshazzar (Dan 5:27), the suggested change has been weighed on the scales and found wanting, for several reasons: it diminishes the internal coherence of the surrounding text; it fails the test of where the bulk of the evidence points; it is based on a spurious source; and it appeals to an unknown or unlikely meaning for the word in question.[144] It fails the tests for truth in multiple ways.

The reason I cite this example is not to push a personal agenda on gender roles, but to show that I recognize the danger of suggesting changes to ideas that have been translated consistently for centuries. Such a suggestion for change has to be justified and justifiable. I am about to suggest just such changes, and I hope to demonstrate that they are both justified and justifiable.

From Counting Coins to Paying According to Value

Consider the Greek words that are translated *chosen* and *elect* in the New Testament. Because there are several, and because they appear in many verses, I have attached an appendix with a listing of all the verses in which they appear, and a summary, from a variety of dictionaries and lexicons, of the ways in which they have been translated historically, inside and outside of the New Testament.

The more I research this issue, the more convinced I become that our Bibles are biased to favor "individual predestination for salvation." In almost every single use of the word *chosen*, or *elect*, there are other words which are well within the range of meaning of the original word, which could have been used.

I will show a few examples to demonstrate what I am suggesting. If you want to consider it in more detail, refer to Appendix A. Rather than footnote every point here, the details are in the appendix.

In the following verse, the Apostle Paul is countering false teaching concerning "the coming of our Lord Jesus Christ and our being gathered to him" (2 Thes 2:1) Apparently, someone was teaching that "the day of the Lord" had already happened, and they were attributing their false teaching to Paul himself (2 Thes 2:2). Paul attempts to calm the Thessalonians' fears, and he uses the occasion to give them some further teaching on their security as believers. In 2 Thessalonians 2:13, he says:

> **KJV** 2 Thes 2:13 But we are bound to give thanks alway to God for you, brethren beloved of the Lord, because God hath from the beginning **chosen** you to salvation through sanctification of the Spirit and belief of the truth: (Strong's # 138)

> **NIV** 2 Thes 2:13 But we ought always to thank God for you, brothers loved by the Lord, because from the beginning God **chose** you to be saved through the sanctifying work of the Spirit and through belief in the truth.

The word that is translated *chosen* (KJV) and *chose* (NIV), is used three times in the New Testament. Basically, the word means to *choose, prefer, take, take for oneself.* In Classical Greek, it was a very broad word. In the Septuagint Old Testament, this one word was used to translate six Hebrew words: *to declare, to choose, to delight in, to love, to offer or give, to lay aside.*

Now consider a perfectly legitimate alternative to the translations above:

Alternative rendering 2 Thes 2:13 But we ought always to thank God for you, brothers loved by the Lord, because from the beginning God **took you for himself** to be saved through the sanctifying work of the Spirit and through belief in the truth.

The change is totally faithful to the original word, but it completely changes the meaning of the verse. Now, instead of the Thessalonians being saved because they have been *chosen* by God, they are saved because of the work of the Holy Spirit and their response to it, by believing. If the choosing were monergistic as Calvinists claim, that is, accomplished entirely by God with no participation on the part of the person, why would Paul bring in their belief as a factor? (Keep in mind that Paul is talking to "brothers" – plural – in keeping with his communal worldview.) In Chapter 7, we are going to consider the foreknowledge of God in more detail, but for now, suffice it to say that this alternative rendering is completely consistent not only with the meaning of the original Greek, but also with God's foreknowledge being his motivator, rather than arbitrary choosing.

Consider another example. Toward the end of Jesus' ministry, he made an effort to prepare his disciples for his departure, and what would happen in the end time. In both Matthew's and Mark's Gospels, Jesus describes a time of severe trial, so difficult that if it were allowed to continue, all human life would perish. The days are shortened, Jesus says, "for the sake of the elect." Who are the "elect"? The word used here is one of three Greek words from the same root – the second and third words being derived from the first one. The three words occur as verbs, adjectives, and nouns. Together, these three words are found over fifty times in the New Testament, making them by far the most commonly used words for this concept that is usually translated as *chose, chosen,* or *elect.* The point that is missed when the words are translated simply as *chose, chosen* or *elect,* is that the Greek word carries with it a sense of high quality, or superiority: *to choose because of superiority, beauty, or value; favorite, select, of the best quality, choice ones, excellent, outstanding.* The words can even mean *to say, to name,* or *to call.* The adjective form was used in the Septuagint Old Testament to translate 26 different Hebrew words, almost all of which carry with them the sense of being the best: *choicest, fattest, polished, pure, desirable, ornamental, highest,* etc. The verb form was used in the Septuagint to translate Hebrew words that meant to *receive, gather,* or *search,* as well as the more common usage of *choose* or *chosen.*

THE MEANING OF A BROAD GREEK WORD, RICH IN MEANING IN THE ORIGINAL LANGUAGE, HAS BEEN DEEPLY IMPOVERISHED AND NARROWED IN THE TRANSLATION

This is what I was leading up to earlier when I described the narrowing of meaning when certain words are translated into Latvian. It has happened as these Greek words have been brought into the western European languages. The meaning of a broad Greek word, rich in meaning in the original language, has been deeply impoverished and narrowed in the translation. Only a part of the original word has been captured by the translation, and – I would suggest – that narrowing does a real disservice to what the original speakers and writers were conveying.

Armed with this knowledge of the wider range of meaning of these words, let's look at the text. As before, the words under consideration (Strong's # G1588) are **bold and underlined**.

KJV Matt 24:22 And except those days should be shortened, there should no flesh be saved: but for the **elect's** sake those days shall be shortened.

NIV Matt 24:22 If those days had not been cut short, no one would survive, but for the sake of the **elect** those days will be shortened.

Alternative rendering Matt 24:22 If those days had not been cut short, no one would survive, but for the sake of the **choice ones,** those days will be shortened. (**Choice ones**, those picked out, gathered, or named because of some quality which sets them apart from others – in this case, like Abraham, they believed God and it was credited to them as righteousness.)

Remember, it's not the word that's important. It's the concept. With this in mind, and the fact that the Greek word has an element of "superior quality" contained within it which the English translation fails to capture, the word *elect* could even legitimately be translated as *faithful*.

Alternative rendering Matt 24:22 If those days had not been cut short, no one would survive, but for the sake of the **faithful ones**, those days will be shortened.

One consideration in the mind of the translator or reader, is whether or not "the elect" are future believers, or already believers. If they are future believers, then the observer's theological perspective will sway their belief in how God knows they will become believers – because of his foreknowledge, or because he has chosen them. If the elect are already believers, the theological perspective will sway the observer's belief in how they got there – because God chose them, or because they believed and as a result, God put his name on them and they became part of those he is gathering for eternity in heaven. If "the elect" are already believers, the verse could just as accurately have been worded:

Alternative rendering Matt 24:22 If those days had not been cut short, no one would survive, but for the sake of the **gathered ones**, those days will be shortened.

or

. . . but for the sake of the **named ones**, those days will be shortened.

One reason to consider that "the elect" in this verse are already believers, is because this is exactly the same usage of the word as in 1 Timothy 5:21, when it describes the angels who did not rebel. In other words, the elect angels are not *future* faithful ones because God has predetermined they will be, or foreknows they will be, they are part of a group who are already faithful, not because God chose them, but because they themselves chose to be – when the other angels rebelled, they did not.

> **KJV** 1 Tim 5:21 I charge *thee* before God, and the Lord Jesus Christ, and the **elect** angels, that thou observe these things without preferring one before another, doing nothing by partiality. (Strong's # 1588)

> **NIV** 1 Tim 5:21 I charge you, in the sight of God and Christ Jesus and the **elect** angels, to keep these instructions without partiality, and to do nothing out of favoritism.

> **Alternative rendering** 1 Tim 5:21 I charge you, in the sight of God and Christ Jesus and the **choice** angels, to keep these instructions without partiality, and to do nothing out of favoritism.

> **Alternative rendering** 1 Tim 5:21 I charge you, in the sight of God and Christ Jesus and the **faithful** angels, to keep these instructions without partiality, and to do nothing out of favoritism.

In Luke 18:1-8, Jesus tells the story of the persistent widow and the unjust judge, to encourage his disciples to "always pray and not give up." There is even a distinct possibility that this story connects with those believers observed by the Apostle John in Revelation 6:9-11, who were clamoring for justice.

> **KJV** Luke 18:7 And shall not God avenge his own **elect**, which cry day and night unto him, though he bear long with them? (Strong's # 1588)

> **NIV** Luke 18:7 And will not God bring about justice for his **chosen** ones, who cry out to him day and night? Will he keep putting them off?

> **Alternative rendering** Luke 18:7 And will not God bring about justice for his **choice ones**, who cry out to him day and night? Will he keep putting them off?

Alternative rendering Luke 18:7 And will not God bring about justice for his **faithful ones**, who cry out to him day and night? Will he keep putting them off?

Alternative rendering Luke 18:7 And will not God bring about justice for his **named ones**, who cry out to him day and night? Will he keep putting them off? (will not God bring about justice for **those upon whom he has put his name**, who cry out to him day and night? Will he keep putting them off?)

One of the most powerful parallels regarding the translation of these words, is related to what happens with those who are God's people. At the end of the famous blessing of Aaron (Num 6:22-27), God says of the priests, "So they will *put my name* on the Israelites." The idea of God naming, or putting his name on his people, is well within the meaning of these Greek words, except the words have been translated as *chosen*.

Consider another one. This time, it is related to titles of honor in the greeting of the Apostle John, in his second letter. Preliminary question: In a greeting, which is more likely, to use a title of honor, or to describe a person's destiny? Surely John is describing a quality of the two ladies in question, rather than their predetermined destiny. If the ladies are churches rather than people, then the argument for "chosen" might be defensible, but even then, the word "choice" would be equally faithful to the Greek (Strong's # 1588).

KJV 2 John 1:1 The elder unto the **elect** lady and her children, whom I love in the truth; and not I only, but also all they that have known the truth;

NIV 2 John 1:1 The elder, To the **chosen** lady and her children, whom I love in the truth – and not I only, but also all who know the truth –

Alternative rendering 2 John 1:1 The elder, To the **most excellent** lady and her children, whom I love in the truth – and not I only, but also all who know the truth –

Alternative rendering 2 John 1:1 The elder, To the **choice** lady and her children, whom I love in the truth – and not I only, but also all who know the truth –

KJV 2 John 1:13 The children of thy **elect** sister greet thee. Amen.

NIV 2 John 1:13 The children of your **chosen** sister send their greetings.

Alternative rendering 2 John 1:13 The children of your **most excellent** sister send their greetings.

Alternative rendering 2 John 1:13 The children of your **choice** sister send their greetings.

The alternative renderings are not only well within the broader meaning of the original word, but make much more sense in the context in which the word is used.

Consider another. One of the Greek words used in the New Testament means *to choose by raising the hand* (Strong's G5500). It often means to vote by raising the hand, but in this case, it seems clear that it is Paul and Barnabas who are choosing by raising the hand, so it probably implies that they indicated their choice by pointing to certain people. Rather than creating that mental image, the translation creates a more institutional impression.

KJV Acts 14:23 And when they had **ordained** them elders in every church, and had prayed with fasting, they commended them to the Lord, on whom they believed.

NIV Acts 14:23 Paul and Barnabas **appointed** elders for them in each church and, with prayer and fasting, committed them to the Lord, in whom they had put their trust.

Alternative rendering Acts 14:23 And when they had **selected** elders in every church, and had prayed with fasting, they commended them to the Lord, on whom they believed.

I suspect that here we are seeing a similar translation issue as with the word *baptism*. By the time the vernacular translations were started, the level nature of the church that Jesus initiated had been gone for centuries – replaced by a hierarchy with a paid professional clergy and an uneducated, and to a great extent, uninvolved laity. Jesus told his disciples to call no man "father" (Matt 23:9), but the implication of that had long been lost. The ordination of clergy does not appear in the New Testament, although it is often justified by the admonition of 1 Timothy 3:10, that deacons first be tested before they are allowed to serve, and it is something of a natural continuation of the concept of priests from the Old Testament. But it was neither Jesus nor the early church who developed the notion of a professional clergy. By the time the translations of the Bible started to proliferate, however, the hierarchical system was so well established, supported by monarchies in the background, that nobody questioned it. So when the verse above was translated about the selection of elders, the use of the word *ordained*, or later *appointed*, served the interests of the leaders of both the institutional church and the government better than any other word. Bible translation is an ideological act.

Consider one more. On Paul's first missionary journey, at Antioch in Pisidia, he gave an extensive presentation of the history of Israel, leading up to Jesus as the messiah. The local people were so impressed, that the second Sabbath, "almost the whole city gathered to hear the word of the Lord" (Acts 13:44). When the Jews saw the crowds, they became jealous and started verbally abusing Paul. In response (Acts 13:47), Paul quoted Isaiah 49:6 as his commission from God: "I have made you a light for the Gentiles, that you may bring salvation to the ends of the earth." The next verse is the one of interest to us:

KJV Acts 13:48 And when the Gentiles heard this, they were glad, and glorified the word of the Lord: and as many as were **ordained** to eternal life believed.

NIV Acts 13:48   When the Gentiles heard this, they were glad and honored the word of the Lord; and all who were **appointed** for eternal life believed.

Alternative rendering Acts 13:48   When the Gentiles heard this, they were glad and honored the word of the Lord; and all who were **concerned** about eternal life believed.

Remember, again, that it is not the word that is critical, it is the concept. The Greek word that is translated as "ordained" or "appointed" is a derivative of Strong's G5021 (τάσσω , tassō). The basic word means "to arrange in an orderly manner, that is, assign or dispose (to a certain position or lot): – addict, appoint, determine, ordain, set." In the middle voice, which is used in this verse, it can even mean to "set one's heart,"[145] and that is logical, since the middle voice usually expresses reflexive action, that is, one acting upon oneself. The word implies that someone is the agent of the action – either God or humans. Notice how a bias can affect our understanding. In Thayer's Lexicon, he says regarding this verse: "as many as were appointed [A.V. *ordained*] (by God) to obtain eternal life, or to whom God had decreed eternal life."[146] But does the text say that, or even imply that? Note the fact that the action is specifically *not* attributed to God. It would have been so easy for Luke to use the active voice and say, "and all whom God had appointed to eternal life, believed." He does not, but the Calvinist does. I am convinced a more accurate translation would capture the idea that the people are themselves the agents of the action – they are *addicted* to eternal life, or *compelled* toward eternal life, they have *set their hearts* on eternal life, or their background has *predisposed* them to be *concerned* about eternal life. Thayer demonstrates a bias in one direction, toward predestination of individuals to salvation. The more I study Scripture, the more I believe the original text supports a bias in the opposite direction – that it *never* supports predestination of individuals to salvation.

What I have demonstrated here can be done for every verse in the New Testament that seems to imply that God chooses individuals for salvation. In Appendix A, I look at every occurrence of the words *chose*, *chosen*, and *elect* that occur in the New Testament. In many instances, the use of the words *chose* or *chosen* are fitting, because the situation really does involve a simple choosing, with no theological implications involved. However, in many theologically critical cases, an alternative rendering that captures more of the breadth of the original word is just as legitimate in terms of translation, and more than legitimate in terms of the principles and theological themes that are woven throughout Scripture. To translate the words as *chosen* and *elect* is not only not necessary, it is not even justified. It grossly narrows the original meaning. It is a clear case of counting coins instead of paying according to value, and we get badly cheated in the exchange. We get a coin, but it's worth only half, a quarter, or even less of the original value. An argument can even be made that it's a counterfeit coin. It promotes an understanding that is inconsistent with other parts of Scripture, so that what could be clear and consistent, is now a matter of debate and division. In the chapters ahead, I will attempt to demonstrate how that consistency was originally there, how it can be restored, and how it impacts our view of God, our view of his plan, and our part in it.

Endnotes

[1] Gonzalez, *Story of Christianity*, xvii.

[2] Manuel Jinbachian, "Introduction: The Septuagint to the Vernaculars," in *A History of Bible Translation*, ed. Philip A. Noss (Rome: Edizioni di Storia e Letteratura, 2007), 34.

[3] G. Darshan, "The Twenty-Four Books of the Hebrew Bible and Alexandrian Scribal Methods," in *Homer and the Bible in the Eyes of Ancient Interpreters: Between Literary and Religious Concerns (JSRC 16)*, ed. M.R. Niehoff (Leiden, Netherlands: Brill, 2012), 221-244.

[4] Menachem Cohen, "The Idea of the Sanctity of the Biblical Text and the Science of Textual Criticism," in *HaMikrah V'anachnu*, ed. Uriel Simon, (Tel-Aviv: HaMachon L'Yahadut U'Machshava Bat-Z'mananu and Dvir, 1979). English translation edited by Isaac B. Gottlieb. http://users.cecs.anu.edu.au/~bdm/dilugim/CohenArt/, accessed 25 June 2015.

[5]   Philip R. Davies, "The Jewish Scriptural Canon in Cultural Perspective," in *The Canon Debate*, ed. Lee Martin McDonald and James A. Sanders (Peabody, MA: Hendrickson Publishers, 2002), 50.

[6]   Lee Martin McDonald and James A. Sanders, "Introduction," *The Canon Debate*, (Peabody, MA: Hendrickson Publishers, 2002), 5.

[7]   Burke, 69, citing L .McDonald, *The Formulation of the Christian Biblical Canon* (Peabody, MA: Hendrickson, 1995), 89, and E. Würthwein, *The Text of the Old Testament*, 2nd rev. ed., trans. E.F. Rhodes (Grand Rapids, MI: Eerdmans, 1995), 53.

[8]   P.R. Ackroyd and C.F. Evans, eds., *The Cambridge History of the Bible: Vol. 1 From the Beginnings to Jerome* (Cambridge, New York, Melbourne: Cambridge University Press. 1970), 308.

[9]   David G. Burke, "The First Versions: The Septuagint, the Targums, and the Latin," in *A History of Bible Translation*, ed. Philip A. Noss (Rome: Edizioni di Storia e Letteratura, 2007), 59.

[10] Philip A. Noss, *A History of Bible Translation* (Rome: Edizioni di Storia e Letteratura, 2007), 8.

[11] Martin Hengel, *The Septuagint as Christian Scripture: Its Prehistory and the Problem of Its Canon*, trans. Mark E. Biddle (Grand Rapids, MI: Baker Academic, 2002), 19.

[12] Frederick W. Danker, *Multipurpose Tools for Bible Study*, rev. ed. (Minneapolis, MN: Fortress, 1993), 63.

[13] Danker, *Multipurpose Tools*, 62ff.

[14] Danker, *Multipurpose Tools*, 63.

[15] Burke, "The First Versions," 62.

[16] Burke, "The First Versions," 62.

[17] J. Trebolle Barrera, *The Jewish Bible and the Christian Bible*, trans. W.G.E. Watson (Leiden, Netherlands: Brill; and Grand Rapids, MI: Eerdmans, 1998), 318.

[18] Burke, "The First Versions," 63.

[19] Jinbachian, "The Septuagint to the Vernaculars," 35.

[20] Burke, "The First Versions," 60;

[21] Lamin Sanneh, *Translating the Message: The Missionary Impact on Culture* (Maryknoll, NY: Orbis Books, 2009), 1.

[22] Sanneh, *Translating the Message*, 53; Amos Yong, *Missiological Spirit: Christian Mission Theology in the Third Millennium Global Context* (Eugene, OR: Cascade Books, 2014), 41.

[23] These four divisions are an exact quote from Jinbachian, "The Septuagint to the Vernaculars," 29.

[24] Jinbachian, "The Septuagint to the Vernaculars," 39.

[25] Jinbachian, "The Septuagint to the Vernaculars," 50.

[26] Jinbachian, "The Septuagint to the Vernaculars," 50-51.

[27] Jinbachian, "The Septuagint to the Vernaculars," 40; http://armenianbible.org/, accessed 30 June 2016.

[28] Jinbachian, "The Septuagint to the Vernaculars," 43-44, quoting Sidney Jellicoe, *The Septuagint and Modern Study* (Oxford: Clarendon, 1968), 261.

[29] Stefan Rebenich, *Jerome: The Early Church Fathers* (London, New York: Routledge, 2002), 28.

[30] Rebenich, *Jerome*, 9, 13.

[31] Rebenich, *Jerome*, 28.

[32] Rebenich, *Jerome*, 24.

[33] Rebenich, *Jerome*, 26-28.

[34] Burke, "The First Versions," 84-88.

35 Erroll Rhodes, "Secondary Versions: Arabic to Old Slavonic," in *A History of Bible Translation,* ed. Philip A. Noss (Rome: Edizioni di Storia e Letteratura, 2007), 102.

36 Jinbachian, "The Septuagint to the Vernaculars," 54; Christopher de Hamel, *The Book. A History of the Bible* (London, New York: Phaidon Press, 2001), 190ff.

37 Jinbachian, "The Septuagint to the Vernaculars," 54; de Hamel, *The Book,* 196; https://www.britannica.com/place/Ottoman-Empire, accessed 30 June 2016.

38 Jinbachian, "The Septuagint to the Vernaculars," 54; de Hamel, *The Book,* 218-220.

39 Paul Ellingworth, "From Martin Luther to the English Revised Version," in *A History of Bible Translation,* ed. Philip A. Noss (Rome: Edizioni di Storia e Letteratura, 2007), 134.

40 Ellingworth, "From Martin Luther," 134.

41 Wycliffe Global Alliance, as of Oct, 2015. http://www.wycliffe.net/statistics, accessed 1 July, 2016.

42 Sanneh, *Translating the Message,* 97.

43 Sanneh, *Translating the Message,* 149, 162-3.

44 Robert D. Woodberry, "The Missionary Roots of Liberal Democracy," *American Political Science Review,* Vol. 106, No. 2, May 2012, pp. 244-274. Quotes p. 244, 245.

45 de Hamel, *The Book,* 283-286; William Carey, British missionary, *Encyclopedia Britannica,* https://www.britannica.com/biography/William-Carey, accessed 1 July 2016.

46 Eugene A. Nida, "Principles of Correspondence," in *The Translation Studies Reader,* ed. Lawrence Venuti (NY: Routledge, 2004), 153.

47 Philip A. Noss, "A History of Bible Translation: Introduction and Overview," in *A History of Bible Translation,* ed. Philip A. Noss (Rome: Edizioni di Storia e Letteratura, 2007), 23.

48 Burke, "The First Versions," 73.

49 H.J. Haskell, *This was Cicero* (New York: Alfred A. Knopf, 1964), 300–301; Elizabeth Rawson, *Cicero, A Portrait* (London: Penguin Books Ltd., 1975), 303.

50 Michael Grant, "Introduction" to Cicero, *Selected Works,* trans. Michael Grant (London: Penguin Books, 1971), 24.

51 Jinbachian, "The Septuagint to the Vernaculars," 31.

52 Jinbachian, "The Septuagint to the Vernaculars," 44, who cites the Babylonian Talmud, *Kiddushin* 49a, and Tosephta, *Megillah* 4(3):41.

53 Gordon Campbell, *Bible: The Story of the King James Version 1611-2011* (Oxford, UK: Oxford University Press, 2010), 81.

54 As any Greek-English lexicon will show. Cf. Ethelbert W. Bullinger, *A Critical Lexicon and Concordance to the English and Greek New Testament* (Grand Rapids, MI: Zondervan, 1975), 151.

55 As any Greek-English lexicon will show. *The New Testament Greek-English Dictionary, Vol. 11* (Springfield, MO: The Complete Biblical Library, 1990), 525, 527.

56 *The New Testament Greek-English Dictionary Vol. 16* (Springfield, MO: The Complete Biblical Library, 1990), 236.

57 *The NT Gr.-Eng. Dict. Vol. VI,* 236.

58 Bullinger, *Lexicon,* 150.

59 Grant R. Osborne, *The Hermeneutical Spiral: A Comprehensive Introduction to Biblical Interpretation* (Downers Grove: InterVarsity Press, 1991), 72.

60 Osborne, *The Hermeneutical Spiral,* 75.

61 D.A. Carson, *Exegetical Fallacies* (Cumbria, UK: Paternoster; Grand Rapids, MI: Baker Books, 1996), 36.

[62] *The NIV Study Bible, 10th Anniversary Edition*, ed. Kenneth Barker (Grand Rapids, MI: Zondervan, 1995), 1925.

[63] Osborne, *The Hermeneutical Spiral*, 72.

[64] Anthony Pym, "On the Historical Epistemologies of Bible Translating," in *A History of Bible Translation*, ed. Philip A. Noss (Rome: Edizioni di Storia e Letteratura, 2007), 196-197.

[65] Campbell, *Bible*, 65-66.

[66] de Hamel, *The Book*, 16, 55.

[67] With spaces and punctuation, the illustration reads, "A sentence would look something like this except the letters were handwritten so they were not uniform. The next sentence would start without a break, and so on and so on."

[68] Lynne Truss, *Eats, Shoots and Leaves: The Zero Tolerance Approach to Punctuation* (New York, NY: Penguin, 2006), 7.

[69] Truss, *Eats, Shoots and Leaves*, 9.

[70] English has four cases, but that fact is not commonly known or taught because it makes no practical difference. Except for personal pronouns (*he* becomes *his* or *him*, etc.) and possessives (*car* becomes *car's*, etc.), there are only one or two words (like *who* and *whom*) where spelling changes based on the case of the words.

[71] Hiebert, *Missiological Implications*, xiii.

[72] See Cornelius Augustijn, *Erasmus: His Life, Work and Influence*, trans. J.C. Grayson (Toronto: University of Toronto, 1991).

[73] J.I. Packer and O.R. Johnston, "Historical and Theological Introduction, Erasmus to 1517," in Martin Luther, *The Bondage of the Will*, trans. J.I. Packer and O.R. Johnston (Grand Rapids, MI: Baker Academic, 2012), 13. Originally published in 1957, Cambridge, UK: James Clark & Co; Westwood, NJ: Revell.

[74] Packer and Johnston, "Introduction," 14.

[75] Packer and Johnston, "Introduction," 14.

[76] Packer and Johnston, "Introduction," 15.

[77] Packer and Johnston, "Introduction," 15.

[78] "Epistle 337" in *Collected Works of Erasmus Vol. 3,* trans. R.A.B. Mynors and D.F.S. Thomson; annotated by Wallace K. Ferguson (Toronto: University of Toronto Press, 1976), 134.

[79] "Epistle 273," *Collected Works of Erasmus Vol. 2*, 253.

[80] Most of the manuscripts Erasmus had available were later Byzantine manuscripts, "selected more for convenience than for textual supremacy." de. Hamel, 226. For more evidence that he used the oldest manuscripts the least, see: Bruce Metzger, *The Text of the New Testament. Its Transmission, Corruption, and Restoration* (Oxford University Press, 1992), 102; Paul Arblaster, Gergely Juhász, Guido Latré , eds., *Tyndale's Testament* (Turnhout, Belgium: Brepols, 2002), 28.

[81] de Hamel, *The Book*, 226. "The New Testament volume of the Complutensian Polyglot was already printed, but it was still in its loose sheets in storage in Alcalá and it was not yet published or available for study."

[82] Eric W. Gritsch, "Luther as Bible Translator," *The Cambridge Companion to Martin Luther*, ed. Donald K. McKim (Cambridge, UK: Cambridge University Press, 2003), 63; Campbell, *Bible*, 70.

[83] de Hamel, *The Book*, 226.

[84] Ellingworth, "From Martin Luther," 110; Gritsch, "Luther as Bible Translator," 62.

[85] For Luther's New Testament, the original texts on which his translation was based, was Erasmus' 1516 bilingual Greek and Latin New Testament. See Ellingworth, "From Martin Luther," 110.

[86] Hans Volz, "German," *The Cambridge History of the Bible: Vol. 3 The West from the Reformation to the Present Day*, ed. S.L. Greenslade (Oxford, UK: Oxford University Press, 2001), 94.

[87] de Hamel, *The Book*, 229-230.

[88] Ellingworth, "From Martin Luther," 110-111; Gritsch, "Luther as Bible Translator," 63.

[89] Viggo Hjørnager Pederson and Per Qvale, "Danish and Norwegian Traditions," *Routledge Encyclopedia of Translation Studies,* ed. Mona Baker and Kirsten Malmkjaer (London and New York: Routledge, 1998), 385.

[90] Ellingworth, "From Martin Luther," 112.

[91] "Johann Ernst Glück," University of Texas Linguistics Research Center, https://lrc.la.utexas.edu/eieol/litol/100, accessed 8 July 2016.

[92] Ellingworth, "From Martin Luther," 125.

[93] "Glück," UT Linguistics Research Center.

[94] "Glück," UT Linguistics Research Center; Lindsey Hughes, "Catherine I of Russia, Consort to Peter the Great". In Clarissa Campbell Orr, ed. *Queenship in Europe 1660-1815: The Role of the Consort* (Cambridge, UK: Cambridge University Press, 2004), 131-154.

[95] Ellingworth, "From Martin Luther," 124.

[96] According to Salla Korpela, April 2012, "Religion in Finland," http://finland.fi/life-society/finnish-church-aims-to-be-down-to-earth/, accessed 16 July 2016.

[97] Ellingworth, "From Martin Luther," 122.

[98] Ellingworth, "From Martin Luther," 122.

[99] Ellingworth, "From Martin Luther," 119.

[100] de Hamel, *The Book,* 230.

[101] Roland H. Bainton, *Here I Stand: A Life of Martin Luther* (New York: Mentor, 1955), 261. Carter Lindberg, ed., *The European Reformations Sourcebook, 2nd Ed.* (West Sussex, UK: John Wiley & Sons, Ltd., 2014), 49; Michael A. Mullett, *Martin Luther* (London: Routledge, 2004), 148-150; Ellingworth, "From Martin Luther," 316; Pym, "Historical Epistemologies," 203; Derek Wilson, *Out of the Storm: The Life and Legacy of Martin Luther* (London: Hutchinson, 2007), 185.

[102] Ganoczy, "Calvin's Life," 5.

[103] Ganoczy, "Calvin's Life," 6.

[104] The Holy Roman Empire was made up of what is now Austria, Belgium, Croatia, Czech Republic, France, Germany, Italy, Liechtenstein, Luxembourg, Monaco, the Netherlands, Poland, Slovenia, and Switzerland.

[105] "Holy Roman Empire," *Encyclopedia Britannica Online*, https://www.britannica.com/place/Holy-Roman-Empire/Empire-and-papacy, accessed 8 July 2016; "History of The Holy Roman Empire," historyworld.net, http://www.historyworld.net/wrldhis/plaintexthistories.asp?historyid=aa35, accessed 8 July 2016; Lonnie R. Johnson, *Central Europe: Enemies, Neighbors, Friends* (Oxford, UK: Oxford University Press, 1996), 23.

[106] Ellingworth, "From Martin Luther," 114; de Hamel, *The Book,* 240.

[107] Catholic Encyclopedia, http://www.newadvent.org/cathen/02091a.htm, accessed 31 Oct 2016, citing Thomas Netter Waldensis, *Doctrinale*, Book I, Ch. 34, para. 5.

[108] Mary Dove, "Wyclif and the English Bible," in *A Companion to John Wyclif: Late Medieval Theologian*, ed. Ian Christopher Levy (Leiden, UK; Boston, MA: Brill, 2006), 365.

[109] See, for example, Martin Luther's Preface to Jan Hus, *Letters of John Huss Written During His Exile and Imprisonment*, ed. François Paul Émile Boisnormand de Bonnechose, trans. Campbell Mackenzie (Edinburgh: William Whyte & Co., 1846).

[110] David Daniell, *William Tyndale: A Biography* (London and New Haven, CT: Yale University Press, 1994), 18.

[111] Robert Demaus and Richard Lovett, *William Tindale: A Biography* (St. Paul's Churchyard, UK: The Religions Tract Society, 1904), 86; Daniell, *Tyndale*, 79.

[112] L. Franklin Gruber, *The Truth About the So-Called "Luther's Testament in English," Tyndale's New Testament* (St. Paul, MN: E. Mussgang, 1917), 26.

[113] Henry W. Hoare, *The Evolution of the English Bible: A Historical Sketch of the Successive Versions from 1382 to 1885*, 2nd ed. (London: John Murray; New York: E.P. Dutton & Co., 1902), 140. Hoare's statement is confirmed by Daniell, *Tyndale*, 267, quoting Sir Thomas More, from *The Complete Works of Sir Thomas More, Book VI* (London and New Haven, CT: Yale University Press, 1969), 28.

[114] Hoare, *English Bible*, 122.

[115] Gruber, *The Truth*, 22.

[116] Daniell, *Tyndale*, 112.

[117] de Hamel, *The Book*, 243; Michael Farris, *From Tyndale to Madison: How the Death of an English Martyr Led to the American Bill of Rights* (Nashville, TN : Broadman & Holman, 2007), 37.

[118] Campbell, *Bible*, 18.

[119] Campbell, *Bible*, 18.

[120] Campbell, *Bible*, 22.

[121] David Daniell, *The Bible in English: Its History and Influence* (New Haven, Conn: Yale University Press, 2003), 277.

[122] Daniell, *The Bible*, (2003), 304.

[123] Daniell, *The Bible*, (2003), 292.

[124] Campbell, *Bible*, 25.

[125] Campbell, *Bible*, 28; Daniell, *The Bible*, (2003), 339.

[126] Campbell, *Bible*, 27.

[127] Campbell, *Bible*, 30.

[128] Daniell, *The Bible*, (2003), 358.

[129] Daniell, *The Bible*, (2003), 362-366.

[130] Ellingworth, "From Martin Luther," 124.

[131] Campbell, *Bible*, 35.

[132] Campbell, *Bible*, 35.

[133] Brian Moynahan, *William Tyndale: If God Spare my Life* (London: Abacus, 2003), 1-2. See also *Naomi Tadmor, The Social Universe of the English Bible: Scripture, Society, and Culture in Early Modern England* (Cambridge: Cambridge University Press, 2010), 16. Both authors cite John Nielson and Royal Skousen, "How Much of the King James Bible is William Tyndale's? An Estimation Based on Sampling", *Reformation* **3**: (1998), 49-74.

[134] Joan Bridgman, (2000), "Tyndale's New Testament", *Contemporary Review* 277 (1619): 342-346.

[135] Gruber, *The Truth*, 68.

[136] William Cunningham, *The Reformers & the Theology of the Reformation* (London: Banner of Truth, 1967), 109; James, *Peter Martyr Vermigli and Predestination*, 30; Trueman, *Luther's Legacy*, 69.

[137] Plass, *What Luther Says*, Selection 1348, p. 456.

[138] Calvin, *Institutes*, Book III, Ch. 21, para. 5, p. 568.

[139] Campbell, *Bible*, 84-85.

[140] Pym, "Historical Epistemologies," 195-196.

[141] Berkeley and Alvera Mickelsen, "The 'Head' of the Epistles," *Christianity Today* 25/4 (Feb. 20, 1981), 20-23.

[142] Carson, *Exegetical Fallacies,* 37.

[143] Wayne A. Grudem, *Countering the Claims of Evangelical Feminism* (Sisters, OR: Multnomah Publishers, 2006), 122-123. See also Grudem's extensive research on this subject in Wayne A. Grudem, *Evangelical Feminism & Biblical Truth : An Analysis of More Than One Hundred Disputed Questions* (Sisters, OR: Multnomah Publishers, 2004), 202, and Appendix 3, 544-551; John Piper and Wayne Grudem, ed., *Recovering Biblical Manhood and Womanhood: A Response to Evangelical Feminism* (Wheaton, IL: Crossway, 2006), 424-425; and Wayne A. Grudem, *Biblical Foundations for Manhood And Womanhood* (Wheaton, IL: Crossway Books, 2002), 145-202.

[144] Carson, *Exegetical Fallacies,* 36-38.

[145] *The New Testament Greek-English Dictionary Vol. 16,* 256.

[146] Joseph H. Thayer, *Thayer's Greek-English Lexicon of the New Testament* (Grand Rapids, MI: Baker Book House, 1977), 615.

Chapter 6
Ephesians 1 and Romans 8-10

The notion that we read the New Testament exactly as the early Christians did, without any weight of tradition coloring our interpretation, is an illusion. It is also a dangerous illusion, for it tends to absolutize our interpretation, confusing it with the Word of God.
– Justo L. Gonzalez[1]

In Chapter 2, we looked at worldviews and culture, and how they affect our thinking. It was my developing understanding of those things while I was in seminary that changed my views about predestination. I was working on a degree in intercultural studies, in preparation for working cross-culturally. Since the educational institution was a seminary, everybody there studied theology, but those of us who were not majoring in theology were also studying "practical" things like worldviews and how they affect cross-cultural communication. One of the things I kept seeing was the difference in the worldviews of the people who were walking the earth when Jesus did, and those in our times, as well as those who have come and gone in the centuries between.

Students who study hermeneutics (Bible interpretation) are taught that in order to really understand the message the writer intended, we must understand the cultural context in which the original message was sent. When that is not done, we accuse people of "taking a verse out of context," and by that, we are implying that they are using a verse to teach something (or justify something) that was not what the original writer intended. A simple illustration was the country preacher talking about "putting your hand to the plow" to make a straight furrow. A more important one was the acquaintance who uses certain verses to insist that baptism is necessary for salvation.

In my cross-cultural communication classes, I learned that "messages are sent, meaning is received." Both halves of that statement are saying the same thing – that the worldviews of the individuals determine both the message sent, and the way the message is received (its meaning). As I was studying the apostle Paul's letter to the Ephesians, I realized for the first time how really important that is. Years earlier I had learned from a pastor that if you really want to understand a book of the Bible, then read it every day for a month, and that was what I was doing with Ephesians. As I read and re-read the book, I thought I was starting to see the whole argument Paul was making. Part of that argument, I discovered in chapter 2, verses 11-22, was that God was making one new thing out of two former ones.

Notice a couple of distinct points Paul makes in this passage.

1. There used to be two groups: those near, and those far away. From Paul's descriptions, it seems obvious beyond debate that those two groups were (1) the Jews – Israel, the "circumcised," those near, those included in the covenants of the promise, those with hope and with God in the world, those who had the law with its commandments and regulations, God's people; and (2) the

Gentiles – described as Gentiles by birth, the "uncircumcised," those separated from the messiah, excluded from citizenship in Israel, foreigners to the covenants of the promise, without hope and without God in the world, those who were far away, foreigners and aliens to God's people.

2. Now those two groups have been made into one new group, called "one new man" in v. 15, "this one body" in v. 16, "God's household" in v. 19, "a holy temple" in v. 21, and "a dwelling in which God lives" in v. 22. I think it is safe to say, and consistent with other Scripture, that this new group is the church.

The reason this is important is because the first chapter of Ephesians is one of two places in the New Testament that is often understood to teach "predestination of individuals for salvation." In the first 12 verses of that chapter, Paul makes such statements as these: "he chose us in him before the creation of the world" (Eph 1:4); "he predestined us to be adopted as his sons through Jesus Christ" (1:5); "in him we were also chosen, having been predestined according to the plan of him who works out everything in conformity with the purpose of his will" (1:11). Then in 1:13, Paul says, "And you also were included in Christ when you heard the word of truth, the gospel of salvation." The problem is, in Ephesians 1, Paul never really says who "us" and "we" are, or who "you" are. He just says "we" and "us" have been chosen and predestined, and "you" have been included in Christ.

From looking at Ephesians 2, however, we can see that Paul clearly identifies "you" as the Gentiles (2:11). He does that again in 3:1, then says that he has been called to clear up the mystery of the ages, which he explains in 3:6, "This mystery is that through the gospel the Gentiles are heirs together with Israel, members together of one body, and sharers together in the promise in Christ Jesus."

I realized in my study that it was clear who "you" were, but it was still not clear who "we" were in chapter 1. I suspected it was the Jews, since chapter 2 makes it so clear that God was making one out of two, and the two were the Jews and the Gentiles. Still, chapter 1 does not specify who "we" were, so I looked in the rest of the book for clarity. As I studied, I also realized another thing that has been helpful many times since then, and that is, in order to understand Paul's letters well, you have to pay *really* close attention to his use of pronouns. At the human level, Paul was nobody's fool, and at the spiritual level, we assume that he was inspired by the Holy Spirit in his writing. That presupposes no mistakes in the original texts. As I mentioned earlier (in Chapter 4), when Bible translators have been casual with Paul's pronouns, the result is that verses have been given completely different meanings from what they would have had if the proper pronouns had been used.[2]

Since both "we" and "you" are plural pronouns,[3] and since Paul was a communal/collectivist thinker, I asked myself what groups were possible within the context Paul was writing from. He had already cleared up the "you" question (they were clearly the Gentiles), so I was looking for groups of which Paul himself was a member, since he called the group "we," and it also had to be a group which his audience would have automatically connected Paul with, since he did not actually state it. Paul was a Roman citizen (Acts 16:38), a Jew, a Pharisee, a member of the tribe of Benjamin (Phil 3:5), and a believer and follower of Jesus Christ. His readers might have known all of that, but they might not. His "we" could not have meant believers, because Paul was writing to other believers, so both he and those he was writing to were in that same group together. It's also clear that he was contrasting the "we" against "you, the Gentiles." Logically, then, "we" had to be a group of which Paul was a member, but who were not Gentiles. That leaves a limited number of options. "We" could not mean Roman citizens, because most of the Gentiles were also Roman citizens, nor could "we" mean the sect of the Pharisees, of which Paul was a member, because that was not a direct contrast to being a Gentile. So I concluded that "we" logically has to be the Jews.

When I realized what I had just discovered, I went back to reading the book over and over, but now with a new understanding – "we" are the Jews, and "you" are the Gentiles. That new understanding works very well until you get to about chapter 3 and verse 13, when in Paul's mind, apparently, he had completed the task of making the two into one new unit, so he stops using the words to refer to the two ethnic groups, and starts using them to simply refer to "you, the ones to whom I am writing," and "we, the ones in whom Christ is at work." This change in focus is typical Paul, in that the early parts of his letters often lay a theological base, then the later parts show the practical implications it has.

The importance of what I had discovered cannot be overstated, because of the impact it has on the doctrine of "predestination of individuals for salvation."

I asked myself why Paul would have written this book in such a vague way that it has to be figured out, instead of in a way that would be obvious at even a casual reading. It turns out that, to his original audience, it *would* have been obvious at even a casual reading. We are hindered in our understanding because of translation issues, and those translation issues lead to one of the most basic ideas – a completely wrong idea, I contend – on which Calvinism is based.

Ephesians 1

Watch what this understanding of Paul's pronouns does to the first part of Ephesians. I will edit it to show what I see when I read it, and you, like the Bereans in Acts 17:11, should examine the Scriptures to see if what I say is true. Keep in mind that Paul was a Jew, writing in Greek. That's important to remember, so I won't be accused of taking liberties with the Scripture when I change the word "Christ" to read "messiah." To Paul, as a Jew, Jesus was not "Jesus Christ," but "Jesus, the messiah," or "Jesus, the anointed one." However, when he wrote, he was writing in Greek, so he translated the word "messiah" into Greek, and it came out as "Jesus Christ." Keep in mind, also, that "messages are sent, but meaning is received." What Paul was sending was coming from a first century Jew, with all the assumptions and meanings that would have been attached to that cultural perspective, and what was being received would have been read through the same sort of assumptions in the minds of the original readers. Since nobody was expecting a messiah but the Jews, when you substitute the word "messiah" for the word "Christ," Paul's Jewishness becomes *so* clear, that it explains why he felt no need to specifically state who he meant by "we."

Eph 1:1-14 (My rendering)

[1] From: Paul, a messenger sent out by the messiah, Jesus, according to the will of God,

To: The saints in Asia (see note[4]), those faithful to the messiah, Jesus:

[2] Grace and peace to you from God our Father and the Lord Jesus, the messiah.

[3] Praise be to the God and Father of our Lord Jesus, the messiah, who has blessed us (my people, the group I am a part of but you are not – the Jews), in the heavenly realms with every spiritual blessing in the messiah. [4] For he chose us (the Jews), in him before the creation of the world to be holy and blameless in his sight. In love [5] he predestined us (the Jews) to be adopted as his sons through Jesus, the messiah, in accordance with his pleasure and will— [6] to the praise of his glorious grace (undeserved favor), which he has freely given us (the Jews) in the One he loves.

[7] In him we (the Jews) have redemption through his blood, the forgiveness of sins, in accordance with the riches of God's grace [8] that he lavished on us (the Jews) with all wisdom and understanding (through the symbols and sacrifices of the Jewish law). [9] And he made known to us (the Jews) the mystery of

his will according to his good pleasure (through the law and the prophets), which he purposed [10] to be put into effect in the messiah, when the times will have reached their fulfillment – to bring all things in heaven and on earth together under one head, even the messiah.

[11] In him, we (the Jews) were also chosen, having been predestined according to the plan of him who works out everything in conformity with the purpose of his will, [12] in order that we (the Jews), who were the first to hope in the messiah, might be for the praise of his glory (by being the means through which he revealed himself to the nations).

[13] And you (Gentiles) also were included in the messiah when you heard the word of truth, the gospel of your salvation. Having believed, you were marked in him with a seal, the promised Holy Spirit, [14] who is a deposit guaranteeing our inheritance until the redemption of those who are God's possession – to the praise of his glory.

Notice that when the word "Christ" is changed to the word "messiah," the whole passage suddenly becomes totally Jewish. The Jews were the only ones expecting a messiah. They were the only ones given the law and the prophets. To the original audience, Paul's introductory argument makes perfect sense in light of the whole Old Testament story, and lays a logical foundation for what he is going to say next. The Jews, chosen before the creation of the world to be blessed in order to be a blessing (Gen 12:2-3), and on whom the grace of God had been lavished (his unmerited favor), were the ones given the first hope, through the law and later through the prophets, of a Redeemer – the Messiah, the Anointed One – who by redeeming them, would bring

WHEN THE WORD "CHRIST" IS CHANGED TO THE WORD "MESSIAH," THE WHOLE PASSAGE SUDDENLY BECOMES TOTALLY JEWISH

praise to his glory by removing the sin barrier and restoring fellowship with God. Now, Paul says in 1:13, you Gentiles have been included in the promise as well, and when you believe, you are marked with a seal, the Holy Spirit – like earnest money on a pending contract, or an engagement ring before the permanence of the marriage – as a guarantee that you will also receive what you have been promised – the complete and final redemption with all the other people throughout the ages who belong to the eternal God.

The importance of what this means cannot be overstated. There are no chosen, predestined individuals in Ephesians 1. Only groups. "We" are the Jews, chosen before the foundation of the earth, and "you" are the Gentiles, included when you believed.

Paul then goes on in the next two chapters, to make clear what he started in chapter 1 – to show the making of one group out of two. Earlier, we discussed the way in which the early church reinterpreted itself over time (in Chapter 3). We saw the church at Antioch reinterpreting itself from being a Jewish movement that also included Gentiles (Acts 11ff), to "the church" made up of "Christians" in which Jews and Gentiles had equal status and there was no obligation to keep the Jewish law. In the process, as Lamin Sanneh points out, the Gentile culture was *destigmatized* while the Jewish culture was *relativized*. "Thus it was that the two subjects, the Judaic and the Gentile, became closely intertwined in the Christian dispensation, both crucial to the formative image of the new religion."[5] That is what Luke described in Acts. Now, in Ephesians, Paul is showing that that was God's exact intention: "the mystery of Christ, which was not made known to men in other generations . . . is that through the gospel the Gentiles are heirs together with Israel, members together of one body, and sharers together in the promise in Christ Jesus" (Eph 3:4-6).

That's Paul's argument. As he continues to lay that foundation, he shows that salvation is a gift of grace, not of works, but for a purpose that includes works (Eph 2:8-10). Then he builds on that foundation. With the gift comes the responsibility to "walk" in such a way that God's plan is not hindered, but implemented – in unity, with appropriate submission and leadership, using the spiritual armor provided by God, and so on.

Paul lays the historical and theological foundation in chapter 1 for everything else he will say later in the book. For the first two and a half chapters, he is making it very clear that even though the Jews were the chosen ones, God's plan includes the Gentiles, and Jesus has cleared all the barriers away to make that possible.

If that's Paul's argument, then why do so many people today read "individual predestination for salvation" into Ephesians chapter 1, when Paul is talking about groups? I see two explanations for why Paul's message has been obscured for later readers, and they are what I have been describing in previous chapters.

The first lies in the worldviews of the people reading Paul's writings. As we have already established, there is no evidence that individual predestination was ever considered at all for over four centuries after Paul wrote the letter, and it was not accepted in any real sense for almost 15 centuries. By the time the new understanding was accepted, the worldview of those reading the material had changed from being generally "communal" to generally "individualistic." A communal thinker would automatically see groups in Paul's writings, and an individualistic thinker would see individuals. So when Paul writes in Ephesians 1:3, "Praise be to the God and Father of our Lord Jesus, the messiah, who has blessed us in the heavenly realms with every spiritual blessing in the messiah," the communal thinker would ask, "What group is 'us' that has been so blessed? What group has been blessed in the messiah?" To the communal thinker of the first century, the answer is obvious – the Jews. But fifteen centuries later, the individualistic thinker doesn't even need to ask such questions, because the answer is already clear – "we," as individuals, have been blessed in the heavenly realms with every spiritual blessing in Christ. Not in the messiah, but in Christ.

That's the second explanation – the use of the word "Christ" instead of the word "messiah." By the 16th century, as today, the word "Christ" did not clearly mean "the messiah," or "the anointed one," as it did to the first century Gentile reading Paul's letter. Over time, and with changing languages, it had come to essentially be the last name of Jesus, or at least to add formality to the name of Jesus. He has become "Jesus," the man; "Jesus Christ," the savior; the "Lord Jesus," God; and the "Lord Jesus Christ," both God and savior. But to the first century reader, he would have been "Jesus," the man; "Jesus Christ," the Jewish messiah; the "Lord Jesus," the divine one, to the Gentiles; and the "Lord Jesus Christ," the man who was both divine to the Gentiles and messiah to the Jews.

As we have already considered, it is easy to see the progression in the gospels and Acts as the writers alter the way Jesus is described. Until Acts 11:17, he is generally called "Lord" by his disciples, and "Jesus" or "Jesus the messiah" by the writers, and very rarely, the "Lord Jesus." Those few exceptions when the Jews call him "Lord Jesus," would have been heard as the "sovereign authority, Jesus," closer to "Jesus the master" than divine. That changes in Acts 11:17, when Luke makes it clear that for the benefit of the Gentiles, Jesus is called the "Lord Jesus" to connect with the way they talked about their gods. To the Gentiles, when they heard "Lord Jesus," they heard "the divine Jesus," closer to "God Jesus" than just "Jesus the master" that the Jews heard. The Jews thought of him as "Jesus the messiah," the promised redeemer; the Gentiles thought of him as the "Lord Jesus," God of the universe. Often, both are brought together, and he is called the "Lord Jesus Christ."

For those of us in the world of Christian missions, who deal with cross cultural communication and different languages, it is obvious that John Calvin was a tightly bound captive of the culture of his day. His education has been described as humanist classicism – based on the Greek classical thinking, and with understanding derived from human reasoning rather than spiritual discernment. In spite of his knowledge of Latin and Greek and theology, he viewed the world so differently from the first century Romans and Jews, that when he read the Bible, he could not even envision what they would have seen there.

Calvin quotes Ephesians 2:16, "That he might reconcile both into one body by the cross," then he explains it this way: "The nature of this mystery is to be learned from the first chapter to the Ephesians, where Paul, teaching that we were chosen in Christ, at the same time adds, that we obtained grace in him."[6] If the argument I have just outlined has any validity at all, then Calvin completely missed Paul's message in Ephesians. *Completely missed it.* To repeat, John Calvin viewed the world so differently from the first century Christians, that he could not even remotely envision what they saw when they read the writings of Paul.

> JOHN CALVIN VIEWED THE WORLD SO DIFFERENTLY FROM THE FIRST CENTURY CHRISTIANS, THAT HE COULD NOT EVEN REMOTELY ENVISION WHAT THEY SAW WHEN THEY READ THE WRITINGS OF PAUL

Calvin's sixteenth century, western European perspective affected his view of Ephesians, but it also affected his view of Romans. The whole argument for individual predestination for salvation rests in those two books. We have now seen that in Ephesians, Paul said nothing to his original audience about individual predestination for salvation. If he said nothing in Romans about it, then he said nothing at all about it, and there is no biblical basis for it.

So let's consider Romans.

Romans

This book is often said to be the Apostle Paul's *magnum opus*, his greatest work. Dr. Gordon Johnson, President Emeritus of Rio Grand Bible Institute in Edinburg, Texas, and a person I deeply respect, says, "The truths of Romans have challenged the greatest minds and have never been fathomed in centuries of exposition."[7] I once had a pastor who spent three years preaching through the book of Romans. That means he covered roughly three verses each Sunday. When he finished, I did not understand Romans any better than when he started. But while I was in seminary, I studied Romans the same way I studied Ephesians. I divided it into three sections and read each section every day for thirty days. By the time I had spent 90 days in Romans, I had an idea of what Paul's basic message was. Granted, the book is deep theologically. Maybe it's even unfathomable, as Johnson says, but if it is, why write it in the first place? Surely, Paul wanted his readers to understand his message. Surely, the Holy Spirit, prompting Paul to write, and guiding the process, wanted the readers to understand the message. Surely the original readers weren't all theologians with multiple PhDs. Surely there is a message there that the average reader can understand and benefit from.

Maybe, just maybe, there is. I believe that the pastor who spent three years scrutinizing every word in the book of Romans, retranslating every sentence, mulling over subtle innuendoes, and presenting his findings in weekly three-verse summaries, did both Paul and the Holy Spirit more of a disservice than a service. Paul did not write the book in weekly, three verse segments; he wrote it as a total unit. It has a starting point, an ending point, and supporting arguments between those two. I think Paul expected people to hear or read the book in one setting, and understand it. When pastors and theologians break the book up into smaller segments, they typically conclude that what Paul is using as supporting arguments for his larger argument, are major arguments themselves, maybe even his MAJOR arguments. From my viewpoint, they're not.

I think of the book as a bridge – you get on at one end, and you get off at the other end. The bridge has decking that connects those two ends. Along the way, the bridge has supports that hold it up. It's a long bridge, so it needs those intermediate supports. The supports are important, even critical to holding up the bridge, but they are not the bridge itself. An individual support can be examined by itself, but if it is, it will appear to be detached from the bridge, standing alone. That's fine. There is nothing wrong with a post standing alone in the middle of a river. But standing alone, the relationship to a bridge is no longer visible, and Paul did not construct a bunch of independent posts standing alone in a river. If we look at each support in even more detail, we will see that they are made up of individual pieces held together with nuts and bolts. Again, there is nothing wrong with examining the component parts of a support. But they, also, are not designed to stand alone. Paul connected them together to form supports, and he connected the supports together to form the bridge.

So what does the bridge look like?

Paul starts the book by greeting his audience and inviting them to join him on the bridge. Like them, we get on the bridge with the proclamation that there is good news of which Paul is not ashamed, the power of God for the salvation of everyone who believes. It starts by faith and ends by faith (1:16-17). We get off the bridge with the challenge to live in such a way that God is glorified (15:1-7), so that the Gentiles may glorify God (15:8ff), so that all nations might believe and obey him (16:26). That's the bridge. It starts with salvation for everyone who believes, and ends with all nations potentially believing and obeying God. That's the argument. Everything else is provided to support that argument.

Let's look at it in a little more detail, but without breaking it apart into three-verse segments – the nuts and bolts of the supports – and without spending three years to do it. In the next chapter, we will look at the plan of God for the ages, but in a very real sense, Paul does that here, in the book of Romans. I should point out that the references I show to reflect the points that Paul makes, are not as clearly separated as I show them to be. There is a lot of overlap and intermingling of the ideas as Paul develops his thoughts and connects the supporting arguments to each other and to the main argument. I hope it will become clear that Paul makes a clear distinction in this book between the way God deals with groups and individuals.

Summary of Romans

* Paul's premise statement: I am not ashamed of the good news, because it is the power of God to everyone who believes – to the Jew first, then for the Gentile. In the good news, a righteousness from God is revealed that is based on believing, from beginning to end (1:16-17). [From this point forward, over and over again, Paul hammers home the fact that despite the favored status of the Jews as God's chosen people – as a group – there is no difference in how God sees and treats the Jews as individuals, and how he sees and treats the Gentiles (see esp. 2:11).]

* There are entire groups of people who used to know the truth of God, but because they ignored it, even suppressed it, and lived for their selfish desires, they are now in complete spiritual darkness (1:18 - 1:32).

* Paul lays the foundation of one of his main supporting arguments – that all are under sin and therefore under judgment – by pointing out a universal tendency of people to hold others to a standard that we ourselves do not live up to (2:1 - 2:4). By doing so, Paul argues, we demonstrate that we are aware of a standard outside of ourselves, leaving us culpable, accountable to God, both Jew and Gentile alike. It is possible for people with no special revelation of God to have eternal life, by seeking noble things and living in a selfless manner (2:5 - 2:16). Paul returns to this point in chapter 10, to point out that it is not likely that there will be that spontaneous belief, without a messenger to point them to Jesus as the focal point of God's eternal plan. But here, in chapter 2, he says it's possible, through Jesus Christ.

* Being part of God's chosen ethnic group is not enough to please him, nor can we please God by obeying rules, but by genuinely believing in him and living in a way that is consistent with that belief (2:17 - 2:29). Paul's argument attacks the very idea that being part of the chosen group guarantees salvation.

* In case the point was missed in chapter 2, Paul rewords and repeats it in chapter 3: both Jews and Gentiles are equally under sin, and being part of God's chosen ethnic group did not make people righteous, nor did obeying rules. Instead, righteousness comes through believing in Jesus, the messiah. That righteousness is for all who believe, with no difference between the Jew or the Gentile, that is, between the chosen and the not chosen (3:1 - 3:30).

* In chapter 4, Abraham is used as an example to further reinforce Paul's argument that it is believing, not being chosen, that gains us righteousness before God. He shows that Abraham believed before he was circumcised, and that even now, he is the father of all who believe, whether they have been circumcised or not – that is, whether they are part of the chosen group, or not. Paul belabors this point, an indication of how important he considers it to be. Several different ways in chapter 4, he says that Abraham is the father of all who believe, regardless of whether or not they are Jews. Those who believe God, as Abraham did, are reconciled to God, and are given the righteousness of Jesus Christ (4:1 - 4:25).

* Then in chapter 5, he says the same thing again, a different way. We have peace with God, he says, and it's all by grace, a gift which leads to holiness and results in eternal life, and we obtain this gift simply through believing. He makes an extensive argument that sin entered the world through one man, and that one man's sin applies to every living human, but that the reversal of that effect has also been made possible by one man, and it also applies to every living human. A critical point is visible in the text: the

191

justification that brings life is "for all men," but the *gift of grace* overflows "to the many." Why is one universal, and the other not? Because of the argument Paul has already made – even though the justification that brings life is available to all, only those who believe become "children of Abraham" (5:1 - 5:21).

* Paul expands on this in chapter 6, showing the spiritual implications of believing. When the grace of God is accepted through believing, we are immersed in, placed under, the Anointed One, Jesus. In a spiritual sense, we have participated in his death, the death that God requires for sin (6:23). In the same way that we are immersed in Jesus, we are immersed in his death – it covers us. Jesus' death becomes the substitute for our own. This atonement sets us free from bondage both to sin and death. We are now free to serve righteousness (6:1 - 6:23).

* In chapter 7, Paul extends his argument to show that our immersion in Jesus, our atonement, also frees us from the bondage of the law. Now, we are free to follow the spirit of the law, rather than the letter of the law. Paul even makes the argument that as long as we are living in our human bodies, with its emotions and hormones and prior conditioning, we will break the letter of the law, even while we are loyal to the spirit of the law in our desires (7:1 - 7:25).

* However, even when our lives don't match our desires, we are not condemned because we are in Christ, set free from the law of sin and death. We no longer have to live under the control of our sinful nature. We can live according to our spirit, which wants to honor and serve God. Success is not guaranteed, though. Paul makes the argument that we contribute to the success of our own moral lives – we have the responsibility to no longer live according to our sinful nature, but to "put to death the misdeeds of the body." The Spirit of God leads us, Paul says, testifying with

our spirit that we are God's children, and if we are children, then we are heirs – heirs of God (8:1 - 8:17a) ...

* ... and co-heirs with Christ, if we are willing to co-share in his suffering, in order to co-share in his glory (character). For those who accept that responsibility, nothing can separate us from the love of God (8:17b - 8:39).

* In times past, God selected one specific ethnic group through which to demonstrate his love, and to be his messengers to those societies in spiritual darkness, but they did not do it. Instead, they concentrated on obeying God's rules themselves, rather than having a genuine attitude of love for God and love for other people. Again, Paul emphasizes his message that being in the chosen group does not make a person a child of God, or a child of Abraham. To be a child of Abraham, all that is required is to genuinely believe the truth about Jesus, and to openly follow him as Lord. And again, Paul makes it clear that there is no difference in the Jew and the Gentile – every individual who calls on the name of the Lord will be saved. It has nothing to do with being in the chosen group (9:1 - 10:13).

* Then Paul asks, reaching back into chapters 1 and 2 to address those who do not have access to the word of God, "How can these people know of God's love for them and his plan to reconcile humanity to himself, unless someone tells them?" (10:14-15).

* Israel had the good news, but many of them did not believe it, and as a nation, they failed to pass it along to others. As a result, God has turned his attention away from using them as his means of revealing himself to others, to using the Gentiles to do it. Those of us who have heard the message of God's love and who have responded to it, have experienced the mercy of God. This is not related to being among the chosen, because the chosen have been set aside due to their unbelief, and those who have believed have

become the ones God is using (10:16 - 11:36).

* Therefore, in light of the entire argument Paul has just made about believing being necessary for salvation, and about the role that hearing plays in that process, he begs us, if we have experienced the mercy of God, to make ourselves totally available to God and change our way of thinking so that our focus is on eternal things rather than on temporary things. By doing this, we can experience God's perfect will (12:1-2). [This point marks the end of Paul's theological argument, and transitions into the practical application of it.]

* Being totally available to God and having a different focus in life will result in a sincere love for others that will be reflected in several ways:

  • We will live in humility within a community of other believers, neither independent nor dependent (12:3-21).

  • As much as we can, we will live in harmony with the local social and political system (13:1-7).

  • We will make sure that our actions do not promote failure in people weaker than ourselves (13:8 - 15:4).

* If we do these things, the work of God in our lives will reveal God to other people, and the good news of his plan to reconcile humanity to himself will spread, so that all nations might believe and obey him (15:5-13, 16:25-27).

That's it. That's the summary of the book. To revive our analogy, it's like a bridge, with a starting point and an ending point, and supporting structures that are connected with decking. The summary reveals the decking, making it distinct from the supporting structures. The decking is believing. Over and over, Paul uses it to tie the rest of the argument together. We get on the bridge with believing, we cross the entire bridge on believing, and we get off with believing. It is helpful to remember that there is only one word in Greek for the two English concepts of "faith" and "believing," so whichever one is used, it is part of the same structure.

I stated earlier that I could not accept that Paul expected his letter to be so deep that people had to study it for a lifetime to understand it. The social conditions of the time, and the last chapter of the book, support that position. One of the distinct possibilities for why Paul wrote the book in the first place, could be to attempt to ease tensions in the Roman church between Jews and Gentiles. In Acts 18:2, Luke documents that all the Jews were expelled from Rome, with the date usually thought to be between 49 and 51 C.E.[8] Unavoidably, with all the Jews gone, Gentiles would have had to fill the leadership vacuum in the churches, then when the Jews were later allowed to return, there could logically have been tension between the new leaders and those returning from exile. That could explain why Paul, writing after the Jews were allowed to return, goes to such lengths to say, "the Jew first, and also the Gentiles." He repeatedly emphasizes the Jews' chosenness as the people of God, then in the next breath removes any sense of privilege that might bring. Their chosenness should encourage the Gentiles to treat them with respect, and the fact that they gain no special status in God's eyes by being a Jew, should encourage them to interact with others in humility.

The last chapter supports my expectation that the essential message of the book could be understood easily. From the greetings Paul extends, it appears that there were at least three house churches in Rome. He sends greetings to several individuals, presumably in the house church to which Phoebe would deliver the letter, but also to two other groups of "brothers" and "saints" (16:14-15). If Paul was assuming that the letter would be taken to the other house churches and read, he must have assumed the hearers would understand what they heard.

The basic argument itself is not so deep – the depth comes with the way each supporting thought connects with the rest of Scripture.

When viewed from that perspective, Johnson is not exaggerating when he calls the book unfathomable – its depths cannot be fully plumbed. But the basic message is not unfathomable. As already stated, it starts with salvation for everyone who believes, and ends with the goal of all nations believing and obeying God. Those two points alone, with their inclusivity and the fact that they are based on believing rather than predestination, should cause us to question Calvinism, with its exclusivity and divine determinism. If the starting and ending points are inclusive, it stands to reason that the arguments Paul uses to support that inclusivity, will themselves be inclusive. As it turns out, when they are viewed through the lenses of Paul's original readers, they are. Let's consider what Paul's initial audience would have seen.

Predestination in Romans

There are two basic passages in Romans that are problematic in the debate over divine determinism. They are Romans 8:28-30, and 9:10-24. Romans 8:28-30 says:

> And we know that in all things God works for the good of those who love him, who have been called according to his purpose. For those God foreknew he also predestined to be conformed to the likeness of his Son, that he might be the firstborn among many brothers. And those he predestined, he also called; those he called, he also justified; those he justified, he also glorified.

The good Calvinist reads "predestination of individuals for salvation" into those verses. Let's connect these verses to some others to see if another, better understanding is possible. First, I find it helpful to recognize a hierarchy among believers, not in terms of salvation, but in terms of usefulness to God. All of us know people who appear to be true believers, but who do little or nothing to actually further the kingdom of God. If we are honest, we know that we ourselves are not consistent in how useful we are to God. We can identify times in our own lives that reflect the situation Paul described in Romans 7:18ff: "I have the desire to do what is good, but I cannot carry it out. For what I do is not the good I want to do; no, the evil I do not want to do – this I keep on doing." By contrast to those who accept the gift but don't pass it along, it seems that most of the work of the kingdom of God is done by a very small percentage of those who call themselves Christians. This observation is supported by both the parable of the sower, and the ending of the book of the Revelation, when John is describing the way things will function for eternity in heaven.

In the parable of the sower (Matt 13:3-23; Mark 4:2-25; Luke 8:4-18), Jesus told a story to a large group of people, then left without explaining it. His disciples approached him later and asked for an explanation. Jesus said the parable makes a double comparison – first, between the saved and unsaved, and then between the saved who do not bear fruit, and those who do. Seed is sown in four different soils. The seed represents the word of God, and the soil represents the hearts of people. In the first soil, the seed is snatched away by the birds, representing Satan, so that the person does not believe and be saved. In each of the other three soils, the seeds produce life – the word of God produces a new life spiritually. In the three soils in which life is produced, Jesus makes a comparison between two that do not produce fruit, and the one that does. Jesus makes two points through this second comparison – first, that the person who really takes the word of God to heart, who really understands the implications of eternal life, will respond by passing it along. The passing along is what produces fruit. Second, Jesus makes the point that not all believers produce fruit. Some are saved, but then attend a dead church or no church at all, so there is never enough spiritual nourishment to stimulate growth, so they never produce fruit. Others have plenty of nourishment, but are distracted by the cares of this world, so they never put their efforts into eternal things.

It is noteworthy that in two of the Gospels (Mark and Luke), the parable of the sower is followed immediately by Jesus' challenge not to hide the light of our candle. That challenge is usually separated in the Bible text from the parable of the sower by an artificial heading, *A Lamp on a Stand* or something similar, but it is not a separate passage – it is the practical application of the parable. Letting our light shine is an illustration of passing along our understanding, which is what produces fruit. This is consistent with Paul's challenge in Romans 12:1-2, where he says that if we are going to know the perfect will of God, it requires that we make ourselves totally available (presenting our bodies as living sacrifices) and end our conformity to the world (which focuses on earthly things, which is what happens in the third soil). For Paul to make such a challenge implies that not every believer automatically takes up the mantle and gets involved in the work of the kingdom, which is exactly what Jesus says in the parable of the sower.

LETTING OUR LIGHT SHINE IS AN ILLUSTRATION OF PASSING ALONG OUR UNDERSTANDING, WHICH IS WHAT PRODUCES FRUIT

The last chapters of the Revelation support this as well. When God has vanquished his enemies, we are presented with the new heaven and new earth, and the new Jerusalem, in which God will dwell with his people for eternity (Rev 21). The "nations" will live in that new city (21:24-26) and the servants of God will reign with him for ever and ever (22:3-5). We will deal with this in more detail in the next chapter, but for now, it simply supports the idea that in heaven, there will be two major groups of believers – the nations, and those servants who will reign with God for eternity. What separates them is their faithfulness, their fruitfulness, in this life.

Remember when we changed the position of the comma in Romans 8:17? I'm convinced that that verse is crucial to understanding everything Paul writes in the rest of chapter 8 and in chapter 9. It is his way of making the distinction we just made – between the nations, and the faithful servants of God. Paul calls the two groups "children who are the heirs of God," and "those who are co-heirs with Christ because they co-suffer with him in order to have co-glory with him." (The three uses of the "co" prefix is consistent with the original Greek construction.) This verse marks a turning point in the book. Before it, Paul has been talking primarily to the children of God, the heirs of eternal life, who will be among the nations in eternity. But now, he turns his attention to the co-heirs who co-suffer and will have co-glory. He turns his attention to those faithful servants of God who will rule with him for eternity, who are the fruit bearers in this life.[9]

With this in mind, let's return to Romans 8:28-30, and consider what the text actually says, not what it is often assumed to say. To begin with, it is worthy of note that salvation is never mentioned. We see God at work in all things for the good of those *who love him* – and we can stop there for another point of clarification.

If we consider 1 John 2:15, we can realistically conclude that love for the world and love for the Father are mutually exclusive. But love for the world and salvation are not mutually exclusive, as Jesus showed in the parable of the sower (the third soil). Armed with that insight, we can return to Romans 8:28 and suggest that God is not working all things for the good of all believers, but for those *who love him*. I suggest that those who love him are that select group of the faithful ones who produce fruit now, and who will reign with him for eternity. They have been called according to God's purpose. And what is God's purpose? It's the bridge. This passage is not a major point in Paul's argument – it is here simply to support the bridge. The bridge starts and ends with believing – it starts with the salvation of everyone who believes, and it ends with the goal of all nations believing and obeying him. That's God's purpose. God calls those he knows in advance will help push that agenda, then he works all things for their good, to enable their growth – that they be conformed to the image of his son. Jesus was not distracted by the cares of this life. Neither are his disciples, but most believers are. When they are, they do not look like Jesus – they are not conformed to the image of God's son.

Notice how our previous assumptions affect our understanding of a verse. "For those God foreknew he also predestined to be conformed to the likeness of his Son . . ." (Rom 8:29). If we have already been taught that these verses are talking about salvation, then we will understand "predestined" to mean *for salvation*. But if we keep the bridge in mind, and if we keep the concepts consistent within this passage, we will see that "predestined" does not refer to salvation, but to shaping events in the lives of those believers who have the potential to produce fruit.

Here's what I see when I read these verses: God looks at every person and evaluates their integrity and potential for faithfulness. This is Paul's expression of what Hanani the seer said to King Asa – "the eyes of the Lord range throughout the earth to strengthen those whose hearts are fully committed to him" (2 Chron 16:9). When God finds a person he can trust, that he knows in advance will be faithful, he starts rearranging events to facilitate the development of that person. When the time is right, he calls that person and starts arranging events to enable that person to answer the call – not to salvation, but to a life of producing fruit. The person may already be saved, but if not, at some point along the way, salvation will occur, as it did in the life of Paul. But salvation is not what the calling is to. The calling is to a life of fruitfulness.

This is exactly what Jesus said to his disciples: "You did not choose me, but I chose you and appointed you to go and bear fruit – fruit that will last" (John 15:16). This is one of the verses most commonly used to justify the idea that individuals are chosen for salvation. But Jesus did not choose his disciples for salvation – there is serious reason to doubt that Judas Iscariot was ever saved, and there is every reason to believe that all the other disciples were already God-fearing believers, which constituted salvation in that day. So the choosing was not for salvation, but *for a purpose* – to go and bear fruit. When did Jesus choose his disciples? After studying them and testing them. When he could be reasonably certain of their future potential, including that of Judas Iscariot, he picked the ones he could trust to help him carry out God's mission. I suggest that it is no different today.

In *The New International Dictionary of New Testament Theology*, Colin Brown says, "We can only speak of election, when we also give weight to what John in particular emphasizes, but which is always implicit: the commission to fruit-bearing service, obedience and a God-fearing and God-trusting life."[10] That is Paul's point.

The progression in Romans 8:28-30 is important: from foreknowledge to predestination, to calling, to justification (salvation), to glorification. It is interesting that for this person – foreknown, predestined, called, and justified – the final stage will be glory. In the next chapter, we will look at the glory of God in more depth, but for now, it is worth noting that glory is something worthy of praise. Psychologist Larry Crabb helped me a lot when he mentioned what he learned from his own father – that the glory of God is simply God's character[11] – his infinite goodness, his infinitely loving, infinitely holy nature. This foreknown, predestined person, the one conformed to the image of Christ, will receive glory. We tend to think of "glory" as "praise," but is it closer to the term "character," of being "praiseworthy." In Romans 2, Paul has already promised eternal life to those "who by persistence in doing good seek glory, honor and immortality," then he extended that, saying that there will be "glory, honor and peace for everyone who does good" even if they have no access to the Word of God.

The point is that glory is connected to character, to "doing good." There is no doubt that every believer will be "glorified" in heaven, in the sense that we will have new bodies and will live in the presence of God for eternity. But from 1 Corinthians 3, we also know that what we do in this life will be tested by fire, and everything we do that has no eternal value will be burned up. We will receive no reward for wasted effort – for remaining in shallow soil or being distracted by the cares of this world.

Paul has also just made the point that we will share in Christ's glory, *that which makes him praiseworthy,* "if indeed we share in his sufferings" (Rom 8:17b). In the western church, most Christians seem to be determined *not* to share in his sufferings. The progression, then, is not to salvation, but to something worthy of praise – to glory, to bearing fruit – and that happens only through effort – the "persistence" in Romans 2:7. Salvation – justification – is an intermediate point along the progression, not the final goal. In the same way that Jesus lived his life with an eternal purpose, and suffered, and so was worthy of praise, of being glorified – the one who catches God's attention "as his eyes range throughout the earth," "one whose heart is fully committed to him," one who is a potential fruit bearer – that is the one described in this passage.

John Calvin read Romans 8:28-30 through the lenses of his culture, which was steeped in both individualism and Aristotle's fatalism, and he saw "individual predestination for salvation." But it's not there in the words Paul used, and when this passage is understood within the backdrop of Paul's larger argument – the bridge – it's not there at all.

The second problematic passage in Romans is 9:10-24. This whole chapter, understood through the lenses of a first century Jew, says exactly the opposite of what Calvinism teaches, yet it is one of the major foundations of that theology. Early in the chapter, Paul expresses his anguish over the plight of the people of Israel. Why? Because they have rejected the messiah. Paul cites all the blessings they have been given as the chosen ones of God, then he concludes that being chosen is not what brings righteousness. It is faith – believing God. Paul has already spent most of chapter 4 laying a supporting argument that it is not works, but faith, that commended Abraham to God. At least four times, Paul quotes Genesis 15:6: "Abraham believed God, and it was credited to him as righteousness" (Rom 4:3, 5, 9, 22). Now, in 9:23-

24, Paul deliberately extends that principle to us: "The words 'it was credited to him' were written not for him alone, but also for us, to whom God will credit righteousness – for us who believe in him who raised Jesus our Lord from the dead." In chapter 4, Paul makes the point that Abraham is the father of all who believe, whether they are circumcised or not (Rom 4:11-12ff). Stated another way, Abraham is the father of all who believe, whether they are among the chosen, or not. The Israelites were the chosen people of God – they were "the circumcised," a group distinguished from "the uncircumcised" group. But Paul is stressing that it is not chosenness that commends a person to God, but faith.

Now Paul connects his current supporting argument to the supporting argument he laid in chapter 4. He makes the point that not all descendants of Israel are Abraham's children – some are not people of faith. They are not believers (Rom 9:6-7). Paul could hardly emphasize this point more. Over and over, in this chapter and the next, he says that it is not chosenness, but faith, that brings righteousness: Romans 9:24, both Jews and Gentiles are called; 9:30, the Gentiles (the unchosen), who did not pursue righteousness, obtained it, but the Jews (the chosen) failed to obtain it because they were trying to earn it; 10:4, the messiah is the end of the law, so that righteousness is available to everyone who believes; 10:12-13, there is no difference between Jew and Gentile – the same Lord is Lord of all and richly blesses all who call on him – why? – for everyone who calls on the name of the Lord will be saved.

How did Calvin miss this? He missed it because his fatalistic, individualistic worldview caused him to misinterpret the intermediate verses, the problematic passage. That misinterpretation formed the base from which he interpreted all the rest of Scripture. Let's look at the intermediate verses.

Starting in Romans 9:10, Paul outlines God's plan of election – the choosing of some, and the not choosing of others. He starts with Rebekah's twins – Jacob and Esau. Paul is specifically quoting from Malachi 1:2-3 when he says, "Just as it is written: 'Jacob I loved, but Esau I hated.'" When we go back to Malachi and read what Paul is quoting, we find that the passage is using the names Jacob and Esau, not to refer to the individuals, but to refer to the nations that arose from their descendants. "Jacob, the nation, I have loved; but Esau, the nation, I have hated." Obadiah does the same thing – calling the two nations Esau and Jacob (Obad 6, 10). Paul is doing the same thing here, and by doing so, he is establishing that this election was corporate, not individual.[12] Paul makes the point even more clearly in Romans 11:28, which is dealt with in Appendix A. Here, however, he is comparing two nations.

If you read the history of Jacob and Esau, you will find that at birth (Gen 25:21-26), God did not say that he loved Jacob and hated Esau. He did tell Rebekah, however, that two *nations* were in her womb, and that the older would serve the younger. God knew in advance that Esau would not be a spiritual person, but Jacob would be. Notice how consistent this is with the argument Paul has just made in Romans 8:28-30. Based on his foreknowledge of their potential for faithfulness, God predestined events in the life of Jacob that he did not for Esau. Their legacies passed down to the nations they fathered. By the time God said through the prophet Malachi that he hated Esau, the nation of Edom that had started with Esau had refused Israel passage during their time in the desert (Num 20), they had warred against Israel during the time of Saul, David, and Solomon (1 Sam 14, 2 Sam 8, 1 Kings 11) until the Israelites subdued them, then they rebelled and were "in rebellion to this day" (2 Chron 21:10), they gloated when Jerusalem was sacked, and even plundered the city (Obad 12-13), and they worshipped false gods (2 Chron 25:20). As Esau their father had been, Edom the nation was prideful and self-reliant (Jer 49:16), rebellious and exploitative (Obad 8-14). When one is in that position, whether individual or nation, one is the enemy of God. God did not hate Esau the twin; he hated Esau, the evil nation that was bent on destroying his chosen people. But he foreknew that Esau the twin would leave that legacy, so he did not predestine events in his life as he did in the life of Jacob, and he gave their mother advance warning of how it would be.

From this introduction, Paul, the communal thinker, asks, "Is God unjust in selecting one group, through which to display his goodness and mercy, and not selecting another group?" We have no choice into which group we are born. So whether the mercy of God extends to us in this corporate election, based on which group we are born into, is not our choice – it does not depend on our desire or effort, but on the mercy of God. Paul uses the example of Pharaoh to show God's ability to choose to whom he will show compassion or mercy – but the example is still extended corporately. Pharaoh represented the nation of Egypt, just as Jacob and Esau represented the nations that came from them. Even if we choose not to see Pharaoh as a corporate representative, his individual selection was still for a purpose, and based on his character, just as Judas Iscariot's was.

> THE PLAN IS GOD'S PLAN. IF HE WANTS TO CHOOSE ONE NATION THROUGH WHICH TO REVEAL HIMSELF TO ALL OTHER NATIONS, HE HAS THE RIGHT TO DO THAT

In the next chapter, we are going to discuss the overall plan of God, including the idea of God hardening hearts. We may not come to any profound conclusions, but one thing we will see, is that God chose to reveal himself through the nation of Israel. We can trace the developments of that choice, that plan, up to and beyond the coming of the messiah, but this side of heaven, we will never fully understand why he chose that plan above all the other options that were available to the infinite God. That is Paul's main point in this supporting argument to his overall argument. God has the right to make that choice. The plan is God's plan. If he wants to choose one nation through which to reveal himself to all other nations, he has the right to do that. All the rest of us are simply players in a much bigger game that we don't fully understand.

Paul supports that argument with one more problematic idea – that of the potter and the clay, in Romans 9:19-21. At first glance, it sounds awfully Calvinistic. "Does not the potter have the right to make out of the same lump of clay some pottery for noble purposes and some for common use?" But where did Paul get the metaphor? Surely from Jeremiah 18:6. Note carefully three things from that original passage: 1) its communal, corporate application – referring to nations, not to individuals, 2) its direct connection to human choice, not the arbitrary choice of God, and 3) the complete opposite of the idea of "eternal decrees," a favorite anchor premise of John Calvin.

> "O house of Israel, can I not do with you as this potter does?" declares the LORD. "Like clay in the hand of the potter, so are you in my hand, O house of Israel. If at any time I announce that a nation or kingdom is to be uprooted, torn down and destroyed, and if that nation I warned repents of its evil, then I will relent and not inflict on it the disaster I had planned. And if at another time I announce that a nation or kingdom is to be built up and planted, and if it does evil in my sight and does not obey me, then I will reconsider the good I had intended to do for it" Jer 18:6-10.

Does history, from Scripture, support the pattern Jeremiah describes? Certainly it does. God's dealing with Nineveh in the book of Jonah shows him relenting from a pronouncement of impending judgment, and his dealing with Israel shows him reconsidering the good he had planned for them. Without doubt, that principle would apply to individuals, but that is not Paul's point here. Here, he is applying the principle corporately. Connecting with the foundation he laid in chapters 1 and 2, Paul continues his argument by reflecting on how God expresses his wrath to those who have been "prepared for destruction."

It is critical to observe that God does not take credit for preparing those "objects of his wrath" for destruction. Paul says they *are prepared* for destruction (a passive verb), but who does the preparing is not identified – possibilities are God (which Calvin believed), or Satan, or themselves, or possibly their ancestors (through a culture which suppressed truth and promoted evil in general and false gods in particular, as Rom 1:18-23 describes). The degree to which we use determinism or free will as our anchor premise, will determine to whom we attribute the preparing. It is significant, though, that Paul distinctly does not attribute it to God, as Calvin does. Paul could easily have done that. As he is concluding this controversial passage, he makes the point mentioned earlier – he deliberately opens up the mercy of God beyond the boundaries of chosenness. "What if he did this to make the riches of his glory known to the objects of his mercy, whom he prepared in advance for glory – even us, whom he also called, not only from the Jews but also from the Gentiles?" (Rom 9:23-24)

IN A GENERAL SENSE, CHOSENNESS IS CORPORATE, UNAFFECTED BY HUMAN DECISIONS; CALLING IS INDIVIDUAL, AND CAN BE ACCEPTED OR REJECTED AT WILL; AND CALLING IS ALWAYS FOR A PURPOSE

Do you see the relationship between the two problematic passages? It is the difference between the chosen and the called, between the corporate and the individual. In a general sense, chosenness is corporate, unaffected by human decisions (9:16); calling is individual, and can be accepted or rejected at will; and calling is always for a purpose. The Jews are the chosen ones, but they are not the only ones called, nor are all of them called. They are not the only ones who are objects of his mercy, nor the only ones he has prepared in advance for glory. The distinction of being called, as the progression of Romans 8:29-30 shows, is reserved for those he knows in advance will help him accomplish his purpose.

From what Paul teaches in Romans to support the bridge – his overall argument from salvation for everyone who believes, to the goal of all nations believing and obeying – I suggest that we can now make a definite statement that completely undermines the very foundation of Calvinism. When Paul's writings are read in light of his larger arguments, and through the lenses of his original readers, it becomes clear: *the election of God, whether corporate or individual, is always for a purpose within his larger plan, never for salvation.*

In Chapter 5, we saw that when Paul was talking about the salvation of the Thessalonians, the word usually translated *chosen* can just as legitimately be translated *took you for himself.* Now we have seen that choosing individuals for salvation is not in Ephesians, and it is not in Romans. In fact, it is not in Scripture.

The coherence of that statement with the rest of Scripture, as the plan of God unfolds, I will attempt to demonstrate in the next chapter.

Endnotes

[1] Gonzalez, *Story of Christianity*, xvii.

[2] 1 Tim 2:15 was used as a classic example of this in the NIV, with the translators substituting the word "women" (a third person *plural noun*) for the word "she" (a third person *singular pronoun*) that was present in the original, thus further obscuring the meaning of the verse rather than clarifying it.

[3] Paul consistently uses the plural "you" in Ephesians. The only times he uses the singular "you" (thou, thee, thy) is in 5:14 and 6:2-3, where he is quoting previous Scripture. That usage of plurals supports my contention that Paul was thinking corporately, or communally, as he was writing this book.

[4] There is strong evidence that Paul did not write this letter specifically to the Ephesians, but as a general letter. Early copies of the document are not addressed to the Ephesians. Plus, in 1:15, Paul says, "...ever since I *heard about* your faith in the Lord Jesus and your love for all the saints..." (emphasis mine). Since we know Paul spent more than two years in Ephesus on his third missionary journey (Acts 19:8-10), it is unlikely that he would imply that he did not personally know the recipients of the letter. More likely, he wrote a general letter which was later copied and sent to various locations, including Ephesus. Later the letter was recopied many times, and fragments of both those without the address to the Ephesians, and those with the address to the Ephesians, have survived and influenced our understanding.

[5] Sanneh, *Translating the Message*, 1.

[6] Calvin, *Institutes*, Book II, Ch. 17, para. 2, p. 326-327.

[7] Comment is from the Introduction to Johnson's *Abundant Life in Christ* series, available at http://kneillfoster.com/Johnson/en/Romans/romans1.html.

8   This event is confirmed by two Roman historians, Suetonius (Gaius Suetonius Tranquillus, c. 69 – c. 122 C.E.) and Cassius Dio (c. 150 – c. 235 C.E.), as well as fifth-century Christian author Paulus Orosius (c. 375 - c. 418 C.E.) Cf. Suetonius, "Claudius 25," *Lives of the Caesars*, transl. Catharine Edwards (Oxford: Oxford University Press, 2001), 184.

9   I am indebted to Zane C. Hodges for alerting me to this distinction. See Chapter 9, "Who Are the Heirs?" in Zane C. Hodges, *The Gospel Under Siege* (Dallas, TX: Redencion Viva, 1981), 109-120.

10   Colin Brown, *The New International Dictionary of New Testament Theology* (Grand Rapids, MI: Zondervan, 1975), 542.

11   Crabb, *Biblical Counseling*, 30. "I am indebted to my father for the suggestion that to glorify God is to reveal His essential Being . . . I glorify God as I reveal Him by walking as He walked."

12   For a more thorough treatment of corporate election, see William W. Klein, *The New Chosen People: A Corporate View of Election* (Eugene, OR: Wipf and Stock, 2001).

Chapter 7
What is the Plan?

It turns out that the truth, or reality, is our home.
– Anne Lamott.[1]

The neurological clock in my head wakes me up a minute or so before the alarm goes off, so on March 20, 1975, I turned the alarm clock off before it sounded. Almost immediately, the telephone rang. Who would be calling me at exactly zero five hundred? I answered officially, "Lieutenant Mauldin."

"Lieutenant, a message has come in about some classified material in the vault. The colonel wants to see it as soon as you can get here."

I couldn't get into the vault, but as the Classified Materials Officer, I was responsible for it. I was stationed at Camp Hansen, Okinawa. I had been there less than six months, fresh out of Marine Corps Engineering

School. My main job was being the battalion's Assistant S-4, which is logistics. Mainly, that meant making sure vehicles and equipment were ready to go, verifying that parts were ordered and tracking their status. The daily routine involved reams of accordion fold computer printouts with the perforated, tractor-feed edges. Each page was about eighteen inches wide, too far to stay on a line, so every other line was light green. My job was to litter the green and white striped paper with red circles and check marks, proof that someone was providing oversight for Motor-T and Heavy Equipment. Being the Classified Materials Officer was an "additional duty" that I didn't mind, because it got me an interim top secret clearance, which bolstered my status a notch above my peers. Every officer had additional duties. I had four more.

Overall, being the Classified Materials Officer wasn't bad, but it did carry a little responsibility. The only two people who could get into the battalion's vault worked for me, in a sense. On the front end, I had to pick up the classified documents. On the back end, I had to destroy them. Monthly, and occasionally on call, a driver and I would check pistols out of the armory and take an open jeep to the division headquarters, on a separate base farther south on the island, to get the new classified material. It always took a while.

The driver would wait with the jeep while I went in. After being checked against an access list, I was locked in a concrete cell with a peep hole about head high in the steel door. The room had a table and a chair, a stack of documents about a foot high, and a typed list of what was supposed to be there. I literally had to count every page of every document. They ranged from a few pages to two hundred or more, and every page had to be accounted for. If a page was missing, I rejected the document. If a page was blank, the list said, "p. 185 - blank". When I finished, I would sign the list verifying that all the material was there and that I was receiving it, then I would pack all the documents in a briefcase, lock the briefcase and grip it in my left hand since my pistol was on my right hip and I am right-handed, then signal that I was ready for the door to be unlocked. When I got back to the battalion, the two Marines who manned the vault went through the same ordeal to receive the material from me. That was the front end.

The back end was no better. Every document had an expiration date on it. Either the date was extended in a classified amendment, or the document had to be destroyed. Shredding was not good enough. Shredded documents are like buried bodies – some have been known to come back alive. Security demanded cremation. When that time came, I had to sign the material out, then burn it page by page in a rotating hopper that had rocks in it, so the ashes were battered beyond any hope of resurrection. Then I had to sign a form saying I had done it, specifying every page so destroyed. It was the system.

So even though I did not have a key to the vault, I was still responsible, which is why I got the five o'clock call. As soon as I got to battalion headquarters, I called the sergeant in charge of the classified materials vault. He got his partner, and they were both there within minutes. In the meantime, the battalion commander showed me the message that had come in, so I knew what document he wanted. My memory will not be exact on the details, but the message was brief. It looked like this:

197503201206ZULU
FROM: SECDEF
TO: WORLDWIDE
CLASSIFICATION: TOP SECRET
MESSAGE:
ACTIVATE OPERATION FREQUENT WIND.
END OF MESSAGE.
CLASSIFICATION: TOP SECRET

My two Marines went into the vault and came out with a paper-bound book, letter sized, about 200 pages thick. It had TOP SECRET plastered in bright red letters on every visible surface. On the front, above the seal of the Department of Defense, it read simply OPERATION FREQUENT WIND. I had no idea what was about to happen, but I knew every US military unit around the world had received the same message and pulled out their copy of Operation Frequent Wind.

By late-afternoon, I was in the Philippines, in charge of about 30 Marines, a "six-by" truck, and a rough terrain forklift – all four tires head-high. Donna and I were engaged, planning a summer wedding. We were in the habit of writing each other every day. I barely had time to get a quick note in the mail – "I'm changing locations. I'll write when I can." The Air Force planes that transported us from Okinawa were C-141s from Tacoma, Washington. Like mine, the lives of their crew had changed on short notice. They also could not tell their loved ones where they were going or when they would be back. They had been in the air for 15 hours by the time they met us, and then another five to get us to the Philippines.

Within an hour of our arrival in the Philippines, our forklift joined others loading hundreds of thousands of C-rations into ships. Earlier in the day, thousands of pallets of the prepared meals had been staged on the dock, and an armada had started assembling. As the planes were leaving the west coast of the US to pick us up, over 40 ships in various places were quietly altering their headings, and as I was drawing my weapon and stuffing gear into my backpack and sea bag along with some 1600 other Marines on Okinawa, floodgates were opened on Philippine warehouses and waves of C-rations and other supplies splashed out onto the dock. It all had two things in common: we were part of the US military, and we were heading for Vietnam, following the plan laid out in Operation Frequent Wind.

Over the next six weeks, almost 139,000 people were evacuated from Saigon, including over 2600 orphans sired by American servicemen. I spent most of the time on a ship off the coast of Vietnam, only dimly aware of what was happening outside of my personal responsibilities. My 30 Marines studied and drilled, trained and complained. Our responsibility was to stay well prepared, not to stay well informed. When the final evacuation started, we responded, even though we had scant knowledge of all that was going on.

Chaos, courage, and creativity characterize military operations, and this one was no different. There was opposition to our efforts, and all around us, mistakes were made, accidents happened, unforeseen events arose, and spontaneous decisions were made. The situation changed minute by minute. Plans were changed, then changed again. But THE PLAN never changed. When it was all over, Operation Frequent Wind had done what it was designed to do. The world was a different place.

"In the beginning, God created the heavens and the earth." Why? What was THE PLAN? If the orthodox view is correct, God himself is without beginning, without end, and without need. He existed from all eternity past as the Trinity, without conflict or confusion, in relationship, without need. *In relationship, without need.* Why change that?

The purpose of creation

Theologians have speculated for centuries about God's reasons for creating, since he logically had no need to do it. The conclusion that I have come to personally, is that God created *simply to have more to love.* No other explanation seems to fit all the biblical data. Scripture does not specifically state this, but the idea is infused throughout. Scripture says "God is love" (1 John 4:8, 16). It is his nature. Assuming that our understanding of love has some merit, it is not loving to enslave, so loving involves giving

GOD CREATED SIMPLY TO HAVE MORE TO LOVE.

the one loved the ability to either return that love, or not. Inherent in the ability to respond is the capacity to choose to do it, or not do it – or the response would not be real. With the capacity to return love, is the capacity to not return it. Hence, philosophically, the necessity of free will is justified, both among humans and angels. Philosophically, it is justified; practically, it could be an illusion, but it appears to be real.

Since God is considered to be infinite, his capacity for love, and the social relationships associated with it – fellowship – would also be infinite. That means he can experience an infinite number of relationships simultaneously, so I'm suggesting the plan was to share his love with such a large number of created beings that altogether, they come close to matching his infinite capacities. It might not be theologically acceptable to imply that God developed his plan over time – considering he is beyond time, and theoretically knows everything anyway. So to imply a progression in thought about the plan, or a process of development, might not be correct. I won't suggest then, that as God *developed* his plan, he chose to do things a certain way. I will suggest, however, that for each part of the complete plan, a virtually infinite number of options were available to the infinite God, and from each of those variables, for each part of the overall plan, he determined to implement one. Those chosen options, together, form the total plan of God for the ages. Using the Bible as our guide, and Paul's counsel to "fit it together to make a whole," let's consider what THE PLAN looks like.

The effects of creation

When creation was complete, the world was effectively in operation. I prefer to believe the Genesis account, that the world was created in mature form in six of what were God's days at the time. We cannot insist that they were the same as the days we experience, because our days are determined by the revolving of the earth on its axis in relation to the sun, and those things did not yet exist – they were part of the creation. It does appear, however, that the Genesis account attempts to make a connection between the days of creation and the way humans experience days, since each day of creation is said to progress through evening and morning. Today, we think of a day literally beginning at midnight, and perceptively beginning at dawn, but the ancient Jews did not. They thought of the day beginning at sundown, so evening preceded morning, and each of the days of creation is described that way. If it is true that the earth was created in six days of some literal length, then the apparent age of the universe that science appears to observe, was built into the original creation, and is exactly that – apparent. But other things were built in, as well.

For one thing, the universe operates according to observable, predictable patterns that are often called laws of nature. They are too numerable and complex to deal with here, but just to make the point, we can mention such things as gravity – the fact that any two bodies with mass are attracted to each other – and heat – the fact that heat causes things to expand, for example. And there is the fact that as water freezes, it expands. If it did not, in extreme cold, lakes and oceans would freeze solid, killing all life in them. The fact that matter exists in three forms, solid, liquid, and gas, was part of creation. The fact that the moon causes tides, has a remarkable affect on the oceans, in terms of circulating the water. The tilt of the earth's axis combined with the earth's revolution around the sun, is responsible for the seasons, triggering all kinds of natural cycles. The fact that white or brown seeds planted in brown soil and watered with clear water produce a plant with brown bark, white wood, green leaves, and fruit of various colors and tastes, was built into creation. DNA and RNA were part of the creation. DNA contains RNA, yet RNA is necessary for the production of DNA – it is the classic case of the chicken and the egg. Each is necessary for the production of the other. How could they exist, dependent as they are on the prior existence of each other, if they were not created simultaneously and complete?

Not only did God create the ability of seeds to reproduce after their kind, but he did the same for animal life. Today we know that our genes control our physical characteristics. It's built in, passed down from our ancestors, a combination of all the pairs of parents in our background. We know how the sperm uses it's tail to swim in seminal fluid to fertilize the ovum, and we know that the one who wins the race, is one of some 300 million who started out. Why 300 million, instead of just one? Because that's the way God made it. There is a lot of redundancy built into nature. A certain number of sperm are defective, but many more simply die unused. Why? A healthy, mature woman produces an ovum every month whether she stands a chance of getting it fertilized or not. Why? A certain number of plant seeds are eaten by birds or even humans, or compromised by weather conditions. A certain number of fish eggs are eaten or washed away. A lot of the reproductive potential of nature never gets used in the reproduction process. Why all that redundancy and apparent randomness in the process, if everything is predetermined ahead of time? The redundancy appears to make propagation more certain than if there was only one, and the randomness appears to promote diversity. It is notable that Genesis does not say that God created the land animals. He told the land to produce them (Gen 1:24). That does not imply that he was not their original source, but it might imply some kind of a different process. Regardless of the details of the original start, however, we see the world functioning today according to natural laws.

THE WORLD WORKS THE WAY IT WORKS, BECAUSE GOD CREATED IT THAT WAY

My point is simply that the laws of nature are part of creation. Stated another way, *the world works the way it works, because God created it that way.* In God's discussion with Job, he made the point that he had no advisor as he set the cosmos in motion and established the laws by which it would be governed (Job 38 - 41). Proverbs 3:19-20 says, "By wisdom the LORD laid the earth's foundations, by understanding he set the heavens in place; by his knowledge the deeps were divided, and the clouds let drop the dew." Later, we will examine Calvin's thinking about decrees, but for now, we can simply assert that the world works the way it does, because God made it that way. Our job, then, is not to state the way things are, it is to humbly explore and find out how they are. We weren't there, so the best we can do is to say, "from my vantage point at this time and in this place, it appears ...." From our observations, we may come to conclusions about the way things are, but those conclusions must meet the tests of truth, or they cannot be said to accurately reflect the reality that is out there.

If we consider the Bible to be inspired of God, and if it is part of what we explore, then for our conclusions to meet the tests for truth, they must: 1) reflect consistency with all that Scripture says, and 2) reflect consistency with all that we experience. It should not surprise us to find a similar principle taught in Scripture. In 2 Peter 1:16-21, Peter briefly relates his memory of the time he witnessed Jesus' transfiguration (Matt 17, Mark 9, Luke 9), which he then connects with prior Scripture. Essentially, he says that his personal experience makes prophesy more certain. It should be that if Scripture is true, our experience will verify it. One of the major criticisms of Calvinism is that the world as we experience it, does not appear to work the way Calvin envisioned it – including the redundancy and apparent randomness in the reproductive process of almost everything.

One effect of creation was the image of God in humans, which we will consider more later. It appears that both male and female were created on day six, the same day God made the land animals and had Adam name them. Along with his image, God gave humans the responsibility, and I will argue later, the right, to rule over the rest of the earth's creation (Gen 1:28).

Finally, one effect of the creation was the response of angels. The morning stars sang together and the angels shouted for joy as the cornerstone of the earth's foundation was laid – metaphorical language, no doubt, but still instructive, because it leads us to believe that the spirit world existed before the physical world (Job 38:4-7). It may also imply, without certainty, that the fall of Satan and the demons who accompanied him, happened after the creation of the physical world, since Satan is thought to have been one of those "morning stars." Traditionally, it has been believed that the fall of Satan may have been related to the creation of humanity, in that Satan coveted the glory that humans brought to God. While that view is not contradicted by Scripture, neither is it clearly supported. Jesus said that he saw Satan fall from heaven (Luke 10:18), so that is certain. The passages following Isaiah 14:12 and Ezekiel 28:11 have often been interpreted to be allegorical descriptions of that fall, but that also is not certain. Since those passages are talking about the king of Babylon and the king of Tyre, it may be that they are figurative language connecting spiritual domination in the background with evil human leadership, similar to the way the angel described the prince of Persia to Daniel (Dan 10:13). There are some things that we cannot say for sure about the spiritual world, but some things do seem certain.

A tri-polar world

Based on the evidence from Scripture, it appears that the world can be called "tri-polar." To illustrate this, consider the characteristics of a triangle. Without being too technical, a triangle is simply a figure made up of three points on a plane that are not in a straight line. When the points are connected, there will always be three lines, and three angles inside the lines. A triangle is stable – nothing about a triangle can change, without changing the length of at least one line. I figured this out long before I took geometry in school. As a boy growing up on a farm, one of my normal summer activities was to repair and build fences. We used barbed wire, which we had to stretch and keep tight.

I learned that animals will take advantage of loose fences to search for that grass that is always greener on the other side, but tight fences resist their efforts. I learned that the way to keep fences tight is to build the braces at the ends so the wire cannot loosen up over time. And, I learned that the way to build those braces well, is to use triangles.

Think of a square or rectangle, with opposite sides parallel and of the same length. Each corner has the effect of a hinge. Without changing the length of any line, a square or rectangle can be collapsed. Not so with a triangle. To collapse or spread a triangle, the length of at least one line has to be changed. When that principle is applied to a fence, the braces can be made strong and stable, and a well built fence will last for decades. Later, as a young man, I anticipated building my own house. As I studied construction techniques, I learned that the principle is applied there as well. Every corner of every building has a triangular brace built into it, to stabilize the structure. As long as no side of the triangle is changed, the entire structure is stable.

For teaching purposes, I use a triangle with lines of the same length to illustrate the way I see the world – as tri-polar. The illustration is simplistic, but still useful as a visual model. At one corner of the triangle, is God. At another corner, there is the created spirit world,

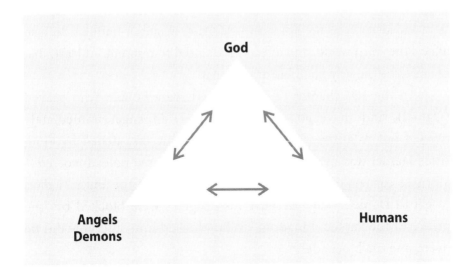

made up of angels and demons. At the other corner, is humans. Although that tri-polar model is not without dispute, it appears to be one that fits the biblical narrative, and below, we will briefly look at alternatives to the model. The point of using a triangle to illustrate the biblical model is related to the stability of the triangle. If you remove any corner of a triangle, you no longer have a triangle. Two of the lines cease to exist, and the whole concept vanishes. That is the way the world seems to work, with the three corners of the tri-polar world being interdependent.

It would be a mistake to imply that God is dependent on anyone or anything, as a matter of necessity. But even without necessity, maybe he has *chosen* to be. We will explore that possibility later, in more detail. If he has chosen to be, it could be that he has designed the world in such a way that both the created spirit beings and the created physical beings play crucial parts in his overall plan – not because there was no other way, but simply because he chose to have it that way. That possibility seems to fit the biblical narrative, so we will explore that further, as well. In the tri-polar world that I visualize, anything that happens on any pole, affects the other poles. Whatever God does, affects the world inhabited by spirits, and the world inhabited by humans. Whatever happens in the spirit world, affects God in terms of his need to respond to it, and also affects the human world. And, whatever humans do, also affects the spirit world, and affects God's need to respond. At least, that seems to be the way the Bible describes it.

In the 10th chapter of Daniel, we have a human who prayed (Daniel), and in response to his prayer, an angel immediately headed out to answer his prayer, presumably dispatched by God, since Daniel was praying to God. That's all three poles involved – all three corners on the triangle. However, it took the angel 21 days to get to Daniel. Why? Because his progress were blocked by "the prince of the Persian kingdom." Who blocked him, and how did he overcome the blockade?

Apparently the prince of the Persian kingdom was a demon, somehow in charge of that territory. His attempt to prevent the angel from reaching Daniel was overcome through aid provided by Michael, "one of the chief princes." Michael was apparently an angel more powerful than the contrary spirit impeding the first angel's journey. That's a lot of "appparentlies" but the picture is fairly clear – we conclude that within that pole of the triangle that represents created spirit beings, there are two teams. One team cooperates with God, and one opposes him, and the two teams function in opposition to each other. Within those teams, there are individual beings with varying amount of strength, or power, so with any given conflict between members of the two teams, whichever team gains the upper hand is determined by the amount of power present on each side of the equation. The term normally used to describe this conflict is "The Spiritual Battle." When humans get involved to try to tip the balance of power, we are said to be participating in "Spiritual Warfare." Neither term is found in the Bible, but both are supported by a variety of passages that, together, shape our understanding. The scenes in the Bible like this one in Daniel may be metaphorical, but the text does not indicate that they are. They are presented as literal occurrences, described in the language and from the understanding of the ones who experienced them and recorded them, and historically, the church has accepted them that way.

If the scene just portrayed from Daniel literally happened, then the conclusions drawn from it bring up a really big question: If God is omniscient, omnipresent, and omnipotent, why is he shown to be 1) waiting on prayers before taking needed action, and 2) dispatching angels to take the needed action, rather than doing it himself? The answer to that question impacts all of theology, including some of the most basic assumptions on which Calvinism rests, so it's worth exploring.

Historically, as already mentioned, the Church has accepted the existence of a spirit world inhabited by angels and demons, as reality. In more recent times, however, that view has been questioned, so today, there are several ideas of what constitutes Spiritual Warfare. Let's look at what Scripture has to say, then briefly consider the variety of ways it is now being interpreted.

Spiritual warfare

The first spirit beings show up soon after creation. It is commonly assumed that the serpent who deceived Eve in the Garden of Eden was Satan in disguise, although that is not stated. After God drove Adam and Eve from the garden, he placed cherubim to guard the tree of life (Gen 3). Apparently there is a hierarchy among angels, and cherubim are one type of angel within that hierarchy.

The next occurrence of angels in Scripture is when Hagar ran away from Sarai (later known as Sarah). The "angel of the Lord" found Hagar near a spring in the desert, told her what to name her son, promised to make her descendants too numerous to count, prophesized about her son's character, and sent her back to submit to her mistress (Gen 16). It is debated as to whether this person was an angel representing God, or a pre-incarnate appearance of Jesus, but it was probably an angel, since in one place (Gen 16:10), it is called simply "the angel."

Thirteen years later, three men appeared near Abraham's tent, later identified as the Lord and two angels. After they ate and conversed with Abraham, the Lord apparently went back to heaven, and the two angels went to Sodom and rescued Lot and his family before the Lord destroyed Sodom and Gomorrah (Gen 18-19). Similar appearances occur throughout the Old Testament narrative.

Most of the time, these spirit beings are said to be "the angel of the Lord," or "the angel of God," with the terms often used interchangeably. When Sarah sent Hagar and Ishmael away, it was the angel of God who helped them survive in the desert (Gen 21). It was the angel of the Lord who stopped Abraham from killing Isaac on Mt. Moriah (Gen 22), and a couple of generations later, Jacob wrestled all night with a man who seemed to indicate that he was God. Jacob certainly interpreted it that way (Gen 32). It was the angel of the Lord who was in the burning bush that caught Moses' attention (Exod 3), the angel of the Lord who blocked the path of Balaam's donkey (Num 22), and who appeared to Gideon (Judg 6).

A common occurrence is for the "angel of the Lord" to appear, but when the being speaks, the speech is attributed to "the Lord" himself. It was that way at the burning bush, and with Gideon. Then there are times when the angel of the Lord is clearly said to be an angel dispatched by God, as in the case when King David brought on God's wrath by counting the available fighting men in Israel (1 Chron 21). Sometimes, however, the spirit being is called a "man," as when Joshua led the Israelites across the Jordan River. He was confronted with a "man" who called himself "the commander of the Lord's army" (Josh 5:13).

One reason to believe that the angel of the Lord was sometimes pre-incarnate appearances of Jesus, is that the being did not protest whenever humans called him "Lord" or "God" and worshipped him. That contrasts with the response of the angel in Revelation 19:10, when John fell at his feet to worship him: "Do not do it!" he said. "I am a fellow servant with you and with your brothers who hold to the testimony of Jesus. Worship God!"

The traditional understanding of the function of angels comes from such places as Genesis 24, when Abraham promised his servant that an angel would precede him on the journey to select a wife for Isaac, and in Exodus 23, when God himself assured Moses that an angel was going ahead of them to protect them and bring them to the place God had prepared for them. Angels appear to be servants of God who arrange matters on earth so that God's will is accomplished. This is consistent with the hills being full of chariots of fire surrounding the city in which Elisha was staying (2 Kings 6), and with Jesus saying that if he asked for them, God would place more than twelve legions of angels at his disposal (Matt 26:53). Statements that support that view include Psalm 91:11, "He will command his angels concerning you to guard you in all your ways," and Psalm 103:20, "Praise the LORD, you his angels, you mighty ones who do his bidding, who obey his word."

By contrast, Satan and demons are portrayed in Scripture as spirit beings who oppose the purposes of God. Satan is shown in 1 Chronicles 21 as the one who incited David to count his potential fighting men. It was apparently David's lack of faith, his thinking that the nation's security depended on human resources rather than God, that brought on the punishment mentioned earlier. In the first two chapters of Job, Satan is shown to be with the angels in heaven who presented themselves before God. From that encounter, God challenged Satan to test Job, and Satan responded in a variety of ways that included everything from causing disease, to killing people and destroying property. He rained fire from the sky, caused a massive storm, and incited tribal raiding parties to steal and kill. Within limitations God placed on him, Satan appeared to have blanket authority to test Job any way he pleased, including manipulating the physical world – including the weather and humans. Since fire from heaven is unnatural, that event suggests that spirit beings have, if not limited ability to create, at least the ability to manipulate physical elements to mimic creation. Or maybe it suggests the ability to arrange for a flaming meteor shower at a precise time and place and with such precise coverage as to do specific damage, but however it occurred, it's pretty impressive. Within certain limitations, God gave Satan the power of life and death over humans, power over nature, and the power to influence human thinking.

Another incident recorded in both 1 Kings 22 and 2 Chronicles 18 gives us insight into the interaction among the three poles of the

SATAN AND DEMONS ARE PORTRAYED IN SCRIPTURE AS SPIRIT BEINGS WHO OPPOSE THE PURPOSES OF GOD

triangle. The prophet Micaiah witnessed God holding a council in heaven, at which various angels proposed ways to kill the wicked king Ahab by natural means. "One suggested this, and another that." Finally, a spirit came forward and suggested being a lying spirit in the mouths of Ahab's prophets to convince him to go into a battle in which he would be killed. The way the impending death was set up is instructive – with a spirit putting ideas in the minds of humans – but the way it played out is equally instructive. Ahab went into the battle in disguise, in order to avoid being specifically targeted, and was killed by an arrow when "someone drew his bow at random" and apparently shot into the air without aiming at any particular target. The arrow "hit the king of Israel between the sections of his armor," at the only place where it could do mortal damage. The obvious implication is that either the precise body position and muscular tension of the archer were controlled by unseen forces, or the path and destination of the arrow were guided by unseen forces. Or both.

This was the same Ahab who, with his wife Jezebel, had promoted the worship of Baal, which Elijah had battled against at Mt. Carmel (1 Kings 18). Baal was the god of the pagan Canaanites, understood to be the god of the weather and the patron of sailors and kingship who gave victory in battles,[2] and the Lord of the Heavens.[3] The drought and then the rain, and the fire from heaven at Mt. Carmel, then the death of Ahab in battle and the way in which Jezebel died, were all designed to completely dispel belief in the powers of Baal. Similar demonstrations of Yahweh's power over false divinities can be seen in the plagues on Egypt prior to the Exodus (Exod 7 - 12) and the time the ark of the covenant was captured by the Philistines and placed in the temple of Dagon (1 Sam 5). The Apostle Paul says that false gods are actually demons (1 Cor 10:20-21), so we can see all three of these confrontations as being between Yahweh and demons.

The life of Jesus was also filled with confrontations with demons. It started as soon as he was baptized, and continued throughout his ministry. For the record, it should be pointed out that the name "Satan" and the term "the devil" are used interchangeably in Scripture, as Jesus' temptation in the desert demonstrates (Matt 4, Mark 1, Luke 4). The term "demon" and "evil spirit" are also used interchangeably, as Luke 4:33 and Acts 19:13 show. In Revelation 12:9 and 20:2, just to make sure Satan's identity is clear, this evil being is called by several names: the dragon, that ancient serpent, the devil, and Satan. Satan appears to be the chief demon, leading the forces of darkness in the fight against the purposes of God (Matt 12:24ff). During the life of Jesus, demons are shown in various capacities: inhabiting humans and animals to the point of controlling their actions (the demoniacs and pigs, Matt 8:28-34); tempting humans to do evil (Jesus in the desert and in the Garden of Gethsemane); inciting humans to do evil (Judas Iscariot, Luke 22:3, John 13:2); testing the character of people (Peter at Jesus' trial, Luke 22:31); and causing physical impairment and disease (Matt 17:14-18, Luke 13:10-16).

Further in the New Testament, a girl is shown to have a "spirit" by which she predicted the future (Acts 16:16), and Paul suggests that believers may receive a "spirit" other than the one that accompanies the gospel (1 Cor 11:4).

I could go on. These references are by no means exhaustive, but they do provide a basic reflection on the biblical worldview as it relates to angels and demons, and the conflict that goes on between the spiritual forces that support God or oppose him – that work for the good of humanity, or work for its destruction. They constitute one pole of the triangle, but the fact that they work for or against God, and for or against humanity, reflect the interdependence of the three poles.

The fact that those spiritual forces are in constant conflict, constitutes the so-called spiritual battle. The impact of the spiritual battle in the physical world is reflected in humans in terms of morality, and probably in certain physical ailments. Within the human sphere, that which promotes morality works for the good of humans, and that which hinders morality, destroys. Historically, influences toward or away from morality have been considered to come from three sources: other humans, our own sinful nature, and demonic forces. The Anglican Common Book of Prayer calls these three deceitful influences "the world, the flesh, and the devil."[4]

As mentioned earlier, when humans get involved in the spiritual battle, we are said to be engaging in spiritual warfare. To a large degree, the way in which spiritual warfare is envisioned today, follows those three sources of influence – the world, the flesh, and the devil. Let's look at some of the more prominent views of spiritual warfare.

In the western world, the classical view of spiritual warfare involves a primary focus on personal holiness, which means fighting against the natural human tendencies to be self-serving at the expense of others, and to doubt the goodness of God. The moral person works to suppress those natural inclinations; the immoral person gives in to those tendencies, or even cultivates them. In this view of spiritual warfare, the primary battle is against the flesh – the sinful nature inherent to being human – and the primary solution is repentance.[5]

An extension of the classical view of spiritual warfare is sometimes called the Deliverance Model, where the primary battle is against the devil, and the primary focus is on casting out individual demons, or, through prayer and other strategies, recovering territory or "strongholds" for God, which have been being held by demonic forces – as we saw from Daniel, and possibly Babylon and Tyre. This view recognizes the need for personal holiness, but contends that personal holiness does not in itself confront the personal, entrenched evil beings who are responsible for oppressing humanity and keeping people locked in bondage through a variety of destructive deceptions.[6]

A third model of spiritual warfare attempts to combine the previous two, so that personal holiness is extended to living a life, as Jesus did, that directly confronts the lies that destroy people. These lies are reflected in greed, sex, racism, violence, religions that put religious observances above people, etc. This view accepts both the need for personal holiness of the classical model and the need for overcoming demons of the deliverance model, but the focus is on a radical lifestyle of revolt against enslaving deceptions.[7]

These three models of spiritual warfare are all based on a similar worldview, which I attempted to reflect above – that of the tri-polar world, in which both angels and demons are accepted as real, and in which they are locked in a battle for control of the fate of humanity. The worldview common to all three reflects a high regard for the divine inspiration of Scripture. The trustworthiness of Scripture is the anchor premise of these models.

A fourth view of spiritual warfare involves a primary focus on the way the culture influences people – specifically, social, economic, religious, and political institutions within the culture. Poverty and various other forms of abuse, exploitation, and oppression are the targets of the spiritual battle. Generally, within this view, demonic forces are not considered to be living, personal beings at all. The "spiritual" aspect of the battle is seen as the "atmosphere" or "environment" of oppression that develops from these evil, human institutions, such that their influence extends beyond their component parts. The influence of an evil political system or an exploitative economic system, for example, extends beyond the power of its leaders and participants, and beyond the natural lives of those who promote it. In this view, the primary focus of spiritual warfare is on the world.[8]

For this fourth model of spiritual warfare, a naturalistic worldview is the anchor premise. Since it has originated within the Christian faith, its proponents typically accept the existence of God, but not the existence of any other living spirit beings. To have such a worldview, they typically take the view that not all of Scripture is inspired, so they assume for themselves the role of judge as to what parts of Scripture to accept as reliable, and what parts to discard. To a large degree, this model appears to be a wedding between Christianity and a secular, materialistic worldview.

A variant of this fourth model is one which describes spirits as emanating from, or emerging from, "complex material and human relationships." This view contends that angels and demons are not created beings. They emerge. Without the material world, and without the human relationships which promote good or evil, angels and demons would not exist.[9] This theory ignores many passages of Scripture, including the one that says angels watched and rejoiced as God laid the foundations of the earth (Job 38:4-7). That implies that angels existed before either the material world existed, or before human relationships existed. Like the fourth model, this one uses recent social science theories as the basis for an understanding that flies in the face of two millennia of church history, which itself follows several millennia of Jewish history. The view suggests an elitist mentality, as if the postmodern academic is somehow superior to those who wrote Scripture, and those in the past who have sought to understand it. Based on the way it disregards not only huge swaths of the written biblical record, but the way it fails to consider the theological implications for the internal consistency of the entire Christian message if the spirit world is removed, this view also does not appear to take the inspiration of Scripture seriously.

It might be appropriate at this point to briefly discuss the inspiration of Scripture. Historically, the Church has held that all of Scripture is inspired of God, and is the supreme authority in all matters of faith and practice. This is consistent with what Paul wrote to Timothy, that "All Scripture is God-breathed and is useful for teaching, rebuking, correcting and training in righteousness, so that the man of God may be thoroughly equipped for every good work" (2 Tim 3:16-17), and what Peter wrote: "Above all, you must understand that no prophecy of Scripture came about by the prophet's own interpretation. For prophecy never had its origin in the will of man, but men spoke from God as they were carried along by the Holy Spirit" (2 Pet 1:20-21).

Typically, the historical position is that the entire Bible "is the word of God." When that position is taken, then disagreement is considered to be related to interpretation – to the *understanding* of the text, not the text itself. In recent times, however, the position is often taken that the Bible "contains the word of God." When *that* position is taken, then when disagreement occurs, the disagreeable text can simply be relegated to a position of non-inspiration, and therefore to a non-authoritative status. In a practical sense, when we pick and choose what Scripture we consider to be inspired, it makes us the final judge of morality, among other things. This is the essence of "liberal theology." Rather than allowing God to impose his will on us, we impose our will on him. Rather than submitting to God, we require that he submits to us. By making ourselves the final judge of what is really the word of God, we usurp God's position as the supreme authority. This applies to all of Scripture, including what it teaches about angels and demons.

Why spend so much time on the spiritual battle and spiritual warfare, in a book evaluating the validity of Calvinism? The answer is actually simple. Throughout the entire Bible, the idea of opposing spirit forces is portrayed as real, and their ability to impact future events, is also portrayed as real – as in the 21 day delay in Daniel, and the death of Ahab. If the Bible can be taken at face value, it appears that the spiritual battle, and human participation in it, is part of the plan of God. Part of THE PLAN. If this is true, then it directly contradicts the Calvinistic insistence that God is in total control of all that happens. If God is in total control, not only of the eventual outcome, but of every step in the process, then the whole idea of a spiritual battle, with the potential for wins and losses, gains and setbacks, becomes a complete fallacy. If it is a fallacy, then why does the Bible portray it as real? And further, why does Scripture seem to indicate that human involvement impacts the outcome? If Scripture gives a consistent description of the way things work, when in fact they do not work that way, is that not deception, rather than truth? Does that not make the Bible untrustworthy, rather than trustworthy?

Augustine contended that "The will of the omnipotent is always undefeated"[10] and Calvin picked up the refrain with such statements as, "every event which happens in the world is governed by the incomprehensible counsel of God."[11] Both of those may be true, in some general sense – eventually – but as Gregory Boyd says, "This perspective, I argue, conflicts with the fundamental motif that runs throughout Scripture in which God battles cosmic powers and humans to establish his will 'on earth as it is in heaven.'"[12] Boyd's point is well made. If God's will is always undefeated, as Augustine and Calvin insist, then not only is the fundamental motif of cosmic conflict fictitious, but for Jesus to instruct his disciples to pray for something that is already true, is nonsensical, and even tends to imply that Jesus himself was either deceived or a deceiver.

The point regarding the spiritual battle is simply part of the evidence that, under scrutiny, Calvin's interpretation of the Bible lacks internal consistency. It fails one of the basic tests for truth. From one side of his pen, Calvin acknowledges the existence of both angels and demons, and gives an accurate reflection of the way they are presented in Scripture. He acknowledges the spiritual battle, recognizing that angels work on behalf of humanity, and demons work to destroy us. Then, from the other side of his pen, he returns to his anchor premise, divine determinism, and contends that all of the actions of the spirit world are under the direct, personal control of God, including God using them to "war against" believers and "exercise dominion over" the wicked. Calvin attributes free will to Satan, but attributes his every action, and those of the "unclean spirits," to the will and control of God.[13] From this position, it seems difficult to exonerate God from being both the originator of the idea, and the instigator of the action, of every evil deed that has ever stemmed from demonic effort. This brings up several issues that are related to the overall plan of God, but more than any other, it appears to impugn the character of God.

The character of God

In Chapter 5, we saw that Martin Luther found himself imagining "that God is a rogue" when he considered the implications of predestination. From Calvin's description of the way the spiritual battle is waged, it is hard to do otherwise. But Scripture teaches that God is not a rogue – God is love, and he is holy. When the Apostle Peter says, "it is written: 'Be holy, because I am holy'" (1 Pet 1:16), he is quoting from Leviticus, where that statement is made at least five times (Lev 11:44-45, 19:2, 20:26, 21:8). Similar statements are found many other times in the Old Testament.[14] The question is, what does it mean when God says he is holy?

In earlier chapters, I attempted to lay the foundation that has affected my own thinking about such issues. Part of that foundation includes the very purpose of language itself – to send messages to other people, and receive messages from them, so that our thinking interacts with theirs. Languages, as we saw, use symbols called words to convey meaning, and they connect those symbols in predictable strings called sentences, so our messages can be understood. The meaning imbedded in the messages is how communication is accomplished. Without common understanding of meaning, there is no understanding of the message. Confusion, not communication, occurs. This proves to be a useful idea.

We saw, courtesy of Grant Osborne, that "meaning is not an inherent property of words," so we concluded that it is not *words* that are important, but the *concepts* the words represent. Without tracing all of the individual verses that could support the contention, I want to suggest that God is ultimately good – in him is no evil at all. He is righteous in all he does. That is the *concept*, the meaning imbedded in the words, when God says, "I am holy." From that position, logic dictates that any description of evil, then, cannot apply to God. This is not a new idea, but it is an important one.

I opened this book with a story of a father who deliberately chooses to leave two of his own children to certain doom, when he had all of the opportunity and capability to do otherwise. I know of no person who could read that story and imagine the terror and eventual death of the abandoned children, without saying that the father was guilty of a moral wrong – in fact, that his actions were evil. As it turns out, Scripture itself says that. James 4:17 says, "Anyone who knows the good he ought to do and doesn't do it, sins." If the father in the story sins by knowing the good that he ought to do, and not doing it, then how can God hold that father to a standard higher than the one to which he holds himself? If God is what we say he is, omniscient, omnipresent, and omnipotent, then the idea that he chooses some to save, as that father did, and fails to save others that he has every opportunity and the capacity to save them, implies that God is as evil as that father. No wonder Luther found himself thinking of God as a rogue.

Every serious critic of predestination throughout history has dealt with this problem. The logic of Calvinism attacks the very character of God.

We met Williams James earlier. In his lecture on "Is Life Worth Living?" [15] he said:

> For my own part, I do not know what the sweat and blood and tragedy of this life mean . . . If this life be not a real fight, in which something is eternally gained for the universe by success, it is no better than a game of private theatricals from which one may withdraw at will. But it *feels* like a real fight – as if there were something really wild in the universe which we, with all our idealities and faithfulnesses, are needed to redeem . . . [16]

This life "feels like a real fight." It should not surprise us then, to see it portrayed in Scripture as a real fight. And if it feels like a real fight, and is portrayed in Scripture as a real fight, but if "every event which happens in the world is governed by the incomprehensible counsel of God," then it is not a real fight, and, as William James concluded, it is nothing more than a game of private theatricals with God as the conductor and us as his puppets – we are living in a delusion, deceived about the way the world is and our part in it. Consistently, Scripture instructs people not to deceive others: Leviticus 19:11: "Do not steal. Do not lie. Do not deceive one another." Proverbs 24:28: "Do not testify against your neighbor without cause, or use your lips to deceive." The character of God is at stake. Does he hold humans to a higher standard than he does himself? Is life a real fight, or is God a deceiver? What is God really like?

The nature of God

It takes all of the Bible to give a full picture of God, and even then, we have to admit that our perception can only be partial. We can get helpful glimpses, however, from specific passages of Scripture.

From 1 John 4:16, we see that God is love – that is, it is his nature. In dealing with the purpose of creation, above, I suggested that God created simply to have more to love. That logic comes from the fact that Scripture says he *is* love. However, it also says he is holy (Ps 99, Isa 57:15, Rev 3:7). It is from this perfect balance of love and holiness that we see redemption provided through the death of God's son. As sinful humans, in our fallen state, we could not restore ourselves to the state of holiness required to enter the presence of God. So God took action himself to do it. That's because God is love. It grieves God when people don't respond to his love. We see that over and over in the prophets, as God grieves, and even expresses anger at the way the Israelites responded to him. Even when he punished them, it grieved him to do so. In Ezekiel 33:11, God said, "Say to them, 'As surely as I live, declares the Sovereign LORD, I take no pleasure in the death of the wicked, but rather that they turn from their ways and live. Turn! Turn from your evil ways! Why will you die, O house of Israel?'" We see God expressing his nature – both his love and his holiness. This entire passage teaches the opposite of the arbitrary God, predetermining the destiny of people before they have ever even lived. It shows God consciously basing his treatment of people on their actions, and even changing that treatment if they themselves change.

Isaiah 40 is another one of those passages that helps us see the nature of God. The chapter starts with, "Comfort, comfort my people, says your God." The natural response is, "How do we do that?" The writer answers (my paraphrase), "Show them that God is coming. Show them what God is like." He is coming with power, in charge, bringing his reward with him. On one hand, he is like a shepherd, tending his flock, carrying the young in his arms, gently leading the nursing ewes. He's a personal, intimate God, aware of the details. He even knows the hairs on your head by number (Matt 10:30, Luke 12:7). He is never too busy. He can take as much time as he needs to know you and deal with you personally. With him, a day is like a thousand years (2 Pet 3:8).

But he is also awesome. He's the creator, the one who set the cosmos in motion, the one who knows each star by name. He causes nations to rise and fall. To him, the great empires of the world are like a drop in a bucket, like dust on the scales. He can see the big picture to such a degree, that a thousand years is like a day to him (2 Pet 3:8).

The chapter continues (Isa 40) – with a God like this, why would you make an idol from wood, and overlay it with some precious metal? How could any substitute ever hope to compete with the everlasting God, the creator of the heavens and the earth? With a God like this, how could you ever imagine that you are invisible to him, that he has forgotten you? Don't you realize that he never gets tired, and never encounters a situation that is beyond his understanding? Don't you realize that you can trust a God like this? In fact, when you see God in these ways, both up close and personal, and out there, big and awesome, it gives you a new sense of security, so that the problems of earth become inconsequential. Like God, you see current problems and opportunities in perspective, not as central to anything, but simply as part of a much bigger plan, which God is guiding to its eventual outcome. You can be like an eagle soaring over a battlefield, undisturbed by what is happening around you. With that kind of God, you can be extremely busy without burning out, and you can have periods of idleness, without falling into depression.

That's a snapshot of God – Isaiah 40. Theologically, he is shown to be both transcendent and immanent – both big and awesome and out there, and also up close and personal. My observation is that churches tend to have difficulty keeping both of those characteristics in perspective. Either they tend to be cerebral in their view of God, or emotional about it. The more intellectually God is approached, it seems, the more he will be viewed as transcendent. This seems to be the approach of John Calvin, the Puritans, and those who follow in their footsteps. "Predestinarianism presupposes the utter transcendence and hiddenness of an all-determining God,"[17] says Peter Thuesen. By contrast, the more emotionally God is approached, it seems, the more he will be seen as immanent. But Scripture teaches us to see him as both. The "fear of God" is a common Old Testament theme, but it is also found in the New Testament (cf. Rom 3:18, 1 Pet 2:17, Rev 14:7). We should hold God in reverence. But we also seem to be invited into a personal friendship with him.

In Exodus 33:11, Moses wrote that God spoke to him as a man speaks to a friend. Several times, Abraham is called God's friend (cf. 2 Chron 20:7, Isa 41:8, James 2:23). In John 15, Jesus said that when his disciples obey his commands, they move from the position of servants to that of friends, and John also indicated in his first pastoral letter that people can know God personally (John 15:15, 1 John 2:13).

Let's think about that. Jesus indicated that the difference between servants and friends is how much they are included in *knowing*. Strict obedience is required of servants, even when they don't know why something has to be done. Not so with friends. Jesus said, "I have called you friends, for everything that I learned from my Father I have made known to you" (John 15:15). In his farewell prayer for his disciples in John 17, often called The High Priestly Prayer, Jesus equated eternal life with *knowing* God the Father, and Jesus Christ, the one he sent. That whole prayer shows a deep, personal love for his disciples – his friends – and in the prayer, he deliberately extends that personal relationship to those of us who later believe (John 17:20). The end of the prayer reflects the desire of his heart, that the love that the Father has for him may be in his disciples as well, and, Jesus says, "that I myself may be in them." That's personal.

The concept is developed further in the New Testament. In Acts 5, after the apostles had been arrested and jailed, then miraculously freed in the night by an angel of the Lord, they were brought back to answer to the highest Jewish council, the Sanhedrin. In making his defense, Peter said, "We are witnesses of these things, and so is the Holy Spirit, whom God has given to those who obey him" (Acts 5:32). I would like to suggest that this hints at a principle that is poorly understood, but one that runs throughout Scripture.

A famous verse that is often used in presenting the gospel is Revelation 3:20. In it, Jesus says, "Here I am! I stand at the door and knock. If anyone hears my voice and opens the door, I will come in and eat with him, and he with me." But in the context in which that invitation is given, it is not an invitation to unbelievers, to salvation, but to believers, to a time of lingering, intimate fellowship with Jesus. But don't detach that invitation from what Peter said, that the Holy Spirit is given to those who obey him. Jesus makes it clear, in John 15 and 16, that he and the Holy Spirit are of one mind: "the Spirit of truth, who goes out from the Father, will testify about me" (John 15:26). As he continued, he said (slightly summarized), "when the Spirit of truth comes, he will guide you into all truth. He will not speak on his own; he will speak only what he hears, and he will bring glory to me by taking from what is mine and making it known to you. All that belongs to the Father is mine. That is why I said the Spirit will take from what is mine and make it known to you" (John 16:13-15).

I think we can be theologically safe saying that the Holy Spirit, who does "not speak on his own," who "will guide you to all truth," who is given to us "as a deposit guaranteeing our inheritance" (Eph 1:13-14), is the means through which Jesus lives in us, as he suggested in his prayer. This is also consistent with his illustration of the vine and branches in John 15, "If a man remains in me and I in him .... If you remain in me and my words remain in you ..." and with his statement that the one who obeys his commands "will be loved by my Father, and I too will love him and show myself to him" (John 14:21).

The point is, there is a principle that runs throughout Scripture, connecting obedience with a close, personal friendship with God. Psalm 15, short but profound, equates being blameless and righteous with being allowed to dwell in the sanctuary of the Lord, to live on his holy hill. King David, one of the few Old Testament saints of whom it was said that they were filled with the Holy Spirit (Ps 51:10), repeatedly connected righteousness with knowing God and being rewarded by him (cf. Ps 18:18-26, 36:10). Following Jesus' time on earth, there is an interconnectedness between the Holy Spirit and Jesus himself, in that it appears that the way Jesus reveals himself today, apart from his Word, is generally, if not exclusively, through the Holy Spirit.

Conversely, we are challenged not to "grieve the Holy Spirit of God, with whom you were sealed for the day of redemption" (Eph 4:30). In fact, writing to believers, Paul indicates that it is possible to quench or extinguish the Holy Spirit (1 Thes 5:19). How do we reconcile these statements?

I think the answer is: they are related to the nature of God. If John Calvin's statement, that "every event which happens in the world is governed by the incomprehensible counsel of God," then the whole idea of the work of the Holy Spirit, like Jesus suggesting that his disciples pray for God's will to be done on earth as it is in heaven, is nonsensical. If God's will is already being done in every event, why imply that humans have a choice in responding to an invitation from Jesus, why imply that it is possible to grieve or even quench the Holy Spirit? Why would God grieve at the death of the wicked? Why would he say that what he has planned for them will change if they change?

The answer, of course, lies in the possibility that humans really do have free will, that the offer God makes is legitimate, that a choice can be made, that the invitation can be accepted or refused, that human decisions affect the future, that humans themselves determine their final destiny. God has the ability to make decisions that affect the future, and he has placed his image in us. If his image is in us, what does that imply?

The image of God

As God's final act of creation, he made humans "in his own image." What that means has been debated over the centuries, and it won't be settled here. But some rational observations can be made. For example, God thinks and feels, and we know we think and feel. God is the creator, and we observe a creative bent in humans. God is relational, and we are as well. God also has the ability to make decisions, and as we experience life, it appears that we do as well. When God makes a decision, it affects future events. From the way we experience life, it appears that the same is true for us.

Every day, we hear of people making wrong decisions on the highway, resulting in accidents that injure or kill people. We all know people who choose to use alcohol or drugs to escape from the pressures of life, and who subsequently become addicted, with all the destruction associated with that. We know of people who have sex for years without pregnancy because they prevent it through actions they take, and others have unplanned pregnancies because they don't take the same precautions. We know people who give birth, and people who abort their unborn babies. No responsible parent fails to teach their kids to look both ways before crossing the street. People who work hard, or choose higher education, tend to have more success in life.

If life actually works the way it appears to work, then the image of God in us includes the ability to make choices that affect the future. But this is the sticking point where the logic of Calvinism seems to run into real problems in terms of internal consistency – if God governs in every event, it seems to preclude the possibility that humans really do have the ability to make decisions that alter the future. So how far does the image of God reach in humans? Consider an illustration.

IF LIFE ACTUALLY WORKS THE WAY IT APPEARS TO WORK, THEN THE IMAGE OF GOD IN US INCLUDES THE ABILITY TO MAKE CHOICES THAT AFFECT THE FUTURE

Sara watched with pride as Benjamin strode to the podium. On one side of her was his wife, and on the other side, their two kids – Sara's grandchildren. It was Benjamin's first official Sunday as senior pastor. He was 36. Sara was glad she could be here. The four-hour drive had been worth it. He looked confident, but she suspected he was nervous. Even if he was, she knew he would do a good job. His dependence on God would sustain him.

Benjamin was named after Jacob's youngest son in the Bible, the one Rachel died giving birth to. Sara named him after that Benjamin because she saw his birth as her own death, like Rachael's. Not physical death, like Rachael, but the death of her life, her hopes, her dreams. And it had turned out that way, to a large extent. Still, she was proud of him, and glad she had kept him.

It hadn't been easy, but it had been her choice. Or choices. The first one had been the night she conceived. She didn't think about it often these days, but over the years, when she did, it had always amazed her, and shamed her in the early days, how one decision could be so life-altering. Her siblings had grown up and left the house, and she was the only one left – a senior in high school. Not wild, but independent. On the fateful evening, her parents had reminded her they had a planning event at the church that would probably run late, and they reminded her of the school night policy – no friends over, no TV, no lengthy phone calls, in bed by 11:00. It was before the days of cell phones or internet. Do your homework, get ready for school tomorrow, and if anything comes up, call the older couple next door. They're always willing to help.

When her parents were gone, Sara called her best friend, and they arranged to meet at the end of the block in a hour. They could hang out for an hour, and she would still be home at least an hour before her parents. She breezed through her homework, then got dressed. She didn't have really short skirts, because her parents wouldn't allow it, but she selected the shortest she had. She knew she had nice legs, and she liked to show them. The guys noticed.

Her friend was waiting as planned, along with her older sister. They needed her to get them into the bar a couple of blocks away, even though nobody really cared. It was a fun time, laughing, talking, feeling grown up, just as they had planned. Sara didn't drink, even though she didn't really share her parent's beliefs about total abstinence. And, when it was time for her to go, she left. It had been fun, but she knew she would be in trouble if her parents found out. It was not worth the risk. Her friends' parents were more lenient, so they were going to stay awhile longer.

Sara was not afraid to walk home alone. It was a safe neighborhood, it was not late, and it was just a couple of blocks.

She had just passed the end of the small shopping center when she heard a noise behind her. It startled her, so she turned to see what it was. She barely got a glance at a young, foreign looking man, when he hit her just below the ear.

When Sara woke up, her first awareness was a general sense of hurting. It took her a minute to get past the fogginess, but as her consciousness returned, it was accompanied by a throbbing in her head. She realized she was moaning, and tried to control it. She was feeling panicked, but tried to control that too. Slowly, she gained possession of her consciousness, sat up, and looked around. She appeared to be alone, in the dark, in the alley behind the shopping center. Movement caused pain in her groin, but other than that and a killing headache, she seemed to be okay. Gradually, the memory of the evening returned, then she remembered the noise behind her, the young man, and him hitting her. Feeling sick, she thought, "So this is what it's like to get mugged. I'm fortunate to be alive." As she struggled to her feet, the pain in her groin was worse. She felt as if she had been kicked by a horse. She also felt a growing sense of shame. How could she be so stupid? So careless? Her parents were going to kill her if they found out. How was she going to explain her wallet getting stolen?

In spite of the pain, now, Sara got up and almost ran the short distance to her house. She had no idea how long she had been out of it, but she was so glad her parents weren't home yet. She felt filthy, violated, so her first thought was to shower. It was only when she started undressing that the full impact of what had happened hit her. Her panties were missing, and there was blood on her legs. No wonder I'm hurting there, she thought, starting to cry. She sat on the toilet for an eternity, sobbing, cursing herself, and praying for some way out. If her parents ever found out, they would kill her.

Finally, Sara gained enough control to shower. No amount of soap and water could wash away the feeling of being dirtied, of being violated, but finally she quit, finished up, and took the strongest pain killer she could find. She was barely in bed when she heard her parents come in. She spent the night in pain, crying and cursing herself for her stupidity.

Somehow, with a little make-up, Sara got to school and through the next day without anybody noticing anything wrong. The first few days were a nightmare. She was exhausted from lack of sleep and the emotional strain, but eventually, she regained control and life normalized. She waited a few days before telling her parents she had lost her wallet, so they helped her sort it out, and slowly, she tried to put the whole sordid event behind her. Things were busy enough that she did not notice when she missed her next period, but a couple of months later, it hit her that she was missing cycles, and the whole sense of panic and shame and dread returned. This time, though, she could not hide and pretend it hadn't happened.

Sara's parents hadn't killed her, as she had told herself they would. They were shocked, but eventually they got over that, and proved to be the godly parents she had always known they were. Even though it had been several weeks, they insisted she report the rape to the police, and when she did, they matched a photo to her description of the young man who had done it. He had been arrested just a few days later not far away, when he had done the same thing again. Only, that time, he had been caught. He was an illegal immigrant, drifting from town to town, robbing and raping. When he got out of prison, they assured her, he would be deported. Sara never had to face him. She had avoided knowing his name, although she was sure she could find it out if she ever needed to know it. School was nearly out, so she graduated before she really started to show. That was a relief. Abortion was out of the question, but adoption was a possibility. In the end, with her parents' support, she made the second life-altering choice – to keep the child. The baby had been due in the fall, so she had not started college. In fact, she never did. Since her parents both worked, they could afford for Sara and her baby to live with them, and Sara got a job as a waitress at a restaurant across town. She went to work just as soon as her mother got home, and it had worked fine. She even made pretty good money, with tips, but it would not have been enough to maintain a decent home for the two of them. She was eternally grateful for her parents' love and support. And Benjamin was raised with godly role models.

Benjamin had proven to be a sensitive child. All boy, always busy, but still compassionate and cooperative. When he was only six, he had committed his life to Christ as Sara prayed with him at bedtime, after her parents had hosted some missionaries in their home. Something in their stories had touched him, and he wanted to serve God with his life, too. He had made it through high school and college without major mishaps, worked for a couple of years, then married a young lady he met at church. Together, they decided he should attend seminary. Afterward, he had been an associate pastor for several years, and they had had two kids so far. He was a godly man. And now here they all were, about to hear his first sermon as senior pastor. Sara was so glad she had kept him.

Does the image of God in us give us the ability to make decisions that affect the future, or are all events controlled by God? Consider the implications of this story based on Calvin's ideas, both of predestination of individuals for salvation, and God's control of all events.

In the story, a teenage girl disobeys her parents and goes out alone while they are gone, gets raped by an illegal alien drifter who is in town for only a few hours, gets pregnant and has a child who is subsequently saved.

Using Calvin's reasoning, not only the salvation of the child was predetermined before the foundation of the earth, but so were the disobedience of the girl, and the illegal immigration and the rape. They were all necessary for that particular pregnancy to occur, considering the lifespan of both the ovum and the sperm and the donors from which they originated and the unlikelihood of the two parents meeting at that particular time and having sex to produce that particular child whose salvation was predetermined before the salvation of the earth. For that particular sperm to fertilize that particular ovum was impossible within a legitimate, God-sanctioned relationship. Two people came into sexual contact with each other through a variety of different acts of sin – the man is in the country illegally, he forcibly rapes the girl, and both of those acts are evidence of a general disregard for the law and the human dignity of others.

The girl is at the scene through an act of disobedience to her parents, and a general attitude of immediate gratification, of seeking pleasure irresponsibly. Yet all of those acts – his and hers – and the attitudes that motivated them, were necessary for the pregnancy. So if Calvin is correct, that the salvation of the child was predetermined before the foundation of the earth, then the child himself was predetermined before the foundation of the earth, requiring that the precise time of the conception was predetermined before the foundation of the earth, so the motivations and the actions that produced the pregnancy must have been predetermined before the foundation of the earth – in order for that particular sperm to fertilize that particular ovum for that particular child to exist so he could be saved and spend eternity in heaven.

It is no wonder that Luther, considering these possibilities, worried about God being a rogue. It is no wonder that the Geneva physician, Jérôme-Hermès Bolsec, accused Calvin of making God the author of sin with his doctrine of predestination. Calvin responded to

Bolsec exactly the way powerful people do when they cannot adequately answer the argument of a critic. They attack the opponent instead of the argument. Jesus was killed under similar circumstances. Bolsec was simply banished from the city.

Maybe there is another way of seeing the world that does not make God a rogue. For one thing, I have already attempted to establish that individual predestination for salvation is 1) a worldview issue, based on paradigms of fatalism and individualism, and 2) a translation issue. In the original understanding of the Bible, I have suggested, the concept was never there, and with better translation, it would never be there.

The other way of seeing the world is related to the nature of God, the way his image is reflected in us, and the way the spiritual battle works. If we allow both Scripture and our own experience to shape our understanding, we will conclude that humans, made in the image of God, do in fact have the ability to make decisions that affect the future. All of us live that way, every day. In practice, we don't even question it. We simply accept it. Why should our theoretical framework not be consistent with what we observe and live out every day?

The question is, how does it work? What is THE PLAN? Numerous concepts converge to provide both a worldview and a theological framework, better than those provided by Calvinism. Let's start with the sovereignty of God.

The sovereignty of God and human free will

The locals call the town "Killie" but officially it's Kilmarnock, a distortion of its Gaelic origin – *Church of My Little Ernan*, named after the saint who founded it. It was here in Kilmarnock that Robert Burns, Scotland's revered poet, published his first book of poetry in 1786, and Johnnie Walker started blending his famous whiskey here around 1819. Until his death in 2012, it was also home to John Peter Houison

Craufurd, twenty-eighth Laird of Craufurd Castle, and holder of the royal ceremonial role, "Washer of the Sovereign's Hands." He inherited the title and the role along with the castle.

Peter Houison Craufurd came from a long line of washers of sovereign hands, the first of which was John Howieson. It seems that James V, King of Scots from 1513 to 1542, was known for wandering around the country disguised as a private person in order to hear complaints which might not otherwise reach his ears. During one such venture, the king was attacked by robbers at Cramond Bridge, near Edinburgh. One John Howieson, a local farm-worker, rescued him, then took him home and washed his injured hands. As a reward, the king granted Howieson ownership of Braehead, the farm on which he worked. The grant carried with it the condition that Howieson and his successors would always be ready to wash the reigning monarch's hands in Holyrood or at Cramond Bridge, a condition enshrined in the role the Howieson descendants fill today. Once in every monarch's reign, they ceremonially wash the sovereign hands from a silver pitcher.[18]

It's a common theme in the history of storytelling – the king who goes away and leaves someone else in charge. Jesus used it himself. In a parable retold in all three of the synoptic gospels, Jesus told of a landowner who planted a vineyard, built a wall around it, dug a winepress, and built a watchtower, then rented the place to some farmers and went away on a journey (Matt 21:33, Mark 12:1, Luke 20:9). In early English literature, the king in disguise was a popular theme.[19]

Every time this story is told, in whatever era, in whatever form, it makes the point: the king has the right to rule, but is temporarily choosing not to do so, and because he makes that choice, he gives others the right to make decisions that may not agree with what the king himself would do. He gives them the right to exercise their free will. He also places himself at the mercy of the free will of his subjects. The stories always make it clear that there is a vast difference between having the right to rule, and exercising that right. Even though King

James V had the right to rule, if John Howieson had not come to his rescue, he might well have been killed by his own subjects. In Jesus' human life, he had the right to rule, but he *was* killed by his own subjects. In the parable he told, the tenants of the vineyard killed the owner's son, the rightful heir and future ruler. The right to rule, and ruling, are two very different things.

One of the central themes of Calvinism is the sovereignty of God. God is sovereign over all. "Every event which happens in the world is governed by the incomprehensible counsel of God." The whole world functions according to the decrees of God. "Are not two sparrows sold for a penny? Yet not one of them will fall to the ground apart from the will of your Father. And even the very hairs of your head are all numbered" (Matt 10:29-30).

If Scripture portrays a tri-polar world, one in which angels and demons are actively engaged in a battle for the good and evil of humanity, and in which humans have the ability to make choices that affect the future, then rather than fighting against that worldview, as Calvin did, why not seek a worldview which harmonizes not only those concepts, but our personal, daily experiences, and other themes of Scripture as well? As it turns out, it is not so difficult.

To begin with, using James V as an illustration, we can dispense with the idea that the sovereignty of God means that *having* sovereignty requires that that sovereignty is exercised, *of necessity*, at all times, in all events. This is one of the major flaws of logic on which Calvinism is based. This will keep coming up, because it is interwoven with other ideas, but for now, we can concede that anytime anyone gives someone else the right to make a decision, it carries with it the possibility that the other person may make a decision that is wrong, or at least different, from what the permission giver would have wanted. By giving authority to others, we necessarily limit our own. To say that God has given humans free will, then, does not in the least impinge on God's sovereignty. It simply says that in his sovereignty, God has made the conscious decision to limit the *exercise* of his sovereignty to the extent that he has given created beings permission to exercise their free will.

To say that humans have free will, does not imply that that free will is limitless. We don't have the free will to do anything we want to do, but we do have the free will to do anything we want to do, *within the parameters* that God has established in this world. We cannot decide to be unborn, or to not die, or to take ourselves out from under eventual accountability to God, but, I contend, we do have the ability to choose our moral path in life, to choose whether we will submit our will to the will of God, to choose our eternal destiny. All of these ideas are supported by Scripture. When Satan was given permission to test Job, he was told he could do anything he wanted to do, except .... He had total free will within the limits God set on him, and he used that free will to kill and destroy. I contend that that concept applies to all of God's living creatures.

> IN HIS SOVEREIGNTY, GOD HAS MADE THE CONSCIOUS DECISION TO LIMIT THE *EXERCISE* OF HIS SOVEREIGNTY TO THE EXTENT THAT HE HAS GIVEN CREATED BEINGS PERMISSION TO EXERCISE THEIR FREE WILL

The eternal decrees of God

One of the foundational premises of Calvin's thinking was that all affairs of the cosmos operate based on the eternal decrees of God. His writings are replete with statements such as, "whatever has been declared by Scripture must be regarded as perpetual, and hence necessary."[20] At the risk of tedium, I make the observation again: his anchor premise was a form of fatalism – divine determinism – and everything he found in Scripture was interpreted through that paradigm. That was the "interpretive framework," the "plausibility structure," through which he evaluated everything.

Generally, theologians attribute the human inability to live a morally perfect life to the sin nature bestowed upon us by Adam's fall.[21] That seems to be Paul's argument in Romans 5:11 through chapter 8. In fact, Paul's argument there even seems to support human free will. He places significant responsibility on those who have been saved, to no longer live under the control of that sinful nature. He says, "**IF** you live according to the sinful nature, you will die," but "**IF** by the spirit, **YOU** put to death the misdeeds of the body, you will live" (Rom 8:13, emphasis added). Calvin refused to accept the sin nature as the cause of human inability to live a life of perfection. Instead, he says, it is the result of the "ordination and decree of God."[22]

Related to this, Calvin rebutted his opponents who believed that "God, by his energy, impressing man with the movement [ability or capacity] by which he can act, agreeably to the nature conferred upon him while man voluntarily regulates his own actions. In short," he summarized, "their doctrine is, that the world, the affairs of men, and men themselves, are governed by the power, but not by the decree of God."[23] Consider that paradigm in light of what we have already discussed. God made humans in his image, with all the aspects included in that – the ability to think, feel, make choices, express themselves creatively, etc. He immediately told them to "fill the earth and subdue it . . . to rule over everything that moves" (Gen 1:28). In other words, he told them *what* to do, but left the *how* to them. That sounds awfully like giving them the *power* to act, but not *decreeing* their actions. And, as it turns out, that is exactly the way we experience life.

I know of nobody who argues against "decrees of God." The question is not whether they exist, the question is whether they control *all that happens*. The laws of nature, and I would even suggest, spiritual laws, fall under the concept of decrees. They are the established parameters, the boundaries determined by God, within which the universe functions. As long as this era that we call "time" is in process, they "govern" what can happen, but even then, it does not appear consistent with Scripture to argue that they are "perpetual, and hence necessary." Miracles and other supernatural events demonstrate that God or empowered spiritual beings can suspend those laws on occasion (as with the bush burning but not being consumed in Exodus 3:2, the provision for the Israelites in the desert for 40 years, and the shadow moving backwards ten steps in 2 Kings 20:9-11). We don't know what laws or decrees operate within the spiritual realm, but it appears that the natural laws that limit human activity, do not limit spirit beings in the same way. Spirits don't appear to be affected by gravity, for example, and they seem to be able to pass through matter that feels solid to us. Think of Jesus suddenly appearing in locked rooms (John 20:19, 26), and the angel of the Lord ascending in the flame (Judg 13:20). At best, then, it seems that the decrees of God provide boundaries that humans and spirits cannot normally cross, but within which, we have complete freedom to act and make decisions.

In fact, that seems to be precisely what God says about the way things work. Consider this passage:

> If I tell the righteous man that he will surely live, but then he trusts in his righteousness and does evil, none of the righteous things he has done will be remembered; he will die for the evil he has done. And if I say to the wicked man, 'You will surely die,' but he then turns away from his sin and does what is just and right – if he gives back what he took in pledge for a loan, returns what he has stolen, follows the decrees that give life, and does no evil, he will surely live; he will not die (Ezek 33:13-15).

Notice three things in this passage: first, it is God talking. Second, he tells a person he will live, but then, based on the person's actions, he changes his mind. And third, he uses the word *decrees* not to mean his determining of the person's actions or destiny, but in a way that could logically be interpreted to mean "inevitable consequences that follow actions."

What God said through Ezekiel, I believe, is the same concept Jesus taught in the Sermon on the Mount. He gave the Golden Rule, then applied it. He said, "So in everything, do to others what you would have them do to you, for this sums up the Law and the Prophets. Enter through the narrow gate. For wide is the gate and broad is the road that leads to destruction, and many enter through it. But small is the gate and narrow the road that leads to life, and only a few find it" (Matt 7:12-14). Notice that there is no break at all between these two statements. I have so often heard these verses applied to heaven and hell – but that is not the context. The context has nothing to do with eternal destinies. Jesus is dealing with how we interact with other people. When we treat others the way we want to be treated, *they* flourish, the *relationship* flourishes – it is life giving. When we compete and abuse, it leads to destruction. And how do most people function? Selfishly, for sure. The self-serving road is indeed broad and well travelled, and destructive. And the self-sacrificing road, the road we would like others to travel in relation to us, is narrow and almost empty. How much better the world works when we cooperate rather than compete. God knew that before Jesus expressed it. He created people to be the way they are, including the way the Fall has affected us. He knows that we blossom with encouragement and wither under criticism. He seems to assume that it is obvious, so he told Ezekiel to remind the Israelites of that several hundred years before Jesus said it. Truly the one who follows the decrees, the principles, that give life will surely live, because that is exactly the way God wants us all to live.

One verse that is often used to suggest that all things must either be decreed by God, or they do not happen, is Lamentations 3:37: "Who can speak and have it happen if the Lord has not decreed it?" This is another example of concepts being more important than the words used to communicate them, and reading a verse within its context. The concept here is how God responds to people. We see the contrast: "The LORD is good to those whose hope is in him, to the one who seeks him" (Lam 3:25), and "Why should any living man complain when punished for his sins?" (Lam 3:39). This is the same passage that is famous for saying that God's "compassions never fail. They are new every morning" (Lam 3:22-23). It also says, "he does not willingly bring affliction or grief to the children of men" (Lam 3:33). In its context, the concept is that no human can defy the God of the universe and win. The very next verse summarizes what 3:25 and 3:39 say, that both the calamities and good things come from God, but, within this context, both of those actions are in response to what the humans do. Only when the verse is detached from its context, can it be understood to make every human action the result of universal decrees of God. Here is a much better rendering of Lamentations 3:37: "Who can speak and have it happen outside of the decrees of the Lord?" This not only allows God's decrees to be limiting boundaries within which we have free will, but it is consistent with the rest of the passage in which the verse is found.

Circumcision

One thing that is not normally discussed in polite company, but which is openly discussed in Scripture, is related to this concept of *boundaries,* the ability of humans to make decisions within certain parameters. It is male circumcision. History documents that the Israelites were not the only nations who practiced circumcision during the Old Testament era.[24] Within the history of Israel, however, Scripture shows that it was God's idea for his people. He made it the evidence of his covenant with Abraham (Gen 17), then formalized it in the Law of Moses (Lev 12:3). Later, it was God who first used physical circumcision as an illustration of a spiritual principle.

In the last chapters of Leviticus, as God was nearing the end of giving the law to Moses on Mt. Sinai, he showed that he assumed human free will – that the Israelites had the ability to choose to obey his law, or disobey it. He promised rewards for obedience, like rain in season and fruitful crops; he promised punishment for disobedience. If after disobedience, however, his people repented, God promised to remember his covenant with them.

Within this ending to the Law of Moses, there are a lot of conditional statements. If . . . then. God says, "if you humans do . . ., then I, God, will do." That in itself seems to contradict Calvin's view on human free will and on decrees of God being perpetual. But that is not the point here. The point here is that God connects disobedience with having *uncircumcised hearts* (Lev 26:41). That illustration was introduced in Scripture by God himself. Why?

Since all Israelite males were circumcised on the eighth day, every person in the nation was familiar with circumcision. The boys grew up with it, and so did the girls. The family structure was very traditional, with clear male and female roles. Young girls would have been changing the local equivalent of diapers on their younger brothers as long as they could remember. *Everybody* in the culture knew about circumcision. So when God used it as a spiritual metaphor, they knew what he was talking about.

At the risk of being graphic and offending someone, it must be understood that circumcision does not remove all of the male foreskin. The procedure removes the *excess* foreskin. Unless an uncircumcised male is sexually aroused, he has no control over whether the foreskin covers the end of his penis or not. It just does. He can choose to pull it back, and even hold it back, but left to itself, it will return to its natural position, covering the end of the penis. With circumcision, however, he has a completely different level of choice. If he chooses, he can pull the foreskin back, and it will stay there, or he can pull it forward, and it will stay there. Circumcision gives him that choice. When God used physical circumcision as an illustration of the condition of the heart, he was saying something that he knew his audience would understand. In Leviticus 26:41, he said, ". . . when their uncircumcised hearts are humbled . . ." so God himself provided the original connection between what happens physically and what needs to happen spiritually, to the heart.

This concept is repeated near the end of Moses' life as he again challenged the people to see the similarity between physical circumcision and what needed to happen to their hearts. "Circumcise your hearts, therefore, and do not be stiff-necked any longer" (Deut 10:16). Then later, ". . . when you and your children return to the LORD your God and obey him with all your heart . . . The LORD your God will circumcise your hearts and the hearts of your descendants . . ." (Deut 30:2, 6). Paul applies this same concept to believers after the time of Christ, when he says in Colossians 2, "In him you were also circumcised, in the putting off of the sinful nature, not with a circumcision done by the hands of men but with the circumcision done by Christ, . . . When you were dead in your sins and in the uncircumcision of your sinful nature, God made you alive with Christ" (Col 2:11,13). Stephen accused the Jewish leaders of having uncircumcised hearts (Acts 7:51), and they killed him for it. They knew exactly what he was saying. Do we? Did Calvin?

WITH SALVATION, THE HEART IS CIRCUMCISED, PART OF THE SIN NATURE IS REMOVED, AND WE HAVE A NEW ABILITY TO CHOOSE WHICH NATURE WE WILL SERVE

Returning to the argument in Romans 5-8, Paul develops the concept that for the unbeliever, the sin nature rules. The heart is uncircumcised. The sinner can choose to be good or do good temporarily, but when the effort stops, the natural tendencies will return. At that point, Paul says, we are slaves to sin. That would have been what the Jewish leaders understood Stephen to be accusing them of. But, Paul argues, with salvation, the heart is circumcised, *part* of the sin nature is removed, and we have a new ability to choose which nature we will serve – the sinful one, or the spiritual one. Even though the believer's old nature has been crucified with Christ so "that we should no longer be slaves to sin" (Rom 7:6), we are still told to "not let sin reign" in our mortal bodies, not to "offer the parts of your body to sin," but to "offer yourselves to God . . . offer the parts of your body to him as instruments of righteousness" (Rom 7:12-13). That was God's point in the Old Testament, and it is Paul's in the New Testament. The critical point here is not the process by which this spiritual circumcision occurs – that will be dealt with later – but the fact that humans have the ability to make choices that affect the future. To make an important spiritual point, God deliberately used a physical illustration that everybody would understand, one that had to do with the human's ability to choose. He placed personal responsibility squarely within the capacity of the human to make decisions that affect the future, rather than controlling those decisions himself.

Control vs. influence

The need for control is the mark of an insecure, needy person, not a confident one. Addictions and the need for control go hand in hand. In a remarkable book called *Blessed are the Addicts*, John Martin makes the point that effective people create change around them through personal *influence*, not through the exercise of control or power. That means, he says, that they must be willing to live with less change than they might like, simply because they don't have enough influence to create more change. He suggests that there is a paradox, however, in that if they try to create more change by exerting control, they may actually get less change, because people resist being controlled. Then, he concludes, the greatest power in the world is the ability to avoid trying to be in control. It brings true freedom – freedom to love, freedom to be oneself with nothing or no one getting in the way.[25]

We would not give Martin's observations the same credibility we give Scripture, but the interesting thing is how similar they are to what Scripture seems to teach. And, how vastly different from what Calvinism teaches.

We are again put in the position of suggesting that if God functions similarly to the way we do, then certain conclusions can be drawn. Again, we admit that we will never match God in any way, but with his image resident in us, it seems to be safe to assume some similarities.

When we consider control, then, we have to examine the motive for wanting to exert it. If one is the parent of a small child, then to control that child's propensity to run headlong into the street, is not selfish, but in the interests of the child. The parent, more knowledgeable than the child, can see the destructive potential of the child's actions, so they take control to prevent harm to the child. The motive is not self centered, but others centered. We will return to that later.

If the same adult attempts to control their spouse, however, the motivation would likely be selfish. In fact, if we're honest, we would probably admit that almost anytime one adult attempts to control another adult who is fully rational, the motives are selfish. Exceptions would be possible, perhaps, when one adult is about to make a decision the results of which they don't fully understand, but generally, power grabs are selfishly motivated. Considering that the ultimate damnation for a human is to spend eternity in hell, it seems that if God were going to control, it would be to keep the irresponsible person, like the irresponsible child who runs into traffic, from taking action to his own harm. If God does exert control, but not to prevent harm to those for whom he has the power to do so, it appears that God's motives must be considered selfish, rather than protective of those who need his care. Would this be loving in a parent? Does this sound like a loving God?

Scripture is full of illustrations that show God attempting to influence people, rather than controlling them. Consider Moses giving his final challenge to the people of Israel, just before they were going to finally enter the promised land. This is what Moses said, slightly condensed:

"Now what I am commanding you today is not too difficult for you or beyond your reach ... See, I set before you today life and prosperity, death and destruction. For I command you today to love the LORD your God, to walk in his ways, and to keep his commands, decrees and laws; then you will live and increase, and the LORD your God will bless you ... But if your heart turns away and you are not obedient ... you will certainly be destroyed ... This day I call heaven and earth as witnesses against you that I have set before you life and death, blessings and curses. Now choose life, so that you and your children may live ..." (Deut 30:11-30).

This is Moses talking, and it sounds much more like influence than control. In fact, it is interesting that he implies that his audience not only has the ability to obey or disobey God's commands and laws, but also God's *decrees*. What is more to our point, however, is that Moses, in his farewell speech, is simply repeating to Israel what God himself had told them years earlier, in Leviticus 26. When God said it, it had the same ring – of influence, not control.

Just before Paul made his observation about circumcision of the sinful nature, which we looked at earlier, he said: "For in Christ all the fullness of the Deity lives in bodily form, and you have been given fullness in Christ, who is the head over every power and authority" (Col 2:9-10). These verses make two important points: 1) Jesus' own power and authority, and 2) the fact that Jesus reflects the fullness of God. Whatever Jesus looked like, God looks like. Jesus even said that himself. When Philip said, "Lord, show us the Father," Jesus replied, "Anyone who has seen me has seen the Father" (John 14:8-9).

When Jesus was about to be arrested in the Garden of Gethsemane, he identified himself as the one they sought. As he did so, "they drew back and fell to the ground" as if knocked off their feet by some invisible hand (John 18:6). Then Peter started swinging his sword, and Jesus asked him, "Do you think I cannot call on my Father, and he will at once put at my disposal more than twelve legions of angels?"

(Matt 26:53). Whatever knocked the arresting mob off their feet, could have kept them there. Jesus could have asked for backup, and ended the whole scene. But he did not. When he could have taken control, he did not. If he is fully representative of God, and if that's the way he functioned, then God functions that way.

Consider the events that led to Jesus' arrest, including his betrayal. I'm actually convinced that Judas Iscariot did not intend to get Jesus killed by betraying him. I'm convinced that he knew who Jesus was – the promised messiah – and he knew what Jesus was capable of. For three years, he had watched Jesus heal people, bring them back to life, feed thousands from one lunch basket, walk on water, still storms, engage the masses through his magnetic personality, win debates with the smartest theologians and lawyers, and on and on. Judas had been present when other disciples jostled for positions of prominence in Jesus' coming kingdom (Matt 20, Mark 9, Luke 9). Like all the other disciples, he expected an earthly kingdom. None of them understood what Jesus was saying when he tried to prepare them for his death and resurrection. They could not get the traditional view of the conquering messiah out of their minds. I'm convinced that Judas did not intend to get Jesus killed, he simply intended to force the situation so Jesus would have to take control and set up his kingdom, when he seemed to be vacillating. That explanation better fits his suicide after Jesus' death, than his trying to get Jesus killed. Judas was a self-serving man (cf. John 12:6). What did he stand to gain by getting Jesus killed? Thirty pieces of silver? He returned those when he saw the outcome of his actions. But if he could force Jesus to set up the kingdom that the Jewish expectation of the messiah portrayed, then as one of the inner circle, he had the potential to suddenly be among the top power brokers in Judea, and possibly in all the world.

> **JUDAS WAS TRYING TO FORCE JESUS TO TAKE CONTROL, WHEN THAT IS NOT THE WAY GOD WORKS**

The problem was, Judas was trying to force Jesus to take control, when that is not the way God works. This returns us to the sovereignty of God issue, and the spiritual battle. In the background, God was directing things in the spiritual world to achieve the outcome he wanted, but at the human level, it was all worked out through a process of influence, not control. This fits perfectly with the translation issues dealt with in Chapter 5, where I suggested that the words in the New Testament that have been consistently translated as *chosen* or *elect*, could be better translated as *gathered* or *choice*.

That should not be a surprise. In 2 Corinthians 3, in a passage we have already touched on in thinking about the use of the word *spirit*, the Apostle Paul contrasts the *spirit* of the law and the *letter* of the law. The spirit of the law is the principle behind a rule. The letter of the law is the rule itself. Principle: do not drive faster than is safe in these conditions. Law: speed limit 60 mph. There are places both on the German autobahn and in some of the western states of the US, where there is no posted speed limit. Drivers are free to drive as fast as they want to, as long as they don't violate the principle. With no speed limit, drivers have freedom. With a speed limit, the freedom is removed. The rule restricts, the principle releases. In summarizing his point, Paul says, "where the spirit of the Lord is, there is freedom" (2 Cor 3:17). God is a God of freedom. He is not choosing, applying irresistible grace – controlling – he is drawing, influencing, and gathering those who respond.

In Chapter 5, we saw that conversionary Protestants provided colonized people groups with the means to achieve freedom, by giving them the Bible in their own language – and with it, literacy and education. We also saw that while both the Muslims and Catholics were conversionary, the countries in which they worked did not achieve the same progress toward democracy, because both of those religions, in that day, attempted to control public discourse and religion. Where there was influence rather than control, there was a new freedom that enabled people to seek a new destiny. It did not work the same way in areas of high control. I suggest it worked the way it worked, because that is the way God himself works.

Hopefully, as we consider a few more pieces of the puzzle, it will be evident that the entire plan, THE PLAN, is not one of control, as Calvin insists, but one of influence at the human level, the deployment of angels at the spirit level, and the bringing of those two things together in a way that never violates the free will of either people or angels.

A final look at the logic of Paul's statement in 2 Corinthians 3:17. "Now the Lord is the Spirit, and where the Spirit of the Lord is, there is freedom." Think back to the point made in Chapter 5, about Paul's use of the word "spirit," and my comment just a couple of paragraphs above. My NIV Bible has the word capitalized here, but I think it should not be. However, consider the flow of logic either way. With the capital S: "Now the Lord is the Spirit, and where the Spirit of the Lord is, there is freedom." In this case, the word Spirit means the Holy Spirit, so where the Holy Spirit is, there is freedom. The Holy Spirit is omnipresent. Therefore, the entire world operates on a principle of freedom. With the small s, which is what I think fits Paul's argument better: "Now the Lord is the spirit, and where the spirit of the Lord is, there is freedom." I think Paul is saying that the Lord is the "spirit" or principle behind the law, and where that principle is allowed to *guide*, rather than a more restrictive law *requiring obedience*, there is freedom. That fits Paul's argument better. But either way, capital S or not, the point is, there is freedom.

The tri-polar world is interdependent, mutually influencing, but not coercive. Even Jesus clearing the temple illustrated the process. It produced a reaction, but did not force it. Jesus consistently took actions that enabled people to respond through decisions of their own. "Anyone who has seen me has seen the Father" (John 14:9). Doing nothing except what he saw the Father doing, Jesus influenced rather than controlled things.

The providence of God

It was a Saturday morning. At 10:00, a conference would start in Riga, the capital of Latvia. I was to be one of the speakers. We lived about an hour away. The previous evening, we had gotten a request to bring several copies of a certain book with us to the conference, so they could be available for a particular purpose. We recognized the importance of the request, so we agreed to do it. We knew that the largest Christian bookstore in Latvia was on our way to the conference, so, we reasoned, we could just leave 15 minutes early, grab the books, and still be at the conference in plenty of time.

The apparent simplicity of our assignment, however, was based on a false assumption – that the bookstore opened at 9:00 on Saturday, as it did on weekdays. In actual fact, it opened an hour later. In our ignorance, we set our departure time and made every effort to meet that schedule. To our dismay, however, one thing after another interfered. Our car had problems it had never had, and other things distracted and delayed us. As we were coming into Riga, we could see that we were barely going to get to the conference on time, even without stopping at the bookstore, But we couldn't *not* stop at the bookstore, because we had promised we would, and the books were important. The stress level in the car was palpable. With the near absence of traffic, I stopped on the street in front of the bookstore by the "no stopping or parking allowed at any time" sign, and Donna was going to run in and get the books while I waited and prayed that no police were around. Then we saw the business hours posted on the door. We were already running late, and they were not going to open until the conference was starting. We simply could not wait.

And at that precise second, we saw the manager of the bookstore unlocking the "Personnel only" door about fifty feet behind us. If he had arrived a minute earlier, he would have been inside when we arrived, and if he had arrived a minute later, we would have already been gone.

With all the delays we had experienced, the timing was precise – he knew us, he was happy to help, and we were on our way within minutes. We eased into the conference seconds before it was to start, to the visible relief of those responsible, and the day went as planned.

Coincidence, or the timing of God?

Another story.

Donna and I had been married about six years, and I had recently been discharged from the Marine Corps. We had been saving money to build our own house with our own hands, and we were in the process of doing that on the wooded acreage we had bought. We had put off having kids until the house was finished, so it was just the two of us. The work was hard, and the process was taking longer than we had anticipated, so we occasionally took a break.

One summer afternoon, after hours of sawing and hammering, we suddenly looked at each other and said, "Why don't we take a break, and go visit the Van der Vekens?" The Van der Vekens were a first generation immigrant family from the Netherlands who were small scale dairy farmers, from a long line of Dutch dairy farmers. So we jumped in our little Toyota pickup, and headed for the Van der Veken farm. It was about a five minute drive.

The instant we pulled into the long driveway that led to the Van der Vekens' house and dairy barn, we saw one of their teenage daughters start running toward us, both hands in the air, waving frantically. When we got to where she was, we found out why she was frantic. Her parents were gone, and her younger sister, less than a minute earlier, had been kicked by a cow in the dairy barn. When the cow kicked, its hoof had smashed the girl's hand against a metal post, so she was in a lot of pain, and the two girls did not know what to do. We did.

As things settled down, it became apparent that the girl's hand was not really seriously injured, but was painful and would be sore for a few days. The interesting thing to us, however, was the timing. We had suddenly and spontaneously decided to visit them about 10 minutes before the accident occurred. We arrived exactly as they needed us.

Coincidence, or the timing of God?

One more story, then I will stop. I could tell dozens more, but I won't. I promise.

My sister and her husband wanted to buy a home, but could not meet the requirements for the down payment. So the husband approached us, knowing Donna worked at the local bank and we had good relations with the bank president, and asked if we could get them a loan to use as the down payment on the house. He felt certain he could manage both the down payment loan and the mortgage with no problem. So we worked it out with the bank, but since the bank did not know my sister and her husband, and there would be no collateral, the loan was contingent on my signature to secure it.

In retrospect, if I had been both wiser and more familiar with biblical principles, I would have graciously declined their request. Twice, the book of Proverbs cautions against being security for the debt of others (Prov 6:1-5, 11:15), and simple wisdom suggests that if the banking institutions don't think it's a good idea, it's probably not. But in my ignorance, I agreed.

On the day we were to sign the papers, the brother-in-law came to our house just before the bank closed, and he and I were to go complete the deal. We headed to the bank in my work van, which was several years old. Visualize the situation. Where we lived was very rural – the wooded acreage mentioned earlier. Our driveway forms the fourth part of the intersection of two gravel roads, so as we exit our driveway, we can choose from three roads, all of which eventually lead to a highway, which then leads to town. On this particular day, I turned right. The highway was over a mile away. About halfway to the highway, we suddenly started smelling smoke, then we started seeing it – coming out from under the hood, and even seeping into the passenger area. We stopped the van, raised the hood, then stood looking helplessly at the engine on fire. We had no fire extinguisher, and couldn't even do anything productive like throwing sand on it. The hard gravel road offered only a few loose pebbles, and it was a dry summer, so the soil nearby was as hard as concrete.

Then, as we thought we were about to watch the entire van burn up, we heard a truck rushing up behind us. Just as we had stopped the van and opened the hood, the driver of a propane delivery truck had walked out of the small store at the end of the gravel road, and as he was getting into his truck, he looked our direction, saw what was happening, and rushed to help. Where could you find more fire extinguishers than on a propane truck? So the fire was out in seconds, and as it turned out, no significant harm was done. Some burned wires were all. The fire was caused by a small gas leak, which was also easily fixed.

But the story does not end there. With the fire out, the crisis was over, so our attention returned to our original goal. The bank loan. We left the van where it was, rushed back to our house, got another car, and got to the bank just before they locked the doors.

The loan was signed, the brother-in-law lost his job, lost the house they bought, defaulted on the loan, and Donna and I had to pay it off. It took several years, and severely crippled our finances until it was behind us. It was a painful experience.

Was the fire in the van a coincidence, or the timing of God?

The first two stories had good endings. Confirmation bias? This one did not have such a good ending. Coincidence, or the timing of God?

Consider some of the details. The gas leak was not instant. I had been smelling gasoline occasionally for several days, but could not find the source. Even a little gasoline on an engine is not a good idea, but if it is too little to find, and doesn't get on anything really hot, it's normally not critical, because there should be no sparks to ignite it, and the heat keeps it evaporated, so it doesn't accumulate. Where did the spark come from at that instant? The van had not been driven earlier, so the engine was not even hot when the fire started. The fire could have happened days earlier, or after the bank appointment, or I could have simply found the problem and fixed it. I had tried. Then there is the choice of road. I had turned right at the end of our driveway, when normally, I would have taken the middle road, because it's the shortest distance to the highway, and smoother road. Then there was the propane truck, whose driver happened to be travelling that particular highway at the time, needed a snack, decided to stop at the small store to get it, happened to park his truck so he could see down the gravel road, then he came out of the store just as the fire started, and just happened to look our direction at the right time. That's a lot of coincidences.

So let's consider if it could be the timing of God. We have already conceded that what we were about to do was unwise, and even violated principles taught in Scripture. Theoretically, then, we can assume that God would be against it taking place. Donna and I were trying to serve God at the time, to the best of our understanding. We were not living in rebellion, or living immorally, or in any other way in opposition to God's purposes. We were simply not well informed. It seems logical, then, that God would be working for us, not against us.

We've also admitted that the consequences of the loan were painful. If the van fire had caused a slightly longer delay, the bank would have closed, the papers would not have been signed that day, and since the brother-in-law had to take time off work and drive for over an hour to get to us, the whole thing might have been delayed for several days before he could arrange to come back – maybe long enough for us to reconsider. But that did not happen. The fire caused a delay, but not enough to prevent the loan being signed. So if God set out to delay us, or get our attention so we would reconsider what we were doing, he failed. Theologically, it is not acceptable that God could fail. Calvin certainly would not allow such a thing.

But maybe there is another explanation. Maybe God dispatched an angel, and said, "We need to prevent that loan being made." Just as God did with Adam in the garden, he tells the angel what to do, but not how to do it. So the angel comes up with a plan that allows it (the angel) to remain invisible and undetectable. It appears from Scripture, that spirit beings can plant thoughts into the minds of humans (remember the lying spirit in Ahab's prophets), and even that they can fail in what they are dispatched to do (the angel being delayed getting to Daniel and having to be rescued by a more powerful angel). So with a few suggestions to prepare the scene, the propane truck is in the right place at the right time, we make a right turn toward the store, a spark ignites gasoline on the engine, and the loan is delayed, without significant damage to our van. Good plan – it should work. Except, instead of taking the hint, we humans rushed around and went to the bank anyway. Both my brother-in-law and I were Christians, and we actually discussed whether this might be God trying to get our attention and stop what we were doing. We decided he could have used other ways, so we discarded the idea, and, with a little help, we rushed around to create a situation that was going to have long, painful results.

If God is in the controlling business, all of the speculation above is senseless. God arranged the loan, arranged the fire, arranged the propane truck, arranged for the brother-in-law to lose his job, arranged for the painful consequences of the loan. However, if God sent an angel to do the job, if the spiritual battle is real, if angels have free will and the ability to fail, and if humans have free will, if there is a tri-polar, interdependent world, then there are no logical or theological contradictions. There is one detail I deliberately failed to mention earlier, however. When the fire was out, the propane truck driver had to leave, so he did, but a neighbor showed up on a tractor to see what was happening. He took us on his tractor back to the house, so we could get another car and get to the bank on time. Without his help, we would have had to walk back to the house, and we could not have been at the bank before it closed. This particular man was an unbeliever, known to be adamantly opposed to things of God. If the demonic world was as interested in crippling our finances as the angelic world was in protecting them, what better human agent to send to help the process along? And if angels had arranged all the other pieces of the puzzle, they might not have been able to anticipate this detail, so the enemy exploited it.

The one theological question left unanswered in this last illustration, is related to the foreknowledge of God. Would God dispatch an angel to do a job when he knows in advance, through his foreknowledge, that the angel will fail? We will deal with that later, but for now, let's consider another implication of these illustrations.

THE PROVIDENCE OF GOD IS "THE DIVINE SUPER-INTENDENCE OF ALL EVENTS TOWARD PREORDAINED ENDS"

Confusion often arises in Christian thinking due to a failure to distinguish between two very different concepts. *Predestination* is the foreordaining of the destiny of individuals, although it is often extended to other things, and sometimes to all things. The *providence of God*, by contrast, is "the divine superintendence of all events toward preordained ends."[26] Few theologians throughout history, and even today, have disputed the providence of God. It is consistent with all of Scripture, consistent with the spiritual battle as Scripture portrays it, consistent with our practical experience (including the stories above), and consistent with the character of a loving, compassionate God. It also allows for human free will. Predestination, by contrast, has problems in all of those areas. Little wonder, then, that Calvin was controversial in his day, and that his doctrine continues to be today. According to Peter Thuesen, in his book, *Predestination: The American Career of a Contentious Doctrine*, "predestination has been one of the most important but unacknowledged sources of discord in churches across the denominational spectrum."[27]

Why can it be said that few theologians throughout history have disputed the providence of God, but predestination has been one of the most important sources of discord? I have already suggested two primary reasons why I challenge predestination: 1) it lacks internal consistency in light of Scripture, and 2) it is based on a worldview of fatalism and individualism. Now, I would like to suggest a third.

Unity is a characteristic of God. Orthodox Christianity teaches that the Trinity existed from eternity past without confusion or conflict, distinct in persons but one in essence, functioning together in perfect unity. There is no reason to think that has changed. Jesus said he had no agenda of his own, but only did what he saw the Father doing (John 5:19). He said, "it is the Father, living in me, who is doing the work" (John 14:10).Then he said that the Holy Spirit would go out from the Father, and "testify about me" (John 15:26). As John is ending his introduction of Jesus in his gospel, he says that the Father has placed everything in the Son's hands, and that God has given the Son the Spirit without limit (John 3:34-35). I think it can be defended theologically to say that Jesus did what the Father wanted done – through the power of the Holy Spirit. Consistently, unity is shown to be a characteristic of God. Paul reinforced that idea in Ephesians 4, pointing out that there is one Father, one Lord, one Spirit, one faith – and believers are to "make every effort" to maintain the unity that comes from the Spirit (Eph 4: 3). Consistently, unity is shown to be a goal among Christians. Jesus prayed for it among his followers (John 17:23), Paul advocated for it several times (Rom 15:5, Eph 4:3, 4:13, Col 3:14), and finally Paul told Titus to withdraw fellowship from a person who insists on being divisive (Tit 3:10). That which is divisive among God's people, is not of the Holy Spirit.

Granted, Jesus said that he did not come to bring peace, but a sword (Matt 10:34). However, the division he brings is between darkness and light, not between two different sections of the light. When the division that Jesus brought is compared with the division that Calvin brought, there is one overarching difference. The more we examine the claims of Jesus, the more it becomes clear that his position is consistent with all Scripture from all times. The more we examine the claims of Calvin, the more it becomes clear that his position is *not* consistent with all Scripture from all times. Those who deny the claims of Jesus are attacking the very nature and purposes of God. They are the enemy. By contrast, I suggest, those who deny the claims of Calvin are *defending* the very nature and purposes of God. It is those who divide God's people who are the enemy, not those who challenge the dividers.

It was Malcolm Muggeridge, the British journalist and agnostic who became a Christian late in life, who said, "Every happening, great and small, is a parable whereby God speaks to us, and the art of life is to get the message."[28] When one looks closely, the providence of God is visible everywhere – but not his predestination. God's providence, the superintending of all things to reach the desired goal, is consistent with influence rather than control, is consistent with the spiritual battle, and is consistent with free will in created beings. It is just one piece of the puzzle that helps us understand the overall plan. There are others.

Prevenient grace

One of the persistent positions of Calvinism is based on Paul's analogy of humans being "dead in transgressions and sins" in Ephesians 2. The reasoning is, that a dead person cannot decide to become alive. Ergo, God must do the work – all of it. This is another example of being able to hold to a theoretical position that does not fit with what we experience. Every person who has ever made a commitment to Christ at the end of a confirmation class, or "accepted Jesus as their personal Savior" in response to some inner or outer invitation to do so, assumes that they made a conscious decision. It *feels* as if we participate in the decision making process, the same way it *feels* as if we make the decision to brush our teeth in the morning, to marry a certain person or not, or to indulge in addictive behaviors. Responsible parents teach their kids to brush their teeth, they attempt to provide them with wisdom regarding spouses, and they warn them of the dangers of addictive temptations. They also diligently and faithfully provide them with instruction regarding the things of God, as Moses instructed the Israelites to do (Deut 6:7, 11:19). Responsible parents observe in real life the consequences of teaching their kids, or failing to do so. And they are motivated by verses such as Proverbs 22:6, "Train a child in the way he should go, and when he is old he will not turn from it," and Proverbs 29:15, "The rod of correction imparts wisdom, but a child left to himself disgraces his mother."

In other words, responsible parents clearly recognize the relationship between human actions and consequences, and they take responsibility for passing that understanding along to the next generation. And through it all, they act as if their decisions, and those of their children, are real, and will produce predictable consequences. In fact, they recognize that the essence of wisdom is the ability to accurately predict the consequences of actions, and to take the appropriate action to bring the best possible results over the longest term. All responsible people accept that life works that way, in practice. But then some disregard all of that at the theoretical level, and say that we don't have any ability at all to consider spiritual matters and make decisions regarding them – because we are dead spiritually. God has to make the decision for us.

If we accept that the decision is made entirely by God, then we have to explain how it works, and, as we have already discussed, why God has created a system that works differently from the way it appears to work. As it turns out, the libraries are full of books attempting to do exactly that.

There is little dispute over the necessity of grace for salvation to occur. It seems reasonably clear, from Ephesians 2:8, that "it is by grace you have been saved." But from that point, it appears, the interpretive framework that necessarily precedes the interpretation, takes over.

Virtually all theologians over the centuries have accepted that idea that the grace of God must already be present for a person to accept the gift being offered. That preceding grace is usually called *prevenient* grace. As we saw at the end of Chapter 4, *prevenient* simply means to precede something in time or sequence. Theologically, it is divine grace that precedes human decision.

In Arminian theology, prevenient grace is given to all people, enabling them to accept or reject the gospel message. To Calvinists, it is simply the first of a series of graces that God gives irresistibly to the elect. It's as if prevenient grace brings the person to life spiritually, but they are still paralyzed, so God must follow it up with *efficacious* grace to remove the paralysis and enable them to actually accept the gift of salvation. But even that illustration is problematic, because to be alive spiritually, and to have salvation, are logically the same thing. But however it happens for Calvinists, it's all done without any participation at all on the part of the individual.

A careful search of Scripture will reveal no such division of the grace of God. Unless, that is, one begins the search with an interpretive framework, a plausibility structure, that simply refuses to release divine determinism, simply refuses to allow humans to have any responsibility for their own destiny. Then it becomes a necessary construct to support the original assumption.

To maintain consistency throughout Scripture, and between our theoretical understanding of the way things work and the practical way we experience it, prevenient grace appears to be both adequate, and resistible. It is consistent with those verses that say clearly that God wants all to be saved (cf. Ezek 18:23, 33:11, 1 Tim 2:3-4, 2 Pet 3:9), and it is consistent with all those passages that either state or assume that humans have responsibility for the decisions they make, and the ability to make those decisions either in favor of, or in rebellion against, the revealed desires of God. From Genesis 1:28, when God gave Adam and Eve instructions to subdue the earth and rule over it, to Revelation

22:17, where John says, "whoever wishes, let him take the free gift of the water of life," there is no teaching in Scripture that humans lack the ability or the responsibility to respond to God.

At this point, the alert predestinarian is going to point to Romans 3:10-18, where Paul says, "There is no one righteous, not even one, no one who understands, no one who seeks God, no one who does good, not even one," and so on. These verses are often used to demonstrate that rejection of God is a universal human condition – after all, Paul does say that no one seeks God, not even one. But the view that this is universal, has two problems: first, this passage follows Romans 2, where Paul has just made the point that some Gentiles, even without having the law of God, follow the principles behind the law and concern themselves with doing good and seeking glory, honor, and immortality, and as a result, they will be given eternal life; and second, in this passage, Paul quotes from six places in the Old Testament, all of which are specifically talking about wicked, rebellious people. Psalms 14 and 53, for example, are contained within Paul's quote. They describe "the sons of men" as those among whom no one does good, not even one, in contrast to "my people" who are their victims.

It is true, that among wicked, rebellious people, none is righteous and none is seeking God. This is simply Paul making clear what he stated in Romans 3:9, that when people are like that, whether they are Jew or Gentile, they are all in the same condition before God – under sin, and in need of the righteousness of God. Then, as he continues his argument, he is going to say that that righteousness cannot be obtained by observing the law (Rom 3:20), but can be obtained by believing in Jesus Christ (3:22). He even clearly extends the availability of that righteousness "to all who believe" (3:22), and makes certain again that we understand the God's plan applies equally to both Jews and Gentiles (3:28-30). Paul's overall point here is not that people are universally opposed to God and require God's active, irresistible intervention to change that, his overall point is that having the law, as the Jews did and the Gentiles did not, is not the issue. It gave the Jews an advantage, but it does not save – believing does. Nowhere in this passage or anywhere else in Scripture, is it taught that God irresistibly imposes his grace on some, and not on others. A much better understanding is that prevenient grace is enough, and is freely given to all.

Several years ago, as we were preparing to serve God as missionaries, one of the things we studied in seminary was past missions efforts. We discussed what worked, and what didn't, and attempted to understand why. One of the apparent mistakes was missionaries working under the assumption that they were "taking God with them" as if he had not been present and already at work where they were going. This attitude sometimes led to assuming that everything about the host culture was evil and to be rejected. An example of this is polygamy. Some missionaries disrupted centuries of social practice and created a lot of confusion and suffering, by insisting that believers submit to monogamous lifestyles, even if they were mature adults and already had a large, polygamous family. Can that be supported by Scripture?

A search of Scripture may reveal that God originally intended for the family to consist of one man and one woman, but when God gave his law to his people, he did not even address polygamy, and it was consistently practiced both before and after the giving of the law. In fact, God said that he himself was polygamous – using the analogy of both Israel and Judah being his wives at the same time (cf. Jer 3:6-14). In other words, in God's mind, apparently, polygamy is not a morality issue but a motivation issue. The missionaries who made monogamy a prerequisite for fellowship within the church, missed the point. Most societies historically have had violent periods that left a shortage of men. If every good gift comes from God (James 1:17) and if polygamy was a good gift within a society to give all women an equal opportunity to experience family life and have children to take care of them in their old age, and to replace those killed in the violence, then it was from God.

The missionaries mistake was that they assumed they were taking God with them. If the Holy Spirit is God, then there is the assumption of divine characteristics – the Holy Spirit is both love and holy. He is omniscient, omnipotent, and omnipresent. *Omnipresent* – everywhere at once. He is also the one Jesus said would "testify about me" (John 15:26) and "guide you to all truth" (John 16:13). Paul connects Jesus Christ with the possibility of favorable judgment for Gentiles who do not have the law (Rom 2:14-16). If the Holy Spirit is everywhere, loving and holy, and in the business of revealing Jesus Christ, then the concept of prevenient grace must be considered to be universal. It does not presume that the culture, or false religions, or the devil, or a combination, will not block understanding of the seeds the Holy Spirit plants (remember the parable of the sower), but it does presuppose the activity of the Holy Spirit in all people, in all places, at all times. That's prevenient grace.

Hardening the heart

Another issue that Calvinism uses to defend its position of God's complete control over human actions and destinies, is the hardening of the heart. It is primarily associated with God's dealing with Pharaoh prior to the exodus, but is spoken of in several other instances as well. Paul even cites it in Romans 9:18 when he is defending God's right to be the author of his own plan. Once again, there is little dispute over whether or not God hardens hearts, or as Paul indicates, hardens people. There is confusion, however, over why or how it occurs.

First, in attempting to understand this, it might be helpful to try to define the term in common language. A hard heart, it appears, simply means to make a decision, or to believe something, from which one is not willing to be dissuaded. More than anything else, it seems to imply a stubborn refusal to relent from a position taken. Jesus used it to describe the Israelites who wanted the right to divorce (Matt 19:8,

Mark 10:5). He also used it to describe his disciples when they were clinging to their preconceived notions of the messiah in the face of his miracles and teaching (Mark 6:52, 8:17). Daniel used it to describe Nebuchadnezzar in his pride (Dan 5:20), and the writer of Hebrews quoted Psalm 95, where it is used to describe the Israelites during their time in the desert (Heb 3:7-9). Both Jeremiah and the historians who compiled the Chronicles, connected it with being stiff-necked (cf. 2 Chron 36:13, Jer 6:28, 7:26). It appears that stiff-necked was more than being stubborn, but a defiant refusal to bow one's neck in a posture of submission.

Second, it is clear that normally, Scripture places responsibility for the hardening of hearts on the people themselves. In almost every usage, it is connected with a plea for the reversal of the condition, a threat of punishment if it is not reversed, or a warning to avoid it. Of fourteen separate instances in Scripture where hearts are said to be hardened, in only four instances is the hardening attributed to God. Even then, there is another pattern visible. It is that God only hardens hearts after the position is obstinately taken by the person (or people) first. An exception to this, arguably, might be where Paul is defending God's right to choose the people who would represent him to the other nations, in Romans 9, but even this is questionable, as we will see below.

This pattern is particularly visible in the case of Pharaoh. Before the event, God told Moses that he, God, would harden Pharaoh's heart (Exod 4:21). But he did not say when, or how. Then, as Moses started interacting with Pharaoh, we see the process described like this: 1) Pharaoh's heart became hard, 2) Pharaoh's heart became hard, 3) Pharaoh hardened his heart, 4) Pharaoh heart was hard, 5) Pharaoh hardened his heart, 6) Pharaoh's heart was unyielding, 7) the Lord hardened Pharaoh's heart. From that point forward, the text never again says that Pharaoh hardened his own heart. God takes credit for doing it. Originally, though, it was Pharaoh's decision. God did not make it irreversible until Pharaoh's own obstinacy was clear.

God does say that he raised Pharaoh up for the very purpose he served (Exod 9:16) and Paul quotes that in Romans 9:17. That does not mean, though, that God was responsible for Pharaoh's character, or his decisions. It may well be that God arranged for this particular person to come to power, simply because his character was such that he would respond in predictable ways that would enable God to work out his larger plan. That is consistent with the providence of God, and does not require that God violate Pharaoh's free will in the process.

In Isaiah 63:17, the prophet accuses God of hardening the people's hearts. There are two possible explanations for that accusation: one is that Isaiah was attributing something to God that God was not doing. Another is that God was in fact hardening their hearts, but if he was, it was only after years, or decades, of them already demonstrating hearts hardened toward him.

In the book of Joshua, as Joshua's initial campaign was ending, a summary of the results is given (Josh 11:16ff). Except for the Gibeonites, who had deceived the Israelites earlier (Josh 9), not one city attempted a peace treaty with Israel. Instead, they defended their territories militarily, so Israel defeated them all in battle. The reason they fought instead of seeking peace, the text says, is because "the Lord himself hardened their hearts to wage war against Israel" (Josh 11:20). Does this contradict the pattern of God only hardening hearts after the people themselves have hardened them? Not at all. These are the same people of whom God told Abram he would delay punishment for four hundred years, because their sin had not yet reached its full measure. Only after centuries of the nations steadily moving in the same direction, did God make their positions irreversible.

Eli's sons "did not listen to their father's rebuke, for it was the Lord's will to put them to death" (1 Sam 2:25). But this is only after "Eli, who was very old, heard about everything his sons were doing to all Israel and how they slept with the women who served at the entrance to the Tent of Meeting" (1 Sam 2:22). Note "very old," "everything his sons were doing to all Israel," and "how they slept with the women" under their influence. This was not something new, or incidental. This was widespread exploitation, decades of abuse of power by those who were supposed to be representing God. It was a lifestyle of evil. At a certain point, God simply let their commitment to do evil stand, then punished it.

This is consistent with the way I understand Scripture to describe the current position of demons. In 2 Peter 2:4, we are told that "God did not spare angels when they sinned, but sent them to hell, putting them into gloomy dungeons to be held for judgment" and in Jude verse 6, it says, "the angels who did not keep their positions of authority but abandoned their own home – these he has kept in darkness, bound with everlasting chains for judgment on the great Day." The word used for "hell" in 2 Peter 2:4 is the word for where the Greeks believed the evil dead were sent, often described as the deepest abyss of Hades.[29] I would like suggest that this is a parallel statement to what God told Adam in the Garden of Eden – that the day they ate of the fruit of the tree of good and evil, they would surely die. In actual fact, they did not literally die the day they ate of the fruit, but the day they ate it, the "surely" part of the promise was activated. God was saying, "On the day you eat the fruit, the certainty of your death will be sealed." I am convinced that the demons are in a similar situation today. The certainty of their eventual fate in hell has been sealed, but in actual fact, they are free to roam the earth, like Satan, and work against the purposes of God. But they are in "everlasting chains of darkness" according to Jude. Peter says they are in "gloomy dungeons," but that was previously translated as "chains of darkness." "Chains of gloom" might be a more accurate reflection of the original. In other words, when they rebelled against God, he simply rendered their decision irreversible, locking them into their eventual destiny, at which time they will be judged not only for their initial rebellion, but also for all the damage they have inflicted on humanity since then.

Paul deals with a similar situation regarding his own people, in Romans 11. In Chapter 5, we looked at the words *chosen* and *elect*, and alternatives to the way they have been translated. In Romans 11, Paul compares the hardening of the heart to those who are among the elect. A remnant of Israel is saved, he says, but the rest are hardened (Rom 11:8). Notice, again, it is not initially an act of God – they were hardened (passive), then, it says, God confirmed the process. As Paul continues his argument, he makes at least two points that argue against God doing the hardening: 1) he says that he himself is working hard to get some to believe (Rom 11:13-14), and 2) he says that if they do not persist in their unbelief, they will be grafted back into the olive tree (Rom 11:23). Why would Paul be working to overcome the unbelief of his fellow Jews, if he was convinced that God had hardened their hearts? Both points imply that the hardening was potentially reversible, with the responsibility being placed on the humans, not God, for how it went.

Jesus made this same point when he told the parable of the sower (Matt 13:3-23; Mark 4:2-25; Luke 8:4-18). As we saw earlier, he gave the parable, then went away without explaining it. When his disciples came later and asked him about it, he said that he used parables to keep some people from understanding. Why would he do that? Well, a good Calvinist would explain that he wants the chosen to believe and be saved, and he is blocking the non-chosen from access to the information they need to believe. But that's not what Jesus said. In Matthew, more than in the other two gospels, he explains that because the hearer's hearts are calloused, he uses parables.

In the parable of the sower, he gave them just enough understanding to understand that they didn't understand. He was forcing them to deal with their own pride, and their rejection of him as the messiah. He told his disciples, "The knowledge of the secrets of the kingdom of heaven has been given to you, but not to them. Whoever has will be given more, and he will have an abundance. Whoever does not have, even what he has will be taken from him" (Matt 13:11-12). The parable of the sower is about understanding – what happens in the human heart, when understanding is offered. In Jesus' illustration, it is not the quality of the seed, or the one who sows it, that is in question. It's the condition of the soil – the heart – in which the seed is sown. The disciples humbled themselves and came to Jesus for more understanding, and they got it. The unbelieving Jews did not. It was not Jesus who hardened their hearts, it was them. He simply left them there. He created a learning opportunity that forced them to take responsibility for their own understanding, and they refused. If they had used what they had, they would have been given more. They had enough understanding to understand that they did not fully understand. It was also clear who had put them in that position, so they knew where to get the complete understanding. They refused the opportunity, so he left them in their condition – with their hard hearts. Paul seems to be making a parallel statement in Romans 11.

Consider one more point related to the hardening of the heart. For Protestants at least, the general consensus is that when a person dies, their eternal destiny is sealed. As the one who gives life, God is also the one who has the right to take it. He has delegated that right to governments under certain circumstances, but basically, he reserves that right for himself. That means that when he ends a life, he effectively hardens the heart of the person, because at the point, the person's eternal destiny is sealed. In other words, whatever decisions the person has made regarding God and eternity, are irreversible at that point. Still, they are the person's decisions. God simply let's them stand. If God renders a person's decisions irreversible earlier than death, would it matter? We will discuss the foreknowledge of God later, but if God can know in advance a person's decisions, then the point at which the person's decision is final, could be the point at which God hardens their heart, and it would make no difference to their future destiny, whether they die the next minute, or live for several more decades.

In John 12:32, Jesus said, "when I am lifted up from the earth, I will draw all men to myself." If we can take that statement at face value, the drawing is universal. We have already seen that the Holy Spirit is the witness to Jesus, and is omnipresent, so I would suggest that the Holy Spirit is the means by which Jesus draws all people to himself. This is consistent with the previous section, that the Holy Spirit is the source of prevenient grace, providing the ability, but not the requirement, to respond to the drawing. We have also already seen that the Holy Spirit, even among believers, can be grieved and even quenched. I actually don't think it is the Holy Spirit that is quenched, but rather his *activity*. It seems logical to me that if the voice of the Holy Spirit is ignored, or suppressed, or rebelled against consistently, and the pattern will predictably continue, then while the literal presence of the Holy Spirit is still there (omnipresence), he can choose to stop working to change our minds. That, to me, would be the same thing as hardening the heart. Assuming that prevenient grace is what enables us to respond to the drawing, if the Spirit of God ceases to work, the prevenient grace would also cease and we would effectively be sealed in our sin, in our decision. At that point, it could be said that God has hardened our heart, but that would be consistent with influence, not control, and without ever impugning the character of God.

The evidence continues to be consistent. The arguments that are used to support the contention of God being in total control of all events, and thereby effectively removing human free will, do not stand up to scrutiny. When they are looked at carefully, they crumble.

The jealous God

Along with accusations that God predestines the unchosen to hell, and that he hardens their hearts to accomplish that, the portrayal of God as a jealous God,[30] is another way his name is often maligned. Let's consider that in light of the foundation we laid earlier.

In the discussion of worldviews and related issues in Chapter 2, we looked at the relationship between "little r" and "Big R" and the relationship between truth and reality. We saw that truth is simply an accurate description of reality, the way things really are "out there." We saw that the closer our "little r" gets to "Big R," the greater our potential for success. Truth brings success, and falsehood brings failure, because the person who is living life based on falsehood, is interacting with an imaginary world. The world is not as they imagine it to be. Driving in darkness, through the fog, they think there is a bridge ahead, but there is not. It collapsed and washed downstream. Unless their understanding of reality changes before they drive off the cliff, their imaginary world is destining them to destruction.

Now apply that principle to God, and his interaction with people. He is the Ancient of Days, the only self-existent being. He is the Creator of all that is, and the sustainer of it all. Without his existence, nothing else would exist at all, and if he did not sustain it continuously, it would simply cease to exist (cf. Col 1:16-17). In short, that means that what he says is, is. One of the things he has said, is that humans will live somewhere for eternity, and that he is the only way for them to live out that eternity in peace and prosperity, rather than in misery.

We saw earlier that God had no need to create, so the best explanation for creation seems to be that he simply wanted to share his love. The very nature of love implies being others-centered. So when Scripture suggests that God is jealous, that he will not share his glory with another, it is not for himself. He has no needs. In reality he *cannot* share his glory with another. There is no *other* to share it with. "They made me jealous by what is no god," he says (Deut 32:21).

Those who appear to be competitors of God – other gods – exist only in the imagination of their followers. Their followers are driving down a road at night, in the fog, toward an imaginary bridge. If God allows them to continue along that path without attempting to warn them, then he is the same as the parent who watches his young child run out into traffic without attempting to intervene. Assume the child's ball is rolling out into a busy street, and someone is saying, "Go get the ball! Go get the ball!" The parent is shouting, "Stop! Listen to me! I'm your parent!" The parent is rightfully jealous for his child to listen to *his* voice, rather than the one that is encouraging the dangerous behavior. The parent's jealousy is not self-centered, it is others-centered. It is the same with God. His concern is for the one blindly driving through the fog. To repeat a point made in Chapter 2, when Jesus said, "You will know the truth, and the truth will set you free" (John 8:32), he was making a profound statement. Anything other than truth is a form of bondage, captivity to a world that exists only in our imagination, and which leads only to failure. God the jealous God is not being selfish or needy or controlling, he is being ultimately loving. His jealousy is others-centered. That is his holy nature.

> GOD THE JEALOUS GOD IS NOT BEING SELFISH OR NEEDY OR CONTROLLING, HE IS BEING ULTIMATELY LOVING. HIS JEALOUSY IS OTHERS-CENTERED

The foreknowledge of God

Next to predestination itself, there is probably no theological issue so controversial as the foreknowledge of God. The reason is clear: the foreknowledge of God also connects with the sovereignty of God, the nature of human freedom, and the problem of evil. We will not likely settle the complex questions here, but maybe we can shed some helpful light on the subject. To begin with, it might be useful to consider the views that are commonly held.

In Chapter 3, we briefly considered the view of C.S. Lewis, that God does not actually "foresee," but that he is "outside and above the Time-line," so whatever happens, he simply watches it happen. He is eternally in the present, so what is past for us is still present for him, and what is still future for us, is already present for him. The view may be difficult for us to understand, but that should not be surprising, since God has told us that his ways and thoughts are not the same as ours, and are as much higher than ours as the heavens are higher than the earth (Isa 55:8-9). We try to understand God and how he works, but do so with the recognition that there will always be some limits. Still, views such as Lewis's are helpful. And, as already suggested, his view does have some scientific support, in that the more we understand, the more it seems that time and gravity are related, and God, as the omnipresent spirit, would also be outside of and above all gravity. Lewis's view is consistent with the idea that God is omniscient, knowing everything, and it is consistent with Scripture indicating that he knows things about people even before they are born.

Lewis's view also allows for complete human free will, because it explains the foreknowledge of God without falling into the trap of fatalism – that if something can truly be known ahead of time, then when the time comes for the event to happen, it cannot happen other than as it was foreknown. And the view allows God to be sovereign without attributing evil to him.[31]

The truly opposite of Lewis's view is the one suggested by Augustine first, but later made famous by Calvin. It is that God knows all that will happen because he preordains (or foreordains) that it will happen. This is classic divine determinism. It denies that either angels or humans truly have the ability of self-determination. Its proponents typically state that agents (human or spirit beings) have the freedom to do what they want to do, but at the same time, it attributes their choices to the sovereign plan of God. Everybody, in essence, wants to do what they do because God has foreordained that they will both want to do that, and then do it. This view moves beyond *knowing ahead of time,* to *determining ahead of time,* or stated another way, it replaces *knowing* ahead of time that something *will* happen, with *making* it happen.[32]

The Calvinist view places so much importance on the sovereignty of God, that it in effect eliminates free will, and that, in effect, makes God the author of all evil. It denies the point that the illustration of King James V makes, that a ruler can be sovereign, without always exercising their sovereignty.

Another view of foreknowledge attributes God with what the view's proponents call "middle knowledge" – he knows what free agents will do, because in his omniscience, he is able to anticipate all of the possible options that could be chosen within the conditions present when a decision needs to be made, and from all of those possible choices, he knows which one that particular free agent, with its unique genetics, background, personality, and character, will choose. He can accurately anticipate, 100 % of the time, what people will do, but he does not foreordain it. Like the Calvinist view, this one leaves the sovereignty of God intact, but in contrast to the Calvinist view, it also leaves free will intact, and does not attribute evil to God.[33]

THE CALVINIST VIEW PLACES SO MUCH IMPORTANCE ON THE SOVEREIGNTY OF GOD, THAT IT IN EFFECT ELIMINATES FREE WILL, AND THAT, IN EFFECT, MAKES GOD THE AUTHOR OF ALL EVIL

Another view, which is probably the most common one, is that God simply knows the future. Within this view, both humans and spirit beings are seen as free agents with complete free will. God knows what they will choose to do of their own free will, not because he foreordains it, and not because he is able to accurately anticipate it through his "middle knowledge."[34] No complicated explanations. He simply knows.

Like the middle knowledge view, the simple foreknowledge view leaves the sovereignty of God intact, leaves free will intact, and does not attribute evil to God. Lewis's perspective would be included in this view. Lewis simply attempts to explain how God could foreknow events without foreordaining them, by placing God eternally in the present, so that time is not a factor that affects God's knowledge.

Another view of the foreknowledge of God, one of fairly recent origin, is based on what is called open theism. It expands the two basic views that, in the past, have attempted to explain the way the created world functions – deism and theism.

Deists believe that God created the world much the way a clockmaker makes a clock. When the clock is finished, the maker winds up the clock's mainspring, then walks away, and the complex mechanisms and the energy provided by the spring work together to keep the clock running, but the maker is detached and his direct, personal involvement is not necessary for the system to continue to function. From the deist viewpoint, what happens from that point on is determined by human action. For this reason, deists place great importance on morality and personal responsibility. "The only thing necessary for evil to triumph, is for good men to do nothing."[35]

Theists, on the other hand, view God not only as the creator of the universe, but as the constant sustainer of that creation. He is not detached, he loves his creation deeply, and he is continuously involved in all that happens within that creation. At the theoretical level, most Christians call themselves theists. However, many function on a day-to-day basis as if deism is true. At one point in our time as missionaries, we had a leader who sent out weekly emails, not the typical newsletter type correspondence common to missionaries, but simply sharing his thoughts along his spiritual journey. In one of those emails, he dealt with the issue of faith and prayer (which we will also deal with later). Referring to Luke 17:6, he said, "I have to admit, I have always had to move my own mulberry trees." That is deism at the practical level.

At the theoretical level, however, deism is hard to justify, if a person considers the Bible to be inspired of God, and to a large degree literal. Scripture portrays God as a loving creator and sustainer who is deeply involved in his creation (cf. Col 1:16-20). So the vast majority of Christians are theists, at least theoretically.

Within the theistic view, in recent times, open theism has offered a new explanation of how things work. This view is included in our discussion because it provides an alternative view of the foreknowledge of God. The proponents of open theism contend that God's foreknowledge is limited. In essence, this view accepts human free will, but does not accept Lewis's suggestion that God is outside of and above the time-line. Open theists believe God sovereignly acts to bring about certain events, so regarding those things, God has complete foreknowledge. His knowledge is limited, however, regarding future decisions of free agents, in that he cannot know what choice they will make until the decision has been made. At that point, God has an infinite capacity to respond to that decision, but the response is genuine, a literal response to a completely free and previously unknown choice. This view is an attempt to deal fairly with the multiple passages of Scripture where God is portrayed as changing his mind, testing people to see what their response will be, making conditional statements ("if you do…, then I will"), and even expressing regret.[36] For those who might be interested in reflecting more deeply on these passages, a list is provided in Appendix B.

The view offered by open theism leaves free will completely intact and exonerates God of any evil, but it reduces the sovereignty of God significantly from the way it has traditionally been understood. It redefines omniscience.

As I have reflected on these various explanations for the foreknowledge of God, the two views that seem the most problematic to me are the Calvinist view and the open theism view. The Calvinist view, I reject for all the reasons already dealt with in this book – first, its lack of consistency with so many things revealed in Scripture, and second, for the conclusion it leads to, if it is true, that God is evil and we are robots, simply playing the game of God's private theatricals, as we saw earlier. Open theism, I credit with trying to deal honestly with the multiple passages in Scripture that seem to indicate that God does not, in fact, always know the future. I have seldom seen that same honesty in other explanations for those passages. I have come to believe, however, that we can deal with those problematic passages that open theism addresses, without abandoning our belief that God has full knowledge of the future (as open theism does), and without assuming that God foreordains everything (as Calvinism does).

I have found Lewis's suggestion very helpful, and credible. I also find the point made by the middle knowledge view to be logical. If God is infinite, truly omniscient, then he would surely be a formidable chess player, as a friend of mine has frequently pointed out, even if he could not foresee the future. There is no doubt that he could not only anticipate all of the possibilities his opponent has for the next move, but from there, imagine all of the future options they open up to all of their eventual resolutions. If Lewis is right, however, it is unnecessary for God to have to use middle knowledge. If all events of all times are visible as present events to God, then he already has all knowledge of all decisions, and does not need to anticipate what they will be. Still, Lewis's suggestion is just that – a suggestion. I would like to suggest one more idea that has helped me in dealing with the foreknowledge of God.

As I ponder deep issues, I find it helpful to consider what God says in Isaiah, that he is so much bigger than I am, that he is capable of dealing with things on a level I cannot really comprehend. For example, Scripture seems to indicate that God experiences emotion, and that he experiences emotion in response to what people do.[37] When we consider that he is interacting with billions of people at the same time, then we also have to realize that he is capable of experiencing hilarious joy, sadness and disappointment to the point of weeping, and intense anger, multiplied millions of times over, all at the exact same time. We find that hard to comprehend, but logically it must be true.

If we apply to the foreknowledge of God that same level of complexity and the same ability to deal with apparently contradictory things simultaneously, we get another possibility. It is that God can know in advance, but in practice, continue to function in relation to us as if he did not know, so that his actions in response to our choices are really just that, honest responses to our free will choices. He can laugh and cry at the same time. Why could he not also know in advance, but act as if he doesn't know?

As a possible illustration of this, let's consider a broad look at Jesus' time on earth. The entire Old Testament provides the illustration of a lamb without blemish being used as a sacrifice for sin. At the very beginning of Jesus' ministry, John the Baptist twice referred to Jesus as "the Lamb of God" (John 1:29, 36). The writer of Hebrews makes it clear that Jesus was the final sacrifice, "once for all" (Heb 7, 9, 10). It appears that it was always God's plan to use his son as the final sacrifice, from before the creation of the world (1 Pet 1:18-20). That is why Jesus came to earth. However, Jesus spent the first half or so of his ministry offering a kingdom to the Jews. When it became clear that they were rejecting him as their messiah, Jesus expressed intense disappointment (Matt 23:37, Luke 13:34). It appears that God made the Jews a legitimate offer to have Jesus as their messiah, and they refused that offer. They had every opportunity to accept the offer, but when they rejected it, then God responded to their rejection, and used the circumstances to carry out what had already been his plan.

> GOD CAN KNOW IN ADVANCE, BUT IN PRACTICE, CONTINUE TO FUNCTION IN RELATION TO US AS IF HE DID NOT KNOW, SO THAT HIS ACTIONS IN RESPONSE TO OUR CHOICES ARE REALLY JUST THAT, HONEST RESPONSES TO OUR FREE WILL CHOICES

I am convinced that at the beginning of his ministry, Jesus did not think that he was going to the cross – at least not immediately. I think the gospels demonstrate that his understanding changed over time, so that his focus changed, and he stopped preaching the "kingdom of God" and concentrated more on preparing his disciples for the upcoming events and what they would be doing afterward. That change is visible in Matthew and Mark with Jesus' question to the disciples, "Who do people say that I am?" (Matt 16:13, Mark 8:27). "*From that time*," Matthew says, "Jesus *began* to explain to his disciples" about his upcoming suffering. Mark says, "He *then began* to teach them" that he would suffer. Both writers show that it was the beginning of a new focus. To say that his focus changed does not *require* that he was not aware of his destiny before, but I think the probability of that is logical. Such a theological position often leads to debate and confusion, because to some people, it indicates that Jesus did not know everything while he was on earth, so he did not have the divine characteristic of omniscience, so he must not have really been God. Once again, the illustration of King James V is helpful. King James did not cease being king simply because he put on ordinary clothes and went for an extended walk. But he did give up the *characteristics* of being a king, one of which was the *ability* to exercise power over his subjects. He did not give up his royalty, but he did give up the *characteristics* of his royalty.

From Jesus' own statements, we can conclude that he did not know everything while he was here on earth (Matt 24:36), nor could he do everything. In Matthew 13:58, whether he *could not* or *did not* do miracles, because of their unbelief, is open to debate, but he *could not* overcome their unbelief. He also was not everywhere at the same time while he was on earth. So in his humanity, he was not omniscient, omnipotent, nor omnipresent. But that doesn't mean he was not God, as some conclude. It means – to repeat – that even though he kept his divinity, he laid aside the *characteristics* of that divinity, in order to fully experience what we experience, in our humanity. I am convinced that Jesus did not heal or do miracles through his own power, but through the power of the Holy Spirit (John 3:34), which means that he was as fully dependent on God in his humanity as we are (John 5:30). To be otherwise would not have been a truly human experience, and he could not have fully experienced every temptation that we have, yet without sin (Heb 4:15).

From God the Father's perspective, then, he could have been watching the events of Jesus' life, knowing the eventual outcome, but *acting as if he did not know*. So at the same time that the plan was the cross, the offer of a kingdom to the Jews could also have been completely legitimate.

It is entirely feasible that both things could have happened – the Jesus both set up an earthly kingdom, and died on the cross. The Jews could have accepted Jesus' offer to be their messiah, in which case he would have set up a government and ruled them, and thrown off their oppressors. Then later, whether a few years, or many, the people could have experienced a change of attitude that ended up with Jesus being overthrown and assassinated even while or after being their earthly king. And if it had happened that way, the circumstances would have exactly fit what had been prophesied centuries earlier. In other words, the particular time and events of Jesus' death were not the only possible way it could have occurred and still fit perfectly into God's bigger plan, considering that God is infinite. Whether or not God is outside of time, as Lewis suggests, I am convinced that God can know our future actions, yet act as if he does not know. If that is true, God remains sovereign, the free will of humans remains real, and God is not the author of evil. God knows the future, but does not have to foreordain it.

My main point, in taking so much time to consider the foreknowledge of God, is simply to demonstrate that the Calvinist position lacks validity – that *knowing ahead of time* also necessitates *determining ahead of time*. That's fatalism. It is not only not a necessary logical conclusion, it also does not adequately address all of Scripture, so it is not even the best logical conclusion.

The missional God

When my wife and I were visiting a church recently, we arrived a few minutes early. As we entered the church, we encountered the pastor doing his duty, standing just inside the front doors and greeting as many people as possible. Normally, when we just visit a church, we try to be invisible, but when the pastor is intent on getting to know people, and make them welcome, he reaches for your hand, and starts asking questions. So, where are you from and what do you do there, led to us revealing that we were missionaries. Immediately, the pastor warmed up, told us he has also been a missionary for several years, and he said, "Mission is the heart of God."

I agree. Mission *is* the heart of God.

Earlier, we saw that it was always God's plan to use his son as the final sacrifice, from before the creation of the world (1 Pet 1:18-20). It also appears that God's plan was always inclusive. When he initially called Abraham, he indicated that Abraham's calling was for a purpose, and that purpose included "all peoples" on earth – all groups of people, plural.

> The LORD had said to Abram, "Leave your country, your people and your father's household and go to the land I will show you. I will make you into a great nation and I will bless you; I will make your name great, and you will be a blessing. I will bless those who bless you, and whoever curses you I will curse; and *all peoples* on earth will be blessed through you" (Gen 12:1-3, italics added for emphasis).

Over the years, this combined promise and calling has often been expressed as two blessings – one called the "top line" blessing, and the other the "bottom line" blessing.[38] The point made is that God's plan has always included everybody, and his plan has always been to use people as the means of reaching others. When a person is blessed (the top line), their calling is not to hoard the blessing, they are called to pass the blessing along (the bottom line, responsibility). Once that paradigm is adopted, it becomes visible throughout Scripture. It's in the parable of the sower. It's in the Great Commission. It's in the books of history. It's in the prophets. It's spread throughout the psalms. It's in the gospels. It's in the epistles. It's in the Revelation. From the beginning to the end, God's plan has always included everybody, and he has always used people to carry out the plan. Always, we are blessed to be a blessing.

To avoid being tedious here, I will avoiding citing all the passages in Scripture that support the intention of God to include "all peoples, all nations" in his plan from the beginning to the end. In case someone is interested, however, I have included such a list in Appendix C. That list is by no means exhaustive, but it shows the pattern.

To make the point, however, let's consider a few examples.

We've already looked at the Israelites' exodus from Egypt, including the hardening of Pharaoh's heart. But what we did not mention was that it was not just the Israelites who left Egypt. As Moses led them out, "Many other people went up with them" (Exod 12:38), so God's interaction with Pharaoh convinced "many other people" to follow the God of the Hebrews. Then God sent his people to a specific location. Why? Why not any of a hundred other locations around the globe? It was the land God had promised Abraham centuries earlier, but why this spot?

If you draw a large circle around Israel, that circle could be thought of as the rim of a wheel. Around that rim were all the major nations of the time. Israel would be the hub of that wheel. The trading routes were the spokes. Every caravan moving between nations had to go through Israel, and the traders were the carriers of the news – the newspapers, the televisions, the Internet of the day. By positioning Israel where he did, God made sure they were prominent players on the world scene, rather than obscure. As he demonstrated his existence and love to Israel, he was also demonstrating it to all who observed it or who heard about it.

Moses made this point in his farewell address, just before the Israelites were about to enter the promised land. He said, "The Lord will establish you as his holy people, as he promised you on oath, if you keep the commands of the Lord your God and walk in his ways. Then *all the peoples on earth* will see that you are called by the name of the Lord, and they will fear you" (Deut 28:9-10, italics added for emphasis).

Just a short time later, Joshua led the Israelites across the Jordan River, which had conveniently dried up as they approached it. As they crossed, one man from each of the twelve tribes hefted a large rock from the riverbed onto his shoulder and carried it with him to the other side. When everybody was safely across, Joshua had the twelve rocks stacked up together to form a memorial. "When your descendants ask what this pile of rocks means," he said, "tell them 'Israel crossed the Jordan on dry ground.'" Then he added, "God did this *so that all the peoples of the earth* might know that the hand of the Lord is powerful and so that you might always fear the Lord your God." (Josh 4, italics added for emphasis).

Generations later, Solomon finally finished the temple, for which his father, David, had planned and gathered materials. Solomon had a monumental dedication service, which involved sacrificing thousands of animals, and which included some profound words from the king himself. In his prayer of dedication, among other things, Solomon prayed that when a foreigner visited the temple and prayed, that God would answer his prayer, "*so that all the peoples of the earth* may know your name and fear you, as do your own people Israel" (1 Kings 8:43, italics added for emphasis). Solomon had knelt to pray, but when he finished, he stood up and blessed the assembled crowd. I picture him with his arms extended upward and outward, so that he symbolically applied the blessing to all the assembled people. He said,

> And may these words of mine, which I have prayed before the Lord, be near to the Lord our God day and night, that he may uphold the cause of his servant and the cause of his people Israel

according to each day's need, *so that all the peoples of the earth may know that the Lord is God and that there is no other* (1 Kings 8:59-60, italics added for emphasis).

Why would God bless Israel? Top line blessing only? No, bottom line blessing as well. *"So that all the peoples of the earth may know that the Lord is God and that there is no other."* That's the plan.

In their singing, the Israelites acknowledged this. Psalm 67 is just one of many that say similar things. "May *the peoples* praise you, O God; may *all the peoples* praise you. May *the nations* be glad and sing for joy, for you rule *the peoples* justly and guide *the nations* of the earth. May *the peoples* praise you, O God; may *all the peoples* praise you" (Psalm 67:3-5, italics added for emphasis).

The theme is continued in the Prophets. In a passage quoted by Jesus as he was clearing the temple just before his death (Matt 21:13, Mark 11:17, Luke 19:46), Isaiah records a message from the Lord encouraging the disenfranchised to have confidence before God. He specifically names eunuchs and foreigners who have committed themselves to the Lord. Both of these were forbidden from entering into the temple itself.[39] These were people who were outside the group due to irreversible limitations. Don't think I will exclude them, God says, "these I will bring to my holy mountain and give them joy in my house of prayer. Their burnt offerings and sacrifices will be accepted on my altar; for my house will be called a house of prayer *for all nations*" (Isa 56:7, italics added for emphasis).

In Daniel, in three incidents spanning decades, God's plan is shown to include all nations. The night Daniel spent in the lion's den resulted in a letter going out from the king "to all the peoples, nations

> *"SO THAT ALL THE PEOPLES OF THE EARTH MAY KNOW THAT THE LORD IS GOD AND THAT THERE IS NO OTHER." THAT'S THE PLAN*

and men of every language" requiring that they fear and reverence "the living God" who "endures forever" (Dan 6).

The same theme, that God's plan includes all nations, is also reflected in several of the minor prophets.

As already mentioned, Jesus carried on with the same theme. It has been suggested that he centered his ministry in Capernaum due to its proximity to the Gentiles, while still having access to all of Judea.[40] Matthew seems to indicate that this was a clear fulfillment of Isaiah's prophecy: "he went and lived in Capernaum," Matthew says, "to fulfill what was said through the prophet Isaiah: the Gentiles – the people living in darkness have seen a great light" (Matt 4:13-16, quoting Isa 9:1-2). Matthew continues: "News about him spread all over Syria, and people brought to him all who were ill . . . and he healed them. Large crowds from Galilee, the Decapolis, Jerusalem, Judea and the region across the Jordan followed him" (Matt 4:24-25). Syria, the Decapolis, and the region across the Jordan, were all Gentile areas.

The paragraph above shows how Matthew combines two major themes. His book is primarily intended to demonstrate that Jesus was the Jewish messiah – he repeatedly includes "this took place to fulfill what was spoken by the prophet" as part of his narrative.[41] But interwoven with that theme, is the theme of "all nations." In Appendix C, this pattern is shown in more detail, but here, it is worth mentioning that Matthew starts his book by including Gentiles in Jesus' genealogy (1:5) and having the Gentile Magi show up to worship him (2:1), then ends the book by having all nations appear before him to be judged (25:32) and including all nations in the Great Commission (28:19), and in between, there are multiple other such connections.

When Jesus first announced his ministry, he did it in his hometown (Luke 4:16-30). Everybody was amazed at his gracious words and spoke well of him, until he pointed out that God had revealed himself to Gentiles throughout history, then the hometown folk became furious and attempted to kill him at the beginning of his ministry, rather than at the end. He continued to repeat the message right up to the end, however, pointing out that "this gospel of the kingdom will be preached in the *whole world* as a testimony to *all nations*, and then the end will come" (Matt 24:14 italics added for emphasis). He included it in his final instructions to his disciples just before his ascension (Matt 28:16-20, Luke 24:45-49).

Paul understood God's plan. Among other places, he reveals his understanding in the doxology at the end of his letter to the Romans, as we have already seen: "Now to him who is able to establish you by my gospel and the proclamation of Jesus Christ, according to the revelation of the mystery hidden for long ages past, but now revealed and made known through the prophetic writings by the command of the eternal God, *so that all nations might believe and obey him* – to the only wise God be glory forever through Jesus Christ! Amen" (Rom 16:25-27, italics added for emphasis).

In his Revelation, John saw a great crowd of victorious saints singing to God, "Who will not fear you, O Lord, and bring glory to your name? For you alone are holy. *All nations* will come and worship before you, for your righteous acts have been revealed" (Rev 15:4 italics added for emphasis).

The pattern is consistent throughout Scripture. God's message was always for everybody. And, the plan always included those who had the message being the means through which God revealed himself to others. God has always been a missional God. Mission *is* the heart of God, for God so loved the world.

Israel as God's chosen people

Millard Erickson, in his *Christian Theology*, notes the missional aspect of God choosing Israel. "One might conclude from Israel's status as the chosen nation that God's concern for and interest in humanity are limited to the Jewish people. Yet it is apparent that the Jews are chosen not to be exclusive recipients of God's blessing, but rather to be the recipients and transmitters of it."[42]

In the last section, we saw that the purpose of God's calling of Abraham as the father of the people who would be God's chosen nation, was to be a blessing to "all people groups." But the fact that God had chosen Abraham to be the beginning of something new, did not mean that God stopped working with people in other parts of the world. When Abraham pursued the four kings who had sacked Sodom and Gomorrah and taken Lot captive, Melchizedek showed up. He was a priest of God Most High, Creator of heaven and earth (Gen 14:18-19). Four hundred years later, when Moses fled from Egypt after killing the Egyptian, he providentially landed on the doorstep of Jethro, a descendant of Abraham through his second wife, Keturah. Jethro was a priest of Midian, and from all appearances, was still serving the God of his ancestor, Abraham. Moses married Jethro's daughter, and left her and their sons with her family while he went on his mission to confront Pharaoh and rescue the Israelites from slavery. After the exodus, Jethro brought Moses' family to him in the desert, and even though Jethro was not part of the chosen people of God, he verbally and visibly expressed his faith in the same God who had led Moses to free the Israelites (Exod 2, 18).

Earlier we saw that this pattern continued even through the birth of Jesus, when the Magi showed up to worship him. The chosenness of Israel has never been in question. Moses made it clear as he addressed the people just before his death and their entry into the promised land: "For you are a people holy to the Lord your God. The Lord your God has chosen you out of all the peoples on the face of the earth to be his people, his treasured possession" (Deut 7:6). But even though the Jews were the chosen people of God, God was still at work among other people groups in other parts of the world. So the fact that the Jews were the chosen people of God, did not mean they were the only people of God. As Erickson states, and as the biblical record consistently shows, Israel was chosen for a purpose.

In Exodus 19:5-6, God himself says what that purpose is: to be a holy nation, a kingdom of priests. The Lord told Moses to tell the Israelites, "Although the whole earth is mine, out of all nations you will be my treasured possession, a kingdom of priests and a holy nation." Priests are only needed when the larger group needs someone to intercede between them and God. If Israel is to be a kingdom of priests, it presupposes they are interceding between a larger group and God, and in this case it is the whole earth that belongs to God, all the nations, with whom he seeks reconciliation.

Paul, in his letters to both the Romans and the Galatians, comments on that purpose. In Romans 3, Paul points out that the Jews have an advantage because they have been "entrusted with the very words of God." This comment makes two points: 1) that the Jews had the very words of God, and 2) that they had been "entrusted" with them. The very concept of being entrusted with something, implies purpose. Part of that purpose, as we have already seen, was that through the Jews, *all the peoples of the earth* may know that the LORD is God and that there is no other."

Another part of that purpose was the giving of a Redeemer. Isaiah prophesied about the coming Redeemer in chapter 49: The Lord says,

"It is too small a thing for you to be my servant to restore the tribes of Jacob and bring back those of Israel I have kept. I will also make you a light for the Gentiles, that you may bring my salvation to the ends of the earth." This is what the Lord says – the Redeemer and Holy One of Israel – to him who was despised and abhorred by the nation, to the servant of rulers: "Kings will see you and rise up, princes will see and bow down, because of the Lord, who is faithful, the Holy One of Israel, who has chosen you" (Isa 49:6-7).

In Galatians 3, Paul connects four concepts we have just been discussing: 1) the chosenness of the Jews, 2) the giving of the very words of God, 3) the Redeemer, and 4) the missional heart of God for all people. Early in Galatians chapter 3, Paul makes it clear that God "announced the gospel in advance to Abraham: 'All nations will be blessed through you'" (3:8). Later in the chapter, Paul asks, "What, then, is the purpose of the law?" He starts to answer his own question: "It was added because of transgressions until the Seed to whom the promise referred had come" (v. 19).

What transgressions? Not transgressions of the law, because the law did not exist. It was "added" (v. 19) 430 years (v. 17) after the promise to make Abraham's offspring into a great nation – the covenant God made with Abraham. No, the law was added because of transgressions of the covenant. As they settled in the new land, the descendants of Abraham would be in danger of intermingling with surrounding peoples, and thereby losing their identity. So, the law was added to protect against that danger. It was the nanny, the tutor, the schoolmaster, "put in charge to lead us to the messiah that we might be justified by faith" (v. 24). The purpose of the law was to bring the world to the Redeemer – not in a personal sense, but in terms of time and place. The illustration Paul was using would have been very clear to his original audience, but it is not so clear to us today. They were familiar with the practice among wealthy Greek families to have a live-in teacher (παιδαγωγός, paidagōgos, schoolmaster, one "put in charge," Gal 3:24) assigned to a child to protect and teach him until he was old enough to be personally responsible. Aristotle was just such a tutor, protector, and schoolmaster for Alexander the Great, until Alexander was 16.

The purpose of the law, Paul is saying, was literally to give the people of Israel a national identity – to give them some boundaries that they felt compelled to stay within, and in so doing, they also stayed together, they thought the same thoughts, and they could not intermingle with other ethnic groups enough to destroy their national identity. Without that national identity, the concept of the redeemer messiah was meaningless – there would have been no place for a messiah to come to, no purpose for his coming, no people to redeem. Literally, then, Israel as a nation provided the platform for the messiah to arrive on – a nation must exist to need deliverance, to need a deliverer. There must be a nation for the deliverer to interact with, to be rejected by, to be killed by, to provide the means of atonement foreshadowed throughout the law. Without the *nation*, there would have been no platform for the messiah to arrive on. Without the *law*, there would have been no *nation* to be that platform for the messiah to arrive on. The law brought us to Christ through history, as literally as Aristotle brought Alexander to maturity.

In this simple illustration, one that is almost completely invisible in our Bibles today, Paul has provided the key to understanding the entire history of Israel as the chosen people of God. Obviously, protecting the national identity of Israel was not the only purpose of the law, but it was one purpose. And, having a platform for the redeemer messiah to arrive on, was not the only reason God chose the people of Israel. But it was one reason. As part of God's purpose, between the choosing of Abraham and the coming of the messiah – "the Seed to whom the promise referred had come" – God would also have used the Jews to reveal his love to the nations, but generally, they failed to do that.

> WITHOUT THE *LAW*, THERE WOULD HAVE BEEN NO *NATION* TO BE THAT PLATFORM FOR THE MESSIAH TO ARRIVE ON

By the time Jesus came, that failure was not one of neglect, but one of deliberate choice. They were so convinced of their superiority as the chosen ones, that they were deliberately trying to exclude everybody else. That nationalistic pride was why Jesus' hometown neighbors tried to kill him when he announced his ministry, as we just saw. It was why John the Baptist told the Jews to repent and make the path straight for the Lord. He was quoting from Isaiah 40, where the prophet used several similar descriptions: make the highway straight, fill in the valleys, level the hills and mountains, make the rough places smooth. Why? So "the glory of the Lord will be revealed, and all mankind together will see it" (Isa 40:3-5). John the Baptist quoted it as "all mankind will see God's salvation" (Luke 3:5).

What is the difference between crooked, rough, hilly roads, and straight, smooth, level ones? Ease of access, obviously. The Jews were deliberately making it hard for "all mankind" to see "the glory of the Lord," to "see God's salvation." They were digging potholes in the road, and putting up "No entry" signs. Little wonder John the Baptist called on them to repent. Rather than the temple being a "house of prayer for all nations," the money changers and those selling doves were set up in the Gentile court, so there was no place for the Gentiles to worship God in the Jewish temple. When Jesus confronted that practice (Matt 21:12-13, Mark 11:15-17, Luke 19:46), it was the final act that led the religious leaders to conspire for his execution. And it was all part of the chosenness of Israel. Not only did the law preserve their national identity so that a nation existed for the messiah to come to redeem, but preserving the power structure of that nation gave the Jewish leaders the justification for killing the messiah.

In providing the redeemer, the people of Israel lived out their purpose for being chosen, even as they tried not to live out their purpose to reveal the salvation of God to all nations. Like John Calvin, they completely missed the point that God is the missional God who wants all people to be saved.

The will of God

Scripture even states what the passages about the missional God demonstrate.

"This is good, and pleases God our Savior [that we live peaceful and quiet lives in all godliness and holiness, from the previous verse], *who wants all men to be saved* and to come to a knowledge of the truth" (1 Tim 2:3-4, italics added for emphasis).

"The Lord is not slow in keeping his promise, as some understand slowness. He is patient with you, *not wanting anyone to perish, but everyone to come to repentance*" (2 Pet 3:9, italics added for emphasis).

(In both of these verses, the KJV uses the word "will" where the NIV uses the milder "wants.")

From Scripture, it appears that it is God's will for *all men to be saved*, for *everyone to come to repentance.*

These verses have always created problems for predestinarians such as Calvin. Let's look at how Calvin himself addressed these verses in his Commentaries.

Regarding 1 Timothy 2:4, Calvin starts by citing Romans 1:16, that "the gospel is the power of God for the salvation of everyone who believes." Then, he says, this calling to believe is "proof of the secret election, so they whom God makes partakers of his gospel are admitted by him to possess salvation." He goes on to say, "Hence we see the childish folly of those who represent this passage to be opposed to predestination. 'If God' say they, 'wishes all men indiscriminately to be saved, it is false that some are predestined by his eternal purpose to salvation, and others to perdition.'" According to Calvin, when it says that God wants all men to be saved and to come to a knowledge of the truth, it is not talking about "individual men," but "the Apostle simply means, that there is no people and no rank in the world that is excluded from salvation."[43] So Calvin interprets the passage to mean that *the chosen will come from every class and group of people*, not that God our Savior wants all men to be saved.

Now let's quickly review this from what we already know regarding languages and communication. Compare these two sentences:

305

- The chosen will come from every class and group of people.
- God our Savior wants all men to be saved and to come to a knowledge of the truth.

Remember, it's not the *words* that are important, it's the *concept*. Do these two sentences communicate the same concept? If not, why not? Can we not believe that if God is inspiring Scripture, he is also smart enough to communicate the *concept* he wants us to understand? If he had meant, "the chosen will come from every class and group of people," why say, "God our Savior wants all men to be saved"? The truth is, sadly, that Calvin could not read this verse as it is written, because to do so would have challenged his anchor premise, divine determinism, and he could not give that up. *Everything* was interpreted through that grid.

He does the same thing with 2 Peter 3:9: "The Lord is patient, not wanting anyone to perish, but everyone to come to repentance." This is Calvin's explanation: "But it may be asked, If God wishes none to perish, why is it that so many do perish? To this my answer is, that no mention is here made of the hidden purpose of God, according to which the reprobate are doomed to their own ruin, but only of his will as made known to us in the gospel. For God there stretches forth his hand without a difference to all, but lays hold only of those, to lead them to himself, whom he has chosen before the foundation of the world."[44]

At the risk of being tedious, let's do the comparison again:

- In the gospel God stretches forth his hand without a difference to all, but lays hold only of those, to lead them to himself, whom he has chosen before the foundation of the world.
- The Lord is patient, not wanting anyone to perish, but everyone to come to repentance.

Do they communicate the same concept? I suggest, again, that God is smart enough to say what he meant to say, and, that what he said communicates what he wants us to understand. However, if we have an interpretive framework, a plausibility structure that says, "what this says is not plausible," then we have to find another explanation, one that it does not say. This is why the grace of God must be divided – prevenient grace is in the gospel, but efficacious grace is necessary to respond to the prevenient grace. It seems to me, if this is true, then prevenient grace is a fraudulent concept. It is a lie that you are being offered something by grace, when you cannot accept it without another form of grace being administered. "You are being offered freedom from prison, but I have the key to the prison door, and I am not going to use it to free you." I return to the point I made earlier. If God appears to offer that which he is actually withholding, he is not the "God is love" that I find in the Bible. He is a deceiver, and therefore, by his own standards, he is evil. He will not inhabit heaven for eternity, since "Nothing impure will ever enter it, nor will anyone who does what is shameful or deceitful" (Rev 21:27).

One more verse needs to be considered. It is 1 John 2:2: "He [Jesus Christ, the Righteous One] is the atoning sacrifice for our sins, and not only for ours but also for the sins of the whole world." Once again, there seems to be an inclusivity in this verse. Does Calvin agree? Here is his perspective:

> . . . the faithful might be assured that the expiation [*atonement for sin*] made by Christ, extends to all who by faith embrace the gospel.
>
> Here a question may be raised, how have the sins of the whole world been expiated? I pass by the dotages of the fanatics, who under this pretense extend salvation to all the reprobate, and therefore to Satan himself. Such a monstrous thing deserves no refutation. They who seek to avoid this absurdity, have said that Christ suffered sufficiently for the whole world, but efficiently only for the elect. This solution has commonly prevailed in the

schools. Though then I allow that what has been said is true, yet I deny that it is suitable to this passage; for the design of John was no other than to make this benefit common to the whole Church. Then under the word all or whole, he does not include the reprobate, but designates those who should believe as well as those who were then scattered through various parts of the world. For then is really made evident, as it is meet, the grace of Christ, when it is declared to be the only true salvation of the world.[45]

Calvin's logic, if I read it correctly, is that the atoning sacrifice of Jesus extends to the whole *Church*, not the whole *world*, as John stated. But I would like to analyze his logic a little further. We can ask, does he do justice to his opponents (the "fanatics") who "under this pretense extend salvation to all the reprobate, and therefore to Satan himself"? I suggest not. Considering this writer is the same John who wrote the gospel, and said "For God so loved the world," I think we can assume that the "world" John is talking about is made up of humans, not the fallen angels, so few through history have seriously suggested that salvation is going to be extended to Satan. What Calvin has done here is a common debate tactic, in which the opposing argument is exaggerated so that it appears ridiculous, and then is not dealt with at all. That's exactly what he did: "Such a monstrous thing deserves no refutation." It's an "absurdity," he says, not worth addressing.

Then, he shows that others divide this atonement in a similar manner as the grace of God is divided: "They who seek to avoid this absurdity, have said that Christ suffered *sufficiently* for the whole world, but *efficiently* only for the elect" (italics added to clarify the comparison). He agrees with this division, he says, but contends that it does not apply to this verse, since John actually means the whole *Church* when what he actually said was the whole *world*. Calvin is clear that the word *all* or *whole* does not apply to everybody – certainly not the reprobate –

but "designates those who should believe," and apparently other future believers who are "scattered through various parts of the world."

Besides those contradictions just mentioned, there is one more glaring error in Calvin's logic. Look at the verse again. "He is the atoning sacrifice for our sins, and *not only for ours* but also for the sins of the whole world" (italics added for emphasis). When John says, "not for our sins only," who is he talking to? Ten times in this letter, John says who he is writing to, and why. It is the only book in the Bible where the author states his reasons for writing so clearly. "I write to you, dear children, because your sins have been forgiven on account of his name" (1 John 2:12). Whose sins have been forgiven? Those in the church, or those not in the church? "I write these things to you who believe in the name of the Son of God so that you may know that you have eternal life" (1 John 5:13). Who believes and has eternal life? Those in the church, or those not in the church?

John *says* several times that he is writing to those already in the church, so he is saying, "the atoning sacrifice was not only for *our* sins, *those of us already in the church*, but also for the sins of the *whole world*." How much clearer could that be? John doesn't say that everybody in the whole world will take advantage of the atoning sacrifice for their sins, but he does say that it is there for them. And Calvin misread it, because it did not fit into his paradigm of divine determinism.[46]

Obviously, others throughout history have also seen these discrepancies in the logic, that God appears to will one thing, but only brings about something less than that, or different from that. If the three verses considered above are to be taken at face value, and historically they have been, then God has provided atonement for the whole world and does in fact have a basic desire for all people to be saved. But he doesn't save everyone. Why not?

Free will is one obvious answer. God wants all people to be saved, and he offers salvation to all, but some simply refuse it. I believe it was an attempt to be honest with the word of God that prompted John of

Damascus to come up with the idea of the 'antecedent' and 'consequent' wills of God. Thomas Aquinas and many others have picked up on those terms and used them over the centuries. As we saw earlier, the simple version is that the antecedent will of God is what he wants beforehand, and his consequent will is what he wants as a consequence of human action. At the level of the cosmos, they can refer to before and after the Fall, and at the individual level, they can refer to where God starts with each of us, and where we eventually end up.

Calvin, however, completely rejected the idea of more than one will of God. Regarding those who disagree with him, he said, "Their first objection – that if nothing happens without the will of God, he must have two contrary wills, decreeing by a secret counsel what he has openly forbidden in his law – is easily disposed of."[47] Continuing on the topic, he explained, "the will of God is not at variance with itself. It undergoes no change. He makes no pretense of not willing what he wills, but while in himself the will is one and undivided, to us it appears manifold, because, from the feebleness of our intellect, we cannot comprehend how, though after a different manner, he wills and wills not the very same thing."[48]

I actually agree with Calvin in that last statement, that the problem is primarily in our understanding. However, our understanding still has to be consistent with all of Scripture, and it has to be consistent with the nature and character of God as presented in Scripture. We also have to be able to communicate our understanding in such a way that others can understand it, without seeing God as evil rather than good.

As I said, others have wrestled with these issues over the centuries. One explanation I have found helpful comes from Leslie D. Weatherhead (1893 - 1976), an extremely liberal, and therefore controversial, British Methodist who pastored a Congregational church in London for almost 25 years. Despite his beliefs in other areas that appear to be the complete opposite of what Scripture teaches, his observations regarding the will of God, or rather the *wills* of God, I find helpful. He suggests that Scripture shows three wills of God – an *intended* will, which is what God desires, but cannot fully accomplish if he also gives free will to his created beings; a *circumstantial* will, which is what he actually accomplishes on a daily basis in response to the circumstances brought about by human decisions and actions; and an *ultimate* will, which is the overarching plan that he is bringing to fruition through the ages.[49]

Despite my disagreement with Weatherhead on so many other issues, I find his thinking here to be consistent with what I observe in Scripture. Whether we like Weatherhead's descriptive terms or not, we can see the *intended* will of God is such places as John 3:16 and the three verses we considered above, all of which seem to indicate that God wants everybody to be saved. However, it seems equally clear from Scripture, that that is not going to happen. Jesus talked openly about hell (cf. Matt 5:22-30, Mark 9:43-47, Luke 16:23), and John shows it to be the final destiny of the unsaved (Rev 20:14-15). Within the *circumstances* humans create by their choices, God is at work, consistently accomplishing his will. What he accomplishes within the circumstances is not his *intended* will, but is consistent with his *ultimate* will, that humans have his image in them, including the ability to make free choices and be held responsible for them and their consequences. The *ultimate* will, then, not only includes the overall parameters within which the universe functions, but includes the direction in which destiny is progressing, and its final outcome. Isaiah 40, considered earlier, provides a glimpse of the ultimate will of God – God is shown considering world empires to be as insignificant as dust on the scales. This *ultimate* will can be easily traced from the Garden of Eden through God's promise to Abraham in Genesis 12, through the messiah, to the final disposition of time at the end of John's Revelation. The final outcome seems definite, but the time may even be flexible – 2 Peter 3 opens up the possibility that how humans live, combined with the patience of God, may delay or speed up the coming day of final judgment.

Note the consistency Weatherhead's view of the will of God brings to all of the interrelated issues. It leaves the sovereignty of God intact, it allows human free will, it is consistent with what Scripture teaches about the spiritual battle and about the missional God, it is consistent with God working through influence rather than control, it does not attribute evil to God, and so on. In fact, I find no contradiction to it in Scripture, or to any of the issues considered above – the nature of God, the character of God, the foreknowledge of God, prevenient grace, hardened hearts, the providence of God, etc. It is also consistent with the antecedent and consequent will of God observed by others through the ages. All it does, in fact, is add the ultimate will to the other two, to show how God is not limited by his creation in bringing his overall plan to where he always intended it to go. It is even consistent with Calvin's statement that God is "disposing and directing every thing to its proper end by incomprehensible wisdom"[50] even though it refutes the means Calvin requires, that "every event which happens in the world is governed by the incomprehensible counsel of God."[51]

Calvin understood that God has a plan and is working out that plan. What he refused to accept, however, is that God can do that without determining all the details that are part of the process. If the ultimate will of God is a ship that leaves one port and sails on schedule to another port, Calvin would insist that the individual movements of all the people and machinery on the ship are as much determined by the ship's captain as is the schedule of the entire trip. A better explanation, as Weatherhead suggests and Scripture consistently supports, is that God is able to *respond* to "every event which happens in the world" in such as way that his ultimate will is unhindered. In fact, that is where the whole idea of redemption enters the picture.

Redemption

The concept of redemption is one of "buying something back" or "replacing one thing with something else as a substitute," which is actually two ways of expressing the same idea. Redemption is codified in the Law of Moses, in Leviticus 25, but the idea preceded that. Before the exodus, God told Moses he would "redeem" the Israelites from their slavery to the Egyptians (Exod 6:6). God was "buying them back" after 400 years in bondage. Then, connected to the first Passover, God claimed ownership of every firstborn male born to an Israelite, whether human or livestock. They had to be "redeemed" by "substituting something else," usually a lamb (Exod 13).

In the social system God set up through the Law of Moses, provision was made for people who experienced periods of acute financial distress. They could sell the family land, or their house, or even themselves, but the sale was not immediately final. The law included provision for a relative, or even the person himself, to buy back what was sold, under certain circumstances. That's redemption. Boaz acted as the kinsman-redeemer for Naomi's land, and got Ruth as his wife as part of the bargain. God is frequently called the Redeemer, the Holy One of Israel, and as we just saw, Jesus coming as the redeemer messiah is part of the explanation for Israel's chosenness.

But redemption has other applications in Scripture. We've already discussed how Jesus' sacrifice *atoned* for all sins. That is the fulfillment of the sin offering in the Law of Moses. Whenever sin occurred, a sacrifice had to be brought to atone for the sin (cf. Exod 29, Lev 4). But the New Testament writers also connect Jesus' sacrifice with the concept of redemption. Paul writes that "redemption came by Christ Jesus" (Rom 3:24), and "we have redemption through his blood, the forgiveness of sins" (Eph 1:7, Col 1:14). The entry of believers into heaven is called redemption: our bodies will be redeemed (Rom 8:23); we are sealed by the Holy Spirit for the day of redemption (Eph 4:30). Jesus' sacrifice of his own blood is said to "obtain eternal redemption" to provide a new, unobstructed access to God himself (Heb 9:12).

There seems to be another application of redemption in Scripture as well. It is expressed in Isaiah 61, where the prophet anticipates the coming of the messiah – the one who will bring a crown of beauty out of the ashes, who will bind up the brokenhearted, free the captives, rebuild the ancient ruins, and so on. We already considered Jesus announcing the start of his ministry in his hometown, Nazareth. Isaiah 61 is the passage he read, and then he said this about it, "Today this scripture is fulfilled in your hearing" (Luke 4:21). This application spreads the concept of redemption more broadly. I suggest it shows that *redemption is the continuous principle at work in the universe, by which God brings good out of evil.*

REDEMPTION IS THE CONTINUOUS PRINCIPLE AT WORK IN THE UNIVERSE, BY WHICH GOD BRINGS GOOD OUT OF EVIL

Consider almost any evil event in history, particularly the history shown in the Bible, and you can see how good has eventually come out of it. I suggest that that is the redemption of God at work. Job said, "I know that my Redeemer lives" (Job 19:25), and time proved him right. The Jews went into exile as polytheists, and returned as monotheists. The Jewish leaders had Jesus killed, and he became the final Redeemer. It is a consistent principle.

Earlier, we looked at the story of Sara and Benjamin. Sara was raped, and as a result, lost her opportunity for a "normal" life as a married woman. But out of the ashes, Benjamin grew up to be a crown of beauty, a godly man whose influence would impact hundreds of other people for good. The story is not the story of predestination, of God arranging the illegal migration, the rape, the specific sperm fertilizing the specific ovum, the concussion, the theft of Sara's wallet – it is the story of redemption, the story of the nature of God, who brings good out of evil. It is God *responding* to circumstances, not *determining* them. It is an expression of John of Damascus' *consequent* will of God, of Weatherhead's *circumstantial* will of God. Within the circumstances created by human free will, God is continuously at work, bringing about his will for the good of people, without infringing on their ability to make choices, even when those choices victimize others. It is God working out the problem of evil for eternity, which we will soon consider.

Calvin understood about the redemption of God. He cites the following passage from Augustine's *In Psalmos* 111:2: "Great is the work of God, exquisite in all he wills! so that, in a manner wondrous and ineffable, that is not done without his will which is done contrary to it, because it could not be done if he did not permit; nor does he permit it unwillingly, but willingly; nor would he who is good permit evil to be done, were he not omnipotent to bring good out of evil."[52]

There is no question that God is omnipotent to bring good out of evil. That's redemption. But it does not require that God predetermine everything, nor does not require that God permit everything willingly. If God permits everything willingly, how can we grieve the Holy Spirit? Why would God grieve over Israel's disobedience in the Old Testament, if he allowed it willingly?

It is worthy to note that the verse Calvin was addressing, Psalm 111:2, does say, "Great are the works of God" but it does not say anything about the will of God, nor any of the other rapturous comments that Augustine added to it and Calvin quoted. Those are derived assumptions, drawn directly from the worldview, the interpretive framework, through which the Psalm was being viewed. How can God be grieved that he had made humans at all, and his heart be filled with pain (in the days of Noah, Gen 6:6), if there is not an element of unwillingly permitting of the process going on? How can God express a desire to destroy the entire Israelite people as a result of their sin (Exod 32:10), if there is not some unwilling permitting going on?

If Calvin is right, that "every event which happens in the world is governed by the incomprehensible counsel of God," then the concept of redemption is nonsense. There is nothing to redeem, because everything that apparently needs to be redeemed, is directly from the hand of God – including Sara's rape and the birth of Benjamin. It parallels the nonsense we saw earlier of the Lord's Prayer, in which Jesus instructs us to pray for God's will to be done on earth as it is in heaven, when it is already being done. As we have noted over and over, this perspective portrays God as a deceiver who has people living in an illusion, in a world that appears to function one way, but in actual fact operates completely differently.

The god of this world

As we have already seen, a better explanation than God governing every event that happens, is the worldview that Scripture presents, of a tri-polar world with a spiritual battle that involves humans in the struggle between good and evil. We have already considered Satan's attack on Job, and the spiritual delaying tactics in relation to Daniel. But those are not the only Scriptures that give us insight into how the whole process works. There are many others, but for the sake of brevity, consider these:

> The devil led him up to a high place and showed him in an instant all the kingdoms of the world. And he said to him, "I will give you all their authority and splendor, for it has been given to me, and I can give it to anyone I want to. So if you worship me, it will all be yours" (Luke 4:5-7).

> The god of this age has blinded the minds of unbelievers, so that they cannot see the light of the gospel of the glory of Christ, who is the image of God (2 Cor 4:4).

> As for you, you were dead in your transgressions and sins, in

which you used to live when you followed the ways of this world and of the ruler of the kingdom of the air, the spirit who is now at work in those who are disobedient (Eph 2:1-2).

For he has rescued us from the dominion of darkness and brought us into the kingdom of the Son he loves (Col 1:13).

"I will rescue you from your own people and from the Gentiles. I am sending you to them to open their eyes and turn them from darkness to light, and from the power of Satan to God . . ." (Acts 26:17-18).

Some Bibles translate 2 Corinthians 4:4 as "the god of this world" rather than the "god of this age," but considering this world as we know it is destined for destruction and replacement at the end of this age that we call "time" (2 Pet 3:12, Rev 21:1), the two translations reflect the same idea. They also reflect the idea that the Creator God is not the authority that this world submits to at the present time.

Some obvious questions arise: If God is not the ruler of this world, who is, why is it that way, how did it come about, and how will it be resolved?

Scripture does not give us a succinct summary that answers those questions, but it does give enough consistent insight throughout the Biblical narrative, that some conclusions can be drawn. The Church has historically believed that Satan is the god of this world, the ruler of the kingdom of the air, the one who has dominion over the world of darkness, the one who blinds the minds of unbelievers, who is at work in those who are disobedient, who exerts power over people who do not recognize and follow God, and so on. It's a consistent picture throughout Scripture.

It also follows a military analogy. Where there is a kingdom, there is a ruler and there are subjects, and there are those who follow the bidding of the ruler to carry out plans for the subjects. Having served for almost eight years in the military, I have no trouble imagining such an arrangement in the spiritual world. In fact, there appear to be two kingdoms – the kingdom of Satan, and the kingdom of God, also known as the kingdom of heaven (Jesus apparently used the terms interchangeably, as shown by Matt 10:7 and Luke 9:2, just one example among many).

Before we look at the kingdom of Satan – the kingdom of darkness – it might be appropriate to make a quick observation regarding the kingdom of God. An analysis of this term as it is used throughout the gospels, shows several descriptions that are very different, and even appear to be contradictory. For example, in Luke 17:21, Jesus said, "The kingdom of God is within you," implying that the kingdom is an inner spiritual experience. Paul supports this idea in Romans 14:17. In other places, however, Jesus implied that the kingdom was heavenly, not of this world (cf. Luke 22:29-30, John 18:36), and Paul also supports this idea in 1 Corinthians 15:50. There are at least six such apparently contradictory statements regarding the kingdom of God. With such different descriptions, how are we to understand it? As it turns out, there is a way.

The key to understanding the kingdom of God is this: *The kingdom of God is the place where Christ rules and the power of Satan is neutralized.* This statement fits every occurrence of the "kingdom" in the New Testament.[53]

- It *can occur now* in an individual life or in the church.
- It *will occur later* in the form of an earthy government.
- It *will last for eternity* in heaven.

However, there is reason to believe that Jesus was serious when he suggested that his disciples pray "your kingdom come, your will be done, on earth as it is in heaven." Even though he told them as he left the earth, that "all authority in heaven and on earth has been given to me" (Matt 28:18), it appears that he has not yet picked up the scepter and started to rule. The writer of Hebrews says, "In putting everything under him, God left nothing that is not subject to him. Yet at present we do not see everything subject to him" (Heb 2:8). All five of the verses noted at the beginning of this section are statements made regarding the present time, and the last four were made *after* Jesus said he had all authority. In fact, based on Revelation 12, it appears that Jesus actually assumes his role as the rightful ruler at some point in the future. This is what John saw in his vision of end-time events:

> And there was war in heaven. Michael and his angels fought against the dragon, and the dragon and his angels fought back. But he was not strong enough, and they lost their place in heaven. The great dragon was hurled down – that ancient serpent called the devil, or Satan, who leads the whole world astray. He was hurled to the earth, and his angels with him.
>
> Then I heard a loud voice in heaven say: "Now have come the salvation and the power and the kingdom of our God, and the authority of his Christ. For the accuser of our brothers, who accuses them before our God day and night, has been hurled down. They overcame him by the blood of the Lamb and by the word of their testimony; they did not love their lives so much as to shrink from death" (Rev 12:7-11).

Several important points can be gleaned from this passage. First, it supports the idea of a vicious spiritual battle going on, which God's forces will eventually win. Second, it makes it clear that Satan is the leader of the army fighting against God. Third, it supports that idea that demons are fallen angels. Fourth, it supports that idea that Jesus has not yet taken up his position as ruler, but he will. And, fifth, it supports the model of the tri-polar world, and the interdependence of the three poles. Of particular note is the fact that the battle is fought in the heavenlies by angels, but the credit for winning the battle is given to humans – those for whom the blood of the Lamb atones, who are outspoken witnesses to what they have experienced, and who are willing to put their lives on the line for it. None of these statements apply to the angels who do the actual fighting.

At this point, it appears that some of the initial questions have been answered. We have seen that it is Satan who is the current ruler of this world, and we know how it will be resolved. What we have not yet answered, is why it is that way, and how it came about.

One explanation that has been offered answers those questions.[54] The explanation appears to be consistent with the biblical record, and fills in many otherwise difficult gaps in our understanding – it suggests that when God instructed the original humans to "fill the earth and subdue it, rule over every living creature" (Gen 1:28), he was giving them more than a responsibility, he was giving them the *authority* to rule. Adam naming all the animals was his first exercise of that authority. When the first couple listened to Satan speaking through the serpent rather than obeying God, however, their submission to Satan transferred their authority to rule, to him. Since God had given humans the right to rule, they also had the right to give that authority away. That leaves God, in his infinite holiness and righteousness, obligated by his own character to respect that decision. This is consistent with what Satan said to Jesus during his temptation in the desert at the start of his ministry. After Satan showed Jesus all the kingdoms of the world, he said, "I will give you all their authority and splendor, for it has been given to me, and I can give it to anyone I want to. So if you worship me, it will all be yours" (Luke 4:6-7). Jesus declined the invitation but he did not dispute Satan's claim. Who gave Satan that authority? Adam?

This understanding explains several critical parts of the way life seems to function. For one, it explains why God has not used his unlimited power to just terminate Satan and his demons ages ago. For another, it explains why the atonement had to be done by a human – only a human can wrest away from Satan the authority that humans gave him. Finally, it explains the interdependence of the tri-polar world, including the observation in Revelation 12 that what humans do on earth, somehow affects what happens in the spiritual battle in the heavenlies. The explanation is consistent with all we have considered about the plan of God – his sovereignty, his character, his image in humans including free will, his use of influence rather than control, and on and on. Now, let's consider how this understanding affects other parts of the plan of God.

Prayer

It was almost midnight, on the last night of a camp for medical students.[55] The setting was an old monastery, now used as a combination nursing home, guest house, and conference center. It was a peaceful setting in an eastern European village surrounded by lakes and wooded mountains. We had taught earlier in the week on personalities, how medical personnel could use an understanding of personalities to have better relationships with both colleagues and patients. Now the closing program was over, the thank yous and awards dutifully given, the camp photos reviewed with hilarity on the big screen, the final party snacks eaten, and a general migration was underway. The cautious would get some sleep; the revelers would continue into the wee hours of the morning. Donna and I intended to be among the cautious.

As we were packing up our computer, a young lady, whom we will call Linda, approached us and said she had hoped she could talk with us about her mother, but she knew it was late and we needed to get some rest before driving home tomorrow. She thought, maybe if she understood her mother's personality, she could have a better relationship with her.

Sensing something important, we invited Linda up to our room so we could visit with more privacy. Once we got settled in, we started asking questions: "What does your relationship with your mother look like?"

"When I walk into a room, she gets up and leaves. She makes me buy my own food, keep it in my bedroom, and eat it there. If I buy salt and leave it in the kitchen, she throws it out and buys more."

"How long has this been going on?"

"All my life."

"Is your father still in the family?"

"Yes."

"How does he respond to the way your mother treats you?"

"He never says anything."

Donna and I looked at each other and said, "She's got him trained."

We asked more questions, and found out that Linda's mother was a doctor, the head of a large department in a state hospital, and Linda's only sister (older) was also a doctor, working for the mother, and apparently the proverbial apple of the mother's eye. Linda was about 30 years old, single, and had just finished her medical residency and become a doctor herself. She had left a previous career in order to go to medical school, because once when she asked her mother why she treated the two girls so differently, the mother had replied, "If you do what your sister does, you will be treated the way she is." When Linda finished her residency, she had moved back into her parents' home while seeking a place to practice, so as we were talking with her, she had been living back in her parents' home for about two weeks. She said her mother had given her until the end of the month, about another two weeks, to be gone permanently. She had found a position in a clinic in a small town, but had not found a place to stay there, so she would start looking for an apartment as soon as she got home.

We visited awhile, then we asked Linda if we could pray for her. We asked God to fill the void in her heart left by her mother's cruelty. We also prayed for God to enable her to feel his presence in the days ahead, and to provide her a place to stay and facilitate the transition she was facing. She found out we were leaving before breakfast the next morning, so she asked if she could ride with us to the next city, where she could catch a bus home much earlier than from the village we were in. We had an empty seat in the car, so it was arranged.

Early the next morning, when we hauled our suitcases down the four flights of stairs, Linda was waiting for us at the car. We dropped her at the appropriate bus stop, entrusting her into the hands of God, in a sense.

The very next day, we were surprised by an email from Linda. She thought we would want to hear what happened after we dropped her off.

As she and an older lady waited together at the bus stop, they exchanged the usual pleasantries – where you from, where you headed? As they talked, they realized the older lady was from the exact village where Linda's new job would be, and where she needed a place to stay. The lady told her, "You don't worry about a thing. We've been needing a full-time doctor for a long time, so we're looking forward to your coming." Giving Linda her phone number, she said, "You call me in a couple of days – I'll find you a place to stay." At that precise moment, a bird flew into the bus stop, crashed into the glass, and fell to the ground dazed. Linda rescued the bird, and attempted to release it, but it couldn't fly. She examined it, and concluded it had injured one wing, so she decided to take it home with her and see if she could nurse it back to health. The two women sat quietly together, admiring the bird sitting peacefully in Linda's hands. After a few minutes, she related to us, the bird stood up, looked around, and flew off, as if nothing had happened.

Linda said she was awed by the whole experience. She felt as if she had been visited by God, in some sense. As soon as she got home, a friend offered to help her move at the end of the month. Within 24 hours of our conversation and prayer, all the insecurity of her immediate future had been removed. And Linda had tangibly felt the presence of God.

We are commanded to pray.

The Apostle Paul tells us to pray continually (1 Thes 4:17), to pray for everyone, for kings and all those in authority (1 Tim 2:1-2), on all occasions, with all kinds of prayers, for all the saints (Eph 6:18), that the message of the Lord may spread rapidly and be honored (2 Thes 3:1), and so on. He says we should be faithful in prayer (Rom 12:12), even devoted to prayer (1 Cor 7:5, Col 4:2). Epaphras, one of Paul's companions, was "always wrestling in prayer" (Col 4:12). We already saw that in Paul's instructions to Timothy regarding principles by which the church should function, the very first principle was for the men of the church "to lift up holy hands in prayer" (1 Tim 2:8). Paul suggests that prayer is the antidote for anxiety (Phil 4:6) and that it helps bring about protection for those prayed for (2 Cor 1:10-11, Phil 1:19).

Paul was simply following and expanding on what Jesus taught. Jesus gave a model prayer, which includes, among other things, the request for daily provision, and protection from both temptation and the evil one (Matt 6:9-13, Luke 11:2-4). He said that if his followers remain in him, and his words remain in them, they can ask whatever they wish, and it will be granted (John 15:7). Both Jesus and Paul modeled devotion to prayer (cf. Mark 1:35, John 17, Rom 1:9-10, Eph 1:16, Phil 1:4, Phm 1:4). James tells us that the prayer of a righteous person is powerful and effective (James 5:16). When we don't know what to pray for, the Holy Spirit helps us (Rom 8:26). In his Revelation, the Apostle John says that there are golden bowls in heaven in which the prayers of the saints are stored, apparently until they can be answered (Rev 5:8).

In fact, there is so much in Scripture about prayer, that hundreds of books have been written about the subject. Why? What makes prayer important? What happens when we pray?

John Calvin recognized the importance of prayer. So much so, in fact, that he wrote an entire chapter in his *Institutes* about it. He says, among other things, "Assuredly it is not without cause our heavenly Father declares that our only safety is in calling upon his name, since by it we invoke the presence of his providence to watch over our interests..."[56] His treatment of the subject of prayer is thorough, practical, and biblical. But how does it fit with his anchor premise, that "every event which happens in the world is governed by the incomprehensible counsel of God"? How does it fit with his insistence that "the affairs of men, and men themselves, are not just governed by the power of God, but by his decree"? It doesn't. Unless, of course, we are robots, so that even our apparent free will is governed by the incomprehensible counsel of God, by his decree, so even our prayers are controlled by God.

This is the lack on internal consistency that causes Calvin's overall theology to fail the test for truth. Maybe there is an better explanation.

Consider prayer in light of the suggestion that Adam transferred to Satan the authority to rule the earth. Humans have the God-given right to rule the earth, but Satan has the human-given right to rule. God, then, in light of his own righteous character, has to wait for humans to request his intervention, in order for him to intervene. How do humans make that request? Prayer.

Instantly, internal consistency is achieved. God is omnipresent, the Holy Spirit is at work in all places at all times, but humans have to *respond* for the power of Satan to be overcome. Humans gave away their rights, they have to take them back again. The prevenient grace of God enables them to do that, but does not force them to. Human efforts do not influence God to save a person, but human *response* to the Holy Spirit does.

Once a person is saved, they have the ability to enter into the spiritual equivalent of the Most Holy Place in the temple, the very presence of God (Heb 10:19-22). In the Old Testament, this place could be entered only by the High Priest, and only once a year. When Jesus died, however, the curtain in the temple blocking entry into the Most Holy Place, was torn from top to bottom (Matt 27:51, Mark 15:38, Luke 23:45), opening up access to God to every believer. We are told to enter into that place with *confidence* (Heb 10:19). When people pray, God, as the Commanding General in charge of the forces for good, sends angels to answer the prayer. But the efforts of the angels are subject to resistance from demons. The battle is real, and humans influence the action. That's why Epaphras "wrestled in prayer."

Apparently the spiritual condition of the one praying, affects how God responds. When one prays within the will of God, an answer is guaranteed (John 15:16; 1 John 5:14-15). Both Jesus and James connect answered prayer to righteousness in the one praying, including right motives (John 15:7, James 4:3, 5:16), and the psalmist says that those who hang on to their sin, forfeit their right to the ear of God (Ps 66:18). This would explain why there are so many admonitions to be "pure and blameless" (cf. Phil 1:10, 2:15) and have a "pure heart and a good conscience" (cf. 1 Tim 1:5, 2 Tim 2:22).

IF CALVIN'S WORLDVIEW IS CORRECT, THE WHOLE CONCEPT OF PRAYER IS NONSENSICAL

Why would so much attention be given in Scripture to prayer, if it did not accomplish something? We are obviously not informing God of something he does not already know. He knows what we need before we ask for it (Matt 6:8), but we are still told to ask.

As already noted in regard to the Lord's prayer, if Calvin's worldview is correct, the whole concept of prayer is nonsensical. Among other things, prayer is requesting God to do something, as if by praying we move the hand of God to do something that without the prayer would not be done. If all things are governed by his decrees, then prayer is not only not necessary, it is nonsense. Even further, if everything is already determined ahead of time, foreordained, how could the purity of a person praying possibly affect what God does? Scripture shows that God *responds* to our prayers. If everything is done according to God's decree, then he is never responding, he is always initiating.

One of the most famous verses in all the Bible contains a conditional statement related to prayer, and the purity of those praying: "if my people, who are called by my name, will humble themselves and pray and seek my face and turn from their wicked ways, then will I hear from heaven and will forgive their sin and will heal their land" (2 Chron 7:14). If . . . then. People praying, turning from their wicked ways, God responding – God doing something that would not be done without the prayer, and without the purity of those praying.

The conclusion is that, for whatever reason, God has chosen to involve humans in what he is accomplishing through his plan. That, I would say, is a decree of God. But another decree of God is the image of God in humans, which even though marred by the fall, was not destroyed (cf. Gen 9:6). Like God, we have free will. We get to choose the degree to which we will participate with God in his plan, and our participation makes a difference in the outcome. We can participate through our purity, and we can participate through prayer, and both affect the future. Or we can participate by rebelling against the plan of God.

The problem of evil

Twelve kilometers southeast of Riga, the capital of Latvia, there is patch of dense forest with sandy soil, selected because it was within walking distance of Riga, close to a local railway station and highway, concealed from sight, yet easy to dig. At the entrance to the site, a granite memorial now stands, with the following inscription in both Latvian and English:

> Here in the forest of Rumbala on Nov 30 and Dec 8, 1941, the Nazis and their local collaborators shot dead more than 25,000 Jews, the prisoners of the Riga Ghetto – children, women, old people, as well as around 1,000 Jews deported from Germany. In the summer of 1944, hundreds of Jewish men from the concentration camp "Riga - Kaiserwald" were killed here.

What is evil? For centuries, if not longer, theologians and philosophers have grappled with this question, and the one that accompanies it: why does evil exist?

The dictionary defines evil as profound immorality or malevolence. It is closely connected to sin, which is defined as an immoral act that violates a divine law. Over the years, I have attempted to restate those concepts in practical terms. First, when one considers that behind every law there is a principle, and that there can never be enough laws to cover every possible situation, then sin is not limited to violating a divine law, it extends to violating the principle behind it. And, at the cosmic level, the principles behind the divine laws are simply reflections of God's character. Sin, then, is anything, thought or action, that violates the character of God. Sin is the opposite of morality. The concept of morality includes that idea of the principle behind the law. Morality implies a standard that can be violated, and all moral standards ultimately end at God, since God is the epitome of holiness. The character of God reflects itself as the creator, the builder, the unifier, the one who loves – so sin shows up as those things that fail to love, that divide, that destroy rather than build.

Evil is entrenched sin, deliberate and sustained. Consider its two expressions – immorality, and malevolence. The immorality connects to the character of God, and the malevolence connects to the impact on people. So at a practical level, evil can be defined as any deliberate act that causes pain and suffering to innocent people. That definition may not cover all conceivable occurrences of evil, but it's a pretty good working definition. The main difference between sin and evil is that sin is an event, while evil is an attitude. The connection is that evil reflects itself in entrenched sin.

When the Nazis and their Latvian collaborators marched 25,000 Jewish women, children, and old people the 12 kilometers from Riga to the forests of Rumbala, shot them and buried them in the sandy soil, that was evil. The fact that those 25,000 were just a small part of the six million Jews the Nazis killed throughout Europe, does nothing to mitigate the evil, but it does raise the question: where was God when all that was happening? It's a legitimate question.

The existence of evil is one of the justifications for atheism. The basic argument goes like this:

1. If there were a God, there would be no evil in the world.
2. There is evil in the world.
   Therefore,
3. There is no God.

The assumption is that God and evil are incompatible.[57] So the basic argument is extended to include the characteristics normally attributed to God:

1. A morally good being *prevents* all the evil that it has the power and opportunity to prevent.
2. An omnipotent being has the *power* to prevent evil.
3. An omniscient, omnipresent, and eternal being has the *opportunity* to prevent evil.
4. God, by definition, is omnipotent, omniscient, omnipresent, eternal, and is creator of all else.
   Therefore,
5. If there were a God, there would be no evil in the world.[58]

However, someone may argue that the first premise of the logic is flawed – that being morally good does not require that *all* evil is prevented. For example, a good person might be justified in causing or allowing pain and suffering, if it is necessary: 1) to prevent a worse evil, or 2) to attain a greater good. So the real argument is that there is no God if there is *morally unjustified* evil in the world. The answer to this is similar to the challenge of proving there are no black cats in Edmonton, and extending that to the assertion that there is no God.

This life is only an infinitesimal segment of an overall existence of infinite duration – a dot on a line of infinite length. A human, living for

70 or 80 years on an insignificant planet in an obscure galaxy, cannot even begin to understand the plans the most exalted Creator God might have that would give him a perfectly good reason for allowing the world to be as it is (including evil, pain, and suffering). There may be spiritual factors involved that we cannot evenly vaguely discern. The best we can do is try to understand what we see, using what God has given us, which includes his image in us, his written word, and our own experiences. So with these resources, we consider such questions as: why does evil exist?

As already established, we are not the first to ask this. Over the centuries, various explanations have been proposed. For what it's worth, a definition might be in order. Any solution to the problem of evil that offers a specific explanation of why God allows it, is called a *theodicy*. The word is a combination of two Greek words, *God* and *justice*. Traditionally, three basic theodicies have been offered. They explain evil as 1) punishment, 2) misuse of free will, and 3) for character development.

All of these solutions are proposed in both extreme forms, and limited forms. The extreme forms say they explain all the evil in the world, the limited forms admit they explain only some of the evil. In a little more detail, then, the three classic theodicies look like this:[59]

1. Evil as punishment – illustrated in Scripture by Jeremiah 6:6-8: "This is what the LORD Almighty says: 'Cut down the trees and build siege ramps against Jerusalem. This city must be punished; it is filled with oppression. As a well pours out its water, so she pours out her wickedness. . .'"

The extreme form says that all suffering is punishment for sin, but it fails to address the problem of innocent sufferers. What about the baby in the womb that is dismembered in the course of a late term abortion? The limited form suggests that some evil is punishment for sin.

2. Evil as misuse of free will – illustrated in Scripture by Deuteronomy 30:15-19: "See, I set before you today life and prosperity, death

and destruction. . . This day I call heaven and earth as witnesses against you that I have set before you life and death, blessings and curses. Now choose life, so that you and your children may live . . ."

The extreme form says that all evil is the result of the misuse of free will by God's creatures: all suffering caused by humans is from misuse of human free will; all suffering caused by natural events is from misuse of free will by spirit beings (demons). The story of Job illustrates suffering caused by demons. The limited form says some evil is justifiably allowed as the price of free will, but that free will may not explain all evil.

3. Evil as a process of character development – illustrated in Scripture by Romans 5:2-4: "We rejoice in the hope of the glory of God. Not only so, but we also rejoice in our sufferings, because we know that suffering produces perseverance; perseverance, character; and character, hope."

This explanation suggests that God has provided the conditions necessary for character development and growth among his creatures:

  i. Beings with free will
  ii. An environment in which those beings can exercise their freedom in morally significant ways
  iii. Problems in life to challenge the character of the free beings
  iv. Opportunities to respond to the challenges of life in both virtuous and vicious ways

The extreme form says that all evil is necessary for the great enterprise of developing character. Critics say that not all evil seems to present an opportunity for character development, so the limited form says some evil is necessary, or is necessarily allowed, for the great enterprise of developing character.

Maybe the best explanation is a combination of the limited forms of all three of the classic theodicies. If so, it would look like this:

4. Evil as a combination of explanations, and with some mystery still – illustrated by all the previous Scriptures, plus Isaiah 55:8-9: "'My thoughts are not your thoughts, neither are your ways my ways,' declares the Lord. 'As the heavens are higher than the earth, so are my ways higher than your ways and my thoughts than your thoughts.'" Some evil is punishment for sin, some evil is from misuse of free will, and some evil is necessary for character development. Even with all these combined, does this explain all evil? Maybe not. Maybe there is still room for some mystery.

Of one thing we can be certain – in heaven, there will be no evil. "There will be no more death or mourning or crying or pain, for the old order of things has passed away. Nothing impure will ever enter it, nor will anyone who does what is shameful or deceitful" (Rev 21:4, 27). In heaven, all punishment for sin will have been accomplished. Everyone will have free will without misusing it. All character development will be complete. Our understanding of God will be complete (no mystery).

But we are not yet in heaven.

Heaven is, but we are not yet. We are in the process of being prepared for heaven.

Where we are now, we can be punished for our own sin, or we can allow another to be punished in our place. We can use our free will for good, or we can use it for evil. Included in the choices available to free will, is the choice to go to heaven or not. We can participate in the character development process, or we can rebel against it. We can assume we understand all we need to know about eternity, or we can accept the possibility of mystery, while living responsibly and with integrity with what we do know.

I want to suggest that in the same way that childhood is the preparation for adult life, this life is preparation for eternity. Childhood is a temporary state. Humans are not designed to be children. We are designed to be adults. Childhood is simply the early, temporary period we have to go through to become what we were designed to be. In the natural process of life, childhood unavoidably gives way to adulthood, and the way in which childhood is used to prepare for adulthood, determines how things go in adulthood. Kids who spend their childhood playing, just living for the present, will not be as successful in adulthood as those who spend their growing up years studying and learning things like self discipline. It is the same with eternity. We were designed for heaven – for endless life in a perfect place, in the presence of God, with unbroken happiness. This life is simply a temporary, preparatory period on our way to eternity. The way this world functions, including the evil in it, and including our free will, provides the environment in which we can either prepare for eternity in heaven, or in which we can refuse that opportunity. We can play our way through this life, or we can spend our time studying and learning things like self discipline.

IN THE SAME WAY THAT CHILDHOOD IS THE PREPARATION FOR ADULT LIFE, THIS LIFE IS PREPARATION FOR ETERNITY

Malcolm Muggeridge has observed that without the Fall, there would be no knowledge of good and evil. The Fall was necessary, he says, because "without it, there would have been no human drama, and so no literature, no art, no suffering, no religion, no laughter, no joy, no sin and no redemption."[60] Even laughter, he points out, is "born of an awareness of the gap between what we are and what we aspire to be, between the perfection we can conceive and the intrinsic imperfection of all our works."[61]

This world as we experience it, is what gives us the ability to make comparisons – not only in terms of quantity and size, but in terms of quality and morality.

And if the Fall had not happened when it did, it would have happened at some other point. So God designed a system in which the problem of evil is being dealt with in such a complete way that both

333

humans and angels can enjoy an eternity of free will without ever again being tempted to use that free will wrongfully.

Consider heaven again for moment. If everybody has free will there, why can God be certain that no one there will ever violate their free will and bring evil into the perfect world, as they did in the Garden of Eden? I want to suggest four reasons:

1. There will be no innocence in heaven. Adam and Eve could not conceive of the   consequences that would follow their disobedience, since it had never happened before. Everybody in heaven will have lived through this life, so we will have a clear understanding of the results of evil. Heaven will be the perfect world that existed in the Garden of Eden, but we will have evil as a part of our experience, so what Adam and Eve could not conceptualize, we will have lived through.

2. There will be no unknowns in heaven. All sin is tied to the insecurities of this life – fear of hunger, fear of rejection, fear of ignominy, fear of pain, fear of the future, etc. The more a person comes to see God as he is, by faith, and the more we experience his care and provision, the more we rise above the tendencies to compete with others for survival, or power, or recognition, or whatever else tends to promote sin. That's the sanctification process. That is the essence of Isaiah 40, considered earlier. In heaven, however, we won't have to rely on faith to give us certainty for what we cannot see but hope for (Heb 11:1). What we hope for now, and believe by faith, will be the daily reality there – we will experience the character and provision of God in personal, living color all the time. All of the comparisons that were not possible before the Fall are now resident in our memories and understanding – without them there, with nothing to compare heaven to, we could not fully experience its richness. Now we can, with no insecurities.

3. The atonement will be complete. What God has accomplished through the final sacrifice, will be *eternal* (Heb 9:12). We are being made perfect *forever* (Heb 10:14).

4. There will be a perfect government in heaven. I remember a preacher once trying to encourage people to sing more enthusiastically in church. He said, "You may as well learn to enjoy singing praise to God now, you will be doing it for eternity in heaven." I don't agree. I actually believe life in heaven with be similar enough to this one, that what we learned in this life, and the creative bents we have in this life, will naturally fit into an infinitely productive life and society in heaven. I envision a farmer growing wheat because he loves horticulture, taking the wheat to a mill where someone loves to grind flour, who then takes it to a baker who loves transforming ingredients into food, who then takes it to a shop where people love meeting others and satisfying their desires, and people will take the food home and enjoy it. And the whole process will occur without currency, because there will be no need for it. There will always be plenty, and the future will be totally secure, so there will be no need to hoard. However, with free will, there will still be the potential for conflict. A lady who loves growing roses, for example, may want to plant a rose garden in the exact spot where another person who loves building and outdoor entertaining wants to build a gazebo. Rather than competing for the spot, however, they will go talk to the local government official, and the result worked out will be perfect – everybody will leave completely happy about the solution.

If you doubt that there will be government in heaven, revisit Revelation 21:24 through 22:5, discussed earlier, and you will find nations in heaven, and God's servants reigning with him for ever and ever. The mere fact that government exists implies that those governed need guidance, because they have the potential to do something that is not in the interests of the society as a whole. In other words, government presupposes free will. Jesus told Martha, the sister of Lazarus, that "whoever lives and believes in me will never die" (John 11:26). If that is true, then eternity is not another life, but an extension of this life. And, if *that* is true, is it even remotely logical that we will have free will in heaven, but do not on earth?

From what I have just described, we again get insight into the "wills of God" and how they work in the overall plan of God. The existence of evil, in the current era, is certainly the will of God. It is what enables all the human drama, and is preparing us for heaven. But it is only within God's ultimate will. When the Nazis marched Jews to death camps and places of mass execution, it was still evil, and still against the will of God – against his intended will. But God – then and now – within the circumstances created by the choices of evil people, continues to work out his ultimate will – to populate heaven for eternity with people who want to be there, and who will never again participate in evil. That's THE PLAN. Everything else is just process.

Calvin actually understood the idea of God having more than one will, although he refused to admit it in theory. Referencing a statement Augustine made, Calvin said, "the apostate angels, by their revolt, and all the reprobate [people], as far as they themselves were concerned, did what God willed not; but, in regard to his omnipotence, it was impossible for them to do so: for, while they act against the will of God, his will is accomplished in them."[62] I would say, God's ultimate will is accomplished in them, but his intended will is not – which is exactly what Calvin said, just without using the terms. If Calvin had incorporated into his theology what he appeared to know deep down inside, what we know as Calvinism would never have existed.

But, in the final analysis, everything will work out to the glory of God.

The glory of God

According to the ordinary Calvinist who has never really examined his belief system, everything happens *by* the sovereignty of God, and *for* the glory of God. We have already looked at the sovereignty of God, so now, let's ask: what is the glory of God?

The first mention of God's glory in the Bible occurs in Exodus 14:4, when the Israelites had left Egypt but had not yet crossed the Red Sea. To prepare Moses for what the Israelites were going to experience next, God said, "I will harden Pharaoh's heart, and he will pursue them. But I will gain glory for myself through Pharaoh and all his army, and the Egyptians will know that I am the Lord."

It is notable that from the very first time the concept of God's glory is introduced in Scripture, it shows evidence of God being the missional God, revealing himself to people other than his chosen ones. Through his interaction with Pharaoh, the Egyptians would know who the real God was.

In the desert, Moses said the Israelites would see the glory of the Lord "in the morning," and the next morning, sure enough, the first manna appeared (Exod 16:7). The Israelites saw the glory of the Lord in the cloud that led and protected them (Exod 16:10). When Moses went up on Mt. Sinai to meet God, the cloud covered the mountain, and to the people watching from the valley, the glory of God looked like a consuming fire on top of the mountain (Exod 24:16-17). When the portable Tent of Meeting was completed, the cloud settled upon it, and the glory of God filled the tabernacle (Exod 40:34-35). Moses asked to see the glory of God in a more personal way, so God hid him in a cleft in the rock and covered him with his hand until he had passed by, then he removed his hand so Moses could see his back, because, God said, "you cannot see my face, because no one can see me and live." I assume the use of the terms *face, back,* and *hand* is metaphorical, but surely there is still a point being made there. God said, "I will cause all my goodness to pass in front of you, and I will proclaim my name, the Lord [Yahweh], in your presence" (Exod 33:18-23).

When Solomon finished building the temple and preparation was being made for its dedication, the priests brought the Tent of Meeting from where it has been located, to the new temple. They moved the ark of the covenant from the tent into the Most Holy Place in the temple, and when they did, "the cloud filled the temple of the Lord. And the priests could not perform their service because of the cloud, for the glory of the Lord filled his temple" (1 Kings 8:10-11).

> THE GLORY OF GOD IS SIMPLY GOD'S CHARACTER – HIS INFINITE GOODNESS, HIS INFINITELY LOVING, INFINITELY HOLY NATURE

This brings us back to what we mentioned earlier – that the glory of God is simply God's character – his infinite goodness, his infinitely loving, infinitely holy nature. Essentially, that is what God said he would show Moses, when Moses asked to see his glory – "I will cause *all my goodness* to pass in front of you, I will proclaim *my name* in your presence" (italics added for emphasis). Somehow, *all his goodness* is connected with *his name*. Remember, to the Israelites, a person's *name* represented *all that one was*. Somehow, just as our prayers become tangible in heaven so that they can be stored in golden bowls, the goodness of God is tangible in heaven – it can be seen. Occasionally, he allows some representation of his glory to be seen on earth.

In one of Ezekiel's visions, he was lifted up between earth and heaven (Ezek 8:3), and there in front of him, he could see the glory of God. As the vision progressed, he followed the movement of the glory of God as it rose up in the temple, moved out over the threshold, then left the temple completely, moved out of the city, and settled on the mountain east of the city (Ezek 8 - 11). The departure of the glory of God from the temple was connected with God's decision to bring judgment on the Jews for following the surrounding nations rather than him (Ezek 11:1-12).

In a similar experience, the Apostle John got to see the new heaven and new earth that will replace the current ones at the end of time. He watched as the Holy City, Jerusalem, came down out of heaven from God. He noted a brilliance to the city: "It shone with the glory of God" (Rev 21:11). He also noted that "The city does not need the sun or the moon to shine on it, for the glory of God gives it light" (Rev 21:23). There will be no night in heaven (Rev 21:25, 22:5). I assume that we will never see a shadow in heaven, since the light will apparently be everywhere, not originating from any specific point.

Both Ezekiel and Daniel had visions of the throne of God. Ezekiel described it as being surrounded with brilliant light (Ezek 1:25-27); Daniel described it as being surrounded with flaming fire (Dan 7:9-10). They may have seen the same thing, but described the brilliance differently. Ezekiel even described the radiance as resembling a rainbow, and said, "This was the appearance of the likeness of the glory of the Lord" (Ezek 1:28).

So, again, what is the glory of God? I suggest it is *all his goodness*, his nature, his character, *his name*, all that he is. One way of thinking about God's glory, is that it is all about him that is *worthy of praise.* That's everything. But his glory is not just resident in him, it emanates out of him, so that it is visible and touches everything in its presence. This connects with the omnipresence of God, the prevenient grace of God being at work through the ministry of the Holy Spirit. In heaven, darkness will be forever eliminated, because of this emanating glory. The Holy Spirit is at work now, illuminating the minds of all people, in all places, at all times. "Your will be done on earth as it is in heaven." Light everywhere, no darkness at all, not even a shadow.

From God's throne, a river will flow, starting as nothing, and becoming a great river of the water of life. It seems to symbolize life itself emanating, as it were, from God. God is the source of all life, so life itself, then, is part of the goodness of God that emanates from who he is. The Apostle Paul seems to agree. He pointed out that in him we live, and move, and have our being (Acts 17:28). In him all things hold together (Col 1:17).

We are told to recognize this, and *give God glory*. But can we, in reality? If God's glory is all that he is, can we add to that? If not, what does it mean to *give God glory*?

When Joshua led the Israelites against Jericho, they were instructed to destroy the entire city and everything in it. The only things to be salvaged were items made of metal, and they were all to be placed in the treasury of the Lord. Achan kept some gold and silver and a nice garment, and as a result, the Israelite army lost the protection of God. When the sin was discovered, Joshua advised Achan to "give glory to the Lord God of Israel" by confessing what he had done (Josh 7:19).

Similar admonitions are throughout Scripture. I am certain that we cannot literally give God anything. God told Job, "Everything under heaven belongs to me" (Job 41:11). Everything came from God, and everything belongs to God. So what can we give him?

If we cannot literally give God glory, then the figure of speech must be symbolic. If so, what is it saying? I'm convinced it is used in two ways: 1) we can give God glory by *recognizing* his glory – all his goodness, all that he is, and 2) we can give God glory be *reflecting* his glory – his goodness, who he is – to others.

The term *give God glory* is synonymous with the term *glorify God*. We glorify God by recognizing him as he is, and by showing who he is to others.

Praising God glorifies him. It recognizes him as he is. Praising God *to others* glorifies him. It shows him as he is to others. It was always this way. When God brought the Israelites out of Egypt, it was not just to get his chosen people to the land he had promised their forefathers. It was so that "the Egyptians will know that I am the Lord." This connects directly with the missional God, with redemption, with God choosing

Israel, with the top line blessing and the bottom line blessing. The reason Israel was situated where they were, geographically, was to make them the hub of the wheel of nations – so the nations could see what God was doing among them. Solomon made that point in the dedication of the temple. The purpose of the temple, the purpose of God blessing Israel, was "so that all the peoples of the earth may know that the Lord is God and that there is no other."

In Isaiah 48:20, God said, "Announce this with shouts of joy and proclaim it. Send it out to the ends of the earth; say, 'The Lord has redeemed his servant Jacob.'" Like any other blessing, redemption is not only for the beneficiary; it is also for observers. "I wish *my* god were like that." "I wish *my* life could be turned around like that." "I wish God provided for and protected *our* nation like that."

Notice how the connections continue.

The fact that God is the source of light literally, shows up in Scripture as a major metaphor. When Paul was converted on the road to Damascus, Jesus told him he was sending him to the Gentiles "to open their eyes and turn them from darkness to light" (Acts 26:17-18). Paul told that to the Jews in Pisidian Antioch, when they became jealous of the crowds who gathered to hear him and Barnabas. Quoting from Isaiah 49:6, he said, "For this is what the Lord has commanded us: 'I have made you a light for the Gentiles, that you may bring salvation to the ends of the earth'" (Acts 13:47).

In the metaphor, darkness equals falsehood, light equals truth. The Psalmist said, "Your word is a lamp to my feet and a light for my path" (Psalm 119:105). God is a jealous God, not for himself, but because those following other gods are in darkness, following a false belief that the bridge is still in place. In darkness, in the fog, people drive off the cliff. In the light, they see the danger ahead of time, and are able to "be saved." Darkness is a form of bondage. The coming of the light enables people to escape from that bondage. So in the metaphor, light not only equals truth, but it provides the way to freedom. Paul captured this connection when he said, "where the spirit of the Lord is, there is freedom" (2 Cor 3:17). John captured it when he said that Jesus was the light of the world (John 1:4-9). Jesus captured it when he said, "I am the way and the truth and the life" (John 14:6), and "you will know the truth, and the truth will set you free" (John 8:32). The light dispels the darkness – it reveals the truth, and the truth provides the possibility of freedom. It glorifies God when we reveal his light, his truth, *all his goodness*. This is one of the major arguments against Calvinism – it does not glorify God, because it does not reveal *all his goodness*. Instead, it actually obscures much of it.

THE MISSION OF GOD, *MISSIO DEI*, WAS FOR ALL PEOPLE TO KNOW HIM

From the very first, the mission of God, *missio Dei*, was for all people to know him. In the Old Testament, one of the means was for observers to see what God was doing through one group of people, to be drawn to that light, and to join themselves to that people (Rahab, Ruth, Uriah the Hittite), or at least join themselves to the God of that people (Naaman, Nebuchadnezzar). It was a drawing toward a center point. In the New Testament, the means was for messengers to go out from a center point. In the Old Testament, the people of God were a nation, a people chosen to draw all nations to the light. In the New Testament, the people of God are the Church, a people chosen to take the light to all nations (remember the Great Commission). The means have changed, but the original goal remains the same.

If God does all things for his glory, as Calvinism claims, I would argue that God's motivation has never been self centered. His purpose, his love, his actions, have always been others centered – his love emanates outward from his very being. THE PLAN has never changed. We are challenged to enter into that plan with the same motivation: "whatever you do, do it all for the glory of God" (1 Cor 10:31). Everything we do, we should do with the intent *to recognize God as he is*, and *to reveal him to others, as he is*. When we do, we experience the providence of God – "Blessed are the pure in heart, for they shall see God" (Matt 5:8). We see God, and he sees us, as his eyes "range throughout the earth to strengthen those whose hearts are fully committed to him" (2 Chron 16:9). We show evidence of being "called according to his purpose" (Rom 8:28). He involves himself in our lives in a fresh, new way, to enable the process to continue: "in all your ways acknowledge him, and he will make your paths straight" (Prov 3:6). As we scatter the seed, "he who supplies seed to the sower will increase your store of seed" (2 Cor 9:9-10).

This is both the spiritual growth process in the individual, and the means God uses to reveal himself to others, through us. It is captured in the phrase "God at work in us and through us." It is a cyclic process in which we participate. I illustrate it like this:

1. I understand truth – I recognize God as he is.
2. By faith, I act as if this new understanding is true (obedience, living as if God is real, including revealing him, as he is, to others).
3. God responds according to his promises, revealing himself even more to me – his glory, his goodness.
4. My faith is reinforced.
5. I understand more & am encouraged to act more as if it is true, further glorifying God.
6. God responds, my faith is reinforced, I am encouraged to act more in obedience.

The cycle repeats itself endlessly. The goal is to move from initial recognition of truth, to being a true disciple – one who follows Jesus in all areas of life. And if we are true disciples, we are also disciple makers, as Jesus was, so the cycle repeats itself endlessly in others. A major principle of missions is that the work of God, done well, is infinitely

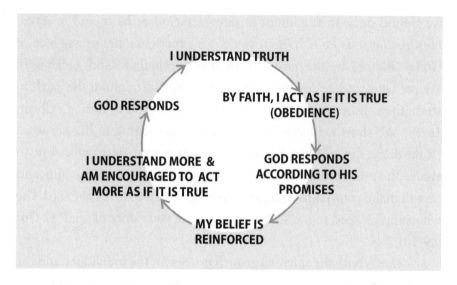

reproducible. Anytime we do anything that cannot be repeated by the ones we are working with, the process grinds to a halt when we leave. The legacy we leave is not the kingdom of God, it is our own empire. God's plan is that we live by the light of God – his glory – and reflect that light to others, and the more we do, the more God reveals himself to us, so we can reveal him to others. That glorifies God. That's THE PLAN.

Endnotes

[1] Anne Lamott, *Bird by Bird: Some Instructions on Writing and Life* (New York: Anchor Books, a division of Random House, 1995), 200.

[2] Wolfgang Herrmann, "Baal," *Dictionary of Deities and Demons in the Bible,* 2nd ed. (Grand Rapids, MI: Wm. B. Eerdmans, 1999), 132-139.

[3] John Day, *Yahweh and the Gods and Goddesses of Canaan* (Sheffield, UK: Sheffield Academic Press, 2000), 75.

[4] "The Great Litany," *The Book of Common Prayer* (New York: Church Publishing, 1979), 149. Credit is given to Paul R. Eddy and James K. Beilby for making this point clear, in the Introduction to James K. Beilby and Paul R. Eddy, eds., *Understanding Spiritual Warfare: Four Views* (Grand Rapids, MI: Baker Academic. 2012), 32.

[5] For a more detailed explanation of this view, see David Powlinson, "The Classical Model,"

Understanding Spiritual Warfare: Four Views, ed. James K. Beilby and Paul R. Eddy (Grand Rapids, MI: Baker Academic. 2012), 89-111.

6   For a more detailed explanation of this view, see C. Peter Wagner and Rebecca Greenwood, "The Strategic-Level Deliverance Model," *Understanding Spiritual Warfare: Four Views,* ed. James K. Beilby and Paul R. Eddy (Grand Rapids, MI: Baker Academic. 2012), 173-198.

7   For a more detailed explanation of this view, see Gregory Boyd, "The Ground-Level Deliverance Model," *Understanding Spiritual Warfare: Four Views,* ed. James K. Beilby and Paul R. Eddy (Grand Rapids, MI: Baker Academic. 2012), 129-157.

8   For a more detailed explanation of this view, see Walter Wink, "The World Systems Model," *Understanding Spiritual Warfare: Four Views,* ed. James K. Beilby and Paul R. Eddy (Grand Rapids, MI: Baker Academic. 2012), 47-71. Wink is best know for his "Powers Trilogy": *Naming the Powers: The Language of Power in the New Testament* (Philadelphia, PA: Fortress Press, 1984); *Unmasking the Powers: The Invisible Forces That Determine Human Existence* (Philadelphia, PA: Fortress Press, 1986); and, *Engaging the Powers: Discernment and Resistance in a World of Domination* (Minneapolis, MN: Fortress Press, 1992).

9   This view originated with Amos Yong, and is explored in *The Spirit of Creation: Modern Science and Divine Action in the Pentecostal-Charismatic Imagination* (Grand Rapids, MI: Eerdmans, 2011), 173-225, as well as in other writings of his.

10   Augustine, *Enchiridion,* in *Enchiridion and Confessions,* ed. Albert C. Outler, Library of Christian Classics (Philadelphia, PA: Westminster, 1955), 7:400.

11   Calvin, *Institutes,* Book I, Ch. 17, para. 2, p. 135.

12   Boyd, "The Ground-Level Deliverance Model," 129. This is the central thesis of Boyd's book, Gregory Boyd, *God at War: The Bible and Spiritual Conflict* (Downers Grove, IL: InterVarsity, 1997).

13   Calvin, *Institutes,* Book I, Ch. 14, para. 3-18, pp. 106-114.

14   Cf. Ezek 28:22, 36:23, 39:7, and Hos 11:9).

15   The address, "Is Life Worth Living," was delivered to the Harvard Young Men's Christian Association, then published in the International Journal of Ethics for October, 1895, and as a pocket volume by S.B. Weston, Philadelphia, 1896.   William James, "Is Life Worth Living?" in William James, *The Will to Believe: And Other Essays in Popular Philosophy, and Human Immortality* (Cambridge MA: Harvard University Press, 1979), 34. Italics in the original.

16   James, "Is Life Worth Living?" 55.

17   Thuesen, *Predestination,* 6.

18   Magnus Magnusson, *Scotland: The Story of a Nation* (London: HarperCollins, 2000), 302-3, quoting Sir Walter Scott in *Tales of a Grandfather,* Chapter XXVII.

19   Linda Hutjens, " The Disguised King in Early English Ballads," in *Literature and Popular Culture in Early Modern England,* ed. Matthew Dimmock and Andrew Hadfield (Burlington, VT: Ashgate Publishing, 2009), 75.

20   Calvin, *Institutes,* Book II, Ch. 7, para. 5, p. 218.

21   Cf. Louis Berkhof, *Systematic Theology* (Grand Rapids, MI: W.B. Eerdmans, 1996), 221; Wayne A. Grudem, *Systematic Theology: An Introduction to Biblical Doctrine* (Grand Rapids, MI: Zondervan, 1994), 496-497.

22   Calvin, *Institutes,* Book II, Ch. 7, para. 5, p. 218.

23   Calvin, *Institutes,* Book I, Ch. 16, para. 4, p. 129.

24   Richard Lewinsohn, *A History of Sexual Customs* (London: Longmans, Green, and Co., 1958), 31-32.

25 John A. Martin, *Blessed are the Addicts: The Spiritual Side of Alcoholism, Addiction, and Recovery* (New York: Villard Books, 1990), 87.

26 Thuesen, *Predestination*, 2, 225.

27 Thuesen, *Predestination*, 4.

28 Quoted in Candi Paull and Lila Empson, *Checklist for Life: For Women* (Nashville, TN: Thomas Nelson, 2002), 12.

29 http://kingjamesbibledictionary.com/StrongsNo/G5020/Hell.

30 God is shown to be a jealous God in Exod 20:5, 34:14; Deut 4:24, 5:9, 6:15, 32:16-21; Josh 24:19; 1 Kings 14:22; Ezek 16:38-42, 23:25, 36:6; Nahum 1:2; Zeph 3:8; Zech 1:14; and James 4:5.

31 Lewis, *Mere Christianity*, 133.

32 For a more detailed explanation of this view, see Paul Helm, "The Augustinian-Calvinist View," in *Divine Foreknowledge: Four Views.*, ed. James K. Beilby and Paul R. Eddy (Downers Grove, IL: InterVarsity Press, 2001), 161-189.

33 For a more detailed explanation of this view, see William Lane Craig, "The Middle-Knowledge View," in *Divine Foreknowledge: Four Views.*, ed. James K. Beilby and Paul R. Eddy (Downers Grove, IL: InterVarsity Press, 2001), 119-143.

34 For a more detailed explanation of this view, see David Hunt, "The Simple-Foreknowledge View," in *Divine Foreknowledge: Four Views.*, ed. James K. Beilby and Paul R. Eddy (Downers Grove, IL: InterVarsity Press, 2001), 65-103.

35 This statement is often attributed to the Irish politician, statesman, and political philosopher Edmund Burke (1729 - 1797), but no to date original source has been found to substantiate its origin.

36 For a more detailed explanation of this view, see Gregory A. Boyd, "The Open-Theism View," in *Divine Foreknowledge: Four Views.*, ed. James K. Beilby and Paul R. Eddy (Downers Grove, IL: InterVarsity Press, 2001), 13-47.

37 For example, In Jer 32, both the anger of God, and God rejoicing, are visible. Isa 49:13 shows God expressing compassion, and Zephaniah 3:17 shows God experiencing great delight and rejoicing.

38 Cf. Bob Sjogren, *Unveiled At Last* (Seattle, WA: YWAM Publishing, 1992), 29; Don Richardson seminar, "Stars, Sand, and Dust," 3-9.

39 Deut 23:1-2.

40 Richardson, "Stars, Sand, and Dust," 6.

41 There may be more, but I have identified 23 times Matthew shows prophecy to be fulfilled: 1:17, 20; 1:22-23; 2:5-6; 2:14-15; 2:17-18; 2:23; 3:3; 4:14-16; 8:16-17; 11:10; 11:14; 12:17-21; 13:35; 15:4; 17:11; 21:4; 21:16; 21:42; 22:41-46; 26:24; 26:31; 26:54,56; 27:9-10.

42 Millard J. Erickson, *Christian Theology* (Grand Rapids, MI: Baker Books, 1998), 561.

43 John Calvin, *Commentary on the Bible, 1 Timothy 2*, https://www.studylight.org/commentaries/cal/1-timothy-2.html.

44 Calvin, *Commentary, 2 Peter 3*, https://www.studylight.org/commentaries/cal/2-peter-3.html.

45 Calvin, *Commentary, 1 John 2*, https://www.studylight.org/commentaries/cal/1-john-2.html.

46 Another verse that could be a problem for Calvin is Matthew 18:14, where Jesus says, "In the same way your Father in heaven is not willing that any of these little ones should be lost." He is talking about little children, and he illustrates his point by stating that a shepherd is happier about finding one sheep that has wandered off, than about his other ninety-nine which did not wander off. Calvin fails to address verse 14 at all, commenting only on verse 12 before it, and

interpreting the wandering off as relating to disciples. It is also worthy of note that all of us start our lives as little children, so at least in our childhood, God is not willing that any of us should perish. See Calvin, *Commentary, Matthew 18,* https://www.studylight.org/commentaries/cal/matthew-18.html.

Hebrews 2:9-10 also supports the idea of Jesus dying for everyone, but only "many sons" being brought to glory.

47 Calvin, *Institutes*, Book I, Ch. 18, para 3, p. 148.

48 Calvin, *Institutes*, Book I, Ch. 18, para 3, p. 148.

49 Leslie D. Weatherhead, *The Will of God, rev. ed.* (Nashville, TN: Abingdon, 1999). Originally published in 1944.

50 Calvin, *Institutes*, Book I, Ch. 16, para. 4, p. 129.

51 Calvin, *Institutes*, Book I, Ch. 17, para. 2, p. 135.

52 Calvin, *Institutes*, Book I, Ch. 18, para 3, p. 149.

53 For my understanding of the kingdom of God, I am deeply indebted to the following authors: J. Sidlow Baxter, *The Strategic Grasp of the Bible* (London: Marshall, Morgan & Scott, 1968); Zane C. Hodges, *The Gospel Under Siege* (Dallas, TX: Redencion Viva, 1981); George Eldon Ladd, *The Gospel of the Kingdom: Scriptural Studies in the Kingdom of God* (Grand Rapids, MI: William B. Eerdmans, 1959; and Howard A. Snyder, *Models of the Kingdom* (Nashville, TN: Abingdon Press, 1991).

54 I am indebted to Edgardo Silvoso for this explanation, from his article "Prayer Power in Argentina," in *Engaging the Enemy:How to Fight and Defeat Territorial Spirits,* ed. C. Peter Wagner (Ventura, CA: Regal Books, 1991), 114-115.

55 A true story, with name and inconsequential details changed to protect the identity of the individual involved.

56 Calvin, *Institutes*, Book III, Ch. 20, para. 2, p. 524.

57 For the logic in this section, I am deeply indebted to Tom Morris, *Philosophy For Dummies* (Foster City, CA: IDG Books, 1999).

58 Morris, *Philosophy*, 264.

59 Morris, *Philosophy*, 269-277.

60 Malcolm Muggeridge, *Chronicles of Wasted Time: 1: The Green Stick* (New York: William Morrow & Co., 1973), 137. He makes this point again in *Jesus: The Man Who Lives* (London: Harper & Row, 1975), 156.

61 Muggeridge, *Jesus*, 156.

62 Calvin, *Institutes*, Book I, Ch. 18, para. 3, p. 148-149.

Chapter 8
The Inconsistencies of Calvinism

**Pride, prejudice and preconceptions are the
big barriers to seeing truth.**
— John White[1]

Judah got a wife for Er, his firstborn, and her name
was Tamar. But Er, Judah's firstborn, was wicked in the
Lord's sight; so the Lord put him to death. Then Judah said
to Onan, "Lie with your brother's wife and fulfill your duty
to her as a brother-in-law to produce offspring for your
brother." But Onan knew that the offspring would not be
his; so whenever he lay with his brother's wife, he spilled
his semen on the ground to keep from producing offspring
for his brother. What he did was wicked in the Lord's sight;
so he put him to death also (Gen 38:6-10).

In the last chapter, I attempted to outline the plan of God, the way the world works – or at least the way it appears to work, based on Scripture and the way we experience life. In this chapter, I want to simply ask several questions that Calvinism seems unable to resolve.

The first is, how does it work that God exercises absolute sovereignty over all that happens, yet holds humans responsible for what they do? In the passage above, it would seem that God, in his absolute sovereignty, decreed that Er would be wicked and die early. It would also seem to be the divine will that Onan spill his semen on the ground to avoid impregnating Tamar, yet God held him responsible for his action and killed him for it. How does that work?

IF DIVINE DETERMINISM IS TRUE, HOW CAN ANYTHING TRULY BE EVIL?

Related to this, is another question: If divine determinism is true, how can anything truly be evil? How is it that both Er and Onan were "wicked in the Lord's sight," when, according to Calvinism, they were simply functioning in a way that God had foreordained and rendered certain? If God plans and purposes all things for his glory, then everything from Er and Onan's motivation to their actions came from God, and what they did glorified God – made him look good in the process. How, then, can what they did be evil, and how can God hold them responsible for what they did, since he predetermined that they do it? And how does the process make God look good?

Carrying the logic further, if God has predetermined who will live and who will be in heaven, then what practical difference does it make if a man ejaculates inside a woman's body or on the ground? If the result of the sex act was already predetermined by God, why should he get angry about the way it actually happened, when the way it happened produced the results that he had predetermined before the foundation of the earth?

In the last chapter, we met Sara and her illegitimate son, Benjamin. The question we considered was, does the image of God in us give us the ability to make decisions that affect the future, or not? But the story also extends to those questions asked above, related to divine sovereignty and human responsibility, and whether anything is ever truly evil. Consider a parallel story from Scripture.

In Genesis 19, we see God destroying Sodom and Gomorrah, and rescuing Lot and his family. Lot's wife disobeyed the command not to look back, so she died. Lot and his two daughters hid in a cave in the mountains for awhile. Over time, the daughters became anxious about the future, aware of the absence of marriageable men, so they conspired together to get pregnant by their own father. They got him drunk in order to sleep with him without his awareness. Each one became pregnant, and each of their son's, Moab and Ben-Ammi, became the father of a nation (the Moabites and Ammonites). Consider the implications of that – if the girls had slept with anybody else in the world, history would have been different. They plotted together to sleep with their own father, and got him drunk to accomplish it. If God renders certain all that happens, if God had predetermined from the foundations of the earth which of their distant offspring would be in heaven, then he first of all had to predetermine who would be born, and that means that he had to determine who had sex with whom, and that means that God was the instigator of the incest, not the daughters at all. And Lot might as well have stayed sober and enjoyed the experience to the full, because it was God's will that it happen.

But the story did not start in that cave in the mountain. It started in Sodom, where Lot had chosen to live when he and Abraham separated, and from which Lot and his daughters were forced to flee when the angel of the Lord was about to destroy the city for its sexual evil. So if all those things were the foreordained will of God, then really the sexual evil of Sodom, for which the cities were destroyed, was part of God's foreordained plan from before the foundation of the earth, because if that evil had never occurred, the angel would not have had to rescue Lot and his family, and the daughters would not have been feeling isolated in the cave in the mountains to the point of wanting offspring from their own father. How does that work, without attributing all of the evil of Sodom and Gomorrah and the incest of Lot and his two daughters, to God?

Is it possible that God was anticipating divine determinism when he had James put pen to paper and write his epistle? James wrote, "When tempted, no one should say, 'God is tempting me.' For God cannot be tempted by evil, nor does he tempt anyone; but each one is tempted when, by his own evil desire, he is dragged away and enticed. Then, after desire has conceived, it gives birth to sin; and sin, when it is full-grown, gives birth to death. Don't be deceived, my dear brothers" (James 1:13-16).

Theoretically, every action taken today, limits all the possible actions that can be taken tomorrow. If I murder somebody today, then he cannot have kids tomorrow, and those potential kids cannot find cures for diseases, nor can they have future offspring who could have future offspring or find magic cures, ad infinitum.

Yet James says that if by our actions we turn a sinner from the error of his ways, we prevent his untimely death (James 5:19-20). How does that work, if God renders all things certain? If we actually do that – alter the date of a death – then our life affected his future, and his continued life will affect other future events. He can have kids who would not have existed if we had not intervened and they can have kids and lead nations either into greater righteousness or greater wickedness, and it would all have hinged on our actions, in preventing a death that otherwise would have occurred.

Consider exactly this situation with Hezekiah and his son Manasseh. Initially, Isaiah told Hezekiah to put his affairs in order, because his illness would be terminal. Hezekiah pouted and prayed, and God granted him 15 years of extra life (2 Kings 20:6). Three years later he fathered Manasseh, who became king at age 12 (2 Kings 20:21, 21:1). Manasseh was one of the most wicked leaders Judah ever had (2 Kings 21:10-15). Decades and four kings later,[2] God said he was still punishing the nation for the direction Manasseh's leadership started (2 Kings 24:1-4). If Hezekiah had accepted death on schedule, Manasseh would never have been born, and his influence would never have existed, so God would not have felt compelled to punish people who were impacted by Manasseh's evil leadership. If God foreordained the extra 15 years of life for Hezekiah, then he must have also foreordained Manasseh's birth and life, so why complain and punish the nation for the evil direction Manasseh's leadership caused? And what did God gain by saying first, that he was going to take Hezekiah's life? Why not just heal him to begin with and let him live another 15 years?

Calvin addressed this in his *Institutes*:

Nor does the Sacred History, while it relates that the destruction which had been proclaimed to the Ninevites was remitted, and the life of Hezekiah, after an intimation of death, prolonged, imply that the decrees of God were annulled. Those who think so labour under delusion as to the meaning of threatenings, which, though they affirm simply, nevertheless contain in them a tacit condition dependent on the result. Why did the Lord send Jonah to the Ninevites to predict the overthrow of their city? Why did he by Isaiah give Hezekiah intimation of his death? He might have destroyed both them and him without a message to announce the disaster. He had something else in view than to give them a warning of death, which might let them see it at a distance before it came. It was because he did not wish them destroyed but reformed, and thereby saved from destruction. When Jonah prophesies that in forty days Nineveh will be overthrown, he does it in order to prevent the overthrow. When Hezekiah is forbidden to hope for longer life, it is that he may obtain longer life. Who does not now see that, by threatening of this kind, God wished to arouse those to repentance whom he terrified, that they might escape the Judgment which their sins deserved?[3]

At least three things are notable from Calvin's observations. One is Calvin's position that God wanted Hezekiah to "obtain longer life." Why? So Hezekiah could father Manasseh, so Manasseh could be wicked and bring judgment on Judah? Another is Calvin's treatment of the Hezekiah incident as if it is parallel to the Nineveh event: "he did not wish them destroyed but reformed, and thereby saved from destruction." Nothing in the biblical record either says that Hezekiah needed reforming or did reform. He simply turned his face to the wall, wept bitterly, and reminded God of how he had tried to be faithful.

A third notable observation is that in Calvin's explanation of "threatenings" of God, he avoids dealing with parallel incidents in Scripture, where the same type of threat is issued, but the one so threatened does not respond, so the threatened punishment is carried out. Jeremiah, for example, gave Zedekiah repeated warnings from God regarding the destruction of Jerusalem, promising good if he would respond, and destruction if he would not. (Jer 38:17-18; Jer 52). How does this work? If a decree has been issued, how can it contain "a tacit condition dependent on the result"? Doesn't that make it not a decree? Doesn't that imply free will of humans, the ability to disregard God's expressed will and act in opposition to it? Can we have a decree, something that God has rendered certain, that also has a condition attached to it?

If God makes a threat of punishment, but relents when the threatened party changes, with "a tacit condition dependent on the result," why would this work in relation to events in this life, but not related to eternity? Calvin says, "Who does not now see that, by threatening of this kind, God wished to arouse those to repentance whom he terrified, that they might escape the Judgment which their sins deserved?" Why use the same technique both with some who respond positively, and some who don't, if the results are foreordained?

Where does the threat of hell come in? Could not a person repent, as Calvin suggests God wants, and "escape the Judgment which their sins deserved" for eternity? How does this work with the Calvinist contention that God selects some people and not others? Can there be both predestination from before the foundation of the earth, and the opportunity of repentance that avoids judgment which their sins deserve?

This brings us to a deeper question: From God's perspective, why create both spirit beings and humans, and allow things to play out over time? Why not just create with the end already in place? If both the final results, and all the pieces of the process along the way are decreed of God – are foreordained before the foundation of the earth, are rendered certain by the will of God – what is accomplished by the process? Wouldn't it be more efficient to just create the finished product without all the drama?

In the last chapter, we considered theodicies – possible explanations of why God allows evil – and one of the most convincing is related to character development of people. If God foreordains everything – renders everything certain ahead of time – then is not character development a delusion? Is not even the Bible unnecessary if God foreordains everything, since it apparently is given to enable humans to know God and his ways in order to develop and grow to live according to God's commands, and by so doing, to experience life as God intended it?

Consider universalism compared to Calvinism's predestination. Universalism is the belief that ultimately, everybody will be saved and spend eternity in heaven. Some versions of universalism even believe that Satan and all the demons will be redeemed – that they will be reconciled to God, and spend eternity in heaven. Universalism takes the few verses that say God wants all to be saved, and uses them to create a theology that overrides and disregards all the other parts of Scripture that talk about judgment and hell. Does not the doctrine of predestination do the same thing? It takes one idea and creates a theology that overrides and disregards all those parts of Scripture that appear to teach exactly the opposite. Both universalism and predestination have the same problem, in that they both deny that created beings really have free will. In the end, in both of those strains of theology, it is not man who chooses his ultimate destiny, but God. In fact, in 1796, Universalist Joseph Huntington argued in his book *Calvinism Improved*, "that the Calvinists were correct on everything except election's extent."[4] What makes Calvinism superior to universalism?

> BOTH UNIVERSALISM AND PREDESTINATION HAVE THE SAME PROBLEM, IN THAT THEY BOTH DENY THAT CREATED BEINGS REALLY HAVE FREE WILL

In Ezekiel 14:14-20, God speaks to the prophet about what will happen "if a country sins against me by being unfaithful and I stretch out my hand against it." He says that the situation will be so bad, the destruction so complete, that if Noah, Daniel, and Job were there, not even their families would be saved. During famine, war, plague, or attacks by wild beasts – four times – God says, "they could save neither son nor daughter. They could save only themselves by their righteousness." How does this work? If God determines the destiny of all humans without regard to anything related to them as individual persons, how could the righteousness of these three men guarantee them special protection which would not even extend to those closest to them?

Typically, Calvinism denies free will in humans – in net effect if not in theory, although typically in theory as well. As Calvin addressed the image of God in humans, he made a distinction between the condition of the human will before and after the Fall. He said:

> In this upright state, man possessed freedom of will, by which, if he chose, he was able to obtain eternal life. It [is] here unseasonable to introduce the question concerning the secret predestination

356

of God, because we are not considering what might or might not happen, but what the nature of man truly was. Adam, therefore, might have stood if he chose, since it was only by his own will that he fell; . . . Still he had a free choice of good and evil; . . . But those who, while they profess to be the disciples of Christ, still seek for free-will in man, notwithstanding of his being lost and drowned in spiritual destruction, labour under manifold delusion, making a heterogeneous mixture of inspired doctrine and philosophical opinions, and so erring as to both.[5]

How does this work? Humans had free will before the Fall, based on the image of God in them, but after the Fall, the freedom of will was removed. Is this logical? Does it fit with the biblical record? Do we assume that the omnipresent Holy Spirit was not present in the Garden of Eden, that the grace of God, prevenient grace, was not being extended before the Fall? Could the human, before the Fall, of his own free will, make a choice of good and evil such that he was able to obtain eternal life? If prevenient grace was present before the Fall, and if it is present after the Fall, what's the difference? Do we see the image of God removed with the Fall? Traditionally, the church has held that the image of God was marred by the Fall, and must be restored, but it was not destroyed. After the flood, God told Noah, "Whoever sheds the blood of man, by man shall his blood be shed; for in the image of God has God made man" (Gen 9:6). That's present tense, well after the Fall. It also implies personal responsibility, which we already questioned as being compatible with the absolute sovereignty of God. After the Fall, the murderer was to be executed based on two factors: 1) he is responsible for his actions and 2) the one he killed was made in the image of God. Where in that is there an absence of free will?

And why is it "unseasonable" to talk about "the secret pre-destination of God" along with the image of God, and the Fall? As Adam faced the choice that would precipitate the Fall, was he not already living in circumstances planned and rendered certain by the purposes of God? If so, how could he freely choose anything other than what God had set him up to do? Is it not when we compartmentalize our theology, rather than harmonizing it, that we can maintain beliefs separately that are inconsistent when considered together? What is the difference in God presenting Adam with a choice of good and evil before the Fall, and Moses presenting the Israelites with a similar choice just before they were about to enter the promised land? Was Adam's choice a genuinely free choice, but the Israelites' choice less so after the Fall?

And what is the "manifold delusion" under which we labor, if we think the Israelites had free will that made them capable of responding to the challenge Moses gave them? The whole history of the Israelite nation as recorded in the Old Testament history books and the prophets – its division into two nations, and their progression into sin and then exile – seems to be related to their failure to use their free will to follow the direction God outlined for them. God repeatedly confronted them, giving them opportunity to reverse the trend, with every confrontation presupposing, on the surface, the possibility that they could change – but how could they, if their free will was removed so that they were dependent on God to provide what they needed to make right decisions? We are back to the prison analogy: "You are being offered freedom from prison, but I have the key to the prison door, and I'm not going to use it to free you," only this time it's more like, "You have to climb this sheer cliff to escape the approaching wildfire, but I have the only rope, and I'm not going to give you access to it." How is it honorable of God on one hand to demand that his people either go in a certain direction or experience judgment, but on the other hand, to withhold from them what only he could provide (free will) to avoid that judgment?

This reveals how paradigms influence what we see. Everywhere I look in Scripture, I see choices presented to humans, and accountability for how those choices are made. Everywhere Calvinists look, they see the sovereignty of God controlling how those choices are made. On one occasion when Jesus talked about hiding a lamp under a bowl, and about the eye being the light of the body, he made an imperative statement: "See to it then, that the light within you is not darkness" (Luke 11:35). Does that not imply that we have both the ability and the responsibility to do so? In Luke's version of the Olivet Discourse, Jesus says, "to whom much is given, much will be required" (Luke 12:48). Is that not evidence of accountability, of the expectation that we can and should use our abilities to influence what is happening? Does it not imply that our actions make a difference?

Other passages raise this same question.

> Jesus went through all the towns and villages, teaching in their synagogues, preaching the good news of the kingdom and healing every disease and sickness. When he saw the crowds, he had compassion on them, because they were harassed and helpless, like sheep without a shepherd. Then he said to his disciples, "The harvest is plentiful but the workers are few. Ask the Lord of the harvest, therefore, to send out workers into his harvest field" (Matt 9: 35-38).

Jesus' observation about the lack of harvest workers is repeated in Luke 10:2, as he sent out the seventy-two. Asking the Lord for more harvest workers, implies that God could do more, if more humans participated. Connect these events with the parable of the landowner who hired workers throughout the day, in Matthew 20. It is not the main point of the parable, but one thing implied by the continued hiring is that there is no shortage of work. Some people get rich, other people become homeless; success in life appears to be a combination of opportunities, and how individuals take advantage of those opportunities, or fail to do so. At the practical level, that's the way life works.

Success also appears to be directly related to how much people understand, which again relates to how well they can take advantage of the opportunities available to them. This is the whole point of schooling. It's also the whole point of leadership. Revisit Manasseh. At the same time that Calvinists say God foreordains every event, they train pastors and missionaries through seminaries, and they teach people in churches, all, ostensibly, to help the people improve so that tomorrow they can be better, and do better, than today. Where is the logic in that? The same Calvin who said that God renders all things certain, sent out over 100 missionaries into France, as we saw in Chapter 1, apparently to influence those people to change their beliefs, and thereby, their future destiny and even the destiny of the nation. How does that work?

If God foreordains all things, why are there differences in beliefs at all? Why would God render certain that Calvin have one set of beliefs, and Jacob Arminius another? And Michael Servetus another?

IF GOD FOREORDAINS ALL THINGS, WHY ARE THERE DIFFERENCES IN BELIEFS AT ALL?

In his early days, "Calvin himself defended the notions of freedom of conscience for the Christian and of tolerance as a special virtue of rulers."[6] Later, however, when he had consolidated his power in Geneva, he used that power to bring about the execution of Michael Servetus, and to silence another critic, Sebastian Castellio. The Genevan church leadership actually cooperated with the Catholic Inquisition in Servetus's execution, which was carried out with the support of Geneva's sister reform communities: Zurich, Bern, Basel, and Schaffhausen. "For all these great leaders of the reform camp there existed no freedom of conscience to affirm a doctrine that deviated from theirs."[7] Doctrine was given greater value than a person's life.

For opposing Calvin, Castellio was removed from his position as rector of the Latin School of Geneva and forbidden to speak in public, a mild reprimand compared to the burning of Servetus.[8] Castellio wrote a rebuttal to Calvin's position, *Whether Heretics Should Be Persecuted (De haereticis, an sint persequendi)*, which "proved even at that time that a theory of toleration could be developed on the foundation of the Christian gospel."[9] Why was Calvin compelled to silence Servetus and Castellio? Do his actions not imply a fear of their influence? And if their presence could produce influence in opposition to his own, does that not imply the opposite of all things being rendered certain? Was the silencing of Calvin's critics foreordained by God? If so, why? To eliminate their influence, when their beliefs, and their prior influence, were also foreordained by God? How does this work? When you factor in the results of the Inquisition itself, successful in Spain but not in Switzerland and Germany, so that Spain and all its exported teachings were distinctly Catholic, how does that work? Why would God foreordain that Catholic positions prevail in one place and Protestants' in another? If Calvin's execution of Servetus was foreordained of God for opposing Calvin's viewpoints, how do we explain the execution of those reformers who supported his viewpoints? How does that work?

This lack of consistent logic can even be seen in the missions efforts of Calvinists. As David Bosch points out, "Belief in predestination can paralyze the will to mission."[10] Why bother? God's got it all under control. Nothing I do will make a difference in the eventual outcome, anyway.

History documents a progression among Calvinists from complete passivity regarding missions, based on their emphasis on the absolute sovereignty of God, to an emphasis on the glory of God, which could be wedded to compassion and thereby justify human effort.[11] In the early days of the settlement of North America, the Puritans saw themselves as the elect, so they thanked God for destroying the Native Americans *en masse* with disease, but just a few years later, as the efforts of John Eliot and others started producing conversions among Native Americans, suddenly the Native Americans were among the elect.[12] How does this work? Did God have elect hidden among the Native Americans in one generation but not in previous ones, so that he foreordained that some become extinct through disease, but others come to repentance through the foreordained settling of the New World and the efforts of John Eliot and others?

Calvin says, "As God is the fountain of all righteousness, he must necessarily be the enemy and judge of man so long as he is a sinner. Wherefore, the commencement of love is the bestowing of righteousness . . ."[13] Is this biblical? "For God so loved the world that he gave his one and only Son, that whoever believes in him shall not perish but have eternal life" (John 3:16). "But God demonstrates his own love for us in this: While we were still sinners, Christ died for us" (Rom 5:8). Are we really to believe that God chooses some based on his "secret predestination" and his "incomprehensible will" but that love is not part of his motivation? That he only starts loving people when they are made righteous by his "efficacious" administration of grace? Are we really to believe that God has no love for the sinner prior to salvation?

ARE WE REALLY TO BELIEVE THAT GOD HAS NO LOVE FOR THE SINNER PRIOR TO SALVATION?

We have already seen that Jesus reflects the fullness of God. Whatever Jesus looked like, God looks like. "Anyone who has seen me has seen the Father" (John 14:8-9). When Jesus lamented over Jerusalem, why was he grieved? "O Jerusalem, Jerusalem, you who kill the prophets and stone those sent to you, how often I have longed to gather your children together, as a hen gathers her chicks under her wings, but you were not willing" (Matt 23:37, Luke 13:34). Was Jesus grieved over missed opportunity? If Jesus is a perfect reflection of the Father, then if Jesus was grieved, the Father was grieved. How could that be, if God foreordains everything? Was Jesus grieved, because he loved the people, and they rejected him? How could that be, if God only starts to love people when he makes them righteous?

I could go on, because these types of questions are endless. Four times in the book of Acts, Luke shows Paul "reasoning" with people and "trying to persuade" them regarding the messiah and the kingdom of God (Acts 17:2-4, 16-17, 18:4, 19:8). Could this be the same Paul whose writings are used to argue that God renders all things certain, including predetermining which individuals will be saved? The more I have examined Calvinism over the past twenty years or so, the more I have seen how poorly it fits the biblical narrative. It appears to me that most Calvinists: 1) don't actually know what John Calvin believed and taught, and 2) have never really examined their own theology in relation to Scripture.

Like the landlord who never left the rural Texas county, and the theologian who made sure that his education always supported what he was raised to believe, they have never really considered the alternatives that are out there. I was in that system. When I examined it, I found it did not stand up to the scrutiny.

Endnotes

[1] John White, *The Fight* (Downers Grove, IL: Intervarsity Press, 1976), 45.

[2] Approx. 44 years – Amon reigned for 2 years (2 Ki 21:19), Josiah 31 years (2 Ki 22:1), Jehoahaz 3 months (2 Ki 23:31), Jehoiakim 11 years (2 Ki 23:36),

[3] Calvin, *Institutes*, Book I, Ch. 17, para. 14, p. 144.

[4] Thuesen, *Predestination*, 109.

[5] Calvin, *Institutes*, Book I, Ch. 15, para. 8, p. 125.

[6] Ganoczy, "Calvin's Life," 6.

[7] Ganoczy, "Calvin's Life," 18.

[8] Ganoczy, "Calvin's Life," 17-18.

[9] Ganoczy, "Calvin's Life," 17.

[10] Bosch, *Transforming Mission,* 258.

[11] Bosch, *Transforming Mission,* 285-286.

[12] Bosch, *Transforming Mission,* 258.

[13] Calvin, *Institutes*, Book II, Ch. 17, para. 2, p. 327.

Chapter 9
Conclusion

The function of freedom is to free someone else.

– Toni Morrison[1]

A different ending . . .

It took the father over half an hour to be back to the foredeck with two of his kids. He was obviously distraught. The captain and one crew member were waiting, clearly anxious to get off the ship. Several of the bright orange, fully enclosed lifeboats were bobbing in the waves to the side of the ship. The crew member helped the father and children put on lifejackets, and was about to help them into the one remaining lifeboat, when the captain asked the father, "Where are your other kids?"

"I brought the ones who're going," the father replied.

"The ones who're going? What does that mean?"

"Two are with me. The two older ones refused to come."

The captain looked at the father as if he had heard something wrong. "Two of them refused to come? Did you explain that this ship is doomed? That once this last lifeboat launches, there is no way to survive? That there won't be another chance?"

In a voice filled with deep pain, the father replied, "I explained all that to them. I pleaded with them. They understood me, but they didn't believe me. I did everything but force them to come. They chose to stay."

What we've seen is that Calvinism, like all theologies, is an organized way of trying to understand the truth of God as given in Scripture. But, as we saw, truth is of divine origin, theology is of human origin – a human attempt, however well-intentioned or not, to organize what Scripture says in order to make it more understandable and teachable. We saw that Calvin developed his theology, as all theologians do, based on the cultural understanding of his day – it cannot be otherwise. That means Calvin's theology was derived from the context in which it arose, as all theologies are. That means it was a contextual theology, simply one of several contextual theologies of the day. It continues to be that today – a contextual theology, and one among many.

We saw that the academic culture of Calvin's day had its roots in Aristotle's Greek worldview, which included fatalism. And we saw that the culture of Calvin's day did not see the world through communal, or collectivistic lenses, but through individualistic lenses, which would have been very foreign to the writers of the Bible and their original audiences.

We saw that our culture provides us with a framework through which we view the world, and that the assumptions contained in that interpretive framework determine the conclusions we come to as we view the available data.

In putting these pieces together, we saw that Calvin applied assumptions of divine determinism and individualism to material written many centuries earlier by writers with very different assumptions, and as a result, Calvin came to conclusions that were never intended by the original writers.

We saw that truth does not stand alone, but is simply an accurate description of reality – that the reality is what is important. And we saw that knowing is not so certain, and proof is elusive, so we use evidence to gain enough certainty to justify a commitment. We saw that success is related to the degree to which our understanding of reality ("little r") accurately matches the reality that is out there ("Big R"). We saw that when we visualize the world differently than it actually is, we are interacting with an imaginary world – we think there is a bridge ahead, when in fact there is not.

We saw that to identify truth in the glut of contradictory information available today, we have to use tests to sift through the mix. We saw that truth *is consistent with observable reality, is consistent with other truth, is internally coherent,* and *is eventually provable.*

When we applied the tests for truth to Calvinism, we found it desperately lacking. It is not *consistent with observable reality,* in that it teaches that humans have no free will, and that all events in life are foreordained by God. We saw how teaching and learning and discipline appear to create human growth in both understanding and character, and that human decisions appear to affect the future. Observable reality leads us to believe that we are morally free agents whose choices are real, and originate in us, and that we could make them other than we do. Calvinism leads us to believe that we are living in a delusion in which God is making all the decisions, and we are merely pawns in his game.

We saw that Calvinism is not *consistent with other truth,* if we accept the Bible as truth. Over and over, we saw instances in Scripture that imply human free will, the reality of a spiritual battle with the possibility of gains and setbacks, and God allowing what happens with grief and anger, because it violates his will. We saw that the Bible reveals God as infinitely good, but Calvinism reveals him as a deceiver, one who seems to give people freedom of choice, but in the background, is determining all that happens.

We saw that Calvinism is not *internally coherent*, as, for example, in its view of the spiritual battle, and in its view that God uses his absolute sovereignty to render certain all that happens. It affirms that there is a spiritual battle going on, but insists that God is controlling all the action within that battle; and it insists that God is absolutely sovereign, yet he is not the author of evil, and humans are responsible for their actions.

The jury may be out about Calvinism being *eventually provable*. We may find as we enter eternity that God has in fact been pulling all the strings, but if we bring this back to Ravi Zacharias's *experiential relevance* – the question of whether we can prove it today in a practical way, we saw that we cannot. By contrast, if we try to prove the opposite viewpoint, that we can alter destiny by our decisions and actions, that appears to be entirely possible.

As we considered the history of Calvin's beliefs, we saw that the idea of individual predestination for salvation was first expressed by Origen in the third century C.E., then by Augustine in the fifth century, and then was picked up about every hundred years or so afterward and promoted by some writer. The mere fact that it took over two hundred years for the very idea to appear, should alert us to the fact that it did not originate in the Bible itself. We also found that every time the view was expressed to the degree that Calvin did, it was denounced as heresy. It is very clear that double predestination, as Calvin believed and taught it, and as the strict Calvinists today teach it, has always been a distinctly minority belief among Christians, and, until it gained a foothold after the Protestant Reformation, was consistently considered heretical.

We saw that Bible translation, no less than any other translation, necessarily reflects the worldview of the translator – short of divine intervention, it cannot do otherwise. We saw that "Bible translation is an ideological act," and we saw the impact that Martin Luther's German translation has had on all successive Bibles – if nothing else, in the mere fact that the weight of prior translation is always considered with new translations. We saw that Luther, like Calvin, was a double predestinarian, and that he admitted that whenever it was legitimately possible, he selected words in his translation that fit with his theology.

We saw that, since there is no absolute correspondence between languages, there can be no fully exact translations. We saw that sometimes a broad word in the original language is severely narrowed in the translation by the choice of word used, and we saw that this is what has happened in our New Testaments regarding the terms "chosen" and "elect." We saw that there are perfectly legitimate alternatives to those narrow words, that better fit with the overall message of Scripture. We saw that if the influence of *opponents* of double predestination had been present in the early vernacular translations, rather than as it happened, our Bibles would logically read something like "gathered ones" or "named ones" rather than "chosen ones," and "choice ones" rather than "the elect."

We also saw how the transliteration of words such as "baptism" and "Christ" have affected and even obscured our understanding of the original message of Scripture.

When we looked at how Calvin's sixteenth century worldview affected his reading of Paul's writings, we saw the distortions created by his individualism and fatalism, and by the use of the title "Christ" rather than the word "messiah." As a result, we saw how Calvin completely missed Paul's message in Ephesians 1 and Romans 8 and 9, leading to the promotion of a doctrine completely foreign to the intent of the original writer, and completely inconsistent with the rest of Scripture.

As we considered the plan of God, we saw how there is always an alternative biblical perspective that retains all that Calvinism attempts to protect – primarily the sovereignty of God and the glory of God – without also attributing evil to God and impugning his character and reputation. We saw that the nature of God is both love and holiness, and that his image is resident in humans – including the ability to make decisions that affect the future. We saw that just as King James V of Scotland could give up the characteristics of a king without giving up his royalty, God can give up the absolute exercise of his sovereignty, without losing any of his character and nature as the living God. We saw that God can be fully in control of the direction and the ultimate destiny of history, without controlling every event in the process. We saw that the decrees of God set the parameters within which the world operates, but do not control everything that happens within those parameters. We saw that God has always been a missional God, with the intention that all nations would follow him. We saw that prayer is part of the plan, that we are commanded to pray, and that our prayers appear to move the hand of God, to alter the balance of power in the spiritual battle, and thereby change the future. We saw that God is both transcendent – awesome and beyond our comprehension – and immanent, the personal God who wants to be our friend.

More than anything else, we saw that Calvinism is not some ultimate form of theological truth that is superior to all other theological expressions. In fact, it is now and has always been a minority view, considered by the large majority of the Christian church to be aberrant at best, and heretical at worst.

I should make it clear that my argument is not with Calvinists themselves. Some of my best friends are Calvinists, and some of them have faithfully supported our missions efforts from the beginning. If lifestyles of consistent morality and personal responsibility are the standard, many evangelical Calvinists are among the best Christians in the world. They really do hold God in high regard, and want to honor him in all they do. I believe that. But at the same time, as this book has demonstrated, I believe that their foundational doctrines are based on false information, both from reading Scripture through lenses very different from those of the original audience, and from biased Bible translation that has narrowed and skewed what we see there. As a result, their doctrine presents an inadequate view of God, attributing to God characteristics that are more consistent with the nature of evil than the nature of good. I have witnessed seekers turned off by the God that Calvinism offers them, and I have seen believers become arrogant and offensive from the conviction that they are among the chosen ones. At a superficial level, Calvinism seems to provide answers to all the basic theological questions. To quote Howard Snyder, "The more basic question, however, is not whether a theory or model provides answers but whether it discloses truth. The two are not necessarily the same."[2]

If there is validity to the case I have presented, Calvinism does not disclose truth. It obscures it.

One of the critical things we saw was that contradictory information in our minds produces cognitive dissonance, such that we experience an internal compulsion to resolve the contradiction. We can assimilate the new information into our belief system, effectively amending the maps in our minds, or we can reject the new information, leaving our mental maps intact. Or, we can decide the information is not important, so we can just disregard it without attempting to resolve the issue.

If you, reading this book, find that what I have presented contradicts what you have believed in the past, remember that I was in that same position 20 years ago. When I first realized that the worldview of the first century Romans and Jews was very different from mine and from the one through which I had been taught to read Scripture, cognitive dissonance occurred. I found myself on a journey, but I had a stronger commitment to truth than to what I already believed. In the short term, it's easier and safer to protect the maps in our minds, but it is not always wise. Wisdom dictates that we examine the contradictory information for validity, and, if the bulk of the evidence supports a change, that we use that new information to revise our maps.

Regarding this process, I offer one final point that has helped me understand my journey.

In his book, *The Different Drum*, psychiatrist M. Scott Peck discusses what he has observed to be stages of spirituality. He represents them something like this:

Stage 1 Chaos / Antisocialism
> Characterized by lawlessness, self interest, absence of spirituality
> *"There is nothing bigger than me in the universe."*

Stage 2 Formalism / Institutionalism
> Characterized by rituals, rules, adherence to the forms of religion – to the letter of the law
> *"There is something bigger than me, and this is how it works."*

Stage 3 Skepticism / Individuation
> Characterized by principled behavior, combined with doubt or disinterest in religion, or combined with reexamination of previous beliefs
> *"There are flaws in the religious systems. What is really true, and what is really important?"*

Stage 4 Mysticism / Communalism
> Characterized by adherence to the spirit of the law, concern for people and their spiritual growth
> *"God has revealed himself to me, and the new relationship has changed what I value."*[3]

Most religious people are in Stage 2, and stay there for life. This is where that theologian lives, the one I mentioned who has always stayed within the confines of the system he grew up in. It is also where virtually every Muslim and every Hindu in the world lives. And virtually every Christian. The problem is, if we have never really examined our beliefs, we are no better off than anyone loyal to any other system that they grew up in. To be fair, though, I should point out that anyone who has experienced a genuine conversion experience, has already gone through Stage 3 to at least some degree – conversion, by definition, is based on a reexamination of past beliefs.

It should also be noted that many people never experience Stage 1. If they are raised in a devout home, they will start in Stage 2, as I did. As I look back, I can see that about the time I was seventeen, I entered Stage 3 – where everything was up for reexamination. It peaked while I was in seminary at almost age 50. I was unaware of Peck's observations, but I was following the path he outlines. He says people enter Stage 3 for various reasons, but usually as a result of disillusionment with what they have already been taught. In my case, as a teenager, I realized that the typical western Christian simply did not hold to the same values that Jesus and Paul did. In seminary, I came across a statement that reflected what I had been observing for decades:

> "Perhaps the most insidious form of syncretism in the world today is the attempt to mix a privatized gospel of personal forgiveness with a worldly (even demonic) attitude to wealth and power."[4]

The fact that that statement originated at a meeting of theologians, anthropologists, linguists, missionaries, and pastors from around the world, is proof that I am not the only one who has made that observation. Syncretism, in case the term is unfamiliar, is the mixture of two religious systems, so that any truth found there may be compromised.

Peck observes that from Stage 3, those who start to reexamine their spiritual beliefs may go to any of the other stages. If the disillusionment is not resolved, they may end up in Stage 1. If they realize that the revamping of the maps in their minds is simply too scary or too complex to pursue, they may return to Stage 2. They will also return to Stage 2 if they value their sense of belonging more than they value truth. However, if the reexamination leads them into a deeper experience with God, they will move to Stage 4. I like to think that is what I experienced. But, the journey was not easy, nor did it make me popular with some of my Christian friends. Time has proven, however, that the process was worth the effort.

If the evidence I have presented has caused cognitive dissonance in your mind, I sincerely hope you will not disregard it as unimportant. Instead, I hope you will follow the path I took, the one Luke observed among the Bereans when Paul presented the gospel to them – I hope you will search the Scriptures, to see if what I have suggested is true. The Bereans were "more noble" than the Thessalonians, who simply held onto their existing beliefs to the point of being willing to destroy the one challenging those beliefs (Acts 17). I hope you will pray for the Holy Spirit to guide you to all truth. If you do, you will go through Stage 3 to Stage 4, and you will be glad you did.

Scott Peck points out that Stage 2 Christians and Stage 4 Christians look much the same in what they do. But they do what they do for very different reasons. The stakes are high. It's eternity we are talking about, not just our own, but of others we impact. It is critical that we have the truth.

In Chapter 2, I pointed out that what religions teach as true can only be ultimately proven at death. But, I said, make no mistake, it will be proven at death. The universal human challenge is to confirm our beliefs before that event occurs. We do that by putting the source of our information through the tests of truth while we are still alive. If it passes those tests in life, that is, if what it says can be experienced in this life, then we have good reason to believe that what it says about the afterlife will also be true. This idea is one of the critical things that sets Christianity apart from other major world religions. All of them can be challenged based on observable reality, internal consistency, and consistency with other truth. And now, as we have seen, so can Calvinism. That is why it is imperative for Christians to move out of Peck's Stage 2, go through Stage 3, and emerge in Stage 4. Rather than depending on those around us to determine what we believe, we are compelled to embark on our own personal journey of faith. Through our own study and personal experience, we prove to ourselves what we cannot prove to others – that the God of the Bible is real, and the path to knowing him is through his Son, Jesus Christ. On that journey, we find that life works the way the Bible says it does, so we expect eternity to also work the way the Bible says it does. And, as we have seen, life does not appear to work the way Calvin says it does.

If there is a God, it matters what we believe. It affects what we do along the path of life. Where *we* go on that journey, we take others with us. It's eternity we're talking about, not just our own, but of others we impact. If there is no God, nothing matters. However, if there is a God, then everything matters. It's all or nothing.

If anything matters, everything matters.

Endnotes

[1] Quoted in Lamott, *Bird by Bird*, 193.

[2] Snyder, *Models of the Kingdom*, 126.

[3] M. Scott Peck, *The Different Drum: Community Making and Peace* (New York: Simon and Schuster, 1987), 187-200.

[4] *The Willowbank Report* (Charlotte, NC.: Lausanne Committee for World Evangelization, 1978), 26.

Epilogue

"The evidence is in, and you are the verdict."
— Anne Lamott[1]

I have been asked what I hope to achieve by writing this book.

The question reminds me of a story I heard as a child, during the height of the Cold War. It seems that a pastor had escaped from the Soviet Union, and over a period of years, had built a successful ministry in western Europe. One day, however, he announced that he was going home. His friends and colleagues were surprised, and even dismayed, because at that time, he was certain to be imprisoned or exiled to Siberia. Another pastor pointedly challenged the wisdom of his decision. "If you go back," he said, "you will become ineffective. If you stay here, you can continue to have a successful ministry." His friend replied, "I'm convinced God wants me to go back. My responsibility is not to have a successful ministry, but to obey. What happens after I obey is God's responsibility."

I don't see myself as an expert at understanding the will of God, although there have been a few times when his leading has been clear. In the case of this book, however, I have been convinced for several years that the Lord has been challenging me to publish what I have come to understand, making it available to a broader audience. Isn't that the most basic principle of helping others – to pass along understanding? Isn't that the principle of evangelism? Isn't that what every teacher does during every class period? Isn't that what every pastor does every time he steps into the pulpit? Isn't that the application of the parable of the sower – to not hide our candle under a bowl?

So . . . I answer the question simply, that what I hope to achieve is to obey God, as nearly as I understand what he wants. But in reality, the answer is much more complex than that.

For one thing, I recognize the unlikelihood of my having much impact on the thinking of Christians worldwide. Who am I? A complete nobody.... One who has limited credibility, in human terms, beyond the circle of people who know me well. With the glut of information available today, this book will become another drop in the ocean. Especially considering my lack of human contacts and financial resources to make sure it doesn't.

As I have pondered the idea of influence, however, I have come to realize that if we worry about our influence, we risk becoming either ambitious or disillusioned, as we take on the responsibility for the world. I have come to believe, and have taught, that we are responsible for our influence, but we are not responsible for the *response* to our influence. In the same way that I become responsible for every new truth to which I am exposed – "anyone who knows the good he ought to do and doesn't do it, sins" (James 4:17); "to whom much is given, much will be required" (Luke 12:48) – the one I influence has that same responsibility. This principle, in fact, is the whole summary of what it means to be a "free moral agent." God will hold me accountable, one day, for how I responded to the truth I encountered along the pathway of life. One of the ways I can respond, is to pass that truth along to others. He will hold others accountable, the same way he will me.

Another thing I am aware of, though, is that God honors faith. It seems to me that many Christians have a very simplistic view of faith – that it is "believing what we cannot see." The biblical definition is much deeper than that. Biblical faith is characterized by action. It does not say, "I believe God can take care of me if I go back into the Soviet Union." Biblical faith *goes back*.

One of my favorite quotes is from Douglas Rumford's book, *Soulshaping*. He says, "God has designed us such that circumstances alter and resources develop to support commitments we make."[2] Donna and I recently spent two years studying and doing intense research, to make this book possible. We have travelled tens of thousands of miles, and spent thousands of dollars that we did not have when we started this journey. Once we made the commitment, the circumstances changed and resources developed to support that commitment. We have seen this before, and we expect to see it again.

"GOD HAS DESIGNED US SUCH THAT CIRCUMSTANCES ALTER AND RESOURCES DEVELOP TO SUPPORT COMMITMENTS WE MAKE."

When we had been in Latvia about two years, we were asked to arrange a team to come to Latvia and teach on creation as an alternative to evolution. The event would be a conference of three to four hundred school teachers from all over Latvia, a regular ministry of a friend of ours. Donna contacted a former physics professor of hers, a brilliant lady who, since teaching Donna in university, had taken a position with one of the leading organizations in the US that researches and teaches on creationism. The professor arranged with several of her colleagues to come, so we committed to providing the team for the conference, which was about a year away. We also started translating a book that examines the claims of evolution, and, since it contained a lot of scientific explanations, we knew that the translation would be challenging. We were introduced to a young man working on his PhD in science, and who had good English, so he agreed to review the translation to make sure the scientific terms used were accurate. As he worked, he used several of his professors as technical sources, so we ended up with a remarkable translation. But the project was expensive, and our resources were limited.

As the project was nearing its end, and the conference was getting near, we started praying specifically for God's intervention. Within the next few weeks, we were going to have to pay the translator, the editors, the graphic designer, and the printer. All together, it would to be around eight thousand dollars. At the time, we were with a large mission organization that paid "salaries" to the missionaries, but the salaries came from money donated specifically for the missionary. In the background, missionaries were responsible for having their own supporters. So if donations exceeded the salary, the extra money was held in reserve by the organization, and if the giving was less than the salary, the salary was paid, and the missionary's account went into deficit. If the deficit continued, the missionary was required to go home and "raise support." Our donations usually exceeded our salary, but not by much.

With the bills for the book coming due, we called the mission headquarters, and asked how much money was in our account. They told us, $6300. That was a surprise, because it had been much less than that, the last we knew. We asked them to send us $4000 immediately and to plan to send us $4000 the next month. After some bureaucratic processing, they sent the first $4000. We paid what bills we could, and prayed. The next month, we received the second $4000. Without our doing anything at all to raise funds, enough extra money had been given to pay our salary and provide the remainder needed for the book.

All the bills were paid on time, the book was scheduled to be published just days before the conference, and our faith became stronger.

But then, when it looked as if everything was on track, several things happened in fairly rapid succession. First, we got a call from the man renting our house in Texas, that he had had a serious fire in the kitchen, so the house was essentially uninhabitable. He was living in an RV until we could resolve the situation. The insurance company assessed the damage, and issued us a check to get the repairs done. Since we had built the house ourselves, we decided to fly home and make the repairs ourselves, which we did. We were there for about six weeks, getting the house back in order, and the schedule allowed us to get back to Latvia just a few days before the conference.

While we were home, since we were so close, we arranged to have dinner with the professor who was leading the team that was planning to come to Latvia for the conference, now just five weeks away. So we ate and visited and discussed who would do what, and when. She told us the team had not really been coordinating their plans, but she would take immediate steps to pull things together. Then three weeks later, with the conference now two weeks away, she called us and told us that the team had completely dissolved – for one reason or another, every other person who had initially committed, had had circumstances develop that were going to prevent their coming. As we talked, we realized that with a little changing of the initial plan, she could come alone and do all of the keynote sessions, rather than dividing them up among a team. With a PhD in physics, she was well qualified to do that. And so it was decided. Our being "home" at that precise time was nothing short of providential, since our visit with the professor prompted her to take immediate action regarding the conference, and it gave all of us time to adjust to the changing situation.

With our house repaired and looking better than it had in years, we returned to Latvia just in time to receive the newly printed books and do the final coordinating for the conference. But a couple of other details are also interesting. Because of who reviewed the translation of the book, we were able to get the book endorsed by the science professor who was the head of the Latvian Academy of Science at the time, and a Christian. We also knew that the Minister of Family Affairs, a government cabinet level position, was also a Christian, so we approached him for an endorsement. He not only endorsed the book, but paid for an extra thousand copies to be printed, which he placed in school libraries across the nation. The book was the first ever to be published in Latvian examining the weaknesses of evolutionary theory from a Christian perspective. And Donna's former professor came and taught about creation from the perspective of a Christian scientist, and beyond that, she deeply ministered to the teachers at the conference, most of whom were women. At the time, the professor was a well-educated Christian educator whose husband was a blue-collar worker, an alcoholic, and not a Christian. The professor's story was parallel to so many of the teachers in the audience, that there was a tangible bonding between them. The outcome of the conference was very likely much more powerful than if the entire team had come – and it had all been accomplished through adversity and through the unlikely. Not long after that, the professor's husband became a believer, and put his alcohol aside.

My point is this: Throughout the process, circumstances changed, and resources developed, to support the commitments we made. God honors faith. We have seen it over and over. In the same way that we started planning for that conference, and for the publication of that book to go with it, we started this writing project. Years ago, as we acted on the commitment regarding that conference, God showed up. As we have pursued the research and writing of this book, God has shown up. Over and over. We have every reason to expect the pattern to continue.

If God is truly leading in this writing, then I don't have to worry about what it accomplishes. I have to be faithful, I have to do everything I can to enable it to succeed, and I have to rest in the certainty that God, through his providence, can accomplish what I cannot in my human strength. I believe the spiritual battle is real, so if God is behind this, the enemy will attempt to defeat it, as he did with the fire in our house and the breakdown of the team of scientists who originally agreed to come for the conference in Latvia. In fact, we have already seen evidence of that opposition. In spite of that, God can redeem the process, and bring good out of it – maybe even more good than if the opposition had never occurred. That's the way the system works.

I have one final concern, however. One thing I hope I achieved, is to demonstrate that Calvinism was simply a contextual theology of its day, and even though it continues to resonate with certain people today, it will never be anything other than that – a contextual theology left over from sixteenth century western Europe. However, it is not the only contextual theology in the world today. In recent years, feminist theology has made its entry on the scene, and even "gay" theology has appeared.[3] In both of those contextual theologies, as with others, one way the theology has developed has been through questioning the traditional understanding of Scripture, to the point that the authority of Scripture is deeply undermined. I sincerely hope that what I have attempted is not seen as being similar in either intent or method.

Nothing could be further from my desire or intentions, than to undermine the credibility or authority of Scripture. In fact, what I hope to achieve, is to strengthen both of those things. It is when Scripture appears to lack internal consistency, and when it appears to teach what is contrary to the way we experience life, that its credibility is compromised, and if its credibility is compromised, it also loses its authority. I am deeply committed to both the belief that Scripture is true – that it is the Word of the living God – and that it is authoritative in all matters of faith and practice. However, that belief applies to Scripture as it was given in its original form, and I recognize that we don't have it in its original form, and I recognize that our cultural assumptions can keep us from understanding what the original message was to the original audience. My desire is to help get Scripture back as close as possible to that original form, and help get our understanding broadened enough that we can understand the original message, and in so doing, to increase not only the credibility of Scripture, but also its authority.

I would be naïve if I thought what I have written will be accepted without criticism. The observation that Thomas Kuhn made decades ago – that the vast majority of intellectual effort is spent defending what we already believe – protecting the maps in our minds rather than seeking genuine truth – is as true today as it was when he observed it among scientists years ago. And, if anything, it is stronger among theologians than scientists, since scientific matters can eventually be demonstrated or refuted, but matters of religious belief are much less definite. I welcome sincere, objective scrutiny of my efforts. I also hope, and pray, that whatever truth is contained in my research, will, over time, become recognized as such.

To that end, to the recognition of truth, to the one who is Truth – to the sovereign God – to God be the glory.

Endnotes

[1] Lamott, *Bird by Bird*, 46, quoting an anonymous acquaintance: "A man I know once said to me,…"

[2] Douglas J. Rumford, *Soulshaping: Taking Care of Your Spiritual Life* (Wheaton, IL: Tyndale House, 1996), 92.

[3] Cf. Joe Dallas, *The Gay Gospel? How Pro-Gay Advocates Misread the Bible* (Eugene, OR: Harvest House, 2007).

Appendix A
The words, their sources, and their meanings

In attempting to determine the original meanings of the words from which the concept of election / predestination has arisen, the following words were researched. For ease of tracing the original word, each one is connected to the numbering system established by James Strong in *Strong's Exhaustive Concordance of the Bible*. If a reference cannot be searched using Strong's numbers, then page numbers are shown, and in some cases, volume and page numbers.

English words	Strong's numbers designating the Greek words from which the English words are translated
Chose, chosen	138, 140, 1586, 1588, 1589, 1951, 2820, 4400, 4401, 4758, 5500
Choose, choosing	138
Chosen beforehand	4899
Choice	1586
Elect	1588
Election	1589

A wide variety of Greek-English references were consulted. Several were duplications, and several were not helpful in any way, so they are not included in the ones cited below.

To be fair, it should be pointed out that even Bible dictionaries and lexicons reflect the worldviews and theological perspectives of those who prepare them. For example, it is evident that both Brown and Liddell favor a corporate view of election, as I do. I did not select them for that reason, I simply realized that in the research process. I argue, in Chapters 4 through 6, that such a view is consistent with the rest of Scripture and with the communal/collectivistic worldview of first century Jews and Romans. Still, I recognize that while I am completely convinced of that, the fact that I believe it does not make it true. However, the fact that major Bible dictionaries and lexicons also reflect that view, adds to the bulk of the evidence pointing in that direction.

It should also be noted that generally, what the references are doing is not saying how the words *should be* translated, they are primarily saying how they *have been* translated in the past.

The references are cited in the sequence they are, because Wigram & Winter was used as the concordance to identify the original Greek word, the number of times the word is used in the New Testament, and where the word is used. Then Strong's was used to get basic definitions, then the other sources were researched. After Wigram & Winter and Strong, the references are cited in alphabetical order. It should be noted that *The New Testament Greek-English Dictionary* assigns its own numbers to the words, so to distinguish between them and Strong's, they are preceded by the # sign.

Alphabetical list of the references cited:

Walter Bauer, William F. Arndt, F. Wilbur Gingrich, and Frederick W. Danker, *A Greek-English Lexicon of the New Testament and Other Early Christian Literature,* 2nd ed. (London and Chicago: Univ. of Chicago Press, 1979). [Bauer's Greek-German Lexicon

Griechisch-Deutsches Wörterbuch zu den Schriften des Neuen Testaments und der übrigen *urchristlichen Literatur*, 4th ed., was translated and adapted by Arndt & Gingrich, then revised & augmented in this 2nd ed. by Gingrich and Danker from Bauer's 1958 5th ed.]

Colin Brown, ed., *The New International Dictionary of New Testament Theology*, 4 vols. (Grand Rapids, MI: Zondervan, 1975).

Gerhard Kittel, G.W. Bromily, and Gerhard Freidrich, *Theological Dictionary of the New Testament* (Grand Rapids, MI: Wm. B. Eerdmans, 1976).

James Strong, *The Strongest Strong's Exhaustive Concordance of the Bible*, rev. & corr. John R. Kohlenberger III and James A. Swanson (Grand Rapids, MI: Zondervan, 2001).

Joseph H. Thayer, *Thayer's Greek-English Lexicon of the New Testament* (Peabody, MA: Hendrickson, 1996).

The New Testament Greek-English Dictionary (Springfield, MO: The Complete Biblical Library, 1990).

George V. Wigram and Ralph D. Winter, *The Word Study Concordance* (Wheaton, IL: Tyndale House, 1978).

Robert Young, *Analytical Concordance to the Bible* (Grand Rapids, MI: Wm. B. Eerdmans, 1975).

Abbreviations used:

1:180 = Volume 1, page 180.

act. = the active voice in Greek

Cl. Gr. = Classical Greek

Heb. = Hebrew

LXX = the Septuagint Old Testament

mid. = the middle voice in Greek

NT = the New Testament

OT = Old Testament

p. 24 = page 24

pass. = the passive voice in Greek

pl. = plural

sing. = singular

The words, their sources, and their meanings:

138

Wigram & Winter: αἱρέομαι, **haireomai,** 4 times in 3 verses, **chosen, chose, choose, choosing**

Strong's: αἱρέομαι, aihreomai, *hahee-reh'-om-ahee,* G138, probably akin to G142 [to take]; to *take for oneself,* that is, to *prefer.* Some of the forms are borrowed from a cognate (ἕλλομαι hellomai, hel-lom-ahee), which is otherwise obsolete: - to choose.

Bauer: p. 24, to choose someone for something, to prefer.

Brown: 1:533-535, Cl. Gr. mid. voice: to take for oneself, seize for oneself, gain for oneself, choose for oneself, decide in favor of something; LXX used 11 times, 4 to choose, choose out, prefer, other 7, to delight in; NT always mid. voice, Phil 1:22 & Heb 11:25, weakened meaning, to prefer; 2 Thes 2:13 to elect someone to something, that is, the church to salvation.

Kittel: 1:180 to choose or elect; NT in Phil 1:22 and Heb 11:25, indicates selective preference between two possibilities; in 2 Thes 2:13, indicates the election of the community of God.

NT Gr-Eng Dict: 1:108, #140, verb, to choose, prefer, take; Cl. Gr. very broad meaning, mid. voice primary meaning, to take for oneself, secondary, to choose; LXX OT used to translate 6 Hebrew words: to declare, to choose, to delight in, to love, to offer or give, to lay aside; NT simple human choice (Phil 1:22 & Heb 11:25), chosen to salvation (brethren, plural) through sanctification and belief in the truth (2 Thes 2:13).

Thayer's: p. 16, to take, to take for oneself, to choose, prefer.

Young's: p. 164, to take, lift up for oneself

KJV Phil 1:22 But if I live in the flesh, this *is* the fruit of my labour: yet what I shall **choose** I wot not.

NIV Phil 1:22 If I am to go on living in the body, this will mean fruitful labor for me. Yet what shall I **choose**? I do not know!

No alternative rendering needed.

KJV 2 Thes 2:13 But we are bound to give thanks alway to God for you, brethren beloved of the Lord, because God hath from the beginning **chosen** you to salvation through sanctification of the Spirit and belief of the truth:

NIV 2 Thes 2:13 But we ought always to thank God for you, brothers loved by the Lord, because from the beginning God **chose** you to be saved through the sanctifying work of the Spirit and through belief in the truth.

Alternative rendering 2 Thes 2:13 But we ought always to thank God for you, brothers loved by the Lord, because from the beginning God **took you for himself** to be saved through the sanctifying work of the Spirit and through belief in the truth.

KJV Heb 11:25 **Choosing** rather to suffer affliction with the people of God, than to enjoy the pleasures of sin for a season;

NIV Heb 11:25 He **chose** to be mistreated along with the people of God rather than to enjoy the pleasures of sin for a short time.

No alternative rendering needed, but a perfectly legitimate one would be Heb 11:25 He **preferred** to be mistreated along with the people of God rather than to enjoy the pleasures of sin for a short time.

140

Wigram & Winter: αἱρετίζω, **hairetizo,** 1 time, **chosen**

Strong's: αἱρετίζω, aihretizoō, *hahee-ret-id'-zo,* from a derivative of G138 [choose, prefer]; to *make a choice:* - choose.

Bauer: p. 24, choose, adopt, choose for oneself

Brown: 1:533-535, Cl. Gr. to make someone eligible, to choose him; LXX to choose or to adopt; NT choose, quoting from Isa 42:1, but the quote is not from the LXX

Kittel: 1:184, to choose, to adopt

NT Gr-Eng Dict: 1:106-107, #139, verb, choose, select, Cl. Gr. one member of a rather large group of words whose basic meaning involves choice or selection; LXX used to translate 7 words: desire, choose, honor, spare, delight in, accept, gone; NT paraphrase of Isa 42:1, one who is taken hold of, chosen, to accomplish the purposes of God.

Thayer's: p. 16, choose; common word in LXX, and in OT Apocryphal & ecclesiastical writings.

Young's: p. 164, to take, choose.

KJV Matt 12:18   Behold my servant, whom I have **chosen**; my beloved, in whom my soul is well pleased: I will put my spirit upon him, and he shall shew judgment to the Gentiles.

NIV Matt 12:18 "Here is my servant whom I have **chosen**, the one I love, in whom I delight; I will put my Spirit on him, and he will proclaim justice to the nations.

No alternative rendering needed.

1586

Wigram & Winter: ἐκλέγομαι, **eklogomai,** 21 times, **chosen, choice, chose**

Strong's: ἐκλέγομαι, eklegomai, *ek-leg'-om-ahee,* mid. voice from G1537 [of, out of, from] and G3004 (in its primary sense [to gather]); to *select:* - make choice, choose (out), chosen.

Bauer: p. 242, choose, select (for oneself) (for a purpose) (from among a number)

Brown: 1:536-542 Cl. Gr. "The words in this group are used in various contexts, but wherever they are found, it is evident that certain things common to them all are implied. First, there are several objects from which to choose; secondly, the person making the choice is not tied down by any circumstances which force his hand, but is free to make his own decision. Thirdly, the person making the choice – at least at the moment of choosing – has the person or thing to be chosen at his disposal. Moreover, the act of choosing (and thus the words in this group) includes a judgment by the chooser as to which object he considers to be the most suitable for the fulfillment of his purpose" (p. 536); LXX no noun usage, verb is usually used to translate choose, select, prefer, but with implied of being suitable, desirable, desirable in comparison with another, election by the people, a considered choice between several possibilities; to set apart, select, purge;

NT (i) appointment by the church to a particular office (Acts 6:5, 15:22, 25, possibly 1:24) (ii) the self-esteem from a special seat at the table (Luke 14:7) (iii) Mary devoting herself to the words of Jesus (Luke 10:42) (iv) God's election (John speaks of Christ electing 6:70, 13:8, 15:16, 19). Luke speaks of Jesus selecting the Twelve (Luke 6:13).

Kittel: 4:69-73, root word 3004, λέγ- (leg-) "to gather," λέγω (lego) very common in the sense "to gather," meaning expanded over time, sometimes to count, to enumerate, to draw up, to enter on a list, to enlist, to narrate, to say; this word (1586) 4:144-176, Cl. Gr. to choose something for oneself, to make one's choice; LXX mainly to choose, occasionally to gather, to sift, to separate, to select, to elect, that which is choice or excellent (p. 145); NT to decide between two.

NT Gr-Eng Dict: 2:341-342, #1573, verb, to choose, select, elect; Cl. Gr. to choose or pick (for oneself) or because of superiority, beauty, or value; LXX used to translate 7 words: three that mean choose, but also chosen, learn or receive, gather, search; NT normal decision making, to choose, to select.

Thayer's: p. 196-197, LXX to pick out, choose; NT to pick, choose out for one's self (from a number of persons, for an office, as special).

Young's: p. 164, to lay out for oneself.

KJV Mark 13:20 And except that the Lord had shortened those days, no flesh should be saved: but for the elect's sake, whom he hath **chosen**, he hath shortened the days.

NIV Mark 13:20 If the Lord had not cut short those days, no one would survive. But for the sake of the elect, whom he has **chosen**, he has shortened them.

Alternative rendering Mark 13:20 If the Lord had not cut short those days, no one would survive. But for the sake of the elect, whom he has **gathered**, he has shortened them.

Alternative rendering Mark 13:20 If the Lord had not cut short those days, no one would survive. But for the sake of the elect, whom he has **searched out**, he has shortened them.

KJV Luke 6:13 And when it was day, he called *unto him* his disciples: and of them he **chose** twelve, whom also he named apostles;

NIV Luke 6:13 When morning came, he called his disciples to him and **chose** twelve of them, whom he also designated apostles:

No alternative rendering needed.

KJV Luke 9:35 And there came a voice out of the cloud, saying, This is my beloved Son: hear him.

NIV Luke 9:35 A voice came from the cloud, saying, "This is my Son, whom I have **chosen**; listen to him."

NASB Luke 9:35 Then a voice came out of the cloud, saying, "This is My Son, *My* **Chosen One**; listen to Him!"

No alternative rendering needed.

KJV Luke 10:42 But one thing is needful: and Mary hath **chosen** that good part, which shall not be taken away from her.

NIV Luke 10:42 but only one thing is needed. Mary has **chosen** what is better, and it will not be taken away from her."

No alternative rendering needed.

KJV Luke 14:7 And he put forth a parable to those

which were bidden, when he marked how they **chose** out the chief rooms; saying unto them,

NIV Luke 14:7 When he noticed how the guests **picked** the places of honor at the table, he told them this parable:

No alternative rendering needed.

KJV John 6:70 Jesus answered them, Have not I **chosen** you twelve, and one of you is a devil?

NIV John 6:70 Then Jesus replied, "Have I not **chosen** you, the Twelve? Yet one of you is a devil!"

No alternative rendering needed.

KJV John 13:18 I speak not of you all: I know whom I have **chosen**: but that the scripture may be fulfilled, He that eateth bread with me hath lifted up his heel against me.

NIV John 13:18 "I am not referring to all of you; I know those I have **chosen**. But this is to fulfill the scripture: 'He who shares my bread has lifted up his heel against me.'"

No alternative rendering needed.

KJV John 15:16 Ye have not **chosen** me, but I have **chosen** you, and ordained you, that ye should go and bring forth fruit, and *that* your fruit should remain: that whatsoever ye shall ask of the Father in my name, he may give it you.

NIV John 15:16 You did not **choose** me, but I **chose** you and appointed you to go and bear fruit –fruit that will last. Then the Father will give you whatever you ask in my name.

No alternative rendering needed.

KJV John 15:19 If ye were of the world, the world would love his own: but because ye are not of the world, but I have **chosen** you out of the world, therefore the world hateth you.

NIV John 15:19 If you belonged to the world, it would love you as its own. As it is, you do not belong to the world, but I have **chosen** you out of the world. That is why the world hates you.

Alternative rendering John 15:19 If you belonged to the world, it would love you as its own. As it is, you do not belong to the world, but I have **gathered** you out of the world. That is why the world hates you.

KJV Acts 1:2 Until the day in which he was taken up, after that he through the Holy Ghost had given commandments unto the apostles whom he had **chosen**:

NIV Acts 1:2 until the day he was taken up to heaven, after giving instructions through the Holy Spirit to the apostles he had **chosen**.

No alternative rendering needed.

KJV Acts 1:24 And they prayed, and said, Thou, Lord, which knowest the hearts of all *men,* shew whether of these two thou hast **chosen**,

NIV Acts 1:24 Then they prayed, "Lord, you know everyone's heart. Show us which of these two you have **chosen**

No alternative rendering needed.

KJV Acts 6:5 And the saying pleased the whole multitude: and they **chose** Stephen, a man full of faith and of the Holy Ghost, and Philip, and Prochorus, and Nicanor, and Timon, and Parmenas, and Nicolas a proselyte of Antioch:

NIV Acts 6:5 This proposal pleased the whole group. They **chose** Stephen, a man full of faith and of the Holy Spirit; also Philip, Procorus, Nicanor, Timon, Parmenas, and Nicolas from Antioch, a convert to Judaism

No alternative rendering needed.

KJV Acts 13:17 The God of this people of Israel **chose** our fathers, and exalted the people when they dwelt as strangers in the land of Egypt, and with an high arm brought he them out of it.

NIV Acts 13:17 The God of the people of Israel **chose** our fathers; he made the people prosper during their stay in Egypt, with mighty power he led them out of that country,

No alternative rendering needed.

KJV Acts 15:7 And when there had been much disputing, Peter rose up, and said unto them, Men *and* brethren, ye know how that a good while ago God **made choice** among us, that the Gentiles by my mouth should hear the word of the gospel, and believe.

NIV Acts 15:7 After much discussion, Peter got up and addressed them: "Brothers, you know that some time ago God **made a choice** among you that the Gentiles might hear from my lips the message of the gospel and believe.

No alternative rendering needed, although the verse would be clearer if it read: "Brothers, you know that some time ago God **chose me from** among you that the Gentiles might hear from my lips the message of the gospel and believe.

KJV Acts 15:22   Then pleased it the apostles and elders, with the whole church, to send **chosen** men of their own company to Antioch with Paul and Barnabas; *namely,* Judas surnamed Barsabas, and Silas, chief men among the brethren:

NIV Acts 15:22   Then the apostles and elders, with the whole church, decided to **choose** some of their own men and send them to Antioch with Paul and Barnabas. They chose Judas (called Barsabbas) and Silas, two men who were leaders among the brothers.

No alternative rendering needed.

KJV Acts 15:25   It seemed good unto us, being assembled with one accord, to send **chosen** men unto you with our beloved Barnabas and Paul,

NIV Acts 15:25 So we all agreed to **choose** some men and send them to you with our dear friends Barnabas and Paul –

No alternative rendering needed.

KJV 1 Cor 1:27   But God hath **chosen** the foolish things of the world to confound the wise; and God hath **chosen** the weak things of the world to confound the things which are mighty;

NIV 1 Cor 1:27   But God **chose** the foolish things of the world to shame the wise; God chose the weak things of the world to shame the strong.

No alternative rendering needed.

KJV 1 Cor 1:28 And base things of the world, and things which are despised, hath God **chosen**, *yea,* and things which are not, to bring to nought things that are:

NIV 1 Cor 1:28 He **chose** the lowly things of this world and the despised things –and the things that are not – to nullify the things that are,

No alternative rendering needed.

KJV Eph 1:4 According as he hath **chosen** us in him before the foundation of the world, that we should be holy and without blame before him in love:

NIV Eph 1:4 For he **chose** us in him before the creation of the world to be holy and blameless in his sight. In love

No alternative rendering needed.

KJV James 2:5 Hearken, my beloved brethren, Hath not God **chosen** the poor of this world rich in faith, and heirs of the kingdom which he hath promised to them that love him?

NIV James 2:5 Listen, my dear brothers: Has not God **chosen** those who are poor in the eyes of the world to be rich in faith and to inherit the kingdom he promised those who love him?

No alternative rendering needed.

1588

Wigram & Winter: ἐκλεκτός, **eklektos,** 23 times, **elect, chosen**

Strong's: ἐκλεκτός, eklektos, *ek-lek-tos'*, from G1586 [gathered, chosen]; *select* (as in high quality); by implication *favorite:* - chosen, elect.

Bauer: p. 242, chosen, select, choice, excellent, outstanding

Brown: 1:536-541, Cl. Gr. the person or thing upon whom the choice has fallen; LXX "appears a number of times for Heb. roots connoting loveliness, preciousness, or excellent condition. Here the adj. does not express the fact of being chosen, but in a wider sense factors which were already present which make choice likely" (p. 537). This latter sense of quality is never used in relation to the selection of Israel; NT In Matt & Mk, this usage is clearly in the same sense as Jewish tradition according to which the object of election (Redemption) is a body of people, even though it is spoken of as many individuals. The sing. is applied to Jesus (Luke 9:35, 23:35, John 1:34, 1 Pet 2:4,6), otherwise it is used only once of an individual (Rom 16:13).

Kittel: 4:181-192, Cl. Gr. choice, selected, the sense of choice for things of the best quality; LXX & Hellenistic Jewish Writings: in general, secular use as an adjective for natural products, the meaning is choice, select, costly, sterling, purified, profitable, best of its kind, of top quality (p. 182). Religious meaning, sacred, pure, holy; NT in the Synoptic Gospels, the word is always used in an eschatological connection; in Matt 22, the use of the word implies an obedience corresponding to grace; election is fulfilled only in obedience, oriented to the right attitude of the elect; in Matt 20, those who give evidence of a right attitude in response to unmerited grace; in Rom 8, communal perspective, the community consists of the chosen, same in Col 3:12, but Rom 16:13 shows the term can also be used of an individual; in 1 Peter 1:1, the construction reveals that the goal of election is obedience; universal calling of the elect people of God is to proclaim the powerful mercy revealed in this election and calling.

NT Gr-Eng Dict: 2:344-348, #1575, adjective, chosen, select, elect; Cl. Gr. chosen, select, outstanding, of the best quality; LXX used to translate 26 words: branch, choice man, short, chosen, test, tested or tried, best or chosen, perfect or undefiled, trampled, fattened or well fed, choicest or fat, colored or multicolored, choice or polished or pure, large blocks or great blocks, pure myrrh oil, desirable or fine, jewel or stone, saddlecloth, diligent, precious, choicest, choicest or fine, delicacies, fruit, ornament or glory, treetop or highest branch, moisture; NT four primary usages (1) God's election of Israel, (2) choosing certain individuals for particular services, (3) God's choice to provide salvation in Christ for humankind, (4) God's election of the church.

Thayer's: p. 197, picked out, chosen, rare in Cl. Gr.; LXX mostly 2 words, both chosen; NT chosen by God, chosen or elect of God, choice ones, choice, select, excellent, preeminent.

Young's: p. 165, 293, laid out, choice, chosen.

KJV Matt 20:16 So the last shall be first, and the first last: for many be called, but few **chosen**.

NIV Matt 20:16 "So the last will be first, and the first will be last."

Alternative rendering Matt 20:16 So the last shall be first, and the first last: for many are called, but few **choice ones respond**. (The concept here is that the more noble, like the Bereans – the select ones, the choice ones – respond.)

Alternative rendering Matt 20:16 So the last shall be first, and the first last: for many are called, but few **are gathered**.

KJV Matt 22:14 For many are called, but few *are* **chosen**.

NIV Matt 22:14 "For many are invited, but few are **chosen**."

Alternative rendering Matt 22:14 "For many are invited, but few **choice ones respond**." (As before, few noble, few higher quality ones, respond.)

Alternative rendering Matt 22:14 "For many are invited, but few are **outstanding**."

Alternative rendering Matt 22:14 "For many are invited, but few are **gathered**."

KJV Matt 24:22 And except those days should be shortened, there should no flesh be saved: but for the **elect's** sake those days shall be shortened.

NIV Matt 24:22 If those days had not been cut short, no one would survive, but for the sake of the **elect** those days will be shortened.

Alternative rendering Matt 24:22 If those days had not been cut short, no one would survive, but for the sake of the **choice ones**, those days will be shortened.

Alternative rendering Matt 24:22 If those days had not been cut short, no one would survive, but for the sake of the **gathered ones**, those days will be shortened.

Alternative rendering Matt 24:22 If those days had not been cut short, no one would survive, but for the sake of the **named ones**, those days will be shortened.

KJV Matt 24:24 For there shall arise false Christs, and false prophets, and shall shew great signs and wonders; insomuch that, if *it were* possible, they shall deceive the very **elect**.

NIV Matt 24:24 For false Christs and false prophets will appear and perform great signs and miracles to deceive even the **elect** – if that were possible.

Alternative rendering Matt 24:24 For false Christs and false prophets will appear and perform great signs and miracles to deceive even the **choice ones** – if that were possible.

KJV Matt 24:31 And he shall send his angels with a great sound of a trumpet, and they shall gather together his **elect** from the four winds, from one end of heaven to the other.

NIV Matt 24:31 And he will send his angels with a loud trumpet call, and they will gather his **elect** from the four winds, from one end of the heavens to the other.

Alternative rendering Matt 24:31 And he will send his angels with a loud trumpet call, and they will gather his **choice ones** from the four winds, from one end of the heavens to the other.

KJV Mark 13:20 And except that the Lord had shortened those days, no flesh should be saved: but for the **elect's** sake, whom he hath chosen, he hath shortened the days.

NIV Mark 13:20 If the Lord had not cut short those days, no one would survive. But for the sake of the **elect**, whom he has chosen, he has shortened them.

Alternative rendering Mark 13:20 If the Lord had not cut short those days, no one would survive. But for the sake of the **choice ones**, whom he has gathered, he has shortened them.

Alternative rendering Mark 13:20 If the Lord had not cut short those days, no one would survive. But for the sake of the **choice ones**, whom he has searched out, he has shortened them.

KJV Mark 13:22 For false Christs and false prophets shall rise, and shall shew signs and wonders, to seduce, if *it were* possible, even the **elect**.

NIV Mark 13:22 For false Christs and false prophets will appear and perform signs and miracles to deceive the **elect** – if that were possible.

Alternative rendering Mark 13:22 For false Christs

and false prophets will appear and perform signs and miracles to deceive the **choice ones** – if that were possible.

KJV Mark 13:27 And then shall he send his angels, and shall gather together his **elect** from the four winds, from the uttermost part of the earth to the uttermost part of heaven.

NIV Mark 13:27 And he will send his angels and gather his **elect** from the four winds, from the ends of the earth to the ends of the heavens.

Alternative rendering Mark 13:27 And he will send his angels and gather his **choice ones** from the four winds, from the ends of the earth to the ends of the heavens.

KJV Luke 18:7 And shall not God avenge his own **elect**, which cry day and night unto him, though he bear long with them?

NIV Luke 18:7 And will not God bring about justice for his **chosen** ones, who cry out to him day and night? Will he keep putting them off?

Alternative rendering Luke 18:7 And will not God bring about justice for his **choice ones** [**his righteous ones**], who cry out to him day and night? Will he keep putting them off?

KJV Luke 23:35 And the people stood beholding. And the rulers also with them derided *him,* saying, He saved others; let him save himself, if he be Christ, the **chosen** of God.

NIV Luke 23:35 The people stood watching, and the rulers even sneered at him. They said, "He saved others; let him save himself if he is the Christ of God, the **Chosen**

One."

No alternative rendering needed.

KJV Rom 8:33 Who shall lay any thing to the charge of God's **elect**? *It is* God that justifieth.

NIV Rom 8:33 Who will bring any charge against those whom God has **chosen**? It is God who justifies.

Alternative rendering Rom 8:33 Who will bring any charge against those whom God has **gathered**? It is God who justifies.

Alternative rendering Rom 8:33 Who will bring any charge against God's **choice ones**? It is God who justifies.

KJV Rom 16:13 Salute Rufus **chosen** in the Lord, and his mother and mine.

NIV Rom 16:13 Greet Rufus, **chosen** in the Lord, and his mother, who has been a mother to me, too.

Alternative rendering Rom 16:13 Greet Rufus, **outstanding** in the Lord, and his mother, who has been a mother to me, too.

KJV Col 3:12 Put on therefore, as the **elect** of God, holy and beloved, bowels of mercies, kindness, humbleness of mind, meekness, longsuffering;

NIV Col 3:12 Therefore, as God's **chosen** people, holy and dearly loved, clothe yourselves with compassion, kindness, humility, gentleness and patience.

Alternative rendering Col 3:12 Therefore, as God's **choice** people, holy and dearly loved, clothe yourselves with compassion, kindness, humility, gentleness and patience.

KJV 1 Tim 5:21 I charge *thee* before God, and the Lord Jesus Christ, and the **elect** angels, that thou observe these things without preferring one before another, doing nothing by partiality.

NIV 1 Tim 5:21 I charge you, in the sight of God and Christ Jesus and the **elect** angels, to keep these instructions without partiality, and to do nothing out of favoritism.

Alternative rendering 1 Tim 5:21 I charge you, in the sight of God and Christ Jesus and the **choice** angels, to keep these instructions without partiality, and to do nothing out of favoritism.

KJV 2 Tim 2:10 Therefore I endure all things for the **elect's** sakes, that they may also obtain the salvation which is in Christ Jesus with eternal glory.

NIV 2 Tim 2:10 Therefore I endure everything for the sake of the **elect**, that they too may obtain the salvation that is in Christ Jesus, with eternal glory.

Alternative rendering 2 Tim 2:10 Therefore I endure everything for the sake of the **choice ones**, that they too may obtain the salvation that is in Christ Jesus, with eternal glory.

KJV Tit 1:1 Paul, a servant of God, and an apostle of Jesus Christ, according to the faith of God's **elect**, and the acknowledging of the truth which is after godliness; 1588

NIV Tit 1:1 Paul, a servant of God and an apostle of Jesus Christ for the faith of God's **elect** and the knowledge of the truth that leads to godliness –

Alternative rendering Tit 1:1 Paul, a servant of God and an apostle of Jesus Christ for the faith of God's **choice ones** and the knowledge of the truth that leads to godliness

---

KJV 1 Pet 1:1   Peter, an apostle of Jesus Christ, to the strangers scattered throughout Pontus, Galatia, Cappadocia, Asia, and Bithynia,

NIV 1 Pet 1:1   Peter, an apostle of Jesus Christ, To God's **elect**, strangers in the world, scattered throughout Pontus, Galatia, Cappadocia, Asia and Bithynia,

Alternative rendering 1 Pet 1:1   Peter, an apostle of Jesus Christ, To God's **choice ones**, strangers in the world, scattered throughout Pontus, Galatia, Cappadocia, Asia and Bithynia,

---

KJV 1 Pet 1:2   **Elect** according to the foreknowledge of God the Father, through sanctification of the Spirit, unto obedience and sprinkling of the blood of Jesus Christ: Grace unto you, and peace, be multiplied.

NIV 1 Pet 1:2   who have been **chosen** according to the foreknowledge of God the Father, through the sanctifying work of the Spirit, for obedience to Jesus Christ and sprinkling by his blood: Grace and peace be yours in abundance.

Alternative rendering 1 Pet 1:2   who have been **gathered** according to the foreknowledge of God the Father, through the sanctifying work of the Spirit, for obedience to Jesus Christ and sprinkling by his blood: Grace and peace be yours in abundance.

KJV 1 Pet 2:4   To whom coming, *as unto* a living stone, disallowed indeed of men, but **chosen** of God, *and* precious,

NIV 1 Pet 2:4 As you come to him, the living Stone – rejected by men but **chosen** by God and precious to him –

No alternative rendering needed.

KJV 1 Pet 2:6 Wherefore also it is contained in the scripture, Behold, I lay in Sion a chief corner stone, **elect**, precious: and he that believeth on him shall not be confounded.

NIV 1 Pet 2:6 For in Scripture it says: "See, I lay a stone in Zion, a **chosen** and precious cornerstone, and the one who trusts in him will never be put to shame."

No alternative rendering needed.

KJV 1 Pet 2:9 But ye *are* a **chosen** generation, a royal priesthood, an holy nation, a peculiar people; that ye should shew forth the praises of him who hath called you out of darkness into his marvellous light:

NIV 1 Pet 2:9 But you are a **chosen** people, a royal priesthood, a holy nation, a people belonging to God, that you may declare the praises of him who called you out of darkness into his wonderful light.

Alternative rendering 1 Pet 2:9 But you are **a special** people, a royal priesthood, a holy nation, a people belonging to God, that you may declare the praises of him who called you out of darkness into his wonderful light.

KJV 2 John 1:1 The elder unto the **elect** lady and her children, whom I love in the truth; and not I only, but also all they that have known the truth;

NIV 2 John 1:1 The elder, To the **chosen** lady and her children, whom I love in the truth – and not I only, but also all who know the truth –

Alternative rendering 2 John 1:1 The elder, To the **most excellent** lady and her children, whom I love in the truth – and not I only, but also all who know the truth –

Alternative rendering 2 John 1:1 The elder, To the

choice lady and her children, whom I love in the truth –
and not I only, but also all who know the truth –

KJV 2 John 1:13 The children of thy **elect** sister greet
thee. Amen.

NIV 2 John 1:13 The children of your **chosen** sister
send their greetings.

Alternative rendering 2 John 1:13 The children of
your **most excellent** sister send their greetings.

Alternative rendering 2 John 1:13 The children of
your **choice** sister send their greetings.

KJV Rev 17:14 These shall make war with the Lamb,
and the Lamb shall overcome them: for he is Lord of lords,
and King of kings: and they that are with him *are* called,
and **chosen**, and faithful.

NIV Rev 17:14 They will make war against the Lamb,
but the Lamb will overcome them because he is Lord of
lords and King of kings – and with him will be his called,
chosen and faithful followers."

Rev 17:14 They will make war against the Lamb,
but the Lamb will overcome them because he is Lord of
lords and King of kings – and with him will be his called,
outstanding and faithful followers."

1589

Wigram & Winter: ἐκλογή, **eklogee**, 7 times, **election, chosen**

Strong's: ἐκλογή, eklogeō, *ek-log-ay'*, from G1586; (divine) *selection*
(abstractly or concretely): - chosen, election.

Bauer: p. 243, selection, election, choosing, that which is chosen or
selected, those selected.

Brown: 1:536-537, 539-540, Cl. Gr. the act of choosing, a choice;

selection for military service, or for administrative office, but with conditions necessary for that selection and such selection always accompanied by some obligation; LXX never used; NT noun used unambiguously and exclusively for God's act of election, usually related to Israel, but in 1 Thes 1:4 and 2 Pet 1:10 for the church.

Kittel: 4:176-181, In Cl. Gr. careful sifting on the basis of aptness and serviceability for a specific end; seeking out, selecting (field, bride, clothes or equivalent value); in Stoicism, always signifies preferring one thing to another; NT Acts 9:15 appointment to serve; five times in Paul (i) divine selection in the history of the patriarchs, Rom 9:11, (ii) the election of all Israel in the fathers, Rom 11:28, (iii) the election of the whole Christian community to faith, 1 Thes 1:4, (iv) God's selecting of a part of Israel out of the whole, the remnant, Rom 11:5, (v) the remnant as distinct from Israel as a whole Rom 11:7. In Peter, 2 Pet 1:10, the election and calling of the community of believers.

NT Gr-Eng Dict: 2:348-349, #1576, noun, selection, choice, chosen; Cl. Gr. from "out of" and "collect, pick out, select, choose, say, name, call"; LXX, 2 times, choicest; NT the free choice of God in fulfilling his purposes.

Thayer's: p. 197, election, choice, the act of picking out or choosing, the thing or person chosen.

Young's: p. 165, 293, choice, a laying out, selection.

> KJV Acts 9:15 But the Lord said unto him, Go thy way: for he is a **chosen** vessel unto me, to bear my name before the Gentiles, and kings, and the children of Israel:
>
> NIV Acts 9:15 But the Lord said to Ananias, "Go! This man is my **chosen** instrument to carry my name before the Gentiles and their kings and before the people of Israel.
>
> No alternative rendering needed, although there may still be a "high quality, choice" connotation.

KJV Rom 9:11 (For *the children* being not yet born, neither having done any good or evil, that the purpose of God according to **election** might stand, not of works, but of him that calleth;)

NIV Rom 9:11 Yet, before the twins were born or had done anything good or bad – in order that God's purpose in **election** might stand:

No alternative rendering needed, although, again, there may be a connotation of "high quality, choice." Theologically, this is not an issue of whether God chose or not, it is an issue of why. Even though the twins had done nothing before the choice was made, their future was going to be very different, so the choice was logically based on God's foreknowledge rather than being arbitrary.

KJV Rom 11:5 Even so then at this present time also there is a remnant according to the **election** of grace.

NIV Rom 11:5 So too, at the present time there is a remnant **chosen** by grace.

No alternative rendering needed. Again, theologically, this in not a question of whether God chose or not – it is a question of whom he chose. I am convinced that he chose the remnant as a group, just as he chose Israel as a group – not the specific individuals in the group.

KJV Rom 11:7 What then? Israel hath not obtained that which he seeketh for; but the **election** hath obtained it, and the rest were blinded

NIV Rom 11:7 What then? What Israel sought so earnestly it did not obtain, but the **elect** did. The others were hardened,

Alternative rendering Rom 11:7 What then? What

Israel sought so earnestly it did not obtain, but the **choice ones** did. The others were hardened,

---

KJV Rom 11:28 As concerning the gospel, *they are* enemies for your sakes: but as touching the **election**, *they are* beloved for the fathers' sakes.

NIV Rom 11:28 As far as the gospel is concerned, they are enemies on your account; but as far as **election** is concerned, they are loved on account of the patriarchs,

No alternative rendering needed. Once again, theologically, this is not a question of whether choosing has occurred, it is a question of whether the group is chosen, or the individuals in the group are chosen. This passage is particularly potent against a Calvinist view, because Paul is making the argument that the Israelites, even during their long periods of rebellion and unbelief, are still the elect, the chosen of God. It argues strongly for election being corporate, not individual.

KJV 1Thes 1:4 Knowing, brethren beloved, your **election** of God.

NIV 1 Thes 1:4 For we know, brothers loved by God, that he has **chosen** you

Alternative rendering 1 Thes 1:4 For we know, brothers loved by God, that he has **named** you (**placed his name on** you)

KJV 2 Pet 1:10 Wherefore the rather, brethren, give diligence to make your calling and **election** sure: for if ye do these things, ye shall never fall:

NIV 2 Pet 1:10 Therefore, my brothers, be all the more eager to make your calling and **election** sure. For if you do these things, you will never fall

Alternative rendering 2 Pet 1:10 Therefore, my brothers, be all the more eager to make your calling and **naming** sure. For if you do these things, you will never fall (The idea, paying according to value: If you want assurance that God has called you and placed his name on you – that you are secure in him – then do these things . . .)

___

1951

Wigram & Winter: ἐπιλέγομαι, **epilegomai,** 2 times, **called, chose**

Strong's: ἐπιλέγομαι, epilegomai, *ep-ee-leg'-om-ahee,* mid. voice from G1909 [on, in, to, unto, against, etc.] and G3004 [later usage, to say or name]; to *surname, select:* - call, choose.

Bauer: p. 295, to call or name, choose or select someone.

Brown: not found.

Kittel: not found.

NT Gr-Eng Dict: 2:543, #1935B, verb, to call, name; call upon, select, choose; no mention of Cl. Gr. usage; LXX used to translate 3 words: to select or choose for religious, military, or social tasks, to burn or cut off, to gather or bring into; NT to name, call, pick, choose, select for a task.

Thayer's: to say besides, to surname, to name, to put a name upon, to choose for, to choose for one's self.

Young's: p. 138, 164, to be laid out besides, to lay upon.

KJV John 5:2 Now there is at Jerusalem by the sheep *market* a pool, which is **called** in the Hebrew tongue Bethesda, having five porches.

NIV John 5:2 Now there is in Jerusalem near the Sheep Gate a pool, which in Aramaic is **called** Bethesda and which is surrounded by five covered colonnades.

No alternative rendering needed.

___

KJV Acts 15:40 And Paul **chose** Silas, and departed, being recommended by the brethren unto the grace of God.

NIV Acts 15:40 but Paul **chose** Silas and left, commended by the brothers to the grace of the Lord.

No alternative rendering needed.

2820

Wingram & Winter: κληρόω, **eklērōthēmen**, 1 time, **obtained an inheritance, chosen**

Strong's: κληρόω, klēroō, *klay-ro'-o*, from G2819 [heir]; to *allot*, that is, (figuratively) to *assign* (a privilege): - obtain an inheritance.

Bauer: p. 435, active, to appoint by lot; passive, to be appointed by lot

Colin Brown: 2:295-296, 299,

Kittel: 3:764-765, Cl. Gr. to appoint someone by lot, to be appointed by lot, to cast lots, to appoint, to apportion; NT an appointment or determination with a goal assigned with the calling; nuance that the call imparts something to the called, namely, a life's goal.

NT Gr-Eng Dict: 3:397, #2793, to make or obtain an inheritance, allot, apportion; Cl. Gr. to choose by lots, to designate, to have something allotted to one; LXX to be taken, chosen or called, given sickness as inheritance for forgetting God; NT to obtain an inheritance, context shows that believers already possess it.

Thayer's: p. 349, to cast lots; to determine by lot; to allot, assign, by lot.

Young's: p. 708, to choose by lot

KJV Eph 1:11 In whom also we have **obtained an inheritance**, being predestinated according to the purpose of him who worketh all things after the counsel of his own will:

NIV Eph 1:11 In him we were also **chosen**, having been predestined according to the plan of him who works out everything in conformity with the purpose of his will,

No alternative rendering needed, since this is talking about Israel as a corporate entity, as we saw in Chapter 6.

4400

Wigram & Winter: προχειρίζομαι, **prokīrizomai**, 2 times, **chosen, make, appoint**

Strong's, προχειρίζομαι, procheirizomai, *prokh-i-rid'-zom-ahee*. Mid. voice from G4253 [before] and a derivative of G5495 [hand]; to *handle* for oneself *in advance*, that is, (figuratively) to *purpose*: - choose, make.

Bauer: p. 724, to choose for oneself, select, appoint, destine.

Brown: 2:148-150 root word χειρ, cheir (or kīr), "hand" is addressed, but this word and these 2 verses are not specifically mentioned.

Kittel: 6:862-864, to ordain, to choose, to appoint; related to the binding nature of an appointment, as in the military, but in other jobs as well, so that connotation may have influenced Luke's choice of this word.

NT Gr-Eng Dict: 5:368, #4258, verb, to choose, select, appoint; Cl. Gr. to have ready, on hand, easily available for use, to take into one's hands, handle, prepare, equip, recruiting troops, appointing minor officials; LXX used to translate 2 words: take or choose, send; NT emphasis is on a decision that is made and then remains binding.

Thayer's: p. 554, to put into the hand, to deliver into the hands, to take into one's hands, to set before one's self, to propose, to determine, to choose, to appoint (for one's self).

Young's: p. 164, to take in hand.

KJV Acts 22:14 And he said, The God of our fathers hath **chosen** thee, that thou shouldest know his will, and see that Just One, and shouldest hear the voice of his mouth.

NIV Acts 22:14 "Then he said: 'The God of our

fathers has **chosen** you to know his will and to see the
Righteous One and to hear words from his mouth.

No alternative rendering needed.

_____

KJV Acts 26:16 But rise, and stand upon thy feet: for
I have appeared unto thee for this purpose, to **make** thee
a minister and a witness both of these things which thou
hast seen, and of those things in the which I will appear
unto thee;

NIV Acts 26:16 'Now get up and stand on your feet.
I have appeared to you to **appoint** you as a servant and as a
witness of what you have seen of me and what I will show
you.

No alternative rendering needed, although it is
interesting how the same word, in two versions of the same
story, is translated as *chosen* in one and *appoint* in the other.

_____

4401

Wigram & Winter: προχειροτονέω, **prokīrotoneomai**, 1 time, **chosen**

Strong's: προχειροτονέω, procheirotoneoō, *prokh-i-rot-on-eh'-o*, from
G4253 [before] and G5500 [to elect by extending the hand]; to
elect in advance: - choose before.

Bauer: p. 724, to choose or appoint beforehand.

Brown: 1:478, word is combined with 5500, Cl. Gr. & LXX to vote by
show of hands; NT Acts 10:41 apostles appointed by God to
be witnesses of Jesus' resurrection, 2 Cor 8:19, representatives
appointed to accompany Paul, Acts 14:23 Barnabas and Paul
appoint elders in the Galatian churches "from whence, apparently,
it became the standard term for ordination in later ecclesiastical
Greek" (p. 478).

Kittel: 9:437, combined with 5500, as Brown does.

NT Gr-Eng Dict: 5:368, #4259, verb, to choose, designate beforehand.

No Cl. Gr. or LXX usage mentioned; NT combination of three words: before, hand, to stretch out, meaning "to choose or appoint beforehand."

Thayer's: p. 554, to choose, designate beforehand

Young's: p. 164, to extend the hand (elect) before.

KJV Acts 10:41 Not to all the people, but unto witnesses **chosen** before of God, *even* to us, who did eat and drink with him after he rose from the dead.

NIV Acts 10:41 He was not seen by all the people, but by witnesses whom God had already **chosen** – by us who ate and drank with him after he rose from the dead.

No alternative rendering needed.

4758

Wigram & Winter: στρατολογέω, **stratologeo**, 1 time, **chosen**

Strong's: στρατολογέω, stratologeō, *strat-ol-og-eh'-o.* From a compound of the base of G4756 [large group, army] and G3004 (in its original sense) [to gather]; to *gather* (or *select*) as a *warrior,* that is, *enlist* in the army: - choose to be a soldier.

Bauer: p. 770, to gather an army, to enlist soldiers.

Colin Brown: 3:958, 964, the one who enlisted him.

Kittel: 7:701-713, the one who has chosen him to be a soldier.

NT Gr-Eng Dict: 6:127, #4609, verb, to enlist soldiers, recruit an army, usage consistent from 1st century B.C.E.; LXX no usage; NT chosen as a soldier.

Thayer's: p. 590, to gather (collect) an army, to enlist soldiers.

Young's: p. 164, to levy an army, enlist.

KJV 2 Tim 2:4 No man that warreth entangleth himself with the affairs of *this* life; that he may please him who hath **chosen** him to be a soldier.

NIV 2 Tim 2:4   No one serving as a soldier gets involved in civilian affairs – he wants to please his commanding officer.

No alternative rendering needed.

4899

Wigram & Winter: συνεκλεκτός, **suneklektos**, 1 time, **elected together with**

Strong's: συνεκλεκτός, suneklektos, *soon-ek-lek-tos';* From a compound of G4862 [with] and G1586 [gather, choose]; *chosen* in company *with*, that is, *co-elect (fellow Christian):* - elected together with.

Bauer: p. 787, chosen together with; "No individual lady is meant, least of all Peter's wife, but rather a congregation with whom Peter is staying."

Brown: 1:536-542, not addressed separately from εκλεκτός, eklektos (1586), to elect, choose.

Kittel: 4:191, used for the local congregation combined with the other to constitute the whole.

NT Gr-Eng Dict: 6:191, #4749, chosen along with or together.

Thayer's: p. 603, elected or chosen together with.

Young's: p. 293, chosen along with.

KJV 1 Pet 5:13   The *church that is* at Babylon, **elected together** with *you,* saluteth you; and *so doth* Marcus my son.

NIV   1 Pet 5:13   She who is in Babylon, **chosen together** with you, sends you her greetings, and so does my son Mark.

Alternative rendering   1 Pet 5:13   She who is in Babylon, **choice ones together** with you, sends you her greetings, and so does my son Mark.

Alternative rendering   1 Pet 5:13   She who is in

Babylon, **gathered together** with you, sends you her greetings, and so does my son Mark.

5500

Wigram & Winter: χειροτονέω, **kīrotoneo,** 2 times, **chosen, ordained, appointed**

Strong's: χειροτονέω, cheirotoneoō, *khi-rot-on-eh'-o¸* from a compound of G5495 [hand] and τείνω teinoō (to *stretch*); to be a *hand reacher* or *voter* (by raising the hand), that is, (genitive) to *select* or *appoint:* - choose, ordain.

Bauer: p. 881, choose, elect by raising hands

Brown: 1:478, this word is combined with 4401, since they come from the same root.

Kittel: 9:437, raising the hand to express agreement in a vote; in Acts 14:23, not election by the congregation, but appointment by Barnabas and Paul.

NT Gr-Eng Dict: 6:499, #5336, verb, to choose, select, elect by raising the hand. Cl. Gr. to select, nominate, elect, appoint; no LXX usage; NT appointed, chose for specific tasks.

Thayer's: p. 668, to vote by stretching out the hand, to create or appoint by vote; to elect, appoint, create (when the idea of extending the hand is ignored).

Young's: p. 164, 722, to extend the hand (in voting), to elect by stretching out the hand.

KJV Acts 14:23 And when they had **ordained** them elders in every church, and had prayed with fasting, they commended them to the Lord, on whom they believed.

NIV Acts 14:23 Paul and Barnabas **appointed** elders for them in each church and, with prayer and fasting, committed them to the Lord, in whom they had put their trust.

Alternative rendering Acts 14:23   And when they had **selected** elders in every church, and had prayed with fasting, they commended them to the Lord, on whom they believed.

KJV 2 Cor 8:19   And not *that* only, but who was also **chosen** of the churches to travel with us with this grace, which is administered by us to the glory of the same Lord, and *declaration of* your ready mind:

NIV 2 Cor 8:19   What is more, he was **chosen** by the churches to accompany us as we carry the offering, which we administer in order to honor the Lord himself and to show our eagerness to help.

No alternative rendering needed.

Appendix B
Scriptures that argue against divine determinism

If all things were predetermined before the foundation of the earth, as John Calvin's deterministic worldview suggests, then for God to change his mind would never happen, nor ever need to happen. The Bible is replete with examples of God appearing to change his mind, or appearing to be surprised at the outcome of events, or appearing to respond to human actions rather than determining them. If the world is the way Calvin imagined it, for God to appear to change his mind, then, implies that God is being deceitful – he is giving the appearance that things *are* the way that they actually *are not*.

The examples are divided into the following categories:

- Examples of the Lord changing his mind as circumstances change, or in response to prayer
- Examples of God explicitly saying he will change his mind if circumstances change
- Examples of God expressing surprise, regret, or disappointment over how things turned out

- Examples of the Lord testing his people to determine their faith or faithfulness
- Examples of the Lord asking non-rhetorical questions about the future
- Examples of the Lord speaking of the future in terms of uncertainty

For each example, the setting is described briefly *in italics*, then the actual verses are shown.

Examples of the Lord changing his mind as circumstances change, or in response to prayer

Exod 32:14 *God relenting from destroying Israel, in response to Moses' plea, Mt. Sinai*

Then the LORD relented and did not bring on his people the disaster he had threatened.

Num 14:11-23 *God relenting from destroying Israel, in response to Moses' plea*

The LORD said to Moses, "How long will these people treat me with contempt? How long will they refuse to believe in me, in spite of all the miraculous signs I have performed among them? I will strike them down with a plague and destroy them, but I will make you into a nation greater and stronger than they."

Moses said to the LORD, "Then the Egyptians will hear about it! By your power you brought these people up from among them. . . If you put these people to death all at one time, the nations who have heard this report about you will say, 'The LORD was not able to bring these people into the land he promised them on oath; so he slaughtered them in the desert.' . . . In accordance with your great love, forgive the sin of these people, just as you have pardoned them from the time they left Egypt until now."

The LORD replied, "I have forgiven them, as you asked. Nevertheless, as surely as I live and as surely as the glory of the LORD fills the whole earth, not one of the men who saw my glory and the miraculous signs I performed in Egypt and in the desert but who disobeyed me and tested me ten times – not one of them will ever see the land I promised on oath to their forefathers. No one who has treated me with contempt will ever see it."

Deut 9:13-14 *Moses relating his conversation with God, as the Israelites are about to cross the Jordan to occupy Canaan*

And the LORD said to me, "I have seen this people, and they are a stiff-necked people indeed! Let me alone, so that I may destroy them and blot out their name from under heaven. And I will make you into a nation stronger and more numerous than they."

1 Sam 2:30 *A prophet rebukes Eli for not disciplining his wicked sons*

"Therefore the LORD, the God of Israel, declares: 'I promised that your house and your father's house would minister before me forever.' But now the LORD declares: 'Far be it from me! Those who honor me I will honor, but those who despise me will be disdained.'"

2 Kings 20:1-7 *The story of Hezekiah the king*

In those days Hezekiah became ill and was at the point of death. The prophet Isaiah son of Amoz went to him and said, "This is what the LORD says: Put your house in order, because you are going to die; you will not recover."

Hezekiah turned his face to the wall and prayed to the LORD, "Remember, O LORD, how I have walked before you faithfully and with wholehearted devotion and have done what is good in your eyes." And Hezekiah wept bitterly.

Before Isaiah had left the middle court, the word of the LORD came to him: "Go back and tell Hezekiah, the leader of my people, 'This is what the LORD, the God of your father David, says: I have heard your prayer and seen your tears; I will heal you. On the third day from now you will go up to the temple of the LORD. I will add fifteen years to your life. And I will deliver you and this city from the hand of the king of Assyria. I will defend this city for my sake and for the sake of my servant David.'"

Then Isaiah said, "Prepare a poultice of figs." They did so and applied it to the boil, and he recovered.

1 Chron 21:15 *God stopping the angel from destroying Jerusalem in the days of King David*

And God sent an angel to destroy Jerusalem. But as the angel was doing so, the LORD saw it and was grieved because of the calamity and said to the angel who was destroying the people, "Enough! Withdraw your hand."

Jer 26:19 *Jeremiah recounting how God relented regarding Hezekiah's death*

> "Did Hezekiah king of Judah or anyone else in Judah put him to death? Did not Hezekiah fear the LORD and seek his favor? And did not the LORD relent, so that he did not bring the disaster he pronounced against them? We are about to bring a terrible disaster on ourselves!"

Ezek 20:5-22 *God recounting how he relented several times rather than destroy Israel*

> . . . This is what the Sovereign LORD says: "On the day I chose Israel, I swore with uplifted hand . . . that I would bring them out of Egypt into a land I had searched out for them, a land flowing with milk and honey. . . .
> But they rebelled against me and would not listen to me; they did not get rid of the vile images they had set their eyes on, nor did they forsake the idols of Egypt. So I said I would pour out my wrath on them and spend my anger against them in Egypt.
> But for the sake of my name I did what would keep it from being profaned in the eyes of the nations they lived among and in whose sight I had revealed myself to the Israelites by bringing them out of Egypt. Therefore I led them out of Egypt and brought them into the desert. . . .
> Yet the people of Israel rebelled against me in the desert. . . So I said I would pour out my wrath on them and destroy them in the desert. But for the sake of my name I did what would keep it from being profaned in the eyes of the nations in whose sight I had brought them out.

Also with uplifted hand I swore to them in the desert that I would not bring them into the land I had given them . . . because they rejected my laws and did not follow my decrees and desecrated my Sabbaths. . . Yet I looked on them with pity and did not destroy them or put an end to them in the desert.

I said to their children in the desert, 'Do not follow the statutes of your fathers or keep their laws or defile yourselves with their idols'. . . . But the children rebelled against me . . . So I said I would pour out my wrath on them and spend my anger against them in the desert.

But I withheld my hand, and for the sake of my name I did what would keep it from being profaned in the eyes of the nations in whose sight I had brought them out."

Amos 7:1-6 *God relenting after Amos prays*

This is what the Sovereign LORD showed me: He was preparing swarms of locusts after the king's share had been harvested and just as the second crop was coming up. When they had stripped the land clean, I cried out, "Sovereign LORD, forgive! How can Jacob survive? He is so small!" So the LORD relented. "This will not happen," the LORD said.

This is what the Sovereign LORD showed me: The Sovereign LORD was calling for judgment by fire; it dried up the great deep and devoured the land. Then I cried out, "Sovereign LORD, I beg you, stop! How can Jacob survive? He is so small!" So the LORD relented. "This will not happen either," the Sovereign LORD said.

Jonah 3:1-10 *God relenting from destroying Nineveh after Jonah preached to them*

> Then the word of the LORD came to Jonah a second time: "Go to the great city of Nineveh and proclaim to it the message I give you." Jonah obeyed the word of the LORD and went to Nineveh. . . He proclaimed: "Forty more days and Nineveh will be overturned."
>
> The Ninevites believed God. They declared a fast, and all of them, from the greatest to the least, put on sackcloth.
>
> . . .
>
> When God saw what they did and how they turned from their evil ways, he had compassion and did not bring upon them the destruction he had threatened.

Examples of God explicitly saying he will change his mind if circumstances change

Jer 18:7-11 *God instructing Jeremiah to pronounce doom on Judah for stubbornly abandoning God*

> "If at any time I announce that a nation or kingdom is to be uprooted, torn down and destroyed, and if that nation I warned repents of its evil, then I will relent and not inflict on it the disaster I had planned.
>
> And if at another time I announce that a nation or kingdom is to be built up and planted, and if it does evil in my sight and does not obey me, then I will reconsider the good I had intended to do for it.
>
> Now therefore say to the people of Judah and those living in Jerusalem, 'This is what the LORD says: Look! I am preparing a disaster for you and devising a plan against you. So turn from your evil ways, each one of you, and reform your ways and your actions.'"

Jer 26:2-3 *God instructing Jeremiah to give Judah a conditional warning*

> This is what the LORD says: "Stand in the courtyard of the Lord's house and speak to all the people of the towns of Judah who come to worship in the house of the LORD. Tell them everything I command you; do not omit a word. Perhaps they will listen and each will turn from his evil way. Then I will relent and not bring on them the disaster I was planning because of the evil they have done."

Ezek 33:13-15 *God telling Ezekiel what to say to his countrymen*

> "If I tell the righteous man that he will surely live, but then he trusts in his righteousness and does evil, none of the righteous things he has done will be remembered; he will die for the evil he has done.
> And if I say to the wicked man, 'You will surely die,' but he then turns away from his sin and does what is just and right – if he gives back what he took in pledge for a loan, returns what he has stolen, follows the decrees that give life, and does no evil, he will surely live; he will not die."

Joel 2:13-14 *Joel pleading for his people to wake up and avoid the day of judgment*

> Rend your heart and not your garments. Return to the LORD your God, for he is gracious and compassionate, slow to anger and abounding in love, and he relents from sending calamity.
> Who knows? He may turn and have pity and leave behind a blessing – grain offerings and drink offerings for the LORD your God.

Jonah 4:2 *Jonah's prayer following the repentance of Nineveh*
He prayed to the LORD, "O LORD, is this not what I said
when I was still at home? That is why I was so quick
to flee to Tarshish. I knew that you are a gracious and
compassionate God, slow to anger and abounding in
love, a God who relents from sending calamity."

Examples of God expressing surprise, regret, or disappointment over how things turned out

Gen 6:5-6 *God's response to the wickedness in the days of Noah*
The LORD saw how great man's wickedness on the earth
had become, and that every inclination of the
thoughts of his heart was only evil all the time.
The LORD was grieved that he had made man on the earth,
and his heart was filled with pain.

1 Sam 15:10-11, 34-35 *God expressing regret at having made Saul
king of Israel*
Then the word of the LORD came to Samuel: "I am
grieved that I have made Saul king, because he has
turned away from me and has not carried out my
instructions." . . .
Then Samuel left for Ramah, but Saul went up to his home
in Gibeah of Saul.
Until the day Samuel died, he did not go to see Saul again,
though Samuel mourned for him. And the LORD
was grieved that he had made Saul king over Israel.

Isa 5:3-7 *God expressing surprise at Judah's response to his provision and care*

> "Now you dwellers in Jerusalem and men of Judah, judge between me and my vineyard. What more could have been done for my vineyard than I have done for it? When I looked for good grapes, why did it yield only bad?
>
> Now I will tell you what I am going to do to my vineyard: I will take away its hedge, and it will be destroyed; I will break down its wall, and it will be trampled. I will make it a wasteland, neither pruned nor cultivated, and briers and thorns will grow there. I will command the clouds not to rain on it."
>
> The vineyard of the LORD Almighty is the house of Israel, and the men of Judah are the garden of his delight. And he looked for justice, but saw bloodshed; for righteousness, but heard cries of distress.

Jer 3:6-7, 19-20 *God expressing surprise at Israel's response to his love*

> During the reign of King Josiah, the LORD said to me, "Have you seen what faithless Israel has done? She has gone up on every high hill and under every spreading tree and has committed adultery there. I thought that after she had done all this she would return to me but she did not, and her unfaithful sister Judah saw it. . . .
>
> I myself said, 'How gladly would I treat you like sons and give you a desirable land, the most beautiful inheritance of any nation.' I thought you would call me 'Father' and not turn away from following me. But like a woman unfaithful to her husband, so

you have been unfaithful to me, O house of Israel,"
declares the LORD.

Ezek 22:29-31 *God's disappointment at not finding a faithful man in Israel to represent him*

The people of the land practice extortion and commit
robbery; they oppress the poor and needy and
mistreat the alien, denying them justice.
"I looked for a man among them who would build up the
wall and stand before me in the gap on behalf of the
land so I would not have to destroy it, but I found
none. So I will pour out my wrath on them and
consume them with my fiery anger, bringing down
on their own heads all they have done," declares the
Sovereign LORD.

Examples of the Lord testing his people to determine their faith or faithfulness

Gen 22:12 *God testing Abraham's faith regarding his son, Isaac*
"Do not lay a hand on the boy," he said. "Do not do anything
to him. Now I know that you fear God, because you
have not withheld from me your son, your only son."

Exod 16:4 *God testing the obedience of the Israelites in the desert*
Then the LORD said to Moses, "I will rain down bread
from heaven for you. The people are to go out each
day and gather enough for that day. In this way I
will test them and see whether they will follow my
instructions."

Deut 8:2 *Moses reminding the Israelites that God led them through the desert to test them*

> Remember how the LORD your God led you all the way in the desert these forty years, to humble you and to test you in order to know what was in your heart, whether or not you would keep his commands.

Deut 13:1-3 *Moses explaining that God allows false prophets to test his people*

> If a prophet, or one who foretells by dreams, appears among you and announces to you a miraculous sign or wonder, and if the sign or wonder of which he has spoken takes place, and he says, "Let us follow other gods" (gods you have not known) "and let us worship them," you must not listen to the words of that prophet or dreamer. The LORD your God is testing you to find out whether you love him with all your heart and with all your soul.

Judges 2:20 - 3:4 *The writer of Judges explaining why God had not removed the remaining nations after the death of Joshua*

> Therefore the LORD was very angry with Israel and said, "Because this nation has violated the covenant that I laid down for their forefathers and has not listened to me, I will no longer drive out before them any of the nations Joshua left when he died. I will use them to test Israel and see whether they will keep the way of the LORD and walk in it as their forefathers did." . . .
> These are the nations the LORD left to test all those Israelites who had not experienced any of the wars in Canaan . . . . They were left to test the Israelites to see whether they would obey the Lord's commands,

which he had given their forefathers through Moses.

2 Chron 32:31 *The Chronicler explaining events in the life of King Hezekiah*

But when envoys were sent by the rulers of Babylon to ask him about the miraculous sign that had occurred in the land, God left him to test him and to know everything that was in his heart.

Examples of the Lord asking non-rhetorical questions about the future

Num 14:11 *God discussing with Moses the Israelites response to the report of the 12 spies*

The LORD said to Moses, "How long will these people treat me with contempt? How long will they refuse to believe in me, in spite of all the miraculous signs I have performed among them?"

Hos 8:5 *God expressing frustration at Israel's spiritual adultery*

"Throw out your calf-idol, O Samaria! My anger burns against them. How long will they be incapable of purity?"

Examples of the Lord speaking of the future in terms of uncertainty

Exod 4:8-9 *God giving Moses instructions before sending him to free his people from Egypt*

Then the LORD said, "If they do not believe you or pay

attention to the first miraculous sign, they may believe the second. But if they do not believe these two signs or listen to you, take some water from the Nile and pour it on the dry ground. The water you take from the river will become blood on the ground."

Exod 13:17 *God expressing uncertainty about how the Israelites might respond to war*

When Pharaoh let the people go, God did not lead them on the road through the Philistine country, though that was shorter. For God said, "If they face war, they might change their minds and return to Egypt."

Jer 38:17-23 *Jeremiah predicting the final fall of Jerusalem*

Then Jeremiah said to Zedekiah, "This is what the LORD God Almighty, the God of Israel, says: 'If you surrender to the officers of the king of Babylon, your life will be spared and this city will not be burned down; you and your family will live. But if you will not surrender to the officers of the king of Babylon, this city will be handed over to the Babylonians and they will burn it down; you yourself will not escape from their hands.'"

King Zedekiah said to Jeremiah, "I am afraid of the Jews who have gone over to the Babylonians, for the Babylonians may hand me over to them and they will mistreat me."

"They will not hand you over," Jeremiah replied. "Obey the LORD by doing what I tell you. Then it will go well with you, and your life will be spared. But if you refuse to surrender, this is what the LORD has revealed to me: All the women left in the palace of the king of Judah will be brought out to the officials of the king of Babylon. Those women will say to you: 'They misled you and overcame you – those trusted friends of yours. Your feet are sunk in the mud; your friends have deserted you.' All your wives and children will be brought out to the Babylonians. You yourself will not escape from their hands but will be captured by the king of Babylon; and this city will be burned down."

Ezek 12:1-3 *God assigning Ezekiel a task without certainty the observers will understand*

The word of the LORD came to me: "Son of man, you are living among a rebellious people. They have eyes to see but do not see and ears to hear but do not hear, for they are a rebellious people. Therefore, son of man, pack your belongings for exile and in the daytime, as they watch, set out and go from where you are to another place. Perhaps they will understand, though they are a rebellious house."

Source: Greg Boyd http://reknew.org/2007/12/response-to-critics/#sthash.ZET9gXBi.dpuf, accessed 28 June 2016.

Appendix C
The missional God throughout Scripture

In Chapter 7, we saw that the glory of God is his perfect character, so God is gloried as his character is revealed. The mission of God, then, is to reveal his character. Initially it was done through creation, then through a chosen people, then later in his Son, and subsequently through us as we are conformed to the image of his Son – as the image of God that was given at creation and marred by the fall, is restored in us to a degree. God's desire is for people to see him as he is and want to fellowship with him because of who he is. For those who do fellowship with him, God has given the opportunity and ability to reflect him to others as he is, and by doing so, to attract them to him, or repel them from him. This process can be observed throughout Scripture, as the passages below demonstrate. The list is not exhaustive, but it does show the pattern.

The missional God in the Pentateuch

Gen 12:1-3 The LORD said to Abram . . . "I will bless those who bless you, and whoever curses you I will curse; and all peoples on earth will be blessed through you."

Gen 18:17-18 Then the LORD said, "Shall I hide from Abraham what I am about to do? Abraham will surely become a great and powerful nation, and all nations on earth will be blessed through him."

Gen 22:15-18 The angel of the LORD called to Abraham from heaven . . . "I will surely bless you and make your descendants as numerous as the stars in the sky and as the sand on the seashore . . . and through your offspring all nations on earth will be blessed, because you have obeyed me."

Gen 26:4 "I will make your descendants as numerous as the stars in the sky and will give them all these lands, and through your offspring all nations on earth will be blessed,"

Gen 28:14 "Your descendants will be like the dust of the earth, and you will spread out to the west and to the east, to the north and to the south. All peoples on earth will be blessed through you and your offspring."

Exod 12:37-38 [*The exodus*] The Israelites journeyed from Rameses to Succoth. There were about six hundred thousand men on foot, besides women and children. Many other people went up with them, as well as large droves of livestock, both flocks and herds.

Deut 28:10 [*Moses final instructions*] Then all the peoples on earth will see that you are called by the name of the LORD, and they will fear you.

The missional God in the History Books

Josh 4:24 [*The Lord dries up the Jordan River so the Israelites can cross*] "He did this so that all the peoples of the earth might know that the hand of the LORD is powerful and so that you might always fear the LORD your God."

1 Kings 4:34 Men of all nations came to listen to Solomon's wisdom, sent by all the kings of the world, who had heard of his wisdom.

1 Kings 8:41-43 (2 Chron 6:33) [*Solomon's prayer at the dedication of temple*] "As for the foreigner who does not belong to your people Israel but has come from a distant land because of your name – for men will hear of your great name and your mighty hand and your outstretched arm – when he comes and prays toward this temple, then hear from heaven, your dwelling place, and do whatever the foreigner asks of you, so that all the peoples of the earth may know your name and fear you, as do your own people Israel, and may know that this house I have built bears your Name."

1 Kings 8:59-60 [*Solomon blesses the people at the dedication of temple*] "And may these words of mine, which I have prayed before the LORD, be near to the LORD our God day and night, that he may uphold the cause of his servant and the cause of his people Israel according to each day's need, so that all the peoples of the earth may know that the LORD is God and that there is no other."

1 Chron 16:23-31 [*The psalm of David, sung as the ark of the covenant was brought from the house of Obed-Edom to Jerusalem*] Sing to the LORD, all the earth; proclaim his salvation day after day. Declare his glory among the nations, his marvelous deeds among all peoples . . . Ascribe to the LORD, O

families of nations, ascribe to the LORD glory
and strength, ascribe to the LORD the glory due
his name. Bring an offering and come before him;
worship the LORD in the splendor of his holiness.
Tremble before him, all the earth! . . . Let the
heavens rejoice, let the earth be glad; let them say
among the nations, "The LORD reigns!"

The missional God in the Psalms

Psalm 48:10 Like your name, O God, your praise reaches
to the ends of the earth; your right hand is filled
with righteousness.

Psalm 49:1 Hear this, all you peoples; listen, all who live
in this world,

Psalm 57 Be exalted, O God, above the heavens; let your
glory be over all the earth . . . I will praise you, O
Lord, among the nations; I will sing of you among
the peoples. For great is your love, reaching to the
heavens; your faithfulness reaches to the skies. Be
exalted, O God, above the heavens; let your glory be
over all the earth.

Psalm 66 Shout with joy to God, all the earth! . . . "All the
earth bows down to you; they sing praise to you,
they sing praise to your name." Come and see what
God has done, how awesome his works in man's
behalf! . . . He rules forever by his power, his eyes
watch the nations . . . Praise our God, O peoples, let
the sound of his praise be heard;

Psalm 67 May God be gracious to us and bless us and
make his face shine upon us, that your ways may be
known on earth, your salvation among all nations.
May the peoples praise you, O God; may all the

peoples praise you. May the nations be glad and sing for joy, for you rule the peoples justly and guide the nations of the earth. May the peoples praise you, O God; may all the peoples praise you. Then the land will yield its harvest, and God, our God, will bless us. God will bless us, and all the ends of the earth will fear him.

Psalm 72:11-17 All kings will bow down to him and all nations will serve him . . . May his name endure forever; may it continue as long as the sun. All nations will be blessed through him, and they will call him blessed.

Psalm 77:14 You are the God who performs miracles; you display your power among the peoples.

Psalm 87:6 The LORD will write in the register of the peoples: "This one was born in Zion."

Psalm 96 Declare his glory among the nations, his marvelous deeds among all peoples . . . Say among the nations, "The LORD reigns." The world is firmly established, it cannot be moved; he will judge the peoples with equity . . . they will sing before the LORD, for he comes, he comes to judge the earth. He will judge the world in righteousness and the peoples in his truth.

Psalm 97:6 The heavens proclaim his righteousness, and all the peoples see his glory.

Psalm 102:21-22 So the name of the LORD will be declared in Zion and his praise in Jerusalem when the peoples and the kingdoms assemble to worship the LORD.

Psalm 108:3-5 I will praise you, O LORD, among the nations; I will sing of you among the peoples. For great is your love, higher than the heavens; your faithfulness reaches to the skies. Be exalted, O God, above the heavens, and let your glory be over all the earth.

Psalm 117 Praise the LORD, all you nations; extol him, all you peoples. For great is his love toward us, and the faithfulness of the LORD endures forever. Praise the LORD.

Psalm 145:9-13 The LORD is good to all; he has compassion on all he has made. All you have made will praise you, O LORD; your saints will extol you. They will tell of the glory of your kingdom and speak of your might, so that all men may know of your mighty acts and the glorious splendor of your kingdom. Your kingdom is an everlasting kingdom, and your dominion endures through all generations. The LORD is faithful to all his promises and loving toward all he has made.

Psalm 148 Praise the LORD. Praise the LORD from the heavens, praise him in the heights above. Praise him, all his angels, praise him, all his heavenly hosts . . . Praise the LORD from the earth . . . kings of the earth and all nations, you princes and all rulers on earth . . . Let them praise the name of the LORD, for his name alone is exalted; his splendor is above the earth and the heavens.

The missional God in the Prophets
Isa 2:2-4 In the last days the mountain of the Lord's temple will be established as chief among the mountains; it will be raised above the hills, and all nations will stream to it. Many peoples will come

APPENDIX C THE MISSIONAL GOD THROUGHOUT SCRIPTURE

and say, "Come, let us go up to the mountain of the
LORD, to the house of the God of Jacob. He will
teach us his ways, so that we may walk in his paths."
The law will go out from Zion, the word of the
LORD from Jerusalem. He will judge between the
nations and will settle disputes for many peoples.
They will beat their swords into plowshares and
their spears into pruning hooks. Nation will not
take up sword against nation, nor will they train for
war anymore.

Isa 11 A shoot will come up from the stump of Jesse . . .
with justice he will give decisions for the poor of the
earth . . . In that day the Root of Jesse will stand as a
banner for the peoples; the nations will rally to him,
and his place of rest will be glorious.

Isa 25:6-7 On this mountain the LORD Almighty will
prepare a feast of rich food for all peoples, a banquet
of aged wine – the best of meats and the finest of
wines. On this mountain he will destroy the shroud
that enfolds all peoples, the sheet that covers all
nations;

Isa 34:1 Come near, you nations, and listen; pay
attention, you peoples! Let the earth hear, and all
that is in it, the world, and all that comes out of it!

Isa 56:6-8 "And foreigners who bind themselves to the
LORD to serve him, to love the name of the LORD,
and to worship him, all who keep the Sabbath
without desecrating it and who hold fast to my
covenant – these I will bring to my holy mountain
and give them joy in my house of prayer. Their
burnt offerings and sacrifices will be accepted on my
altar; for my house will be called a house of prayer

for all nations." The Sovereign LORD declares – he
who gathers the exiles of Israel: "I will gather still
others to them besides those already gathered."

Isa 61:11 For as the soil makes the sprout come up and
a garden causes seeds to grow, so the Sovereign
LORD will make righteousness and praise spring up
before all nations.

Isa 66:18 "And I, because of their actions and their
imaginations, am about to come and gather all
nations and tongues, and they will come and see my
glory."

Jer 3:17 At that time they will call Jerusalem The
Throne of the LORD, and all nations will gather
in Jerusalem to honor the name of the LORD. No
longer will they follow the stubbornness of their evil
hearts.

Jer 33:9 "Then this city will bring me renown, joy, praise
and honor before all nations on earth that hear of
all the good things I do for it; and they will be in
awe and will tremble at the abundant prosperity and
peace I provide for it."

Lam 1:18 "The LORD is righteous, yet I rebelled against
his command. Listen, all you peoples; look upon my
suffering. My young men and maidens have gone
into exile."

Dan 4:1-3, 17 [*King Nebuchadnezzar, following his period
of insanity*] King Nebuchadnezzar, To the peoples,
nations and men of every language, who live in
all the world: May you prosper greatly! It is my
pleasure to tell you about the miraculous signs and
wonders that the Most High God has performed
for me. How great are his signs, how mighty his

wonders! His kingdom is an eternal kingdom; his
dominion endures from generation to generation.
... The decision is announced by messengers, the
holy ones declare the verdict, so that the living
may know that the Most High is sovereign over
the kingdoms of men and gives them to anyone he
wishes and sets over them the lowliest of men.

Dan 6:25-27 [*King Darius, following the episode with
Daniel in the lions' den*] Then King Darius wrote to
all the peoples, nations and men of every language
throughout the land: "May you prosper greatly! I
issue a decree that in every part of my kingdom
people must fear and reverence the God of Daniel.
For he is the living God and he endures forever; his
kingdom will not be destroyed, his dominion will
never end. He rescues and he saves; he performs
signs and wonders in the heavens and on the earth.
He has rescued Daniel from the power of the lions."

Dan 7:13-14 [*Daniel's vision of the kingdoms of the earth,
from his own time until the end*] In my vision at
night I looked, and there before me was one like a
son of man, coming with the clouds of heaven. He
approached the Ancient of Days and was led into
his presence. He was given authority, glory and
sovereign power; all peoples, nations and men of
every language worshiped him. His dominion is an
everlasting dominion that will not pass away, and
his kingdom is one that will never be destroyed.

Amos 9:11-12 "In that day I will restore David's fallen
tent. I will repair its broken places, restore its
ruins, and build it as it used to be, so that they may
possess the remnant of Edom and all the nations

that bear my name," declares the LORD, who will do these things.

Mic 1:1-2 The word of the LORD that came to Micah of Moresheth during the reigns of Jotham, Ahaz and Hezekiah, kings of Judah – the vision he saw concerning Samaria and Jerusalem. Hear, O peoples, all of you, listen, O earth and all who are in it, that the Sovereign LORD may witness against you, the Lord from his holy temple.

Mic 4:1-2 In the last days the mountain of the Lord's temple will be established as chief among the mountains; it will be raised above the hills, and peoples will stream to it. Many nations will come and say, "Come, let us go up to the mountain of the LORD, to the house of the God of Jacob. He will teach us his ways, so that we may walk in his paths." The law will go out from Zion, the word of the LORD from Jerusalem.

Zeph 3:9 Then will I purify the lips of the peoples, that all of them may call on the name of the LORD and serve him shoulder to shoulder.

Zeph 3:20 "At that time I will gather you; at that time I will bring you home. I will give you honor and praise among all the peoples of the earth when I restore your fortunes before your very eyes," says the LORD.

Hag 2:7 "I will shake all nations, and the desired of all nations will come, and I will fill this house with glory," says the LORD Almighty.

Zech 8:20-13 This is what the LORD Almighty says: "Many peoples and the inhabitants of many cities will yet come, and the inhabitants of one city will go to another and say, 'Let us go at once to entreat the LORD and seek the LORD Almighty. I myself am going.' And many peoples and powerful nations will come to Jerusalem to seek the LORD Almighty and to entreat him." This is what the LORD Almighty says: "In those days ten men from all languages and nations will take firm hold of one Jew by the hem of his robe and say, 'Let us go with you, because we have heard that God is with you.'"

The missional God in the Gospels
In Matthew, "all nations" is one of the major themes
Matt 1:5 [*Jesus genealogy included Gentiles.*] Salmon the father of Boaz, whose mother was Rahab, Boaz the father of Obed, whose mother was Ruth, Obed the father of Jesse,
Matt 2:1 [*The Magi were Gentiles.*] After Jesus was born in Bethlehem in Judea, during the time of King Herod, Magi from the east came to Jerusalem
Matt 4:13-16 Leaving Nazareth, he went and lived in Capernaum, to fulfill what was said through the prophet Isaiah: the Gentiles – the people living in darkness have seen a great light (quoting Isa 9:1-2).
Matt 4:24-25 News about him spread all over Syria, and people brought to him all who were ill . . . and he healed them. Large crowds from Galilee, the Decapolis, Jerusalem, Judea and the region across the Jordan followed him.
Matt 8:5-13 When Jesus had entered Capernaum, a centurion came to him, asking for help. . . . Jesus . . . said to those following him, "I tell you the truth, I have not found anyone in Israel with such great

faith." . . . Then Jesus said to the centurion, "Go! It will be done just as you believed it would." And his servant was healed at that very hour.

Matt 12:18, 21 "Here is my servant whom I have chosen, the one I love, in whom I delight; I will put my Spirit on him, and he will proclaim justice to the nations. . . In his name the nations will put their hope."

Matt 13:38 The field is the world, and the good seed stands for the sons of the kingdom. The weeds are the sons of the evil one,

Matt 15:22-28   [*Jesus listens to the Canaanite woman, then heals her daughter.*] . . . Then Jesus answered, "Woman, you have great faith! Your request is granted." And her daughter was healed from that very hour.

Matt 15:29-38 [*Jesus ministers to people in the Decapolis, then feeds 4000. The location is made very clear in Mark 7:31ff.*] Great crowds came to him. . . and he healed them . . . And they praised the God is Israel . . . They all ate and were satisfied. . . . The number of those who ate was four thousand, besides women and children.

Matt 21:12-13 (Mark 11:15-17, Luke 19:46) Jesus entered the temple area and drove out all who were buying and selling there. He overturned the tables of the money changers and the benches of those selling doves. "It is written," he said to them, "'My house will be called a house of prayer,' but you are making it a 'den of robbers.'"

Matt 21:43 "Therefore I tell you that the kingdom of God will be taken away from you and given to a people who will produce its fruit."

Matt 24:9-14 "Then you will be handed over to be persecuted and put to death, and you will be hated by all nations because of me. . . And this gospel of the kingdom will be preached in the whole world as a testimony to all nations, and then the end will come."

Matt 25:31-32 "When the Son of Man comes in his glory, and all the angels with him, he will sit on his throne in heavenly glory. All the nations will be gathered before him, and he will separate the people one from another as a shepherd separates the sheep from the goats."

Matt 28:18-20 Then Jesus came to them and said, "All authority in heaven and on earth has been given to me. Therefore go and make disciples of all nations, baptizing them in the name of the Father and of the Son and of the Holy Spirit, and teaching them to obey everything I have commanded you. And surely I am with you always, to the very end of the age."

Mark 13:9-10 "You must be on your guard. You will be handed over to the local councils and flogged in the synagogues. On account of me you will stand before governors and kings as witnesses to them. And the gospel must first be preached to all nations."

Luke 4:25-27 [*Jesus announcing the start of him ministry in his hometown*] "I assure you that there were many widows in Israel in Elijah's time, when the sky was shut for three and a half years and there was a severe famine throughout the land. Yet Elijah was not sent to any of them, but to a widow in Zarephath in the region of Sidon. And there were many in Israel

with leprosy in the time of Elisha the prophet, yet
not one of them was cleansed – only Naaman the
Syrian."

Luke 24:45-47 [*Jesus on the road to Emmaus*] Then he
opened their minds so they could understand the
Scriptures. He told them, "This is what is written:
The Christ will suffer and rise from the dead on
the third day, and repentance and forgiveness of
sins will be preached in his name to all nations,
beginning at Jerusalem."

The missional God in Acts

Acts 1:6-8 [*Just before Jesus' ascension*] So when they met
together, they asked him, "Lord, are you at this time
going to restore the kingdom to Israel?" He said to
them: "It is not for you to know the times or dates
the Father has set by his own authority. But you will
receive power when the Holy Spirit comes on you;
and you will be my witnesses in Jerusalem, and in
all Judea and Samaria, and to the ends of the earth."

Acts 2 [*The Day of Pentecost, the giving of the Holy Spirit*]
Acts 2:4-6 All of them were filled with the Holy
Spirit and began to speak in other tongues as the
Spirit enabled them. Now there were staying in
Jerusalem God-fearing Jews from every nation
under heaven. When they heard this sound, a crowd
came together in bewilderment, because each
one heard them speaking in his own language. . .
Acts 2:14-17 Then Peter . . . addressed the crowd:
"Fellow Jews and all of you who live in Jerusalem,
let me explain this to you; listen carefully to what
I say. These men are not drunk, as you suppose.

It's only nine in the morning! No, this is what was spoken by the prophet Joel: 'In the last days, God says, I will pour out my Spirit on all people.'"

Acts 3 [*Peter and John healing the beggar at the temple*] Acts 3:12 Peter said to them: "Men of Israel, why does this surprise you? Why do you stare at us as if by our own power or godliness we had made this man walk? . . . Acts 3:22-25 For Moses said, 'The Lord your God will raise up for you a prophet like me from among your own people; you must listen to everything he tells you. Anyone who does not listen to him will be completely cut off from among his people.' Indeed, all the prophets from Samuel on, as many as have spoken, have foretold these days. And you are heirs of the prophets and of the covenant God made with your fathers. He said to Abraham, 'Through your offspring all peoples on earth will be blessed.'"

Acts 8:2-14 Godly men buried Stephen and mourned deeply for him. But Saul began to destroy the church. Going from house to house, he dragged off men and women and put them in prison. Those who had been scattered preached the word wherever they went. Philip went down to a city in Samaria and proclaimed the Christ there. . . when they believed Philip as he preached the good news of the kingdom of God and the name of Jesus Christ, they were baptized, both men and women… When the apostles in Jerusalem heard that Samaria had accepted the word of God, they sent Peter and John to them.

Acts 8:26-40 Now an angel of the Lord said to Philip, "Go

south to the road – the desert road – that goes down from Jerusalem to Gaza." So he started out, and on his way he met an Ethiopian eunuch, an important official in charge of all the treasury of Candace, queen of the Ethiopian . . . As they traveled along the road, they came to some water and the eunuch said, "Look, here is water. Why shouldn't I be baptized?" . . . When they came up out of the water, the Spirit of the Lord suddenly took Philip away, and the eunuch did not see him again, but went on his way rejoicing. Philip, however, appeared at Azotus and traveled about, preaching the gospel in all the towns until he reached Caesarea.

Acts 9:15 [*Following Saul's Damascus road experience*] But the Lord said to Ananias, "Go! This man is my chosen instrument to carry my name before the Gentiles and their kings and before the people of Israel."

Acts 10 [*The story of Cornelius and Peter*] Acts 10:45 The circumcised believers who had come with Peter were astonished that the gift of the Holy Spirit had been poured out even on the Gentiles.

Acts 11 [*Peter tells the Jerusalem church the story of Cornelius*] Acts 11:18-22 When they heard this, they had no further objections and praised God, saying, "So then, God has granted even the Gentiles repentance unto life." Now those who had been scattered by the persecution in connection with Stephen traveled as far as Phoenicia, Cyprus and Antioch, telling the message only to Jews. Some of them, however, men from Cyprus and Cyrene, went to Antioch and began to speak to Greeks also,

telling them the good news about the Lord Jesus.
The Lord's hand was with them, and a great number
of people believed and turned to the Lord. News of
this reached the ears of the church at Jerusalem, and
they sent Barnabas to Antioch.

Acts 12:24 But the word of God continued to increase
and spread.

Acts 13 [*Paul's first missionary journey*] Acts 13:1-4 In
the church at Antioch there were prophets and
teachers . . . While they were worshiping the Lord
and fasting, the Holy Spirit said, "Set apart for me
Barnabas and Saul for the work to which I have
called them." So after they had fasted and prayed,
they placed their hands on them and sent them
off. The two of them, sent on their way by the Holy
Spirit, went down to Seleucia and sailed from there
to Cyprus.

Acts 13 [*Paul and Barnabas in Pisidian Antioch*] Acts
13:47-49 "For this is what the Lord has commanded
us: 'I have made you a light for the Gentiles, that
you may bring salvation to the ends of the earth.'"
When the Gentiles heard this, they were glad and
honored the word of the Lord; and . . . The word of
the Lord spread through the whole region.

Acts 14 [*Paul and Barnabas at Lystra*] Acts 14:15-17 ". . .
We are bringing you good news, telling you to turn
from these worthless things to the living God, who
made heaven and earth and sea and everything in
them. In the past, he let all nations go their own
way. Yet he has not left himself without testimony:
He has shown kindness by giving you rain from
heaven and crops in their seasons; he provides you

with plenty of food and fills your hearts with joy."

Acts 14 [*Paul and Barnabas at Derbe, then their return trip to Antioch*] Acts 14:20-27 . . . The next day he and Barnabas left for Derbe. They preached the good news in that city and won a large number of disciples. Then they returned [through the other cities they had visited]. . . strengthening the disciples and encouraging them to remain true to the faith . . . [they] appointed elders for them in each church and, with prayer and fasting, committed them to the Lord, in whom they had put their trust . . . they sailed back to Antioch . . . On arriving there, they gathered the church together and reported all that God had done through them and how he had opened the door of faith to the Gentiles.

Acts 15 [*Paul and Barnabas defend their work to the church leaders in Jerusalem*] Acts 15:12-18 The whole assembly became silent as they listened to Barnabas and Paul telling about the miraculous signs and wonders God had done among the Gentiles through them. When they finished, James spoke up: "Brothers, listen to me. Simon has described to us how God at first showed his concern by taking from the Gentiles a people for himself. The words of the prophets are in agreement with this, as it is written: 'After this I will return and rebuild David's fallen tent. Its ruins I will rebuild, and I will restore it, that the remnant of men may seek the Lord, and all the Gentiles who bear my name, says the Lord, who does these things' that have been known for ages."

Acts 16 [*Paul takes Silas and starts his second missionary journey*] Acts 16:9-10 [At Troas] During the night Paul had a vision of a man of Macedonia standing and begging him, "Come over to Macedonia and help us." After Paul had seen the vision, we got ready at once to leave for Macedonia, concluding that God had called us to preach the gospel to them.

Acts 17 [*Paul and Silas at Thessalonica, then Berea and Athens*] Acts 17:11-12 Now the Bereans were of more noble character than the Thessalonians, for they received the message with great eagerness and examined the Scriptures every day to see if what Paul said was true. Many of the Jews believed, as did also a number of prominent Greek women and many Greek men. [Paul speaking at Athens] Acts 17:26-34 "From one man he made every nation of men, that they should inhabit the whole earth; and he determined the times set for them and the exact places where they should live. God did this so that men would seek him and perhaps reach out for him and find him, though he is not far from each one of us. . . . In the past God overlooked such ignorance, but now he commands all people everywhere to repent . . ."

Acts 18 [*Paul at Corinth*] Acts 18:6-10 But when the Jews opposed Paul . . . he said to them, " . . . From now on I will go to the Gentiles." . . . Crispus, the synagogue ruler, and his entire household believed in the Lord; and many of the Corinthians who heard him believed and were baptized. One night the Lord spoke to Paul in a vision: "Do not be afraid; keep on speaking, do not be silent. For I am with you, and no one is going to attack and harm you, because I have many people in this city." [*Paul starts his third missionary journey*] Acts 18:23 After spending some time in Antioch, Paul set out from there and traveled from place to place throughout the region of Galatia and Phrygia, strengthening all the disciples.

Acts 19 [*Paul at Ephesus*] Acts 19:8-10 Paul entered the synagogue and spoke boldly there for three months, arguing persuasively about the kingdom of God. But some of them became obstinate; they refused to believe and publicly maligned the Way. So Paul left them. He took the disciples with him and had discussions daily in the lecture hall of Tyrannus. This went on for two years, so that all the Jews and Greeks who lived in the province of Asia heard the word of the Lord.

Acts 20 [*Paul meets with the Ephesian elders at Miletus*] Acts 20:20-21 "You know that I have not hesitated to preach anything that would be helpful to you but have taught you publicly and from house to house. I have declared to both Jews and Greeks that they must turn to God in repentance and have faith in our Lord Jesus."

Acts 21 [*Paul at Jerusalem*] Acts 21:17-20 When we arrived at Jerusalem, the brothers received us warmly. The next day Paul and the rest of us went to see James, and all the elders were present. Paul greeted them and reported in detail what God had done among the Gentiles through his ministry. When they heard this, they praised God. Then they said to Paul: "You see, brother, how many thousands of Jews have believed . . ."

Acts 22 [*Paul talks to the murderous mob of Jews in Jerusalem*] Acts 22:21-22 "Then the Lord said to me, 'Go; I will send you far away to the Gentiles.'" The crowd listened to Paul until he said this. Then they raised their voices and shouted, "Rid the earth of him! He's not fit to live!"

Acts 23:11 [*Paul in protective custody in Jerusalem*] The following night the Lord stood near Paul and said, "Take courage! As you have testified about me in Jerusalem, so you must also testify in Rome."

Acts 26 [*Paul testifies before King Agrippa*] Acts 26:15-23 "Then I asked, 'Who are you, Lord?' 'I am Jesus, whom you are persecuting,' the Lord replied. 'Now get up and stand on your feet. I have appeared to you to appoint you as a servant and as a witness of what you have seen of me and what I will show you. I will rescue you from your own people and from the Gentiles. I am sending you to them to open their eyes and turn them from darkness to light, and from the power of Satan to God, so that they may receive forgiveness of sins and a place among those who are sanctified by faith in me.' So then, King Agrippa, I was not disobedient to the vision from heaven. First to those in Damascus, then to those in Jerusalem and in all Judea, and to the Gentiles also, I preached that they should repent and turn to God and prove their repentance by their deeds. . . . I am saying nothing beyond what the prophets and Moses said would happen – that the Christ would suffer and, as the first to rise from the dead, would proclaim light to his own people and to the Gentiles."

Acts 28 [*Paul at Rome awaiting trial, speaks to the assembled Jewish leaders*] Acts 28:28-31 "Therefore I want you to know that God's salvation has been sent to the Gentiles, and they will listen!" For two whole years Paul stayed there in his own rented house and welcomed all who came to see him. Boldly and without hindrance he preached the kingdom of God and taught about the Lord Jesus Christ.

The missional God in the Epistles

Rom 1:16 I am not ashamed of the gospel, because it is the power of God for the salvation of everyone who believes: first for the Jew, then for the Gentile.

Rom 3:29-30 Is God the God of Jews only? Is he not the God of Gentiles too? Yes, of Gentiles too, since there is only one God, who will justify the circumcised by faith and the uncircumcised through that same faith.

Rom 4:16-18 Therefore, the promise comes by faith, so that it may be by grace and may be guaranteed to all Abraham's offspring – not only to those who are of the law but also to those who are of the faith of Abraham. He is the father of us all. As it is written: "I have made you a father of many nations." He is our father in the sight of God, in whom he believed – the God who gives life to the dead and calls things that are not as though they were. Against all hope, Abraham in hope believed and so became the father of many nations, just as it had been said to him, "So shall your offspring be."

Rom 5:18 Consequently, just as the result of one trespass was condemnation for all men, so also the result of one act of righteousness was justification that brings life for all men.

Rom 10:11-13 As the Scripture says, "Anyone who trusts in him will never be put to shame." For there is no difference between Jew and Gentile – the same Lord is Lord of all and richly blesses all who call on him, for, "Everyone who calls on the name of the Lord will be saved."

Rom 10:18-20 But I ask: Did they not hear? Of course they did: "Their voice has gone out into all the earth, their words to the ends of the world." Again I ask: Did Israel not understand? First, Moses says, "I will make you envious by those who are not a nation; I will make you angry by a nation that has no understanding." And Isaiah boldly says, "I was found by those who did not seek me; I revealed myself to those who did not ask for me."

Rom 11:11-12 Again I ask: Did they stumble so as to fall beyond recovery? Not at all! Rather, because of their transgression, salvation has come to the Gentiles to make Israel envious. But if their transgression means riches for the world, and their loss means riches for the Gentiles, how much greater riches will their fullness bring!

Rom 15:12-16 And again, Isaiah says, "The Root of Jesse will spring up, one who will arise to rule over the nations; the Gentiles will hope in him." . . . I have written you quite boldly on some points, as if to remind you of them again, because of the grace God gave me to be a minister of Christ Jesus to the Gentiles with the priestly duty of proclaiming the gospel of God, so that the Gentiles might become

an offering acceptable to God, sanctified by the
Holy Spirit.

Rom 16:25-27 Now to him who is able to establish you
by my gospel and the proclamation of Jesus Christ,
according to the revelation of the mystery hidden
for long ages past, but now revealed and made
known through the prophetic writings by the
command of the eternal God, so that all nations
might believe and obey him – to the only wise God
be glory forever through Jesus Christ! Amen.

2 Cor 5:14 - 6:2 For Christ's love compels us, because we
are convinced that one died for all, and therefore
all died. And he died for all, that those who live
should no longer live for themselves but for him
who died for them and was raised again . . . and
gave us the ministry of reconciliation: that God
was reconciling the world to himself in Christ
. . . And he has committed to us the message
of reconciliation. We are therefore Christ's
ambassadors, as though God were making his
appeal through us. "We implore you on Christ's
behalf: Be reconciled to God."

Gal 3:8 The Scripture foresaw that God would justify
the Gentiles by faith, and announced the gospel in
advance to Abraham: "All nations will be blessed
through you."

Eph 2:14-16 For he himself is our peace, who has made
the two one and has destroyed the barrier, the
dividing wall of hostility, by abolishing in his flesh
the law with its commandments and regulations.
His purpose was to create in himself one new man
out of the two, thus making peace, and in this one

body to reconcile both of them to God through the cross, by which he put to death their hostility.

Col 1:19-20 For God was pleased to have all his fullness dwell in him, and through him to reconcile to himself all things, whether things on earth or things in heaven, by making peace through his blood, shed on the cross.

1 Tim 2:3-4 This is good, and pleases God our Savior, who wants all men to be saved and to come to a knowledge of the truth.

1 Tim 3:16 Beyond all question, the mystery of godliness is great: He appeared in a body, was vindicated by the Spirit, was seen by angels, was preached among the nations, was believed on in the world, was taken up in glory.

James 1:1 James, a servant of God and of the Lord Jesus Christ, To the twelve tribes scattered among the nations: Greetings.

2 Pet 3:9 The Lord is not slow in keeping his promise, as some understand slowness. He is patient with you, not wanting anyone to perish, but everyone to come to repentance.

1 John 2:2: He is the atoning sacrifice for our sins, and not only for ours but also for the sins of the whole world.

The nations in the Revelation

Rev 2:26-29 To him who overcomes and does my will to the end, I will give authority over the nations – 'He will rule them with an iron scepter; he will dash them to pieces like pottery' – just as I have received authority from my Father. I will also give him the morning star. He who has an ear, let him hear what the Spirit says to the churches.

Rev 15:2-4 And I saw what looked like a sea of glass mixed with fire and, standing beside the sea, those who had been victorious over the beast and his image and over the number of his name. They held harps given them by God and sang the song of Moses the servant of God and the song of the Lamb: "Great and marvelous are your deeds, Lord God Almighty. Just and true are your ways, King of the ages. Who will not fear you, O Lord, and bring glory to your name? For you alone are holy. All nations will come and worship before you, for your righteous acts have been revealed."

Rev 21:23-26 The city does not need the sun or the moon to shine on it, for the glory of God gives it light, and the Lamb is its lamp. The nations will walk by its light, and the kings of the earth will bring their splendor into it. On no day will its gates ever be shut, for there will be no night there. The glory and honor of the nations will be brought into it.

Rev 22:1-2 Then the angel showed me the river of the water of life, as clear as crystal, flowing from the throne of God and of the Lamb down the middle of the great street of the city. On each side of the river stood the tree of life, bearing twelve crops of fruit, yielding its fruit every month. And the leaves of the tree are for the healing of the nations.

Appendix D
Representative Views on Predestination of Major Christian Churches

Below is a brief comparison of the basic beliefs on predestination of the larger Christian denominations.

To begin with, it should be noted that the larger and more centralized a church system is, the more likely that it will have established, written doctrines and policies. Even so, within all major Churches, there will be theologians and adherents who differ on almost all issues, and predestination is no exception. As a result, the generalizations given below are an attempt to reflect the authorized perspectives, even though they may not reflect the views of all of a particular Church's leaders or devout adherents.

For some, it may be helpful to define a few terms that may appear in the comparison below. One is *Arminianism*. It is similar to Calvinism in that it is a form of Protestant Reformed theology from roughly the same time period, named after its primary early advocate, the Dutch professor of theology at the University of Leiden, Jacobus Arminius (1560-1609). Arminianism is commonly viewed as the opposite of Calvinism, although that is a serious overstatement.[1] The differences in the two veins of theology are enough that countless books have been written on the subject, but the main difference is that Calvinism essentially removes human free will, and Arminianism retains it. So both teach predestination, but Calvin taught that salvation was unconditional, and Arminius taught that it was conditional, "based on God's foreknowledge of who will freely respond to God's gracious offer of salvation and the prevenient enablement to accept it."[2]

Another term that is important in comparing different views, is *prevenient grace*. It was briefly introduced near the end of Chapter 4, and dealt with in more detail in Chapter 7. Like the word *antecedent*, *prevenient* simply means to precede something in time or sequence. Theologically, it is divine grace that precedes human decision. Both Catholics and Arminians use the term, and the concept, to describe how they understand the grace of God to work in salvation, preceding the human decision, and enabling the decision to be made, but not forcing it.

Two other related terms are *monergism* and *synergism*. Basically, the word *synergy* is the combination of two Greek words, *sun* (together) and *ergon* (work), so synergy (Gr. "working together") is collaboration that produces a result greater than could be achieved otherwise. *Synergism*, theologically, is the idea that the grace of God and the free will of humans work together to produce salvation. Pelagianism and semi-Pelagianism are two forms of synergism which essentially eliminate the need for God's enabling grace in salvation, and both have been deemed heretical for centuries. *Monergism* is the opposite of synergism. It is the combination of *mono* (one) and *ergon* (work), so theologically, *monergism* is the idea that salvation is accomplished entirely by God, independent of human response or cooperation. Essentially, Calvinists, some Lutherans, and Anglicans teach monergism (officially if not in practice), and most other Churches teach some form of synergism. With that foundation, let's briefly compare the basic beliefs of the larger Christian denominations, keeping in mind that within them are various divisions and splinters that have broken off over the years over just the kind of theological beliefs we are considering. The order in which the Churches appear is generally related to the age of the individual Church, rather than size or any other factor.

Eastern Orthodoxy – Predestination is related to the foreknowledge of God. God foresees how a person will act, and makes his decision accordingly. Divine determination depends on the life of a person; the life of the person does not depend on divine determination. [3]

Roman Catholics – Since salvation is offered to all, it must be made concretely available to all.[4] Since only those who die in the state of justification or sanctifying grace will be in heaven, all those and only those are the predestined.[5] God predestines no one to go to hell.[6] When God established his eternal plan of predestination, he included in it each person's free response to his grace.[7]

Lutherans – The eternal decree of election or predestination is that God, before the foundation of the world, chose certain people for everlasting life; not based on any good quality or act of the elect, but based solely on God's grace. The Bible does not teach an election of wrath for those who are lost; God earnestly desires the salvation of all; the lost are lost by their own fault. The Bible does not attempt to harmonize the doctrine of universal grace and the doctrines of election and salvation by grace alone.[8]

Church of England, Anglicans, Episcopalians – Officially, human free will is dependent on the prevenient grace of God. Scripture is clear that God predestines some for salvation, but there is nothing in Scripture about God fashioning or making others for damnation. He elects some, but his promises are made to all. This mystery is allowed to stand. The core teaching on predestination is that God chose his elect long before they were born and thus irrespective of anything they may do or not do. His election is gratuitous, completely free, and unaffected by human choices.[9]

In practice, "Because of its gradual evolution as a 'middle way' between Protestant and Catholic extremes, Anglicanism has long encompassed both Calvinist and Arminian perspectives on predestination, with the latter predominating since the Restoration in 1660. To its New England Puritan opponents, Anglicanism was virtually synonymous with Arminianism."[10]

Methodists – "John Wesley particularly identified his understanding of salvation with the theology and writings of the seventeenth century Dutch theologian, Jacob Arminius,"[11] although Methodists typically have minimal focus on predestination, including the conditional election of Arminius. Officially, justification is by faith, not from works or merit, and based on the prevenient grace of God,[12] but generally, the Methodist position is "somewhere in the middle" between predestination and complete personal responsibility, "that our gracious God desires the salvation of all and invites us to freely accept God's grace in our lives."[13]

Baptists – Typically Arminian, but with a small minority of Calvinists. "…the majority of Southern Baptists do not embrace Calvinism,"[14] although there are notable and vocal exceptions. Southern Baptists are by far the largest Baptist denomination, and their position is representative of most other Baptists. There are Reformed Baptist denominations, but their numbers are miniscule in relation to the total number of Baptists worldwide.[15]

Reformed Churches, Presbyterians, Congregationalists – Many are staunchly Calvinist, although some churches which are not Calvinistic call themselves Reformed.[16]

Charismatic Churches, Pentecostals, Assemblies of God – Typically anti-predestination. "Election is always said to be according to

God's Foreknowledge . . . Those who were chosen were those who were in Christ . . . How did they get there? Through faith in his dear Son."[17]

Endnotes

[1] Roger E. Olson, *Arminian Theology: Myths and Realities* (Downers Grove, IL: InterVarsity Press, 2006), 44.

[2] Olson, *Arminian Theology*, 19.

[3] St. Theophan the Recluse, *An Explanation of Certain Texts of Holy Scripture*, as quoted in Johanna Manley's *The Bible and the Holy Fathers for Orthodox: Daily Scripture Readings and Commentary for Orthodox Christians* (reprint Yonkers, NY: St. Vladimir's Seminary Press, 2011), 609.

[4] John Paul II, encyclical *Redemptoris Missio*, Chapter 1, Section 10, 7 Dec 1990. http://w2.vatican.va/content/john-paul-ii/en/encyclicals/documents/hf_jp-ii_enc_07121990_redemptoris-missio.html, accessed 1 Sep 2016.

[5] Catholic Encyclopedia, entry on Predestination. http://www.newadvent.org/cathen/12378a.htm, accessed 1 Sep 2016.

[6] Catechism of the Catholic Church, Section 1037. http://www.vatican.va/archive/ENG0015/_P2O.HTM, accessed 1 Sep 2016.

[7] Catechism of the Catholic Church, Section 600. http://www.vatican.va/archive/ENG0015/__P1O.HTM, accessed 1 Sep 2016.

[8] Christian Cyclopedia, "Predestination," The Lutheran Church, Missouri Synod, http://cyclopedia.lcms.org/display.asp?t1=p&word=PREDESTINATION, accessed 1 Sep 2016.

[9] The Thirty-Nine Articles of Religion, Art. X, Of Free Will, and XVII, Of Predestination and Election, 12 Sep 1801. http://anglicansonline.org/basics/thirty-nine_articles.html, accessed 1 Sep 2016; http://www.churchsociety.org/issues_new/doctrine/39a/iss_doctrine_39A_Arts09-14.asp, accessed 1 Sep 2016; http://www.churchsociety.org/issues_new/doctrine/39a/iss_doctrine_39A_Arts15-18.asp, accessed 1 Sep 2016; Jonathan Mitchican, "The Anglican View of Predestination," The Conciliar Anglican website, https://conciliaranglican.com/2011/12/09/sweet-pleasant-and-unspeakable-comfort-the-anglican-view-of-predestination-part-iii/, accessed 1 Sep 2016;

[10] Peter J. Thuesen, *Predestination: The American Career of a Contentious Doctrine* (New York: Oxford University Press, 2009), 219-220.

[11] http://www.umc.org/what-we-believe/do-united-methodists-believe-once-saved-always-saved, accessed 2 Sep 2016.

[12] The Articles of Religion of the Methodist Church, Art. VIII, Free Will and IX, Justification, http://www.umc.org/what-we-believe/the-articles-of-religion-of-the-methodist-church, accessed 2 Sep 2016.

[13] United Methodist Church News and Media blog, http://www.umc.org/news-and-media/blogs-commentaries/post/listen-to-god-and-mom-as-you-navigate-through-life, accessed 2 Sep 2016.

14 Eric Hankins, "A Statement of the Traditional Southern Baptist Understanding of God's Plan of Salvation," http://sbctoday.com/wp-content/uploads/2012/06/A-Statement-of-Traditional-Southern-Baptist-Soteriology-SBC-Today.pdf, accessed 2 Sep 2016.

15 Robert E. Johnson, *A Global Introduction to Baptist Churches* (Cambridge University Press, 2010), 358.

16 Olson, *Arminian Theology,* 16.

17 Guy P. Duffield and Nathaniel M. Van Cleave, *Foundations of Pentecostal Theology* (Los Angeles, CA: Foursquare Media, 1983), 207.

Bibliography

Ackroyd, Peter R., and C.F. Evans, eds. *The Cambridge History of the Bible: Vol. 1 From the Beginnings to Jerome.* Cambridge, New York, Melbourne: Cambridge University Press, 1970.

Anglicans Online. The Thirty-Nine Articles of Religion, Art. X, Of Free Will, and XVII, Of Predestination and Election, 12 Sep 1801. http://anglicansonline.org/basics/thirty-nine_articles.html. Accessed 12 Sep 2016.

Anselm of Canterbury. *Cur Deus Homo* (lit. "Why the God Man?"). In *Saint Anselm: Basic Writings,* translated by S. N. Deane. La Salle, IL: Open Court Publishing, 1962.

Aquilina, Mike, illus. and ed. *The Fathers of the Church: An Introduction to the First Christian Teachers.* Huntington, IN: Our Sunday Visitor Publishing, 1999.

Aquinas, Thomas. *Summa theologiae,* translated by Fathers of the English Dominican Province. Notre Dame: Christian Classics, 1981.

Arblaster, Paul, Gergely Juhász and Guido Latré , eds. *Tyndale's Testament.* Turnhout, Belgium: Brepols, 2002.

Aristotle, *De Anima* ("On the Soul"). Translated by J.A. Smith. In *Complete Works of Aristotle, Volume 1: The Revised Oxford Translation,* edited by Jonathan Barnes. Princeton, NJ: Princeton University Press, 1984.

Arminian Bible, The. http://armenianbible.org/. Accessed 30 June 2016.

Augustijn, Cornelius. *Erasmus: His Life, Work and Influence,* translated by J.C. Grayson. Toronto: University of Toronto, 1991.

Augustine of Hippo. *City of God,* translated by Henry Bettenson. New York: Penguin, 1984.

Augustine of Hippo. *Enchiridion.* In *Enchiridion and Confessions,* edited by Albert C. Outler, Library of Christian Classics. Philadelphia, PA: Westminster, 1955.

Augustine of Hippo. "On the Predestination of the Saints." In Augustine, *Anti-Pelagian Writings,* translated by Peter Holmes and Robert Ernest Wallis (1887), translation revised by Benjamin B. Warfield. Peabody, MA: Hendrickson, 1995.

Babylonian Talmud, *Kiddushin* 49a, and Tosephta, *Megillah* 4(3):41.

Bainton, Roland H. *Here I Stand: A Life of Martin Luther.* New York: Mentor, 1955.

Bainton, Roland H. *Hunted Heretic: The Life and Death of Michael Servetus, 1511-1553.* Revised edition edited by Peter Hughes and jointly published in Providence, RI by Blackstone Editions and the Unitarian Universalist Historical Society, 2005. Original publication Boston, MA: The Beacon Press, 1953.

Baird, Forrest E., and Walter Kaufmann. *From Plato to Derrida.* Upper Saddle River, NJ: Pearson Prentice Hall, 2008.

Barnes, Jonathan, ed. *Complete Works of Aristotle, Volume 1: The Revised Oxford Translation.* Princeton, NJ: Princeton University Press, 1984.

Barrera, J. Trebolle. *The Jewish Bible and the Christian Bible,* translated by W.G.E. Watson. Leiden, Netherlands: Brill; and Grand Rapids, MI: Eerdmans, 1998.

Barzun, Jacques. *From Dawn to Decadence: 500 years of Western Cultural Life.* New York: HarperCollins, 2000.

Baxter, J. Sidlow. *The Strategic Grasp of the Bible*. London: Marshall, Morgan & Scott, 1968.

Bauer, Walter. *A Greek-English Lexicon of the New Testament and Other Early Christian Literature, 2nd Edition*, translated and adapted by William F. Arndt and F. Wilbur Gingrich, then revised and augmented in the 2nd edition by Gingrich and Frederick W. Danker. London and Chicago: Univ. of Chicago Press, 1979.

Benedict, Ruth. *Patterns of Culture*. Abingdon-on-Thames, UK: Routledge and Kegan Paul, 1934.

Berkhof, Louis. *Systematic Theology*. Grand Rapids, MI: W.B. Eerdmans, 1996.

Besse, Jean. "Rule of Saint Augustine." In *The Catholic Encyclopedia*, Vol. 2. New York: Robert Appleton Company, 1907. Online at http://www.newadvent.org/cathen/02079b.htm.

Betto, Frei. "Gustavo Gutiérrez – A Friendly Profile." In *The Future of Liberation Theology: Essays in Honor of Gustavo Guitiérrez*, edited by Marc H. Ellis and Otto Maduro. Maryknoll, NY: Orbis Books, 1989.

Bevans, Stephen B., and Roger Schroeder. *Constants in Context: A Theology of Mission for Today*. Maryknoll, NY: Orbis Books, 2004.

Beutel, Albrecht. "Luther's Life." In *The Cambridge Companion to Martin Luther*, edited by Donald K. McKim. Cambridge, UK: Cambridge University Press, 2003.

Bosch, David J. *Transforming Mission: Paradigm Shifts in Theology of Mission*. Maryknoll, NY: Orbis Books, 1991.

Boyd, Gregory A. "A Brief Outline and Defense of the Open View." http://reknew.org/2007/12/response-to-critics/#sthash.ZET9gXBi. dpuf. Accessed 28 June 2016.

Boyd, Gregory A. *God at War: The Bible and Spiritual Conflict*. Downers Grove, IL: InterVarsity, 1997.

Boyd, Gregory A. "The Ground-Level Deliverance Model." In *Understanding Spiritual Warfare: Four Views*, edited by James K. Beilby and Paul R. Eddy. Grand Rapids, MI: Baker Academic, 2012.

Boyd, Gregory A. "The Open-Theism View." In *Divine Foreknowledge: Four*

Views., edited by James K. Beilby and Paul R. Eddy. Downers Grove, IL: InterVarsity Press, 2001.

Bridgman, Joan. *"Tyndale's New Testament."* In *Contemporary Review* (2000), 277 (1619): 342-346.

Britannica Encyclopedia Online. Ottoman Empire. https://www. britannica.com/place/Ottoman-Empire. Accessed 30 June 2016.

British Medical Journal. 2000 Jan 1; 320 (7226): 53. Report on a study comparing smokers and non-smokers.

Brown, Colin. *The New International Dictionary of New Testament Theology.* Grand Rapids, MI: Zondervan, 1975.

Bullinger, Ethelbert W. *A Critical Lexicon and Concordance to the English and Greek New Testament.* Grand Rapids, MI: Zondervan, 1975.

Burke, David G. "The First Versions: The Septuagint, the Targums, and the Latin." In *A History of Bible Translation,* edited by Philip A. Noss. Rome: Edizioni di Storia e Letteratura, 2007.

Calvin, John. *Commentary on the Bible.* Online at https://www.studylight. org/commentaries/cal/.

Calvin, John. *Institutes of the Christian Religion,* translated by Henry Beveridge. Grand Rapids, MI: Wm. B. Eerdmans Publishing Company, 1989. Originally published in Latin as *Institutio Christianae religionis,* 1564. Online at: http://www.ntslibrary.com/ PDF%20Books/Calvin%20Institutes%20of%20Christian%20 Religion.pdf. Accessed 9 Sep 2016.

Campbell, Gordon. *Bible: The Story of the King James Version 1611-2011.* Oxford, UK: Oxford University Press, 2010.

Campbell, Ross. *How to Really Love Your Child.* Colorado Springs: Chariot Victor Publishing, a division of Cook Communication, 1977.

Carson, D.A. *Exegetical Fallacies.* Cumbria, UK: Paternoster; Grand Rapids, MI: Baker Books, 1996.

Catechism of the Catholic Church, Section 1037. http://www.vatican.va/ archive/ENG0015/_P2O.HTM. Accessed 1 Sep 2016.

Catechism of the Catholic Church, Section 600. http://www.vatican.va/ archive/ENG0015/__P1O.HTM. Accessed 1 Sep 2016.

Catholic Encyclopedia. "Predestination." http://www.newadvent.org/cathen/12378a.htm. Accessed 1 Sep 2016.

Catholic Encyclopedia. "Teaching of St. Augustine of Hippo." http://www.newadvent.org/cathen/02091a.htm, citing Thomas Netter Waldensis, *Doctrinale*, Book I, Ch. 34, para. 5. Accessed 31 Oct 2016,

Catholic Encyclopedia: Pelagius and Pelagianism. http://www.newadvent.org/cathen/11604a.htm.

Chadwick, Henry, ed. *The Early Church*. London: Penguin Books, 1993.

Chess, Stella, and Alexander Thomas. *Temperament and Behavior Disorder in Children*. New York: University Press, 1968.

Christian Cyclopedia, "Predestination," The Lutheran Church, Missouri Synod, http://cyclopedia.lcms.org/display.asp?t1=p&word=PREDESTINATION. Accessed 1 Sep 2016.

Church Society. The Thirty-Nine Articles of Religion, Art. X, Of Free Will, 12 Sep 1801. http://www.churchsociety.org/issues_new/doctrine/39a/iss_doctrine_39A_Arts09-14.asp. Accessed 1 Sep 2016.

Church Society. The Thirty-Nine Articles of Religion, Art. XVII, Of Predestination and Election, 12 Sep 1801. http://www.churchsociety.org/issues_new/doctrine/39a/iss_doctrine_39A_Arts15-18.asp. Accessed 1 Sep 2016.

Cohen, Menachem. "The Idea of the Sanctity of the Biblical Text and the Science of Textual Criticism." in *HaMikrah V'anachnu*, edited by Uriel Simon. Tel-Aviv: HaMachon L'Yahadut U'Machshava Bat-Z'mananu and Dvir, 1979. English translation edited by Isaac B. Gottlieb. http://users.cecs.anu.edu.au/~bdm/dilugim/CohenArt/, accessed 25 June 2015.

CNN News. http://www.cnn.com/2016/06/08/middleeast/mother-sets-pakistani-woman-on-fire-police-say/. Accessed 8 Jun 2016.

Cottret, Bernard. *Calvin: A Biography*. Translated by M. Wallace McDonald from French [*Calvin: Biographie, 1995*]. Grand Rapids, MI: Wm. B. Eerdmans, 2000.

Crabb, Lawrence J., Jr. *Effective Biblical Counseling*. Grand Rapids: Zondervan, 1977.

Craig, William Lane. "The Middle-Knowledge View." In *Divine Foreknowledge: Four Views.*, edited by James K. Beilby and Paul R. Eddy. Downers Grove, IL: InterVarsity Press, 2001.

Cunningham, William. *The Reformers & the Theology of the Reformation.* London: Banner of Truth, 1967.

Dallas, Joe. *The Gay Gospel? How Pro-Gay Advocates Misread the Bible.* Eugene, OR: Harvest House, 2007.

Daniell, David. *The Bible in English: Its History and Influence.* New Haven, Conn: Yale University Press, 2003.

Daniell, David. *William Tyndale: A Biography.* London and New Haven, CT: Yale University Press, 1994.

Danker, Frederick W., ed. *Multipurpose Tools for Bible Study.* Minneapolis, MN: Fortress, 1993.

Darshan, Guy. "The Twenty-Four Books of the Hebrew Bible and Alexandrian Scribal Methods." In *Homer and the Bible in the Eyes of Ancient Interpreters: Between Literary and Religious Concerns (JSRC 16)*, edited by M.R. Niehoff. Leiden, Netherlands: Brill, 2012.

Davies, Philip R. "The Jewish Scriptural Canon in Cultural Perspective." In *The Canon Debate*, edited by Lee Martin McDonald and James A. Sanders. Peabody, MA: Hendrickson Publishers, 2002.

Day, John. *Yahweh and the Gods and Goddesses of Canaan.* Sheffield, UK: Sheffield Academic Press, 2000.

Deane, S. N., transl. *Saint Anselm: Basic Writings.* La Salle, IL: Open Court Publishing, 1962.

De Greef, Wulfert. *The Writings of John Calvin: An Introductory Guide.* Louisville, KY: Westminster John Knox Press, 2008.

de Hamel, Christopher. *The Book. A History of the Bible.* London, New York: Phaidon Press, 2001.

DeVries, Dawn. "Calvin's Preaching," in *The Cambridge Companion to John Calvin*, edited by Donald K. McKim. Cambridge: Cambridge University Press, 2004.

Demaus, Robert, and Richard Lovett. *William Tindale: A Biography.* St. Paul's Churchyard, UK: The Religions Tract Society, 1904.

Denzinger, Henry. *The Sources of Catholic Dogma*, translated by Roy J. Deferrari from the Thirtieth Edition (1957) of *Enchiridion Symbolorum*. Fitzwilliam, NH: Loreto Publications, 2002.

Dobson, James. *The Complete Marriage and Family Home Reference Guide.* Wheaton, IL: Tyndale House, 2000.

Dobson, James, and Gary Bauer. *Children at Risk.* Dallas, TX: Word Publishing, 1990.

Dove, Mary. "Wyclif and the English Bible." In *A Companion to John Wyclif: Late Medieval Theologian,* edited by Ian Christopher Levy. Leiden, UK; Boston, MA: Brill, 2006.

Duffield, Guy P., and Nathaniel M. Van Cleave. *Foundations of Pentecostal Theology.* Los Angeles, CA: Foursquare Media, 1983.

Ellingworth, Paul. "From Martin Luther to the English Revised Version." In *A History of Bible Translation,* edited by Philip A. Noss. Rome: Edizioni di Storia e Letteratura, 2007.

Encyclopedia Britannica Online. William Carey, British missionary. https://www.britannica.com/biography/William-Carey. Accessed 1 July 2016.

Encyclopedia Britannica Online. "Holy Roman Empire." https://www.britannica.com/place/Holy-Roman-Empire/Empire-and-papacy. Accessed 8 July 2016;

Erasmus. *Collected Works of Erasmus*, translated by R.A.B. Mynors and D.F.S. Thomson; annotated by Wallace K. Ferguson. Toronto: University of Toronto Press, 1976.

Erickson, Millard J. *Christian Theology.* Grand Rapids, MI: Baker Books, 1998.

Eriugena, Johannes Scotus. *Treatise on Divine Predestination*, translated by Mary Brennan. Notre Dame, IN: University of Notre Dame Press, 1998.

Eusebius. *The Church History*. In *Eusebius – The Church History: A New Translation with Commentary,* translated by Paul L. Maier. Grand Rapids, MI: Kregel Publications, 1999.

Fabella, Virginia, and R.S. Sugirtharajah, eds. *Dictionary of Third World Theologies.* Maryknoll, NY: Orbis, 2000.

Farris, Michael. *From Tyndale to Madison: How the Death of an English Martyr Led to the American Bill of Rights*. Nashville, TN : Broadman & Holman, 2007.

Fishkin, Shelley Fisher. *Lighting Out For the Territory: Reflections on Mark Twain and American Culture*. Oxford University Press, 1996.

Fox News. http://www.foxnews.com/world/2016/08/28/two-friends-from-remote-canada-discover-were-switched-at-birth-41-years-ago.html.

Gamble, Richard C. "Calvin's Controversies." In *The Cambridge Companion to John Calvin*, edited by Donald K. McKim. Cambridge: Cambridge University Press, 2004.

Ganoczy, Alexandre. "Calvin's Life." Translated by David L. Foxgrover. In *The Cambridge Companion to John Calvin*, edited by Donald K. McKim. Cambridge: Cambridge University Press, 2004.

Gibbs, Eddie. *ChurchNext: Quantum Changes in How We Do Ministry*. Downers Grove, IL: InterVarsity Press, 2000.

González, Justo L. *Christian Thought Revisited: Three Types of Theology*. London: SCM Press; Philadelphia, PA: Trinity Press Int'l, 1990.

González, Justo L. *The Story of Christianity*. Peabody, MS: Prince Press, 1999.

Grant, Michael. "Introduction." In Cicero, *Selected Works*, translated by Michael Grant. London: Penguin Books, 1971.

Gration, John. "Christianity and Culture." Distance education course at Prairie Graduate School. Calgary, AB, 2001.

"Great Litany, The." In *The Book of Common Prayer*. New York: Church Publishing, 1979.

Gritsch, Eric W. "Luther as Bible Translator." In *The Cambridge Companion to Martin Luther*, edited by Donald K. McKim. Cambridge, UK: Cambridge University Press, 2003.

Groody, Daniel G. *Globalization, Spirituality, and Justice*. Maryknoll, NY: Orbis Books. 2007.

Gruber, L. Franklin. *The Truth About the So-Called "Luther's Testament in English," Tyndale's New Testament*. St. Paul, MN: E. Mussgang, 1917.

Grudem, Wayne A. *Countering the Claims of Evangelical Feminism*. Sisters, OR: Multnomah Publishers, 2006.

Grudem, Wayne A. *Biblical Foundations for Manhood And Womanhood.* Wheaton, IL: Crossway Books, 2002.

Grudem, Wayne A. *Evangelical Feminism & Biblical Truth : An Analysis of More Than One Hundred Disputed Questions.* Sisters, OR: Multnomah Publishers, 2004.

Grudem, Wayne A. *Systematic Theology: An Introduction to Biblical Doctrine.* Grand Rapids, MI: Zondervan, 1994.

Guelzo, Allen C. *Edwards on the Will: A Century of American Theological Debate.* Middleton, CN: Wesleyan University Press, 1989.

Gutiérrez, Gustavo. *A Theology of Liberation: History, Politics, and Salvation.* Maryknoll, NY: Orbis Books, 1973.

Halverson, James. "Franciscan Theology and Predestinarian Pluralism in Late-Medieval Thought," *Speculum* 70 (1995): 1–26.

Hankins, Eric. "A Statement of the Traditional Southern Baptist Understanding of God's Plan of Salvation." http://sbctoday.com/wp-content/uploads/2012/06/A-Statement-of-Traditional-Southern-Baptist-Soteriology-SBC-Today.pdf. Accessed 2 Sep 2016.

Haskell, H.J. *This was Cicero.* New York: Alfred A. Knopf, 1964.

Hassig, Ross. *Mexico and the Spanish Conquest.* London: Longman Group UK Ltd, 1994.

Helleman, Wendy E. "Introduction." In *Christianity and the Classics: The Acceptance of a Heritage,* edited by Wendy E. Helleman. Lanham, MD: University Press of America, 1990.

Hiebert, Paul G. *Missiological Implications of Epistological Shifts: Affirming Truth in a Modern/Postmodern World.* Harrisburg, PA: Trinity Press Int'l, 1999.

Helm, Paul. "The Augustinian-Calvinist View." In *Divine Foreknowledge: Four Views.,* edited by James K. Beilby and Paul R. Eddy. Downers Grove, IL: InterVarsity Press, 2001.

Hengel, Martin. *The Septuagint as Christian Scripture: Its Prehistory and the Problem of Its Canon,* translated by Mark E. Biddle. Grand Rapids, MI: Baker Academic, 2002.

Herrmann, Wolfgang. "Baal." In *Dictionary of Deities and Demons in the*

Bible, 2nd edition. Grand Rapids, MI: Wm. B. Eerdmans, 1999.

History World. "History of The Holy Roman Empire." http://www. historyworld.net/wrldhis/plaintexthistories.asp?historyid=aa35. Accessed 8 July 2016.

Hoare, Henry W. *The Evolution of the English Bible: A Historical Sketch of the Successive Versions from 1382 to 1885,* 2nd edition. London: John Murray; New York: E.P. Dutton & Co., 1902.

Hodges, Zane C. *The Gospel Under Siege.* Dallas, TX: Redencion Viva, 1981.

Hofstede, Geert. *Cultures and Organizations: Software of the Mind.* London: McGraw-Hill, 1991.

Hofstede, Geert, and Gert Jan Hofstede. *Cultures and Organizations: Software of the Mind.* London: McGraw-Hill, 2005.

Horton, Michael. *For Calvinism.* Grand Rapids, MI: Zondervan, 2011.

Hughes, Lindsey. "Catherine I of Russia, Consort to Peter the Great." In *Queenship in Europe 1660-1815: The Role of the Consort,* edited by Clarissa Campbell Orr. Cambridge, UK: Cambridge University Press, 2004.

Hunt, David. "The Simple-Foreknowledge View." In *Divine Foreknowledge: Four Views.,* edited by James K. Beilby and Paul R. Eddy. Downers Grove, IL: InterVarsity Press, 2001.

Hutjens, Linda. "The Disguised King in Early English Ballads." In *Literature and Popular Culture in Early Modern England,* edited by Matthew Dimmock and Andrew Hadfield. Burlington, VT: Ashgate Publishing, 2009.

Iacocca, Lee, with William Novak. *Iacocca: An Autobiography.* New York: Bantam Books, 1984.

Irenaeus, *Against Heresies,* Book 3, Ch. 18, para. 6. https://carm.org/ irenaeus-heresies3-15-25. Accessed 14 Nov 2016.

James, Frank A. III. *Peter Martyr Vermigli and Predestination: The Augustinian Inheritance of an Italian Reformer.* Oxford: Clarendon, 1998.

James, William, *The Will to Believe: And Other Essays in Popular Philosophy, and Human Immortality.* Cambridge MA: Harvard

University Press, 1979.

Jellicoe, Sidney. *The Septuagint and Modern Study*. Oxford: Clarendon, 1968.

Jinbachian, Manuel. "Introduction: The Septuagint to the Vernaculars." In *A History of Bible Translation*, edited by Philip A. Noss. Rome: Edizioni di Storia e Letteratura, 2007.

John Paul II. Encyclical *Redemptoris Missio*, 1990. http://w2.vatican.va/content/john-paul-ii/en/encyclicals/documents/hf_jp-ii_enc_07121990_redemptoris-missio.html, accessed 1 Sep 2016.

Johnson, Gordon. "Introduction." In *Abundant Life in Christ* series. http://kneillfoster.com/Johnson/en/Romans/romans1.html.

Johnson, Lonnie R. *Central Europe: Enemies, Neighbors, Friends*. Oxford, UK: Oxford University Press, 1996.

Johnson, Robert E. *A Global Introduction to Baptist Churches*. Cambridge University Press, 2010.

King James Bible Dictionary. Oneline at http://kingjamesbibledictionary.com/.

Kittel, Gerhard, G.W. Bromily, and Gerhard Freidrich. *Theological Dictionary of the New Testament*. Grand Rapids, MI: Wm. B. Eerdmans, 1976.

Klein, William W. *The New Chosen People: A Corporate View of Election*. Eugene, OR: Wipf and Stock, 2001.

Korpela, Salla. "Religion in Finland." April 2012. http://finland.fi/life-society/finnish-church-aims-to-be-down-to-earth/. Accessed 16 July 2016.

Kraft, Charles. *Christianity in Culture: A Study in Dynamic Biblical Theologizing in Cross-Cultural Perspective*. Maryknoll, NY: Orbis Books, 1979.

Kuhn, Thomas. *The Structure of Scientific Revolutions*. Chicago, IL: University of Chicago Press, 1962.

Küng, Hans, and David Tracy. *Theologie – wohin? Auf dem Weg zu einem neuen Paradigma*. Zürich-Cologne: Benziger Verlag, 1984.

Küng, Hans. *Theologie im Aufbruch: Eine* ökumenische *Grundlegung*. Munich: Piper Verlag, 1987.

Ladd, George Eldon. *The Gospel of the Kingdom: Scriptural Studies in the*

Kingdom of God. Grand Rapids, MI: William B. Eerdmans, 1959.

Lamott, Anne. *Bird by Bird: Some Instructions on Writing and Life*. New York: Anchor Books, a division of Random House, 1995.

"Lausanne Occasional Paper No. 2." *The Willowbank Report – Gospel and Culture*. Wheaton, IL: LCWE, 1978.

Lewinsohn, Richard. *A History of Sexual Customs*. London: Longmans, Green, and Co., 1958.

Lindberg, Carter, ed. *The European Reformations Sourcebook, 2nd Edition*. West Sussex, UK: John Wiley & Sons, Ltd., 2014.

Lingenfelter, Sherwood G., and Marvin K. Mayers, *Ministering Cross-Culturally: An Incarnational Model for Personal Relationships*. Grand Rapids: Baker Book House, 1986.

Levering, Matthew. *Predestination: Biblical and Theological Paths*. Oxford: Oxford University Press, 2011.

Levy, Leonard W. *Blasphemy: Verbal Offense Against the Sacred from Moses to Salman Rushdie*. Chapel Hill, NC: Univ. of North Carolina Press, 1995.

Lewis, C.S. *Mere Christianity*. New York: The MacMillan Co., 1953.

Luther, Martin. "Preface." In Jan Hus, *Letters of John Huss Written During His Exile and Imprisonment*, edited by François Paul Émile Boisnormand de Bonnechose. Translated by Campbell Mackenzie. Edinburgh: William Whyte & Co., 1846.

Maag, Karin. https://calvin.edu/about/history/john-calvin.html?dotcmsredir=1.

Magnusson, Magnus. *Scotland: The Story of a Nation*. London: HarperCollins, 2000.

Maier, Paul L., transl. *Eusebius – The Church History: A New Translation with Commentary*. Grand Rapids, MI: Kregel Publications, 1999.

Manetsch, Scott M. *Calvin's Company of Pastors: Pastoral Care and the Emerging Reformed Church, 1536–1609, Oxford Studies in Historical Theology*. New York: Oxford University Press, 2013.

Manley, Johanna, ed. *The Bible and the Holy Fathers for Orthodox: Daily Scripture Readings and Commentary for Orthodox Christians*. Yonkers, NY: St. Vladimir's Seminary Press, 2011.

Mann, Nicholas. *The Origins of Humanism.* Cambridge University Press, 1996.

Martin, John A. *Blessed are the Addicts: The Spiritual Side of Alcoholism, Addiction, and Recovery.* New York: Villard Books, 1990.

McDonald, Lee Martin. *The Formulation of the Christian Biblical Canon.* Peabody, MA: Hendrickson, 1995.

McDonald, Lee Martin, and James A. Sanders. "Introduction." *The Canon Debate.* Peabody, MA: Hendrickson Publishers, 2002.

McGrath, Alister E. *A Life of John Calvin.* Oxford: Basil Blackwell, 1990.

McNeil, John Thomas. *The History and Character of Calvinism.* Oxford: Oxford University Press, 1954.

Metzger, Bruce. *The Text of the New Testament. Its Transmission, Corruption, and Restoration.* Oxford University Press, 1992.

Mickelsen, Berkeley and Alvera. "The 'Head' of the Epistles." In *Christianity Today* 25/4 (Feb. 20, 1981), 20-23.

Miller, Darrow L., with Stan Guthrie. *Discipling Nations: The Power of Truth to Transform Cultures.* Seattle, WA: YWAM Publishing, 2001.

Mitchican, Jonathan. "The Anglican View of Predestination." The Conciliar Anglican website, https://conciliaranglican.com/2011/12/09/sweet-pleasant-and-unspeakable-comfort-the-anglican-view-of-predestination-part-iii/. Accessed 1 Sep 2016;

More, Sir Thomas. *The Complete Works of Sir Thomas More.* (London and New Haven, CT: Yale University Press, 1969.

Morris, Tom. *Philosophy for Dummies.* Hoboken, NJ: Wiley Publishing, 1999.

Moynahan, Brian. *William Tyndale: If God Spare my Life.* London: Abacus, 2003.

Muggeridge, Malcolm. *Chronicles of Wasted Time: 1: The Green Stick.* New York: William Morrow & Co., 1973.

Muggeridge, Malcolm. *Jesus: The Man Who Lives.* London: Harper & Row, 1975.

Muggeridge, Malcolm. *The End of Christendom.* Grand Rapids, MI: Wm. B. Eerdmans, 1980.

Mullett, Michael A. *Martin Luther.* London: Routledge, 2004.

Newbigin, Lesslie. *The Gospel in a Pluralist Society.* Grand Rapids: Eerdmans, 1989.

New Testament Greek-English Dictionary. Springfield, MO: The Complete Biblical Library, 1990.

Nida, Eugene A. "Principles of Correspondence." In *The Translation Studies Reader*, edited by Lawrence Venuti. NY: Routledge, 2004.

Nida, Eugene A. *Message and Mission.* New York: Harper & Row, 1960. Reprinted by William Carey Library in South Pasadena, CA, 1972.

Niebur, H. Richard. *Christ and Culture.* New York: Harper and Row, 1951.

Nielson, John, and Royal Skousen. *"How Much of the King James Bible is William Tyndale's? An Estimation Based on Sampling."* In *Reformation* 3: (1998), 49-74.

NIV Study Bible, 10ᵗʰ Anniversary Edition, The, edited by Kenneth Barker. Grand Rapids, MI: Zondervan, 1995.

Noss, Philip A., ed. *A History of Bible Translation.* Rome: Edizioni di Storia e Letteratura, 2007.

Noss, Philip A. "A History of Bible Translation: Introduction and Overview." In *A History of Bible Translation*, edited by Philip A. Noss. Rome: Edizioni di Storia e Letteratura, 2007.

Osborne, Grant R. *The Hermeneutical Spiral: A Comprehensive Introduction to Biblical Interpretation.* Downers Grove: InterVarsity Press, 1991.

Olson, Jeannine. "Calvin and social-ethical issues." In *The Cambridge Companion to John Calvin*, edited by Donald K. McKim. Cambridge: Cambridge University Press, 2004.

Olson, Roger E. *Arminian Theology: Myths and Realities.* Downers Grove, IL: InterVarsity Press, 2006.

Origen. *On First Principles*, translated by G. W. Butterworth. Notre Dame, IN: Ave Maria Press, 2013. Original publication, 1936.

Packer J.I., and O.R. Johnston. "Historical and Theological Introduction, Erasmus to 1517." In Martin Luther, *The Bondage of the Will*, translated by J.I. Packer and O.R. Johnston. Grand Rapids, MI: Baker Academic, 2012. Originally published Cambridge, UK: James Clark & Co; Westwood, NJ: Revell, 1957.

Padilla, C. Rene. "The Contextualization of the Gospel." In *Journal of Theology for Southern Africa* No. 24 (September, 1978): 12-30.

Parker, Thomas Henry Louis. *John Calvin.* Tring, Hertfordshire, England: Lion Publishing Plc, 1975.

Parker, T. H. L. *John Calvin: A Biography.* Oxford: Lion Hudson Plc, 2006.

Paull, Candi, and Lila Empson. *Checklist for Life: For Women.* Nashville, TN: Thomas Nelson, 2002.

Peck, M. Scott. *The Different Drum: Community Making and Peace.* New York: Simon and Schuster, 1987.

Peck, M. Scott. *The Road Less Traveled: A New Psychology of Love, Traditional Values and Spiritual Growth.* New York: Simon & Schuster, 1978.

Pederson, Viggo Hjørnager, and Per Qvale. "Danish and Norwegian Traditions." In *Routledge Encyclopedia of Translation Studies,* edited by Mona Baker and Kirsten Malmkjaer. London and New York: Routledge, 1998.

Perry, Ralph Barton. *The Thought and Character of William James,* Vol. I. Nashville, TN: Vanderbilt Univ. Press, 1996. Original publication 1935.

Peterson, Robert A., and Michael D. Williams. *Why I Am Not an Arminian.* Downers Grove, IL: InterVarsity Press, 2004.

Physics World. http://physicsworld.com/cws/article/news/2010/feb/17/gravitys-effect-on-time-confirmed, accessed 3 Nov 2016.

Piper, John, and Wayne Grudem, eds. *Recovering Biblical Manhood and Womanhood: A Response to Evangelical Feminism.* Wheaton, IL: Crossway, 2006.

Plass, Ewald M. *What Luther Says.* Saint Louis, MO: Concordia Pub. House, 1959.

Poster, Carol. "Protagoras." *Internet Encyclopedia of Philosophy.* http://www.iep.utm.edu/protagor/.

Powlinson, David. "The Classical Model." In *Understanding Spiritual Warfare: Four Views,* edited by James K. Beilby and Paul R. Eddy. Grand Rapids, MI: Baker Academic. 2012.

Pym, Anthony. "On the Historical Epistemologies of Bible Translating." In *A History of Bible Translation*, edited by Philip A. Noss. Rome: Edizioni di Storia e Letteratura, 2007.

Rawson, Elizabeth. *Cicero, A Portrait.* London: Penguin Books Ltd., 1975.

Rebenich, Stefan. *Jerome: The Early Church Fathers.* London, New York: Routledge, 2002.

Rhodes, Erroll. "Secondary Versions: Arabic to Old Slavonic." In *A History of Bible Translation*, edited by Philip A. Noss. Rome: Edizioni di Storia e Letteratura, 2007.

Richardson, Don. Seminar, "Stars, Sand, and Dust."

Rumford, Douglas J. *Soulshaping: Taking Care of Your Spiritual Life.* Wheaton, IL: Tyndale House, 1996.

Rydenfelt, Henrik and Sami Pihlström, eds., *William James on Religion.* Basingstoke, Hampshire, England; New York: Pelgrave Macmillan, 2013.

Sanneh, Lamin. *Translating the Message: The Missionary Impact on Culture.* Maryknoll, NY: Orbis Books, 2009.

Servetus, Michael. "Thirty letters to Calvin," *Christianismi Restitutio*, Part 4.

Sjogren, Bob. *Unveiled At Last.* Seattle, WA: YWAM Publishing, 1992.

Skreslet, Stanley H. *Comprehending Mission: The Questions, Methods, Themes, Problems, and Prospects of Missiology.* Maryknoll, NY: Orbis Books, 2012).

Snyder, Howard A. *Models of the Kingdom.* Nashville, TN: Abingdon Press, 1991.

Spitzer, Robert J. *Ten Universal Principles: A Brief Philosophy of the Life Issues.* San Francisco, CA: Ignatius Press, 2011.

Stanford University Encyclopedia of Philosophy. http://plato.stanford.edu/.

Steinmetz, David C. "Calvin as Biblical Interpreter Among the Ancient Philosophers." In *Interpretation* 63 (2) 2009: 142–153.

Strong, James. *Strong's Exhaustive Concordance*, e-Sword electronic version.

Strong, James. *The Strongest Strong's Exhaustive Concordance of the Bible*, revised and corrected by John R. Kohlenberger III and James A. Swanson. Grand Rapids, MI: Zondervan, 2001.

St. Theophan the Recluse. *An Explanation of Certain Texts of Holy Scripture*. In *The Bible and the Holy Fathers for Orthodox: Daily Scripture Readings and Commentary for Orthodox Christians,* edited by Johanna Manley. Yonkers, NY: St. Vladimir's Seminary Press, 2011.

Tadmor, Naomi. *The Social Universe of the English Bible: Scripture, Society, and Culture in Early Modern England.* Cambridge: Cambridge University Press, 2010.

Thayer, Joseph H. *Thayer's Greek-English Lexicon of the New Testament.* Peabody, MA: Hendrickson, 1996.

Townsend, Kim. *Manhood at Harvard: William James and Others.* London and New York: W.W. Norton & Co., 1996.

The Arminian Bible. http://armenianbible.org/. Accessed 30 June 2016.

"The Great Litany." In *The Book of Common Prayer.* New York: Church Publishing, 1979.

The New Testament Greek-English Dictionary. Springfield, MO: The Complete Biblical Library, 1990.

The NIV Study Bible, 10th Anniversary Edition, edited by Kenneth Barker. Grand Rapids, MI: Zondervan, 1995.

The Willowbank Report. Charlotte, NC.: Lausanne Committee for World Evangelization, 1978.

Thuesen, Peter J. *Predestination: The American Career of a Contentious Doctrine.* New York: Oxford University Press, 2009.

Trueman, Carl R. *Luther's Legacy: Salvation and English Reformers, 1525-1556.* Oxford: Clarendon, 1994.

Truss, Lynne. *Eats, Shoots and Leaves: The Zero Tolerance Approach to Punctuation.* New York, NY: Penguin, 2006.

New Testament Greek-English Dictionary, The. Springfield, MO: The Complete Biblical Library, 1990.

United Methodist Church. The Articles of Religion of the Methodist Church, Art. VIII, Free Will and IX, Justification. http://www.umc.org/what-we-believe/the-articles-of-religion-of-the-methodist-church. Accessed 2 Sep 2016.

United Methodist Church. What We Believe. http://www.umc.org/what-we-believe/do-united-methodists-believe-once-saved-always-saved.

Accessed 2 Sep 2016.

United Methodist Church News and Media blog. http://www.umc.org/news-and-media/blogs-commentaries/post/listen-to-god-and-mom-as-you-navigate-through-life. Accessed 2 Sep 2016.

University of Texas Linguistics Research Center. "Johann Ernst Glück." https://lrc.la.utexas.edu/eieol/litol/100. Accessed 8 July 2016.

Viola, Frank, and George Barna. *Pagan Christianity?: Exploring the Roots of Our Church Practices*. Carol Stream, IL: BarnaBooks, 2008.

Volz, Hans. "German." In *The Cambridge History of the Bible: Vol. 3. The West from the Reformation to the Present Day*, edited by S.L. Greenslade. Oxford, UK: Oxford University Press, 2001.

Wagner, C. Peter, and Rebecca Greenwood. "The Strategic-Level Deliverance Model." In *Understanding Spiritual Warfare: Four Views*, edited by James K. Beilby and Paul R. Eddy. Grand Rapids, MI: Baker Academic, 2012.

Walls, Andrew F. *The Missionary Movement in Christian History: Studies in the Transmission of Faith*. Maryknoll, NY: Orbis Books, 1996.

Weatherhead, Leslie D. *The Will of God, rev. edition*. Nashville, TN: Abingdon, 1999. Original publication 1944.

White, John. *The Fight*. Downers Grove, IL: Intervarsity Press, 1976.

Wigram, George V., and Ralph D. Winter. *The Word Study Concordance*. Wheaton, IL: Tyndale House, 1978.

William of Ockham. *Philosophical Writings*, edited and translated by Philotheus Boehner, OFM, revised by Stephen F. Brown. Indianapolis, IN: Hackett, 1989.

William of Ockham. *Predestination, God's Foreknowledge, and Future Contingents*, translated by Marilyn McCord Adams and Norman Kretzmann. Indianapolis, IN: Hackett, 1983.

Willowbank Report, The. Charlotte, NC.: Lausanne Committee for World Evangelization, 1978.

Wilson, Derek. *Out of the Storm: The Life and Legacy of Martin Luther*. London: Hutchinson, 2007.

Wink, Walter. "The World Systems Model." In *Understanding Spiritual Warfare: Four Views,* edited by James K. Beilby and Paul R. Eddy. Grand Rapids, MI: Baker Academic, 2012.

Woodberry, Robert D. "The Missionary Roots of Liberal Democracy." In *American Political Science Review*, Vol. 106, No. 2, May 2012, pp. 244-274.

Würthwein, Ernst. *The Text of the Old Testament, Second Edition,* edited by Alexander Achilles Fischer. Translated by Erroll F. Rhodes. Grand Rapids, MI: Eerdmans, 1995.

Wycliffe Global Alliance. http://www.wycliffe.net/statistics. Accessed 1 July, 2016.

Yong, Amos. *The Missiological Spirit: Christian Mission Theology in the Third Millennium Global Context.* Eugene, OR: Cascade Books, 2014.

Yong, Amos. *The Spirit of Creation: Modern Science and Divine Action in the Pentecostal-Charismatic Imagination.* Grand Rapids, MI: Eerdmans, 2011.

Young, Robert. *Analytical Concordance to the Bible.* Grand Rapids, MI: Wm. B. Eerdmans, 1975.

Young, Wm. Paul. *The Shack.* Los Angeles, CA: Windblown Media, 2007.

Zacharias, Ravi. "What does it mean to be human?" Lecture at Soldiers & Sailors Memorial Hall, Pittsburgh, PA, October 15, 2015.

Chronological Index

(Numbers in parentheses indicate page references in the text.)

489

(C.E.)	
Dates, Periods, Events	Dates, People
c. 112 The Aelia Capitolina is translated (113)	
	c. 125 – 202 Irenaeus (69, 71, 92, 478)
	c. 155 - c. 240 Tertullian (70)
	c. 184 - c. 253 Origen (71, 96, 97, 103, 368, 482)
225 Iran has more than 20 regional bishops (113)	
250 Consensus on NT books (109)	263 – 339 Eusebius (96, 103, 475, 480)
340 Evidence of Bible translation into the Persian language (113)	c. 347 – 420 Jerome (113, 114, 120, 142, 148, 170, 171, 469, 484)
	354 – 430 Augustine of Hippo (97-102, 148, 233, 286, 315, 336, 368, 470, 473)
	c. 360 – c. 418 Pelagius (97)
	c. 386 – c. 450 Nestorius (67)
385 Jerome moves to Bethlehem (114)	c. 386 – c. 455 Julian, bishop of Eclanum (98)
	c. 400 Rufinus the Syrian (114)
late 4th century Jerome's Vulgate is completed (114)	
400 – 1500 Middle Ages, transitioned into Renaissance (69)	unknown – c. 445 Vincent of Lérins (98)
431 Council of Ephesus (67, 97)	
436 The Armenian Bible is published (113)	5th century Gallic priest Lucidus (98, 104)
c. 475 to 480 Council of Arles (98)	
500 – 1500 Second period of Bible translation (112, 114), Hebrew Scriptures to Arabic, Slavonic Bible started	
529 The Second Council of Orange (98)	
553 Second Council of Constantinople (97)	
7th – 11th centuries The Masoretes preserved and copied the biblical texts with a reputation for accuracy (108)	676 – 749 John of Damascus (98, 99, 309-310, 315)
	c. 808 – 868 Gottschalk of Orbais (98)
late 800s, The Hebrew Bible is translated into Arabic (114)	c. 815 – c. 877 John Scottus Eriugena (98, 104, 475)
700 to 1500 The Arab Islamic empire (112)	
c. 863 Translation of the Slavonic Bible is started (114)	
	1033 – 1109 Anselm of Canterbury (69, 92, 469)
1054 The Great Schism occurs between the Catholic Church and the Eastern Orthodox Churches (68, 88)	
	1225 – 1274 Thomas Aquinas (56, 99, 100, 102, 104, 310)

(C.E.)

Dates, Periods, Events	Dates, People
1244 The Augustinian Order is founded (100)	
1262 Strasbourg is a Free Imperial City (147)	
	c. 1285 – 1347 William of Ockham (100, 102, 104, 486)
1300 – 1600 Renaissance, rediscovery of Greek philosophy, leading to humanism (78, 81, 88, 115)	
c. 1300 Renaissance begins in Italy, lasts about three hundred years (78)	c. 1324 – 1384 John Wycliffe (148, 149)
	1372 – 1415 Jan Hus (149, 174, 480)
1382 John Wycliffe completes his first English translation of the Bible (148)	
	c. 1400 – 1468 Johannes Gutenberg (114)
1415 Council of Constance orders that Wycliffe's bones to be dug up and burned, all his written works be destroyed, and Jan Hus to be burned at the stake (148, 149)	
c. 1450s The printing press is invented in Mainz, Germany, by Johannes Gutenberg (114)	1450 – 1536 Jacques d'Étaples Lefèvre (146, 147)
1453 Constantinople falls to the Islamic Turks, scholars flee into western Europe with Greek manuscripts, triggering the Renaissance and from it, the Protestant Reformation (114-115)	1453 – 1504 Jan Standonck (16)
	1460 – 1524 Johann von Staupitz (100)
	1466 – 1536 Desiderius Erasmus (16, 115, 141-143, 146, 150, 172, 173, 470, 475, 482)
	1467 – 1519 John Colet (150)
	1483 – 1546 Martin Luther (17, 19, 71, 82, 89, 100, 102, 115, 142-155, 171-175, 234, 235, 247, 369)
	1484 – 1531 Ulrich Zwingli (17, 82, 151, 154)
	1485 – 1509 Henry VII, King of England (141)
	1489 – 1565 William Farel (19)
	1491 – 1547 Henry VIII, King of England (142, 151)
	c. 1494 – 1536 William Tyndale (143, 149-153, 172, 174, 469, 472, 474, 476, 481)
	1497 – 1560 Philipp Melanchthon (144)

491

(C.E.)	
Dates, Periods, Events	Dates, People
1499 Date of the earliest surviving whole Slavonic Bible (114)	
1499 Erasmus first visits England (141)	
1500 – 1900 Third period of Bible translation (112, 114-115), Erasmus's parallel Greek and Latin NT (115), followed by vernacular versions in all major languages (115)	
	1503 – 1559 Robert Estienne (148)
	1506 – 1538 Pierre Robert Olivétan (146-148, 151)
1509 Birth of John Calvin (16)	1509 – 1564 John Calvin (see Index of Names)
1511 Erasmus publishes Encomium Moriae (In Praise of Folly), satirizing people in general and the Church in particular (142)	c. 1511 – 1553 Michael Servetus (19, 22, 23, 360, 361, 470, 486)
	1512 – 1542 James V, King of Scots (249, 250, 287, 292, 370)
	1514 – 1572 John Knox (18, 152, 474)
1516 – 1522 Erasmus publishes 3 versions of his parallel Greek and Latin NT (143)	1516 – 1558 Mary I, (Bloody Mary), queen of England from 1553 - 1558 (18, 148, 151, 152)
1517 – 1648 Reformation (16, 17, 19, 68, 88, 89, 101, 112, 115, 116, 118, 120, 142, 144, 147, 368)	
	1519 – 1605 Theodore Beza, Théodore de Bèze (148, 155)
1520s City of Strasbourg converts to Lutheranism, early in the Reformation process (147)	
1522 Luther's German New Testament is translated and published while he is in protective custody at Wartburg castle (144)	
1523 Jacques Lefèvre d'Étaples translates the Bible into French (146)	
	1524 – 1579 William Whittingham (18, 152)
c. 1526 First printing of Tyndale's NT (150)	
1528 Calvin moves to Orleans to study civil law (16)	
	1531 – 1594 Corneille Bertram (148)
1532 Calvin finishes his law studies and publishes his first work, a commentary of Seneca the Younger's De Clementia (16)	

(C.E.)

Dates, Periods, Events	Dates, People
1534	Luther's Old Testament is finished with the help of Philipp Melanchthon, making Luther's German Bible complete (144)	
1535	Olivétan's French Protestant Bible first published (147)	
1535	First complete English Bible is published by Miles Cloverdale (151)	
1535	Anne Boleyn, the second of Henry VIII's six wives, financially supports the publication of the first complete English Bible (151)	
1536	William Tyndale is burned at the stake (151)	
1536	Calvin's breaks with the Roman Catholic Church, begins work on his Institutes, and leaves France permanently (16)	
1537	Thomas Matthew Bible is published by John Rogers (151)	
1538	The Great Bible is published (151)	
1540	The Icelandic New Testament is published (144)	
1541 – 1564	Calvin lives in Geneva (17)	
1541	The first complete Swedish Bible is published in Uppsala (144)	
1546	Council of Trent makes the Vulgate official for the Catholic Church (114)	
1547	A threatening letter found in Calvin's church results in the suspect being beheaded (18)	
1549	John Calvin's wife dies (17)	
1550	Translation of the Danish Bible is completed (144)	
1551	Physician Jérôme-Hermès Bolsec is banished from Geneva for accusing Calvin of making God the author of sin with his doctrine of predestination (18)	
1553	The first Polish New Testament appears (145)	
1553	Mary I (Bloody Mary) takes the throne in England (151)	
1553	Calvin's revision of Olivetan's French Bible is the first entire Bible to use Robert Estienne's system of dividing the text into numbered verses (148)	

(C.E.)	
Dates, Periods, Events	Dates, People
1553 Michael Servetus is burned alive, 27 October (19)	
1554 Sebastian Castellio writes Whether Heretics Should Be Persecuted (De haereticis, an sint persequendi) in opposition to Calvin having Michael Servetus executed (360)	
1555 – 1562 Calvin sends 100 missionaries into France (18, 360)	
1555 Insurrection in Geneva against Calvin is suppressed, with four of those involved executed (19)	
1556 Dutch Calvinists produce a Bible (146)	
1558 Bloody Mary dies (152)	
1558 Elizabeth I assumes the throne, reinstates the Church of England (152)	
1560 The English Geneva Bible published (152)	1560 – 1609 Jacob Arminius (84, 89, 360, 464, 466)
1564 John Calvin dies in Geneva (17)	
	1566 – 1625 King James VI of Scotland and King James I of England (152)
1568 The Bishop's Bible published during Elizabeth's reign (152)	
1582 Douay-Rheims version of NT published, OT 1610 (152)	
1584 The complete Icelandic Bible is published (144)	
1584 The first complete Slovenian Bible is translated by a Lutheran pastor, published in Wittenberg (145)	
1588 Calvin's French Geneva Bible is standardized following several revisions after his death (148)	
1600 – 1900 Enlightenment (56, 74, 144)	
1603 Elizabeth I dies, King James of Scotland ascends to the English throne (152)	
1604 King James authorizes a new translation of the Bible (152)	
1610 Douay-Rheims version of OT published, NT 1582 (152)	
1611 New translation of the Bible authorized by King James is published, known as the King James Version, or KJV (152-153)	

494

Topical Index

(For Greek words, see end of Index)

P

Index of Names

A

Abraham, the patriarch, 163, 191, 193, 202, 203, 224, 225, 238, 255, 294, 295, 300, 302, 303, 311, 351, 431, 438, 451, 458, 460

Achan, 340

Adam 158, 219, 224, 252, 268, 274, 280, 320, 325, 334, 357, 358

Ahab, king of Israel, 227, 232, 269

Ahasuerus (Xerxes), 110

Alexander the Great, 302, 303

Anselm of Canterbury, 69, 92, 469

Aquinas, Thomas, 56, 99, 100, 102, 104, 310

Aristotle, 56, 63, 81, 83, 84, 95, 101, 102, 202, 302, 303, 366, 470

Arminius, Jacob, 84, 89, 360, 464, 466

Asa, king of Judah, 200

Augustine of Hippo, 97-102, 148, 233, 286, 315, 336, 368, 470, 473

B

Barnabas, Paul's co-worker, 66, 166, 341, 397, 415, 418, 453, 454

Ben-Ammi, son of Lot, 351

Benjamin, son of Sara, 242, 246, 314, 316, 351; tribe of, 180

Bertram, Corneille,148

Beza, Theodore (Théodore de Bèze), 148, 155

Biema, David Van,102, 105

Bloody Mary (Mary I), 148, 151, 152

Boleyn, Anne, 151

Bolsec, Jérôme-Hermès, 18, 19, 247, 248

Bosch, David ,92, 93, 361, 363, 471

Boyd, Gregory, 233, 345, 346, 435, 471

Brown, Colin, 201, 209, 386, 387, 388, 390, 391, 398, 408, 412-418, 472

Burns, Robert, 248, 433

C

Calvin, John, 10-23, 61, 62, 66, 75-89, 95, 97, 100-104, 115, 124, 141, 146-148, 151, 154, 155, 175, 186, 187, 202, 203, 206-208, 219, 233, 234, 238, 240, 246, 247, 250-252, 256, 257, 263, 268, 270-272, 286, 304-310, 312, 315, 316, 324-326, 336, 345-347, 353-356, 360-363, 366-369, 375, 421, 464, 472-474, 476, 480-484; as Jehan Cauvin, Ioannis Calvinus, Jean Calvin, 16

Campbell, Gordon, 123, 171, 172, 174, 175, 472

Carey, William, 117, 171, 475

Castellio, Sabastian, 360, 361

Catherine I, 145

Catherine the Great, 145

Christie, Jim, 3

Churchill, Winston, 95

Cicero, Marcus Tullius, 121, 122, 132, 171, 476, 477, 484

Colet, John, 150

Constantine, 67, 115

Cornelius, 65, 66, 452

Cortés, Hernán, 87

Craufurd, Peter Houison, 248-249

D

Daniel, the prophet, 159, 220, 222, 223, 269, 278, 297, 316, 339, 356, 445; book of, see Scripture Index

Daniell, David, 150, 174, 474

Darius, 445

Darwin, Charles, 83

David, king of Israel, 204, 225, 226, 240, 296, 424, 439; as the nation of Israel, 445, 454

de Hamel, Christopher, 143, 171-174, 474

Demetrius of Phalerum, 110

Dobson, James, 475

Donna, author's wife, 3, 20, 214, 264, 265-268, 321, 322, 379, 382

E

Eli, the priest, 279, 423
Elijah, the prophet, 86, 227, 449
Eliot, John, 361, 362
Elisha, the prophet, 86, 87, 225, 450
Elizabeth, daughter of Catherine I, 145
Elizabeth I, queen of England, 152
Epaphras, 324, 326
Er, son of Judah, 349, 350
Erasmus, Desiderius, 16, 115, 141-143, 146, 150, 172, 173, 470, 475, 482
Erickson, Millard, 299, 300, 346, 475
Eriugena, John Scottus, 98, 104, 475
Esau, the man, 203-205; the nation, 204
Estienne, Robert, 148
Eusebius, 96, 103, 475, 480
Eve, 224, 274, 334
Ezra, the priest, 110

F

Farel, William, 19

G

Gabriel, the angel, 143
Galileo, 33, 46, 158
Gibbs, Eddie, 84, 85, 93, 476
Glück, Johann Ernst, 144, 145, 173, 486
Gonzalez, Justo L., 25, 62, 107, 169, 177, 208
Gottschalk of Orbais, 98
Gration, John, 65, 92, 476
Groody, Daniel G., 94, 476
Gruber, Franklin, 150, 153, 174, 476
Grudem, Wayne, 159, 175, 345, 476, 477, 483
Guelzo, Allen, 103, 105, 477
Gutenberg, Johannes, 114
Gutiérrez, Gustavo, 92, 471

H

Hagar, 224
Halverson, James, 100, 104, 477

Hanani, the seer, 200
Harvey, Paul, 25, 62
Helleman, Wendy, 81, 93, 477
Henry VII, 141
Henry VIII, 142, 151
Hezekiah, king of Judah, 352, 353, 354, 424, 425, 433, 446
Hoare, Henry, 150, 174, 478
Hofstede, Geert, 58, 63, 75-77, 93, 94, 478
Hofstede, Gert Jan, 63, 93
Horton, Michael, 101, 104, 478
Howieson, John, 249, 250
Huntington, Joseph, 104, 356, 469
Hus (Huss), 149, 174, 480

I

Iacocca, Lee, 55, 63, 478
Irenaeus, 69, 71, 92, 478

J

Jacob, the patriarch, 126, 203-205, 225, 242; the nation, 204, 301, 341, 426, 443, 446
James, King of Scotland, King of England, 152
James V, King of Scots, 249, 250, 287, 292, 370
James, William, 36, 38, 52-54, 58, 63, 235, 235, 345, 478, 483-485
Jeremiah, the prophet, 206, 278, 330, 354, 425, 427, 428, 434
Jerome, 113, 114, 120, 142, 148, 170, 171, 469, 484
Jesus, 20, 45, 47, 62, 65, 66, 67, 69, 74, 79, 85, 86, 87, 89, 109, 126, 127, 128, 132, 133, 134, 135, 156, 158, 160, 161, 164, 167, 177, 179, 180, 181, 182, 185, 186, 190, 191, 192, 193, 197, 198, 199, 200, 201, 202, 203, 208, 219, 220, 224, 225, 227, 228, 229, 233, 238, 239, 240, 241, 248, 249, 250, 253, 254, 260, 261, 262, 263, 271, 272, 275, 277, 281, 282, 283, 285, 291, 292, 293, 297, 298, 299, 300, 303, 304, 308, 311, 313, 314, 316, 318, 319, 320, 324, 325, 326, 336, 341, 342, 343, 346, 347, 359, 362, 373, 375, 392, 394, 399, 405, 406, 415, 447, 448, 449, 450, 451, 453, 456, 457, 458, 459, 460, 461, 481

Scripture Index

(Numbers in parentheses indicate page references in the text.
Whole words are in the text; abbreviations are references cited.)